HISTORIC PHOTOS OF
FRANKLIN DELANO ROOSEVELT

TEXT AND CAPTIONS BY MATTHEW GILMORE

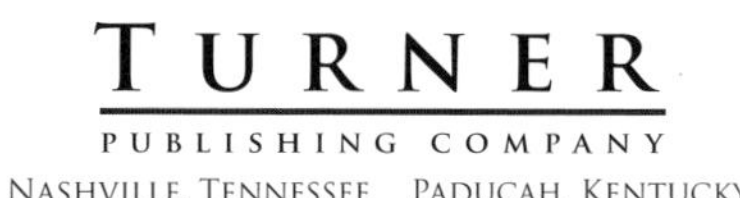

NASHVILLE, TENNESSEE   PADUCAH, KENTUCKY

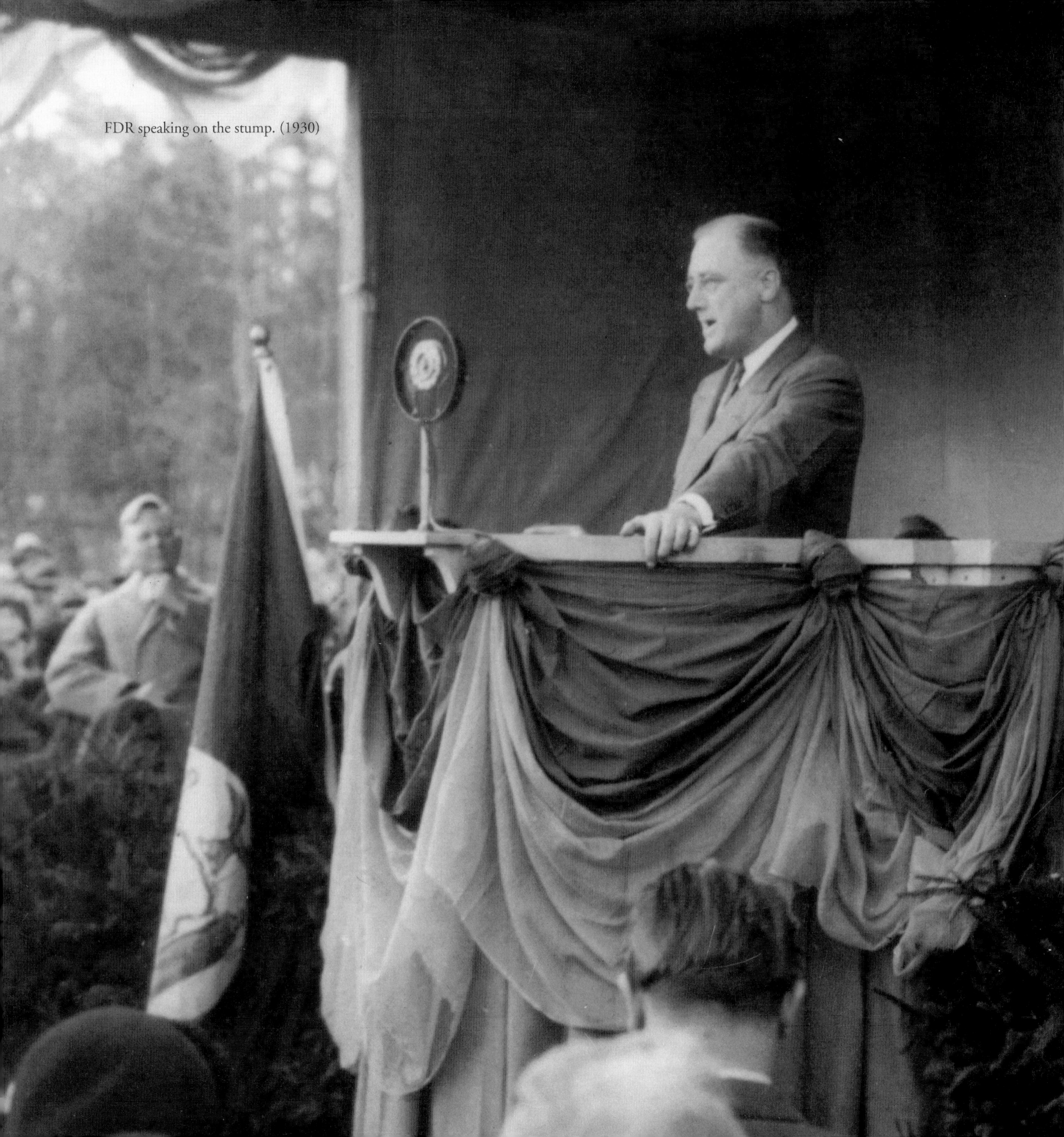

FDR speaking on the stump. (1930)

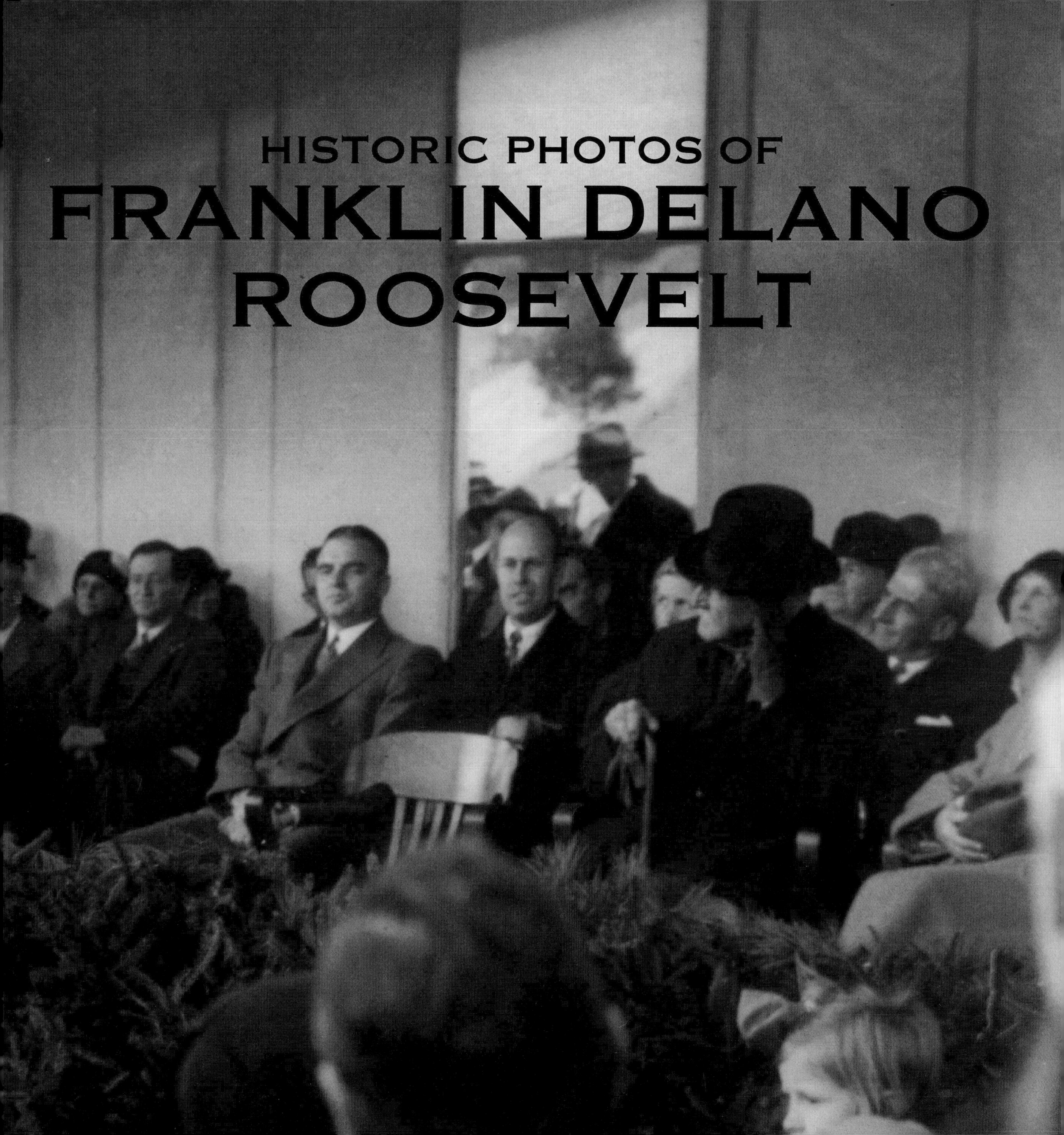

HISTORIC PHOTOS OF

FRANKLIN DELANO ROOSEVELT

Turner Publishing Company
200 4th Avenue North • Suite 950
Nashville, Tennessee 37219
(615) 255-2665

412 Broadway • P.O. Box 3101
Paducah, Kentucky 42002-3101
(270) 443-0121

www.turnerpublishing.com

Historic Photos of Franklin Delano Roosevelt

Library of Congress Control Number: 2007929602

ISBN-13: 978-1-59652-400-2

Printed in the United States of America

07 08 09 10 11 12 13 14—0 9 8 7 6 5 4 3 2 1

Contents

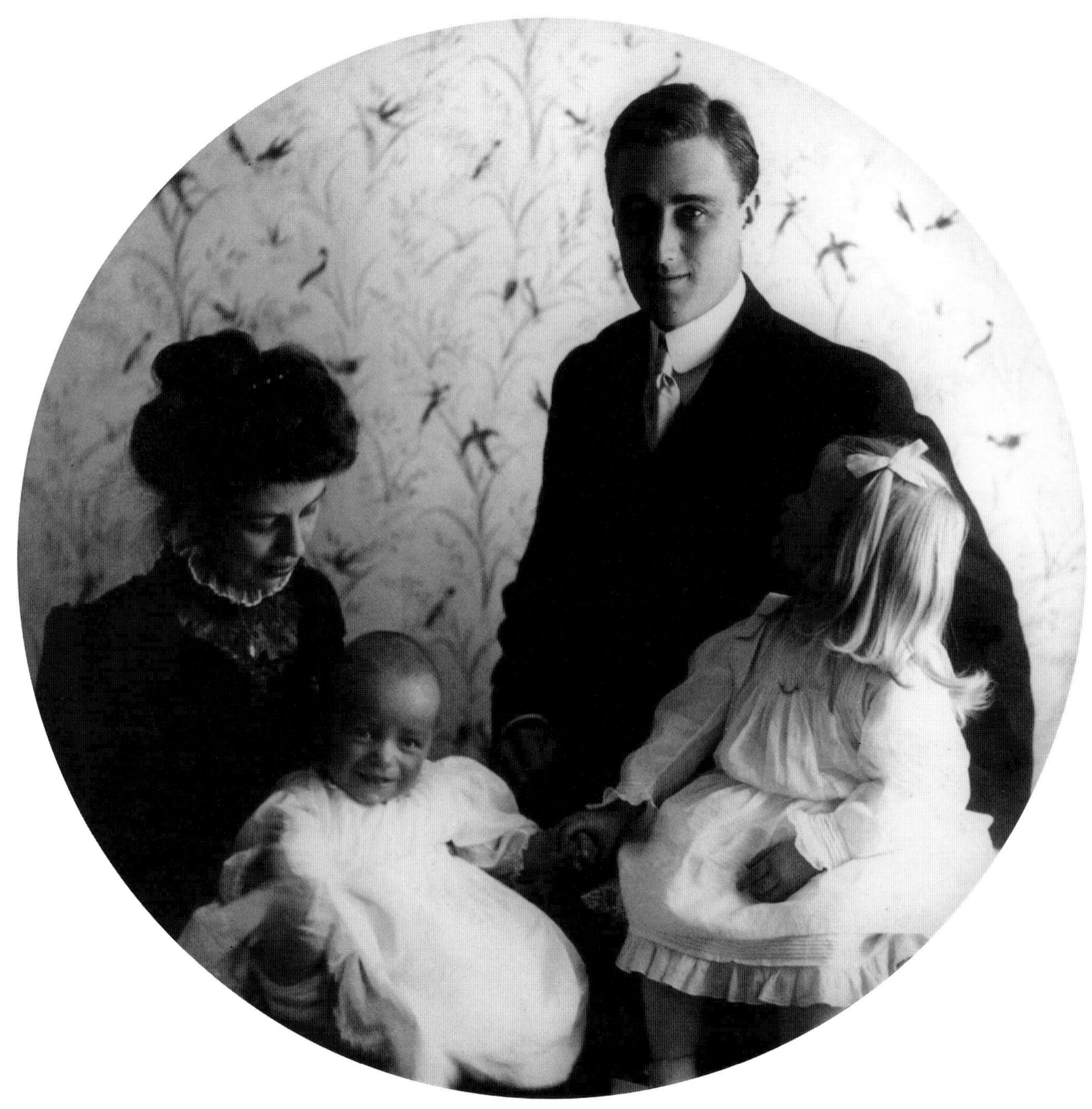

Formal portrait of FDR, Eleanor, and their two children, Anna and baby son James. FDR had left Columbia University Law School without a degree and joined the Carter, Ledyard & Milburn firm. His mother, Sara, gave them a new Charles A. Platt–designed New York brownstone at 49 East 65th (she owned the adjacent number 47). (1908)

Acknowledgments

This volume, *Historic Photos of Franklin Delano Roosevelt,* is the result of the cooperation and efforts of a number of organizations and individuals.

One cannot do research on Franklin Delano Roosevelt without acknowledging the dedicated and resourceful folks at the FDR Presidential Library, from which the photographs come.

And a word of thanks to all those scholars, editors, and memoirists of FDR who have delved into his life and career and produced insightful material.

—*Matthew Gilmore*

Preface

FDR was one of the most significant of American presidents. He came into office facing unprecedented economic crisis, for which he prescribed a "New Deal." That New Deal would radically change American government and transform politics for generations. On the heels of the struggle to restore the economy came the effort to fight and win the Second World War.

The photographs published in this volume encompass the entire career of the man who would become America's 32nd president. Here we see the atmosphere of his childhood—his family, friends, education. Here are his parents, James and (the much younger) Sara (Sallie) Delano Roosevelt. Sallie would remain a constant, influential, and steadying presence in FDR's life until her death a mere four years before his own. His youth as the only child of his parents had its compliment of friends, cousins, aunts, uncles, and even a niece and a nephew of similar age as playmates.

Travel was a constant in his life. There were trips to spas in Europe and to the windswept resort Campobello in Canada. These all had the effect of inculcating and deepening his lifelong love of things maritime. Much of his leisure was spent at sea—on his vacations from political responsibilities he would go sailing. As a political candidate, he would travel thousands of miles crosscountry in pursuit of the presidency. He would travel again and again as president—touring the country to project his concern and make personable connections. And he would retreat to Warm Springs, Georgia, for relief from the whirl of political life in Washington.

He was an avid collector—model boats, stamps, books—so much so that his collections would become the first presidential library. It is from that institution these photographs come.

Much of this is the ordinary life of any man of his class, yet FDR had overweening ambitions. Despite an odd political defeat or two, and his crippling illness, he would persist and succeed in his presidential dreams, backed by strong political advisors. Photographs illustrate his political campaigns from the first in 1910 to the last in 1944. The outlines of his career were unwittingly laid by his cousin (and uncle to his wife) President Theodore Roosevelt. Emulating his uncle, he followed much the same path—from local political office, to Assistant Secretary of the Navy, to vice-presidential candidate, and finally to the presidency. A fierce partisan, the program he offered the nation when he swept into office was unspecific. As *Time* magazine said, declaring him "Man of the Year" for 1932,

> Two months ago, in a lively referendum from ocean to ocean, the people of the U.S. chose their own Man of the Year, and clearly the election of Franklin Delano Roosevelt to the Presidency was without equal elsewhere in the world as an individual accomplishment. To millions & millions of "forgotten men" he was a big-jawed, happy Messiah whose "new deal" would

somehow put money into everybody's pocket. To himself, victory was the sweet reward of long years of careful planning, unremitting work.

Man of the Year Roosevelt's climb to the Presidency represented a physical triumph of the first order. For a decade he had fought a dogged fight to regain control over his paralyzed legs. Today the President-elect can walk in his braces, without crutch, stick, or assisting arm, about 15 steps. Declares his wife: "If the paralysis couldn't kill him, I guess the Presidency won't."

Will he make good in the White House? The country is only too ready to hope so. Yet in spite of his campaign utterances and the activities of his "brain trust," by last week President-elect Roosevelt had apparently only begun to arrive at his answers for the problems of 1933 . . . Cabinet . . . War Debts . . . Farm Relief . . . Economy . . . Tariff . . . Taxation . . . Prohibition. . . . A year from now the U.S. electorate will have a much more real idea of the worth of its 1932 Man of the Year.

If his presidential political platform was a bit of a mystery, his personal life was quite private, in a way almost unimaginable today. FDR married a distant cousin, Eleanor Roosevelt, niece of President Theodore Roosevelt. The marriage, after producing six children (five of whom lived), broke down when Eleanor discovered letters to a mistress. Family pressures left divorce not an option, so the marriage became a kind of political partnership. Franklin's paralysis led to Eleanor's taking the role of stand-in for her husband—as his eyes and ears on the campaign trail. But her story in many ways is a separate one, because they lived very separate lives. She was no enthusiast for his political career and dreaded the thought of becoming First Lady. FDR took pains not to be, and not to be shown as, confined to a wheelchair. Photographs show him swimming, fishing, speaking, campaigning, driving his car—all carefully supported by aides, or by his sons. His disability was no secret, and was commented on by the press, but his sheer gust of activity kept it from defining him as disabled.

FDR exuded a reassuring confidence, as photographs (both posed and candid) abundantly reveal. As president FDR's role was to parlay that sense of confidence into an effective political strategy to bring America out of its economic crisis. In the first hundred days of his term, he rolled out a plethora of political and economic programs, having taken the four months between election and inauguration to craft them. Paradoxically, Congressional resistance to the president's New Deal grew as economic conditions improved. Full-fledged economic recovery proved elusive, however, until America's entry into World War II.

In that war, FDR was a president engaged and in control. He toured war production plants in the Western United States, sailed to Hawaii to meet his admirals, traveled to meet with Allied leaders all over the world, and engaged in personal diplomacy with his fellow Allied leaders to remake the political shape of the postwar world, a world he would not live to see.

FDR's legacy of reshaping American political debate and the world political is both lauded and lamented—he has been excoriated by the left as the savior of American capitalism and by the right as the harbinger of the social welfare state. Speculation has also focused on whether FDR's diplomatic skills could have averted the postwar U.S.-Soviet cold war, even had he lived just a few years longer. Regardless of whether he is blamed or praised, one thing is clear: his legacy is immense.

FDR and Norman Davis on *Amberjack II* at Campobello. FDR would later remark, "I was glad that I had with me the American delegate to the Disarmament Conference in Geneva, Mr. Norman Davis, because he will go back to Geneva and will be able to tell them that he has seen with his own eyes what a border-line without fortifications means between two great Nations." (June 16, 1933)

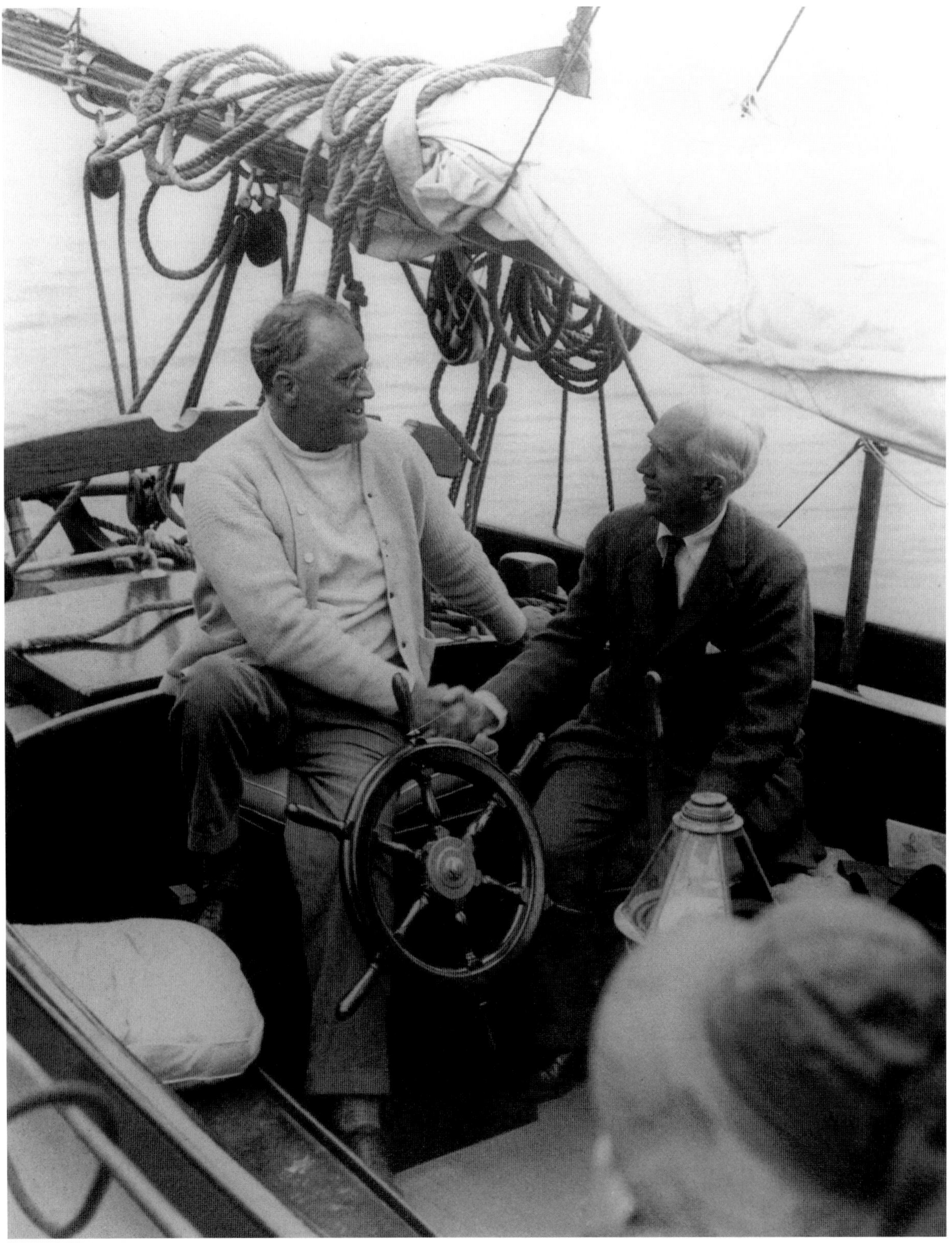

YOUTH
(1882–1910)

Franklin Roosevelt was born into the privilege and comfort of the squirearchy of the mid Hudson Valley, New York. It was an idyllic setting, something out of a Henry James or Edith Wharton novel. He was born January 30, 1882, in Hyde Park, to James Roosevelt and Sara (Sallie) Delano Roosevelt, as the couple's only child. James was the head of the Hudson Valley branch of the Roosevelts, a businessman, and president of the Delaware and Hudson Railroad. In 1867 he had bought Springwood in Hyde Park, near his paternal homestead.

Sallie was James' second wife, a Delano from Massachusetts. Sallie had a rather more exotic or cosmopolitan upbringing; her father Warren had moved the family to Macao during the Civil War to restore his fallen fortunes.

In a harbinger of things to come, when FDR was born, a Roosevelt cousin—Theodore—from the Long Island branch of the family, had just been elected to the New York State Assembly, the first of the large cousinage to enter politics.

The Roosevelts and Delanos moved in rarified New York circles, reaching to the very pinnacle. James' son from his first marriage married an Astor, as did one of Sallie's uncles, Franklin Delano, namesake of the future president. These connections would serve FDR in good stead throughout his life.

As the only son of an elderly father and much younger, doting mother, FDR grew up a precocious lad. Always eager to please and gratify his parents, he also began to reveal an independent streak. When his parents couldn't make a scheduled visit to an English country-house party, he took the train himself—because he wanted to see the stuffed-bird collection. A few years later he and his mother tangled over his acceptance of an invitation to stay with the Theodore Roosevelts at Oyster Bay. Although he had no siblings his own age, his half-brother James had two children just a few years older—they became his playmates, as well as other children on neighboring Dutchess County estates. On family vacations he had numerous Delano cousins to play with in Massachusetts, and the same social swirl existed at family summers in Campobello, New Brunswick.

His parents sent him two years late, at age fourteen, to Groton boys' school, in Ayer, Massachusetts. Despite the late start he managed to make his way at Groton, doing creditably well in the upper 25 percent of his class. After Groton came Harvard, where he again did well, but was more enthusiastic about his extracurricular activities. Hard work paid off and he spent his fourth year as president of the *Harvard Crimson.*

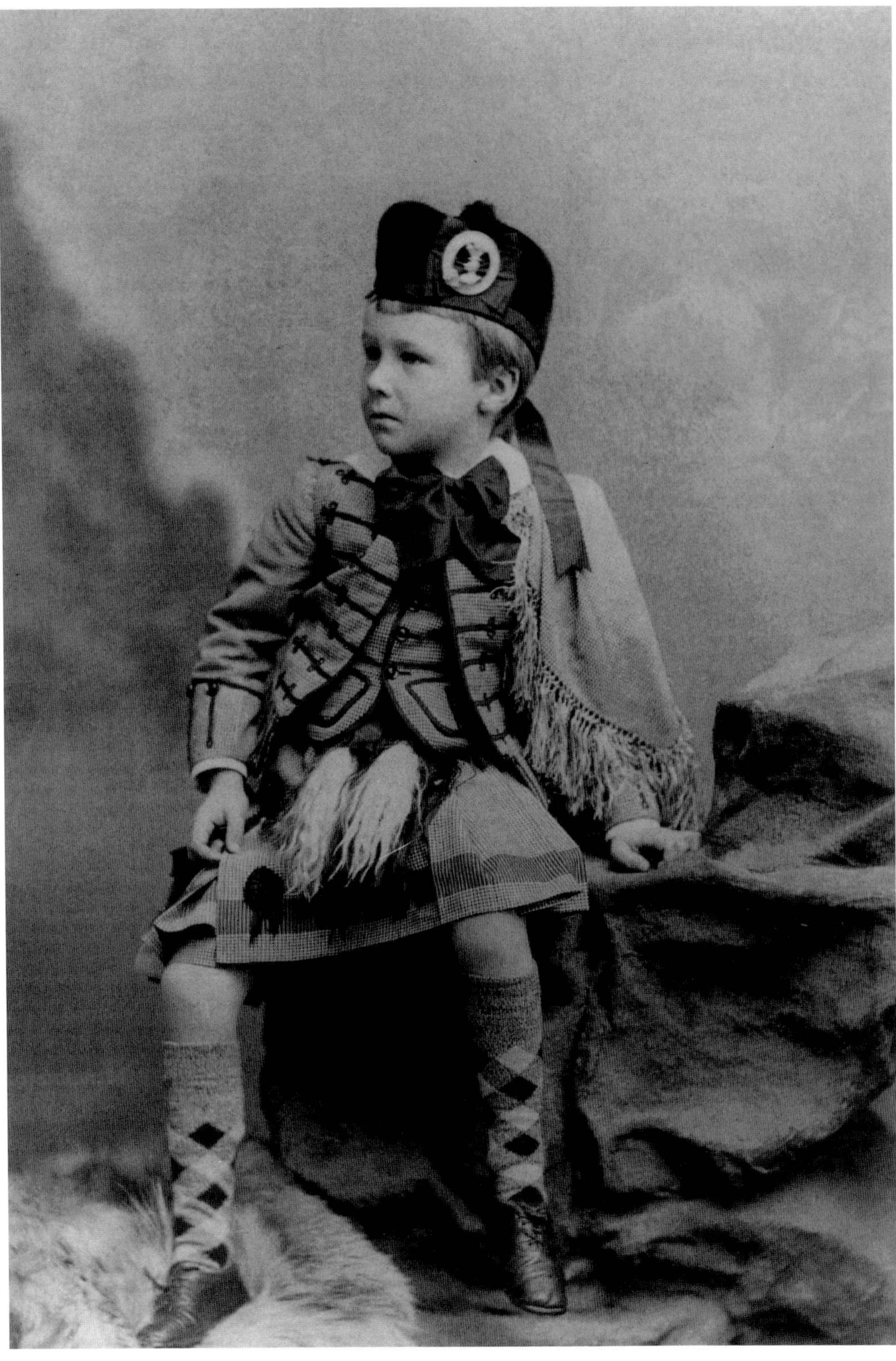

Formal portrait of the five-year-old FDR in full Scottish dress including kilt, taken in Poughkeepsie, New York. Here his boyhood curls have been shorn, but he would not graduate to pants until he was eight years old, kilts being an intermediate step.

Born January 30, 1882, after a difficult day-long labor, he would be James, Sr., and Sara (Sallie) Delano Roosevelt's only child. FDR had a much older half-brother, James Roosevelt Roosevelt (Rosy), born in 1854. It would be Rosy's children Taddy and Helen who would be his playmates. (January 1887)

One of two formal portraits of Franklin taken with each parent, this with his mother Sara. Franklin is in Scottish garb. The Roosevelt family spent the winter of 1887 in Washington, D.C., at 1211 K Street NW, renting the home of the Belgian ambassador in Washington's best neighborhood. They traveled in the highest circles of Washington and Democratic political society, socializing with eminences including William Whitney, Secretary of the Navy, and John Hay, who had been Lincoln's Assistant Secretary of State. As they departed the city, precocious FDR accompanied his father on a White House visit to see President Grover Cleveland. Cleveland, politically embattled, and destined to lose his re-election bid the following year, reputedly wished the five-year-old boy to "never be President of the United States." Yet forty-five years later the man that boy became would sit in the same office. (1887)

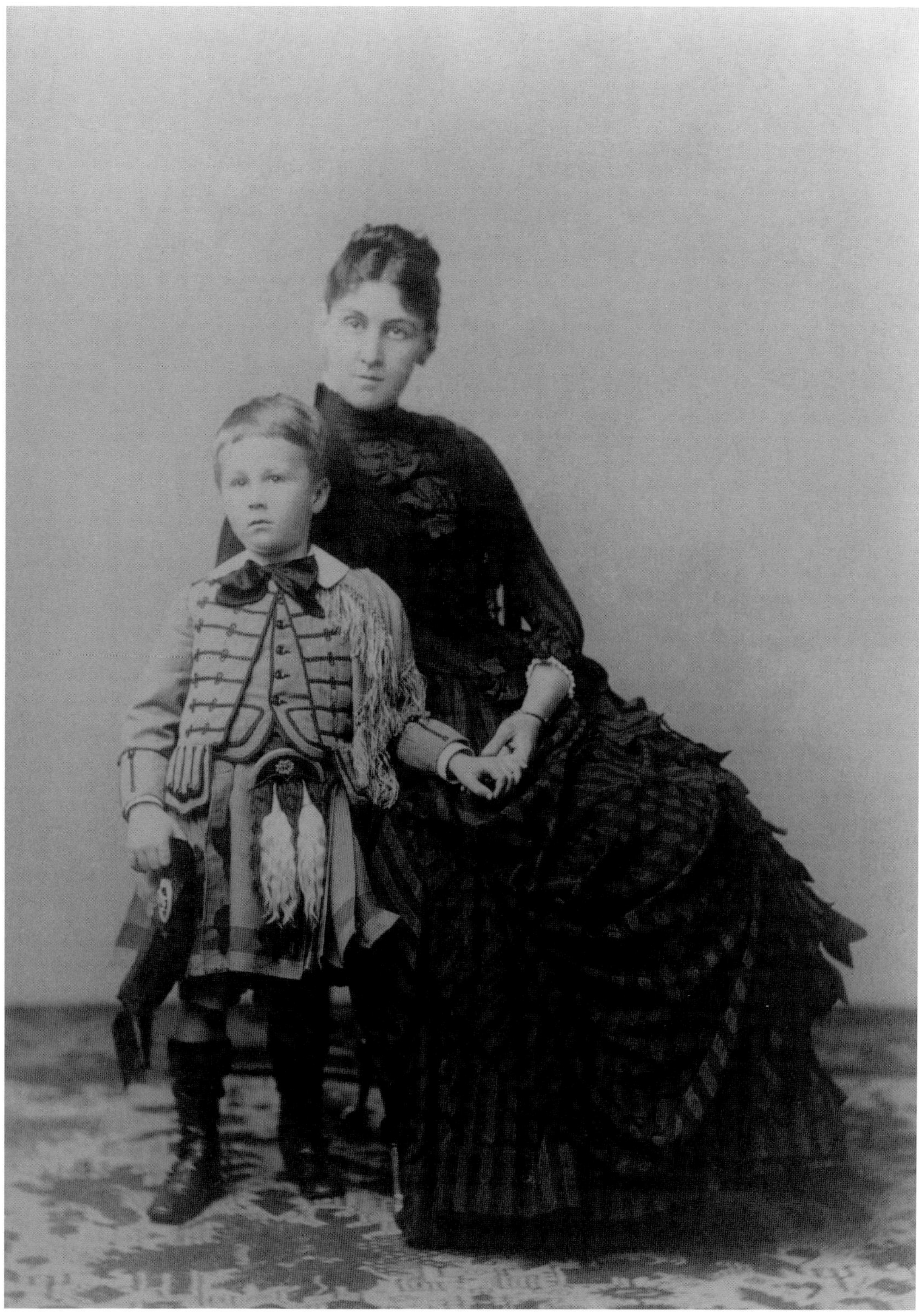

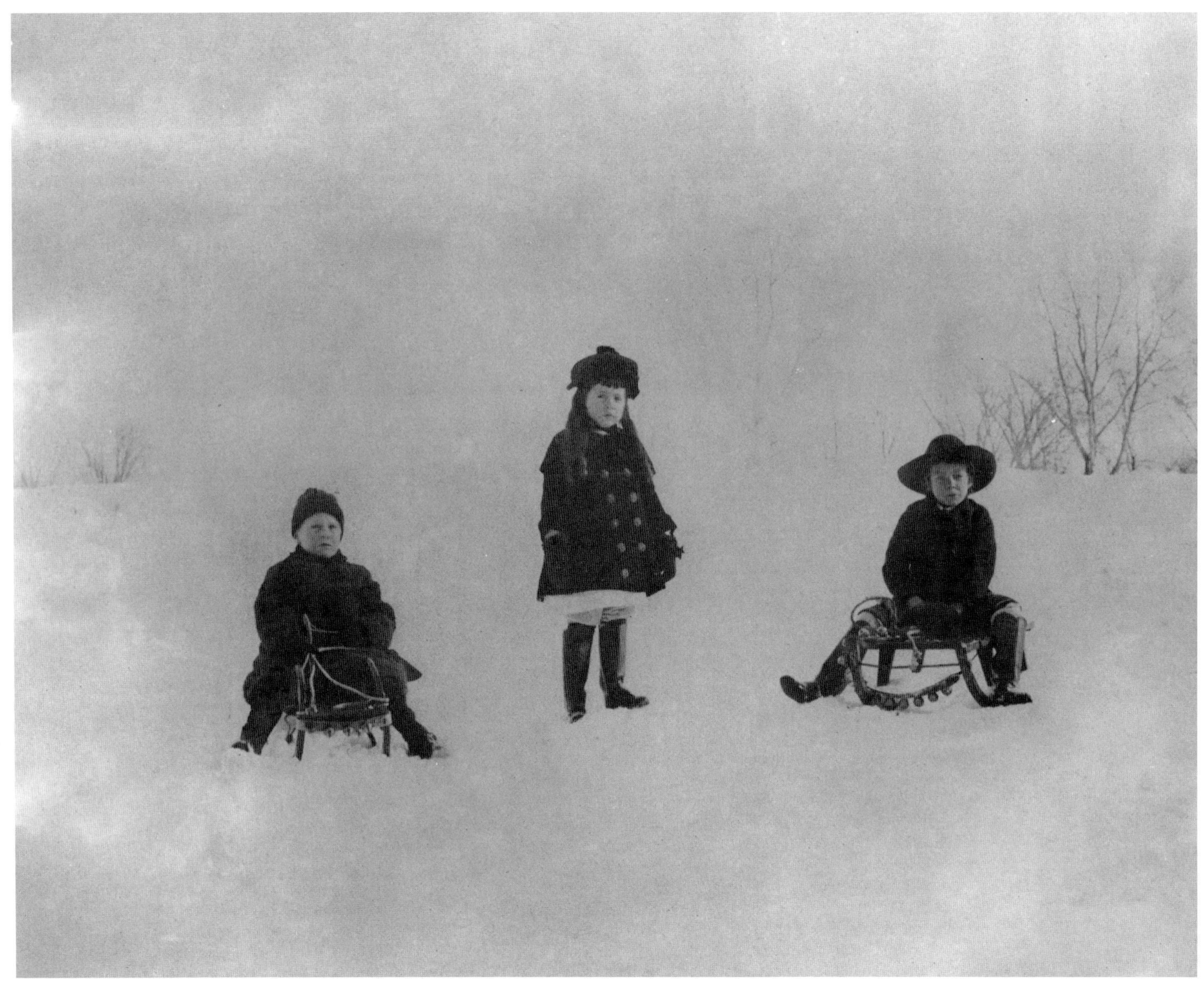

FDR and two playfellows, Helen and James Jr. (Taddy) Roosevelt. The two were actually FDR's niece and nephew, children of his half-brother James and wife Helen Astor. Taddy and Helen, two years and one year older, lived next door until 1893 when their father was posted to London. (1887)

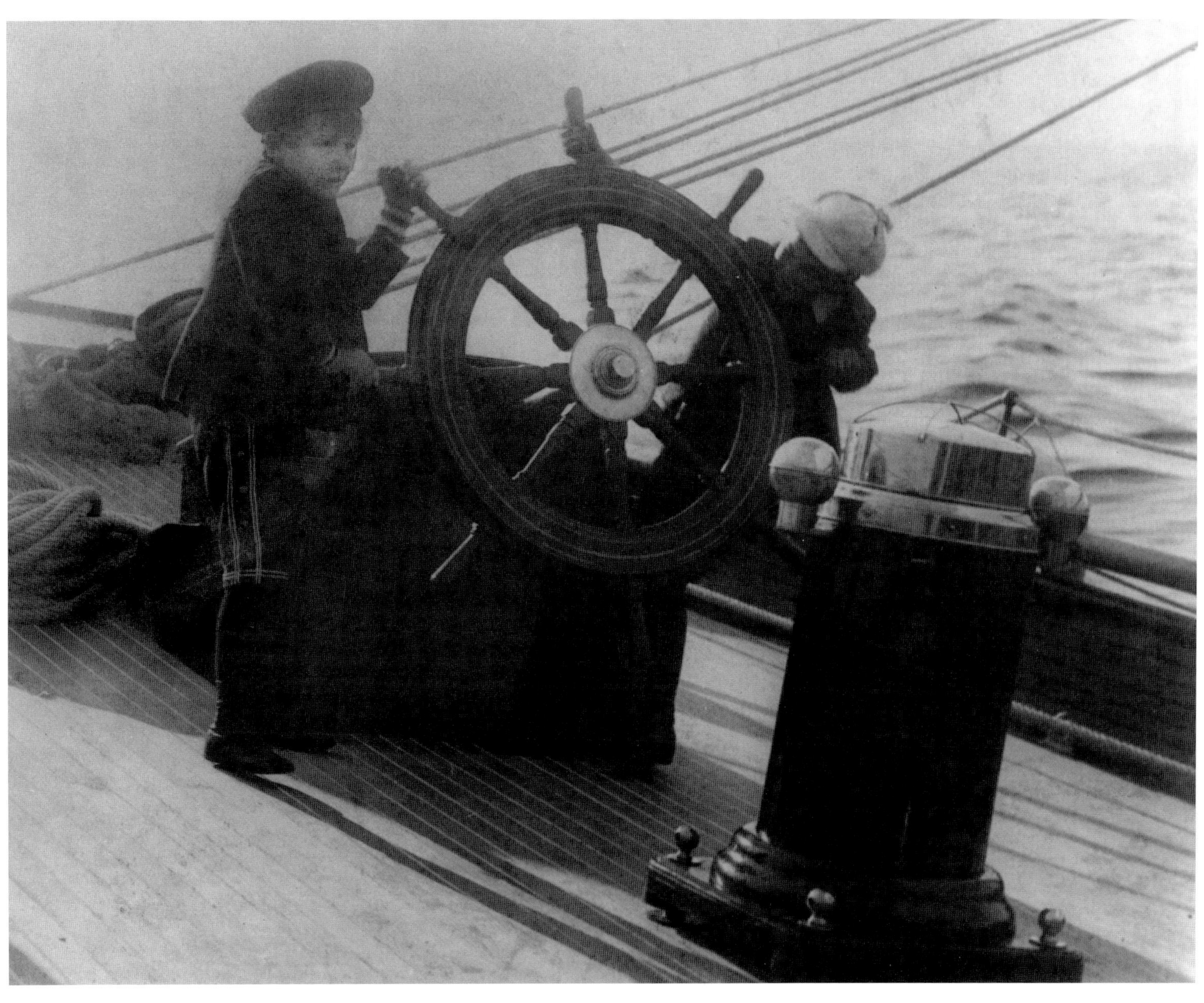

FDR and friend "piloting" the family yacht at Campobello. Campobello, New Brunswick, just across the Canadian border from Maine was developed as a resort in the early 1880s by Bostonians and New Yorkers. The place was touted for "favorable climate, the clean, bracing, salt-tinged, balsam-scented air and the abundant scenic beauty." The Roosevelts and friends summered there starting in 1883. (1888)

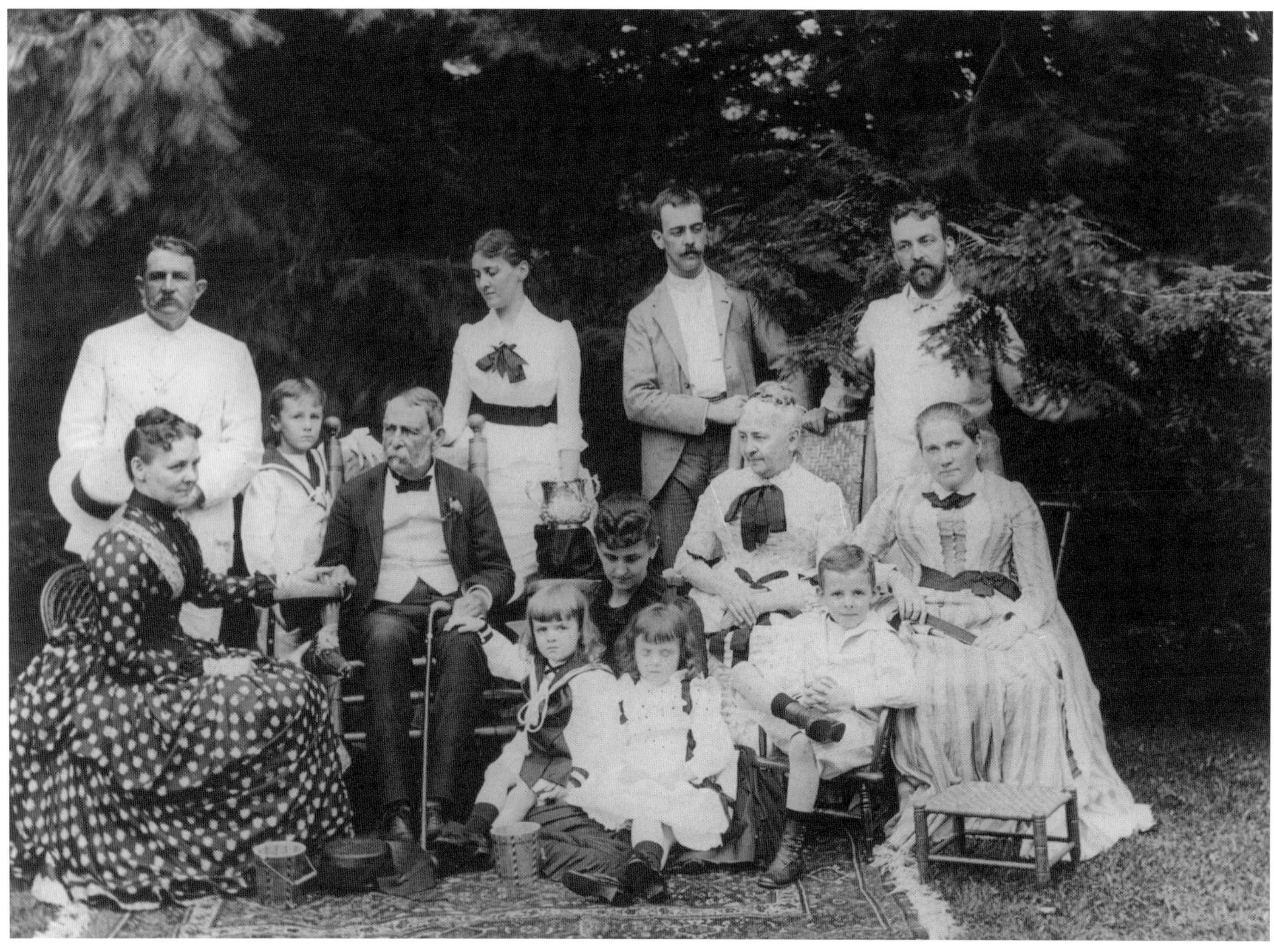

Family portrait for "Papa's 80th birthday" including numerous members of the Delano family—Deborah, Annie, Warren III, Sara, Katharine, and Frederic. "Papa" is Warren Delano II, FDR's grandfather, father of his mother Sallie. The family assembled to present the loving cup on the pedestal to his left. Delano had a rather exotic life—in 1833 he sailed to China and made a career there. He stayed during the Opium War, then married and moved to Macao. He moved back to the United States to Balmville, but after financial reverses, returned to China and Hong Kong to restore his fortune, taking his family including Sara. This image was recorded at Algonac in Balmville, near Newburgh, New York. The hamlet Balmville was a fashionable, mostly rural retreat, filled with stylish houses, including Algonac, which was designed in the popular Andrew Jackson Downing Italian villa style, as was Springwood, the Roosevelt home across the Hudson. (July 13, 1889)

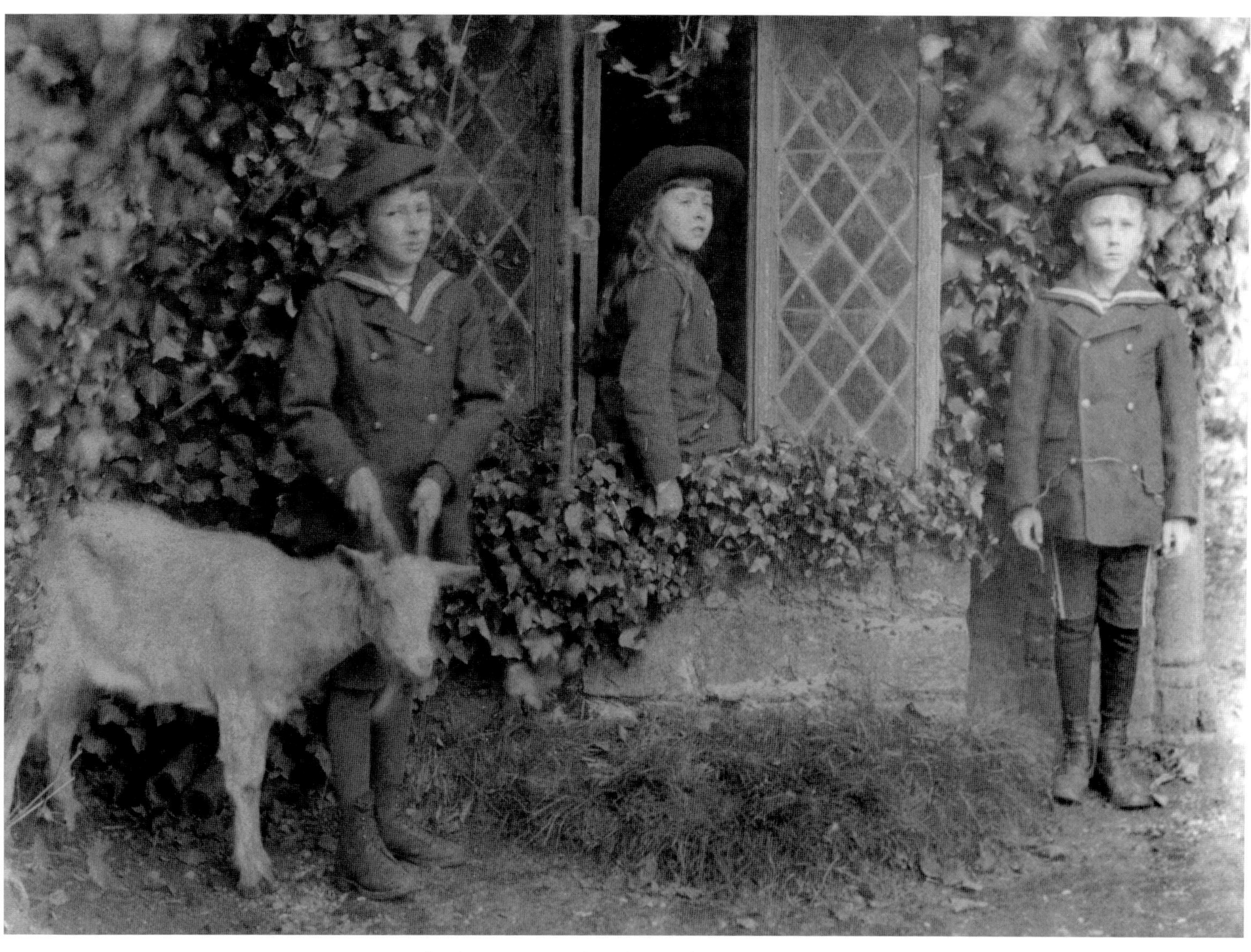

FDR, a family pet goat, and nephew and niece, Taddy and Helen Roosevelt, in Bicester, England. FDR was recuperating from typhoid contracted crossing the Atlantic. FDR and Taddy didn't get along, but he and Helen were great friends. Bicester is a few miles north of Oxford. James Roosevelt had bought a house there; he would be posted to London as a political reward in 1893. (1889)

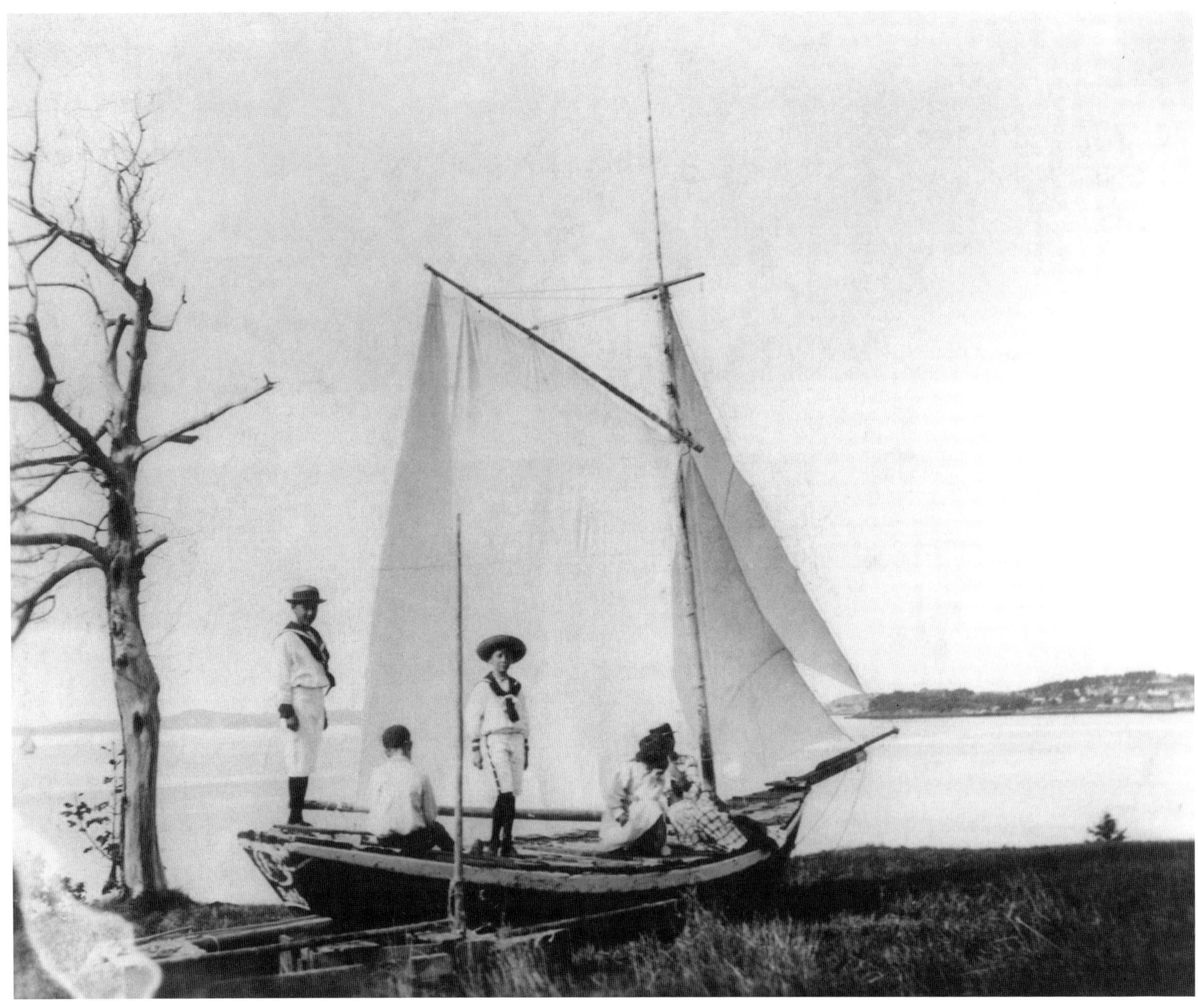

FDR, cousin Russell Sturgis, Henry L. Green, and Betty and Kate Porter during a Campobello outing. Sailing the bay was the primary recreation for those staying at the three hotels. Campobello was the summer retreat for a number of the East Coast elite. (1890)

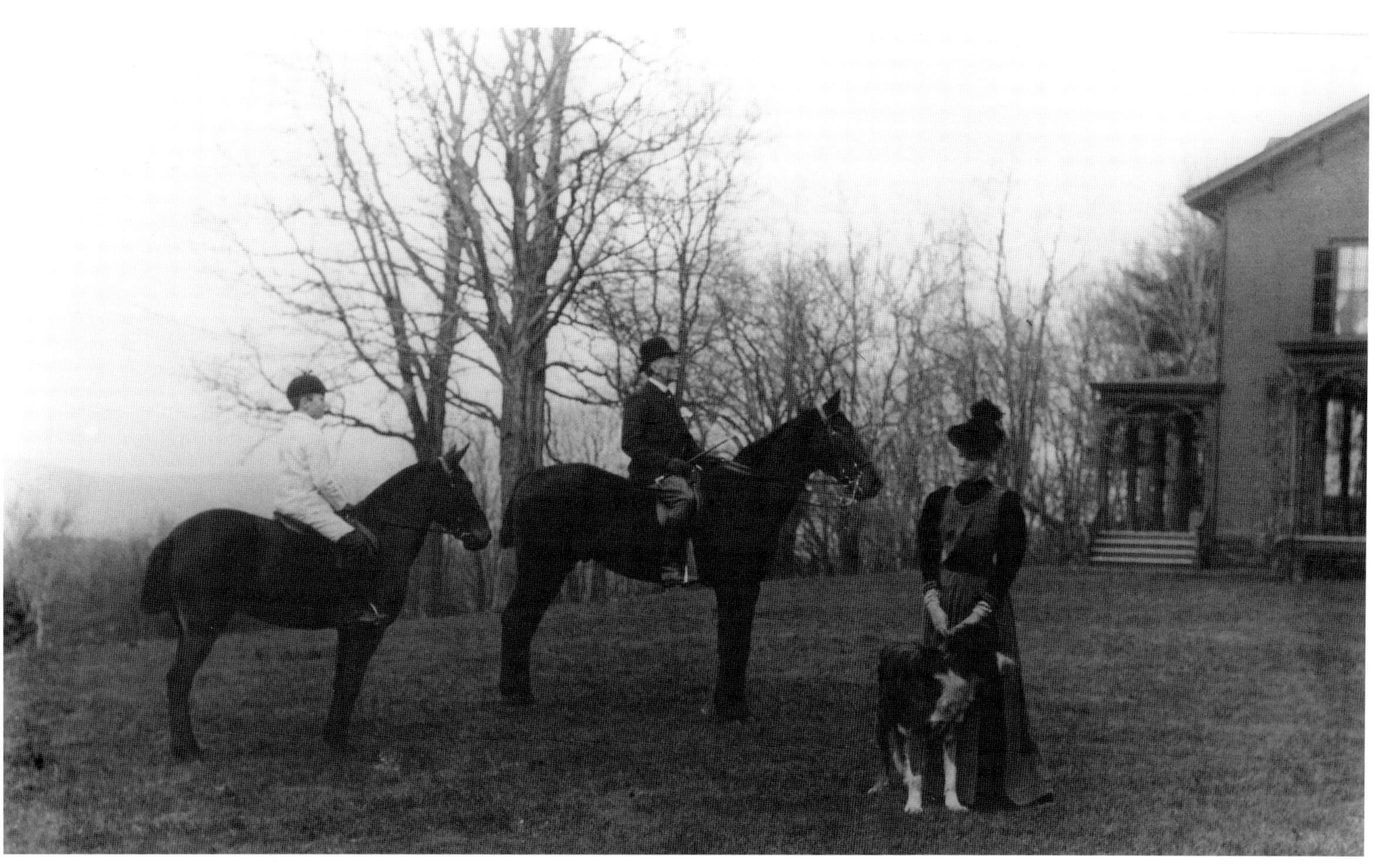

FDR on his Welsh pony at the family home Springwood in Hyde Park with his father, James, and mother, Sallie, and dog. He would write to his aunt Dora Forbes "My pony Debby is well and I rode 12 miles today with Papa and we are going to ride to Algonac as we did last summer." (April 10, 1891)

Formal portrait of the young FDR, now ten years old and graduated to short pants and sailor suit, taken in Poughkeepsie. The previous year he and family had sailed to Germany on the *Teutonic*. His father had taken the cure at Bad Nauheim, where FDR was briefly enrolled in a German school. (January 1892)

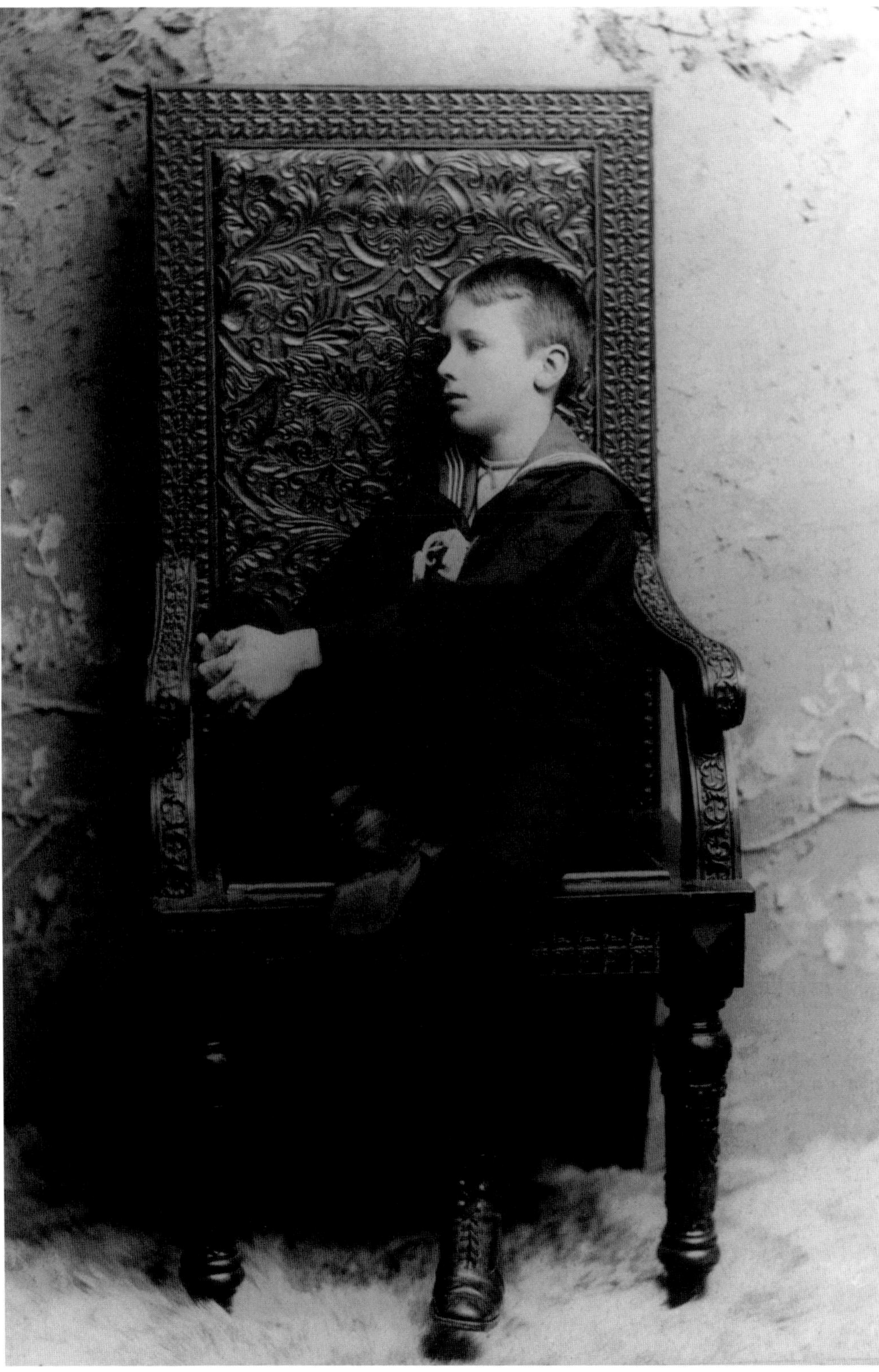

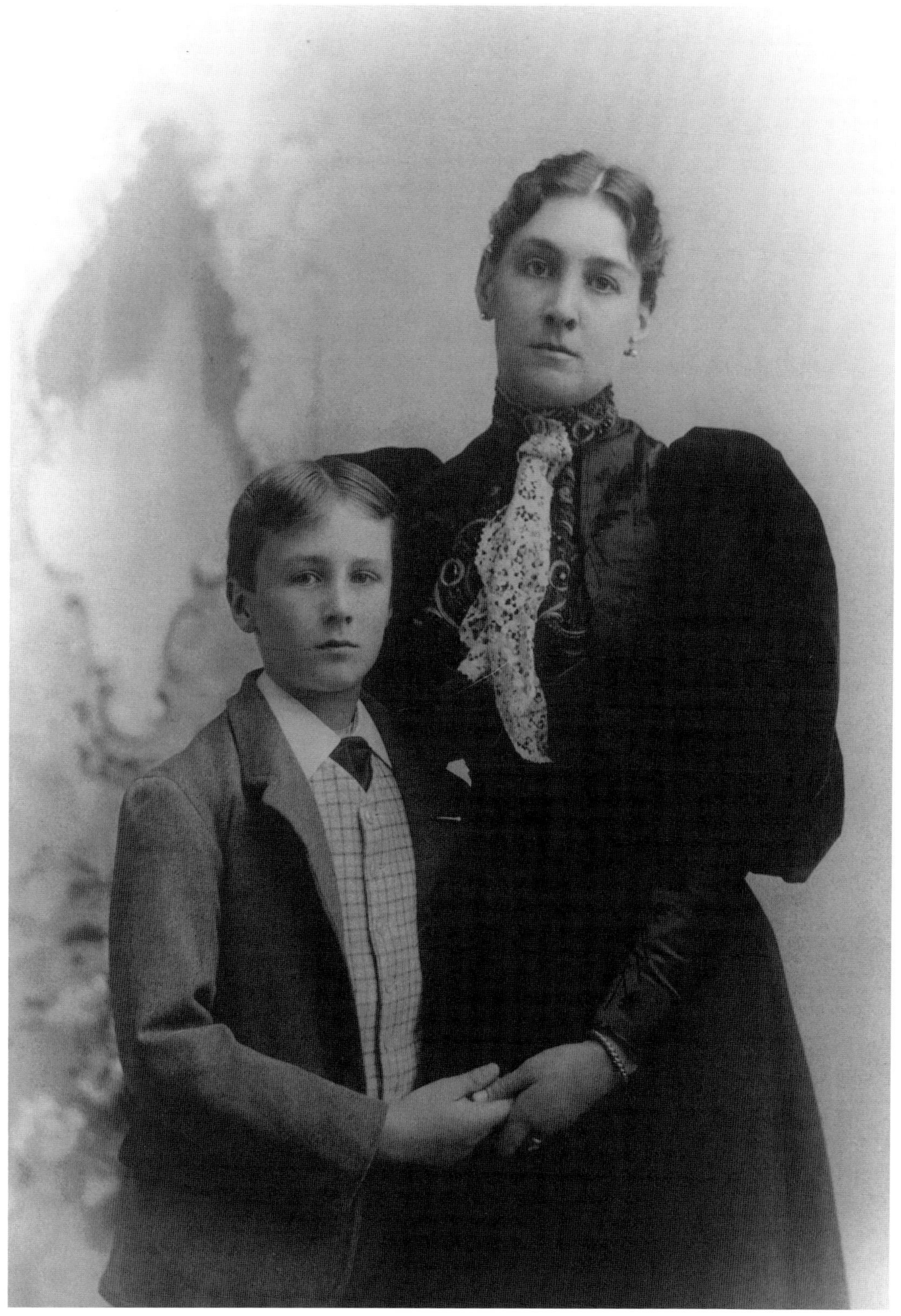

Formal portrait of young FDR (clothed in a young man's clothes) with his doting mother, Sara. Franklin here is eleven years old, and the strong resemblance between mother and son is visible. His mother always considered him far more a Delano than a Roosevelt. (1893)

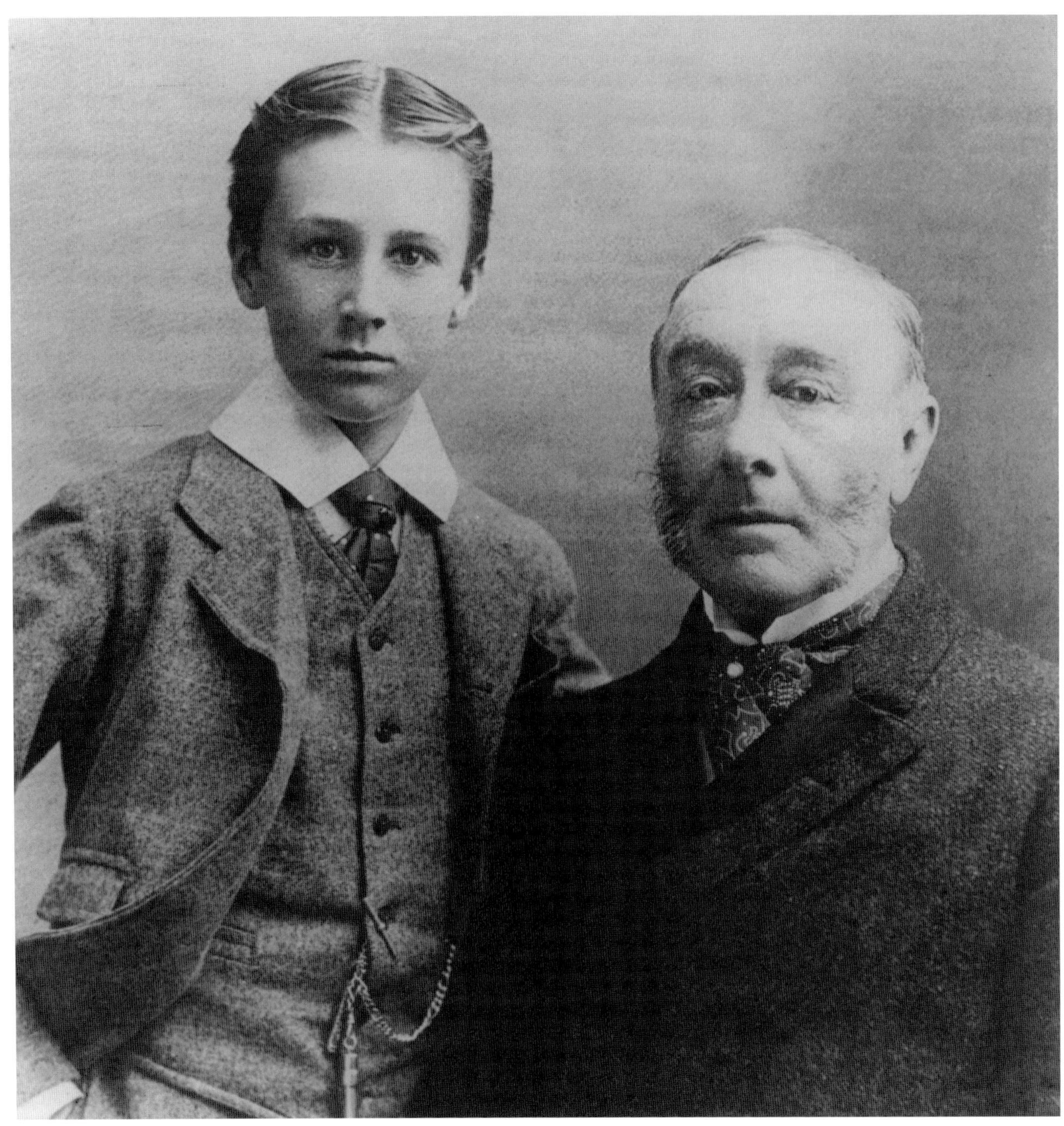

Here is twelve-year-old FDR with his father, James. Franklin's father, now sixty-seven years old, was growing frail. His mother was a much stronger influence on his life—Franklin did not set up his own household until after her death in 1941. (1895)

FDR with Colonel Archibald Rogers and Edith Morton at Loon Lake, New York. Near neighbors, FDR was friends with the Colonel's sons Archibald, Jr., and Edmund. When Archibald, Jr., died in 1889, Edmund became FDR's closest friend and they attended Groton together. Loon Lake was a favorite retreat of President Harrison. Edith Morton was one of Vice-president Levi Morton's four daughters and a Rhinebeck neighbor. This was her coming-out year and in a few more she would marry William Corcoran Eustis and settle in Virginia. (March 16, 1895)

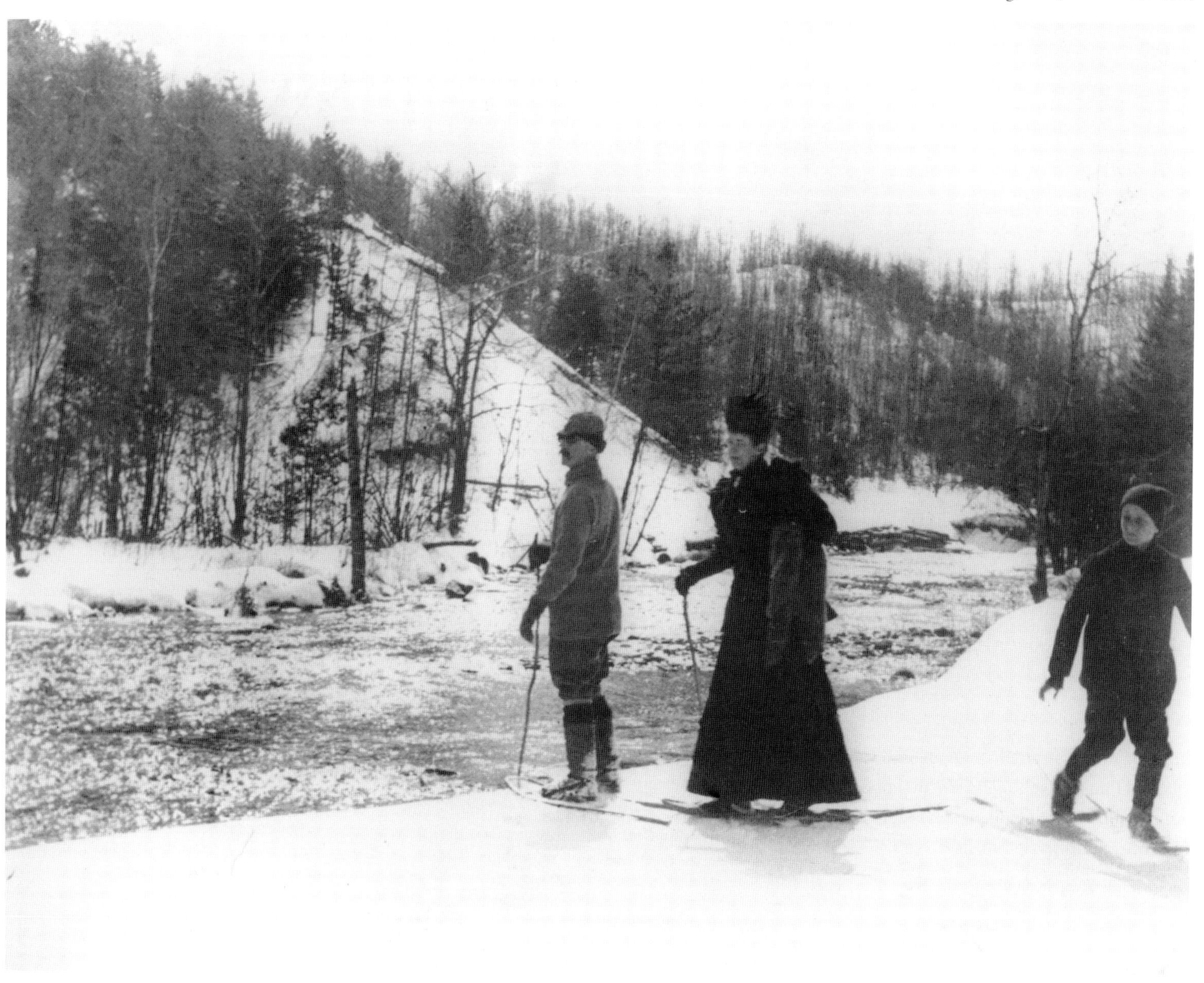

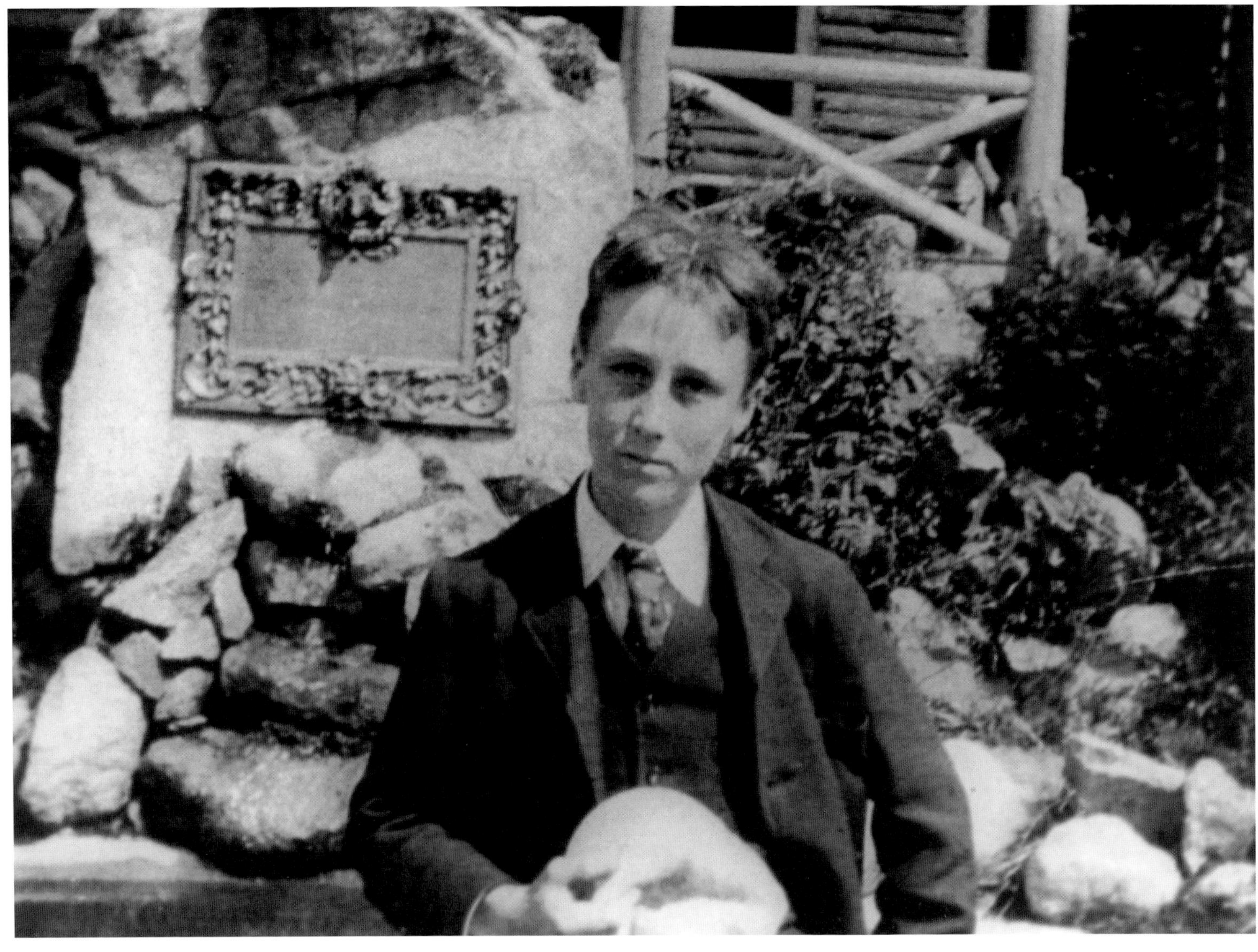

A picture entitled "'Self' (taken by SDR)." "SDR" presumably refers to Sara Delano Roosevelt. The image was recorded at Saint Blasien, Germany. The summer before going to Groton, FDR, now 14, and his tutor Arthur Dumper bicycled through Germany, eventually meeting up with Franklin's parents at Bad Nauheim. Roughing it, the two survived on black bread and cheese. FDR would return here on his honeymoon. (1896)

FDR in a group school portrait, Groton. He entered Groton two years later than the other boys, who entered at age twelve. A boys' school of 110 students, Groton was the brainchild of its headmaster Endicott Peabody—who wanted to instill manly Christian character in his students. Despite the disadvantage of a late start, FDR's twice-weekly letters carry no complaints about the Spartan life at the school. (1897)

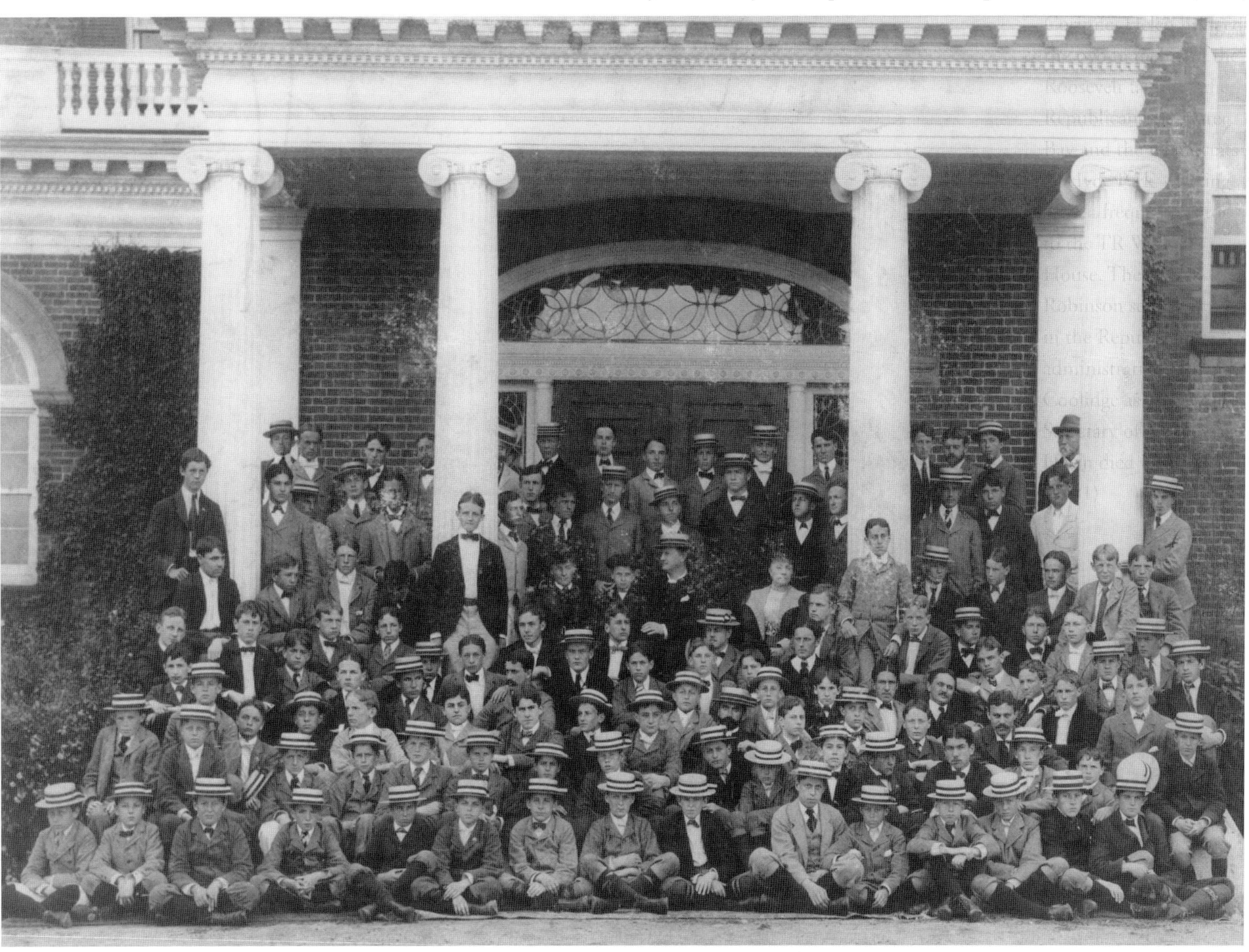

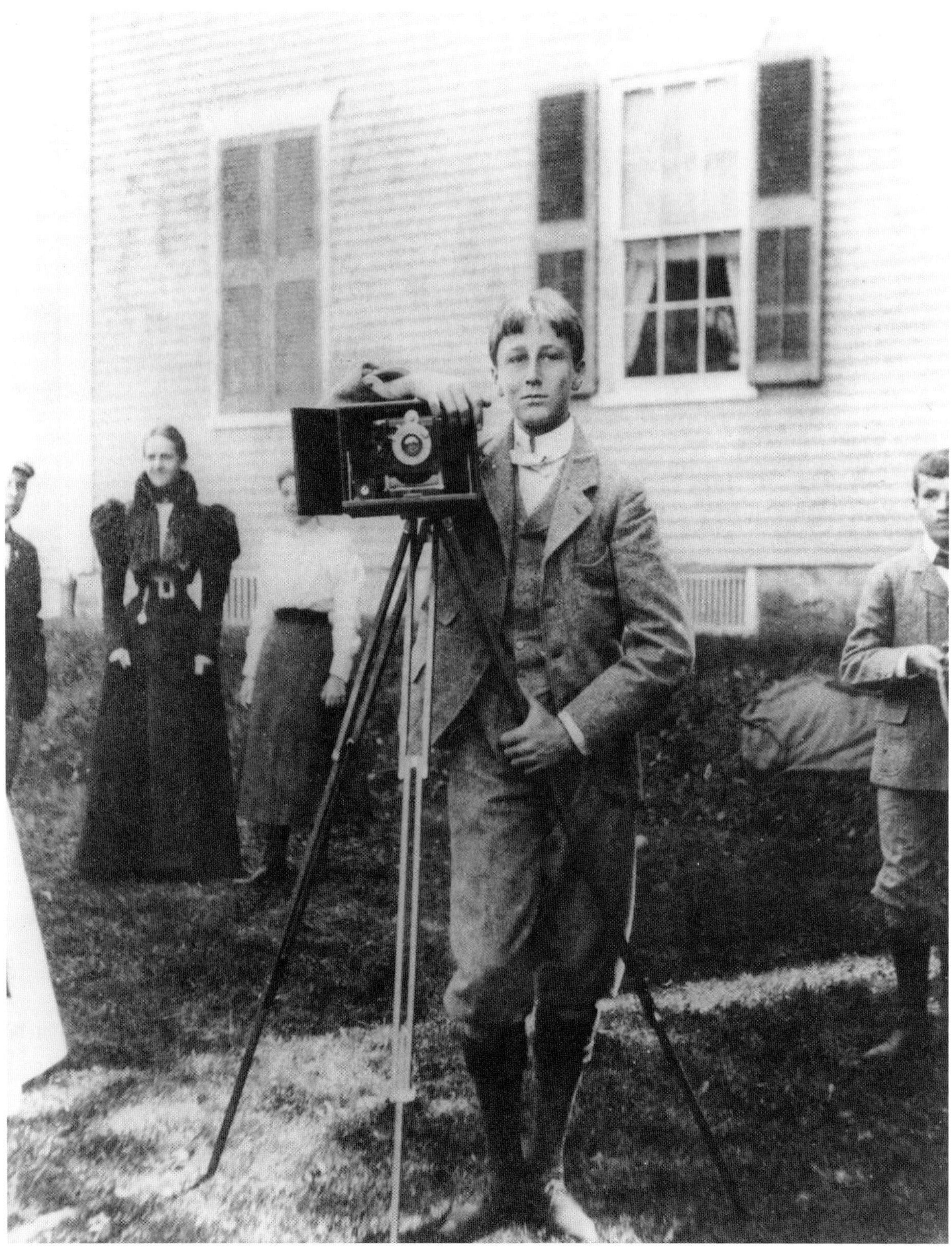

On the other side of the camera, FDR prepares to photograph his Delano grandfather and cousins. (1897)

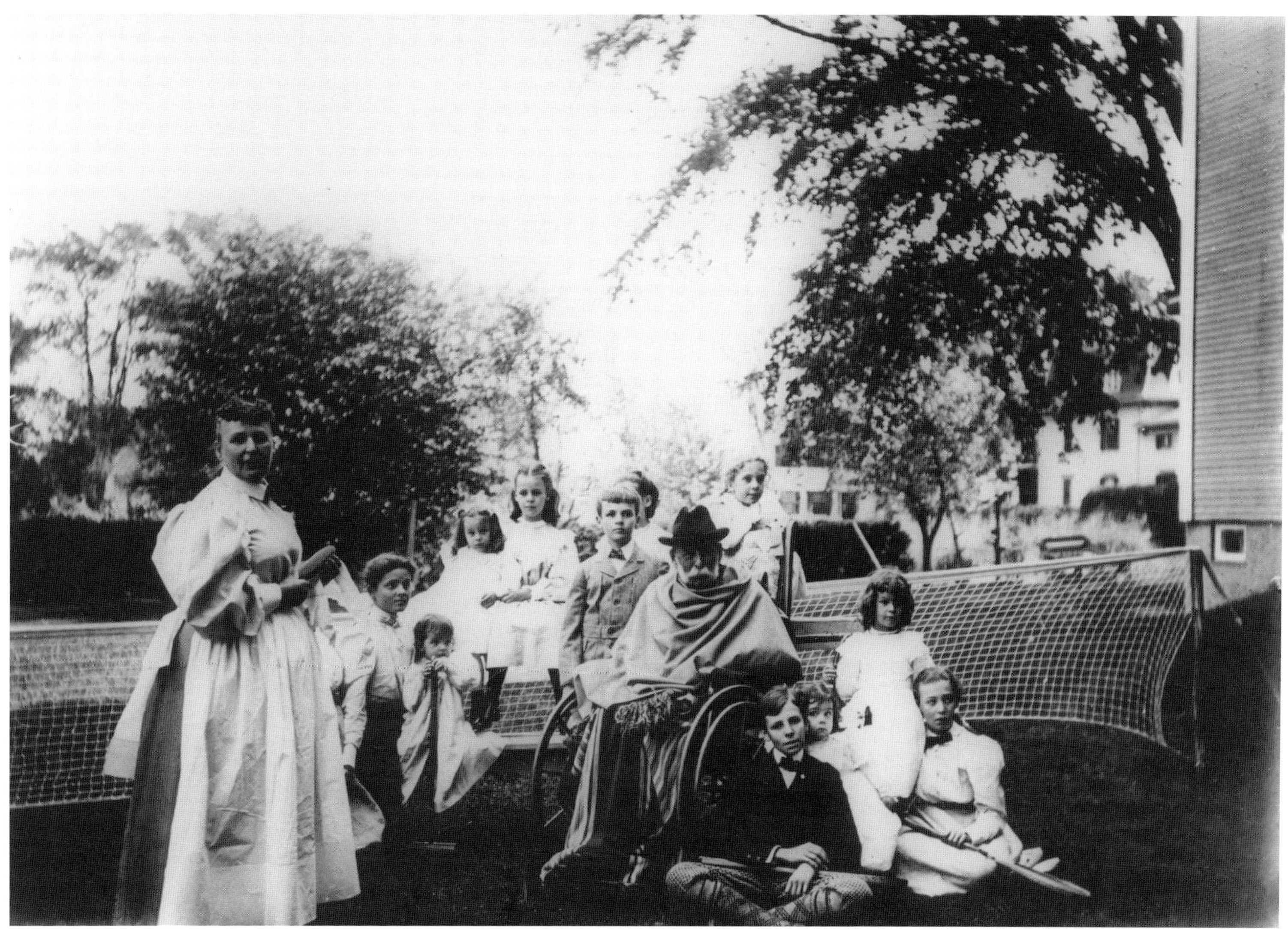

FDR's efforts as photographer yield a candid family portrait of Grandfather Delano and cousins in Fairhaven, Massachusetts. With his grandfather are cousins Lyman, Ellen, Jean, and Sara Delano, Muriel and Warren Robbins, Katherine and Sara Collier, Catherine, Louise, and Laura Delano. Fairhaven was the Delano family hometown, where the first Warren Delano, father of FDR's grandfather built this home in 1832 (and where it still stands at 39 Walnut Street). This was the last summer visit FDR would make to see his grandfather, who died in January 1898, although family gatherings continued for many years more. (1897)

FDR and his father, James, niece Helen Roosevelt, and family friend Frances Pell at Campobello. Perhaps this is the inaugural cruise on James' new yacht, the *Half Moon II,* the previous yacht having accidentally blown up in the Hudson in 1898. (August 1899)

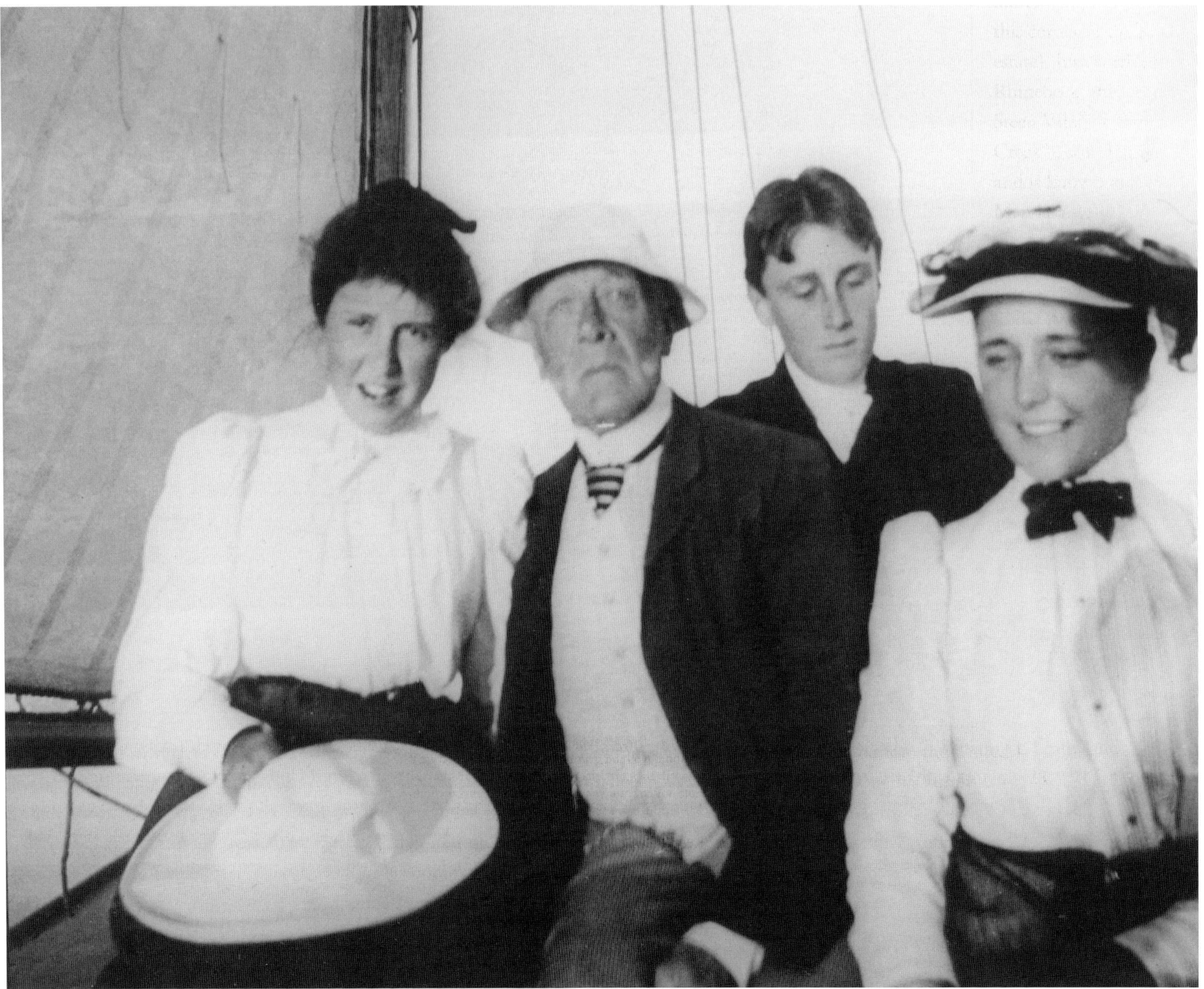

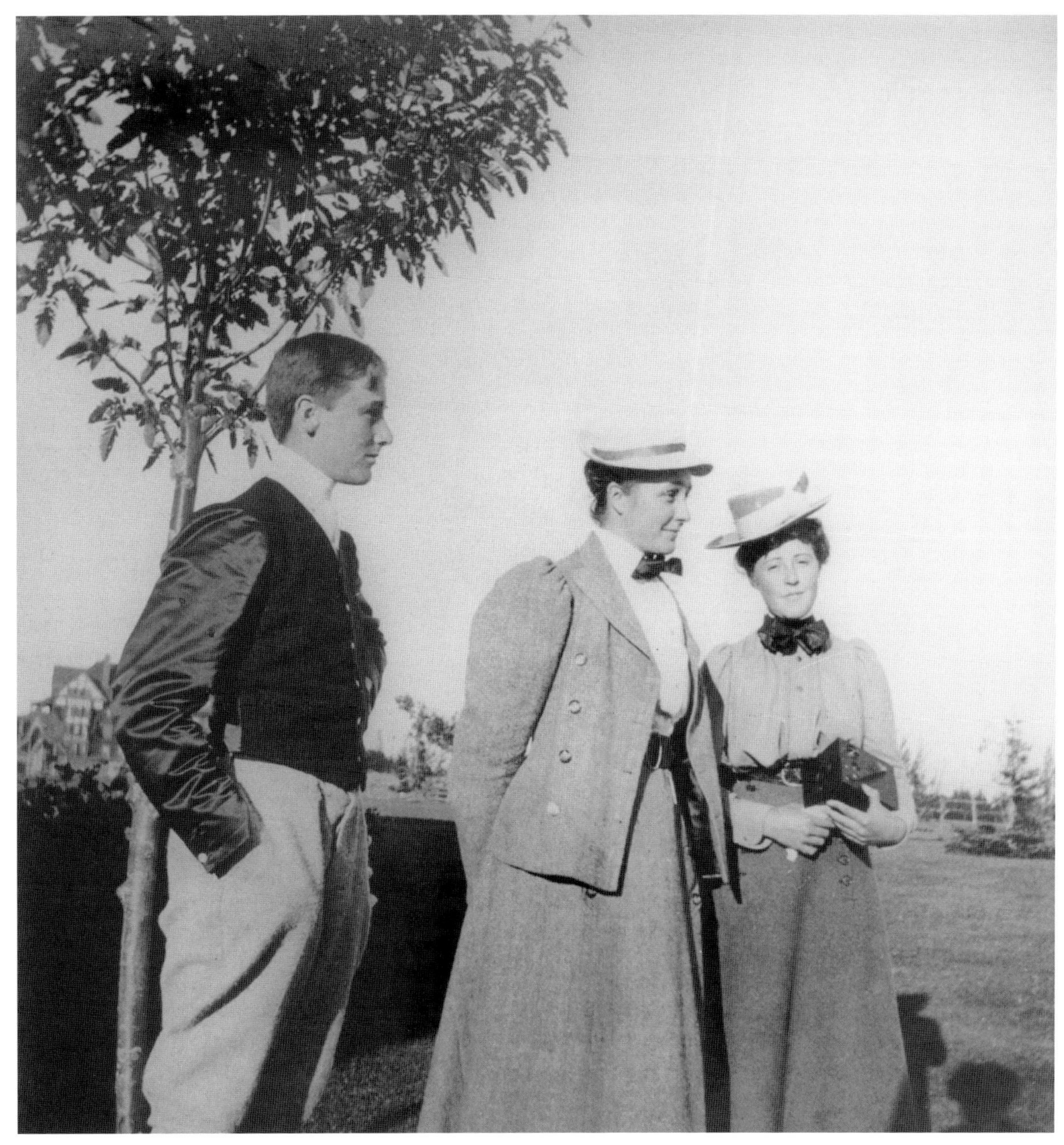

FDR, Frances Pell, and Helen Roosevelt ashore at Campobello. Frances Pell was a childhood friend of FDR's and niece of financier J. P. Morgan. (August 1899)

A lanky FDR and his father, mother, and cousins, Ellen, Laura, Sarah, and Jean Delano in Fairhaven, Massachusetts. Grandfather Delano had died in January; the girls are the daughters of Warren Delano III, who had inherited the family home. This would be one of the last times James would make the trip; he would die in 1900. (September 1899)

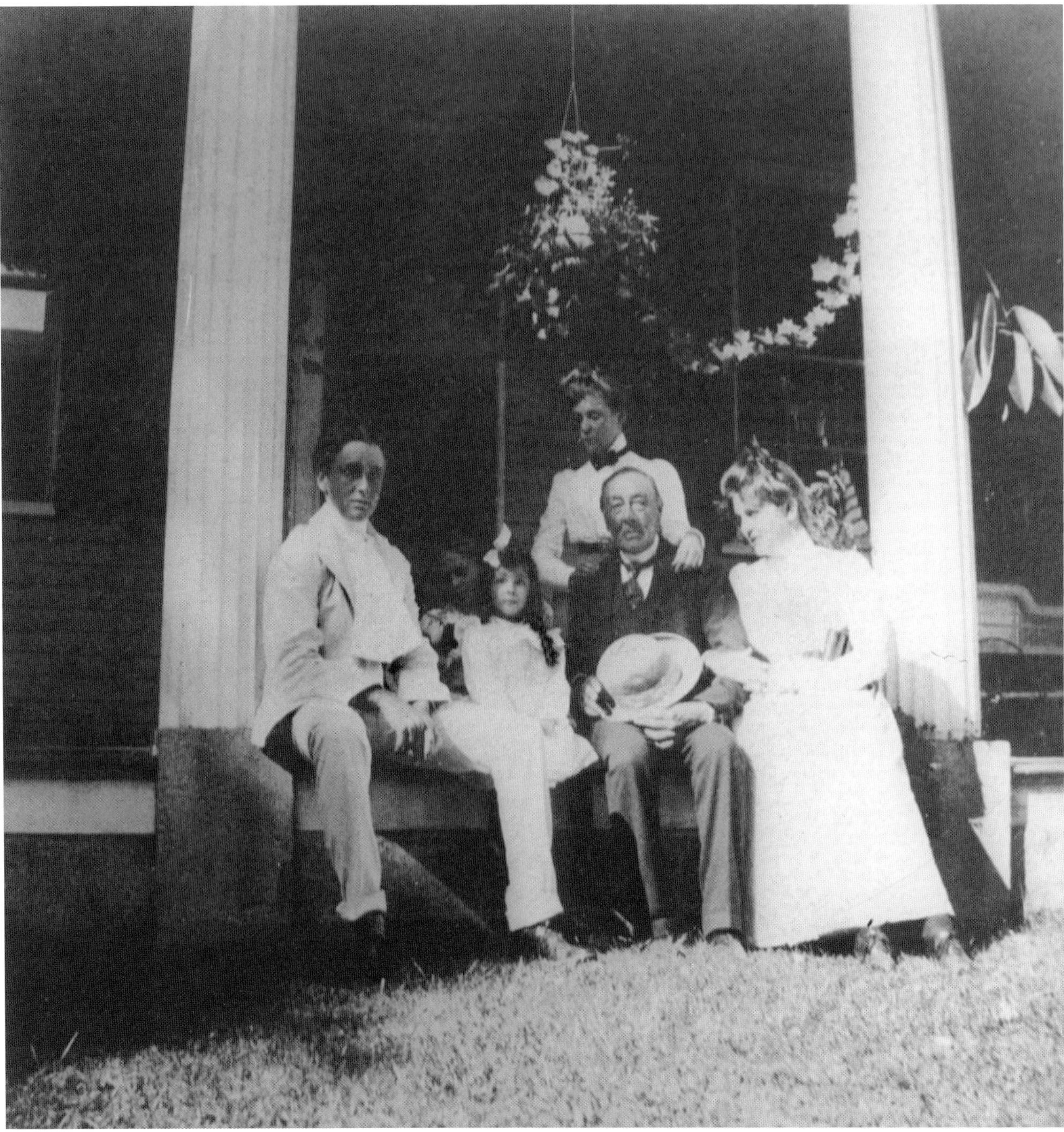

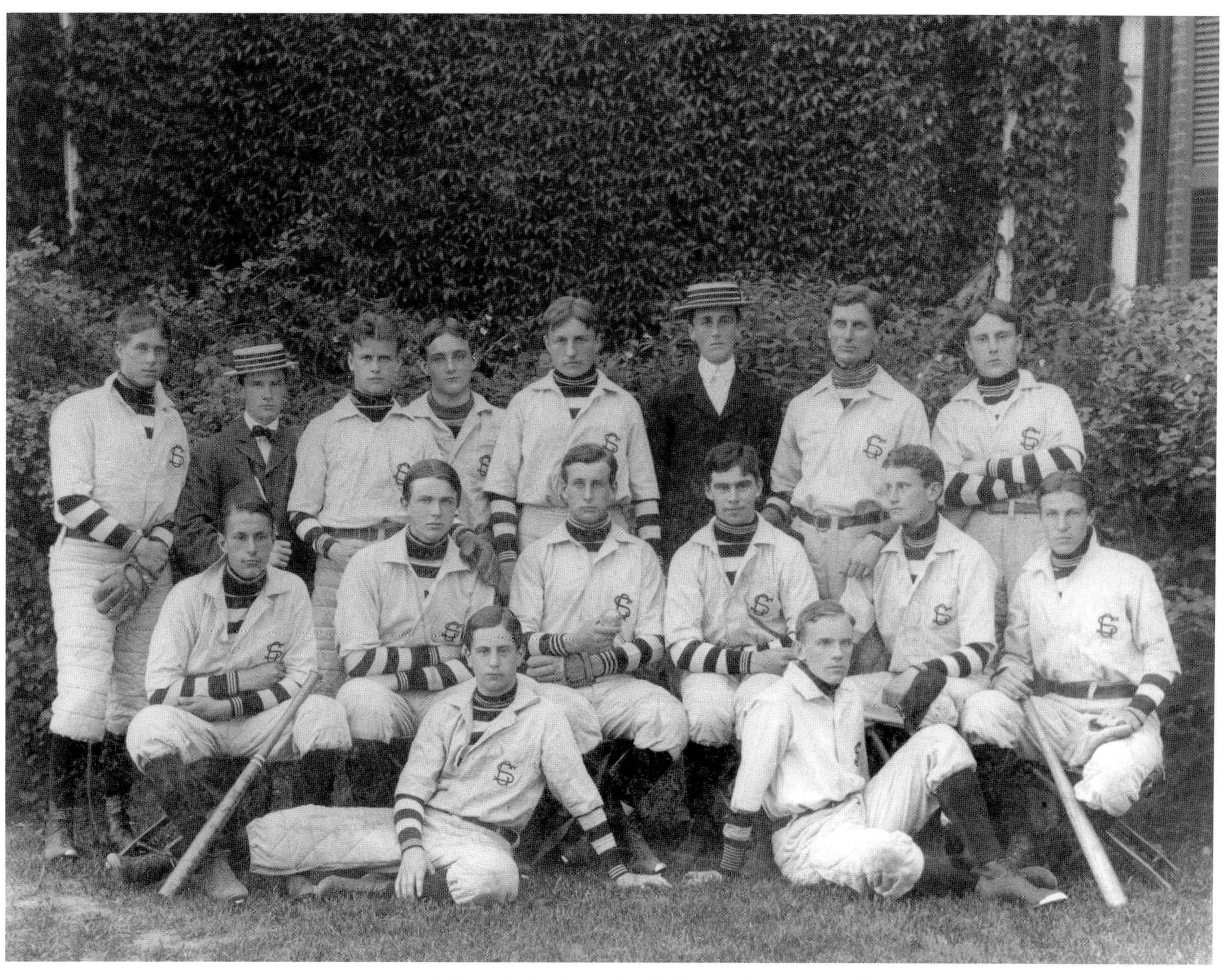

FDR with the Groton baseball team after Groton defeated St. Mark's 7-6 in 12 innings. Franklin was team manager. Baseball would be part of FDR's presidential career more than thirty years later, as he continued the presidential tradition of throwing out the first ball of the season at the Washington Senators game. (1899)

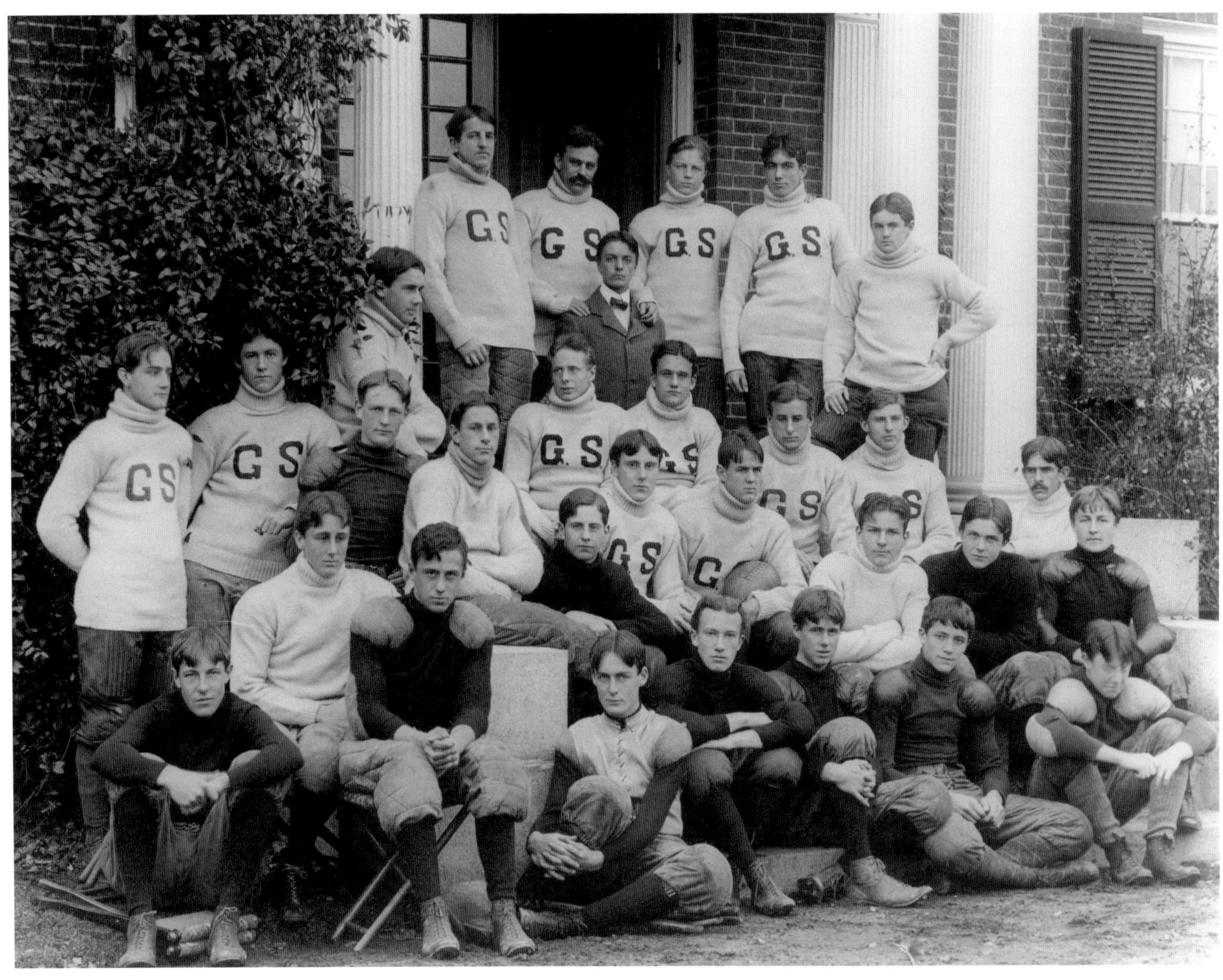

The Groton football team. FDR briefly played fullback on a Groton team, but headmaster Endicott Peabody concluded that he was "too slight for success" athletically. FDR appears to be wearing padding underneath his uniform. (October 1899)

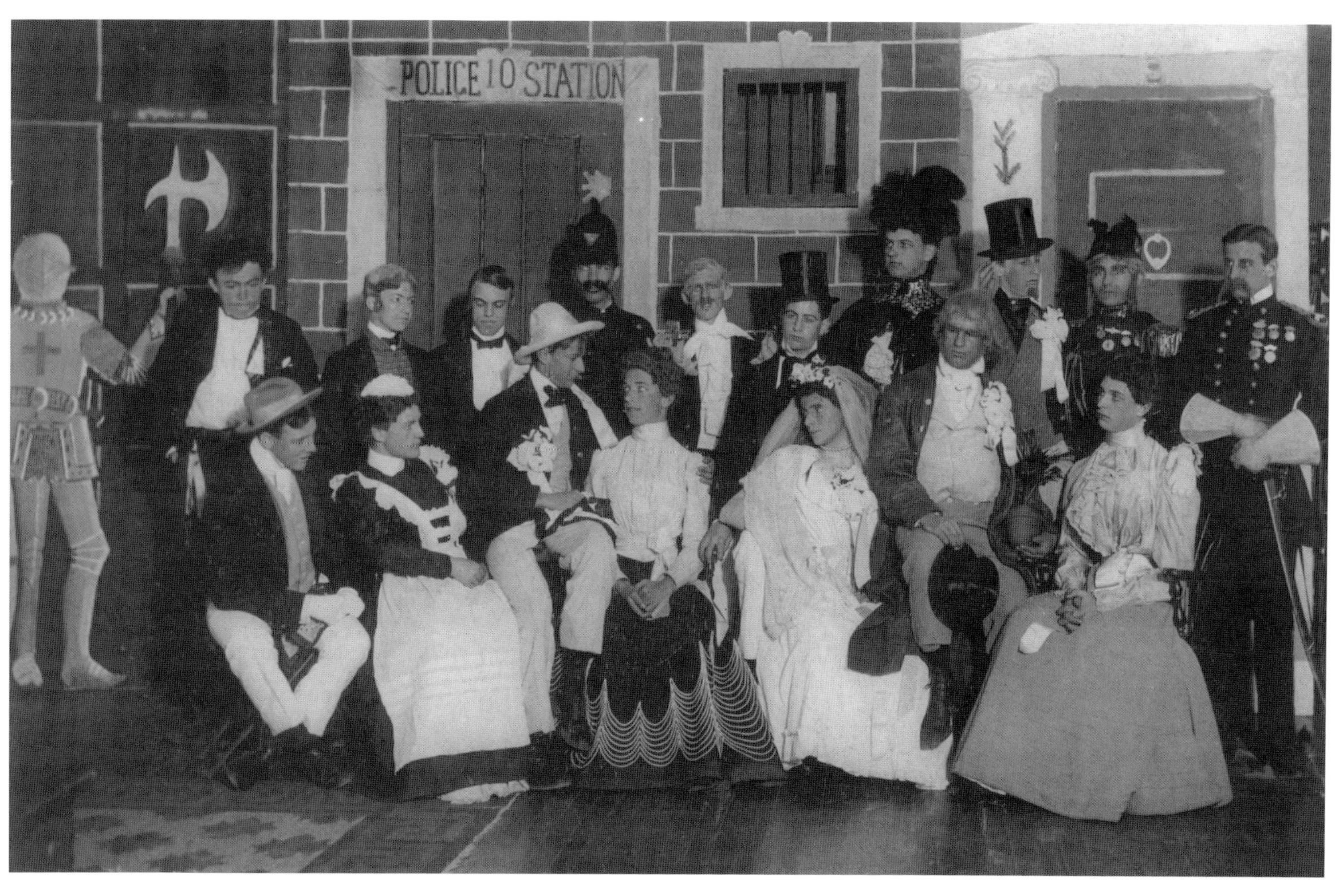

FDR at Groton, playing the part of Bopaddy in the school production of W. S. Gilbert's *The Wedding March*. The boy originally slated for the part fell ill and Franklin served as his replacement. (February 22, 1900)

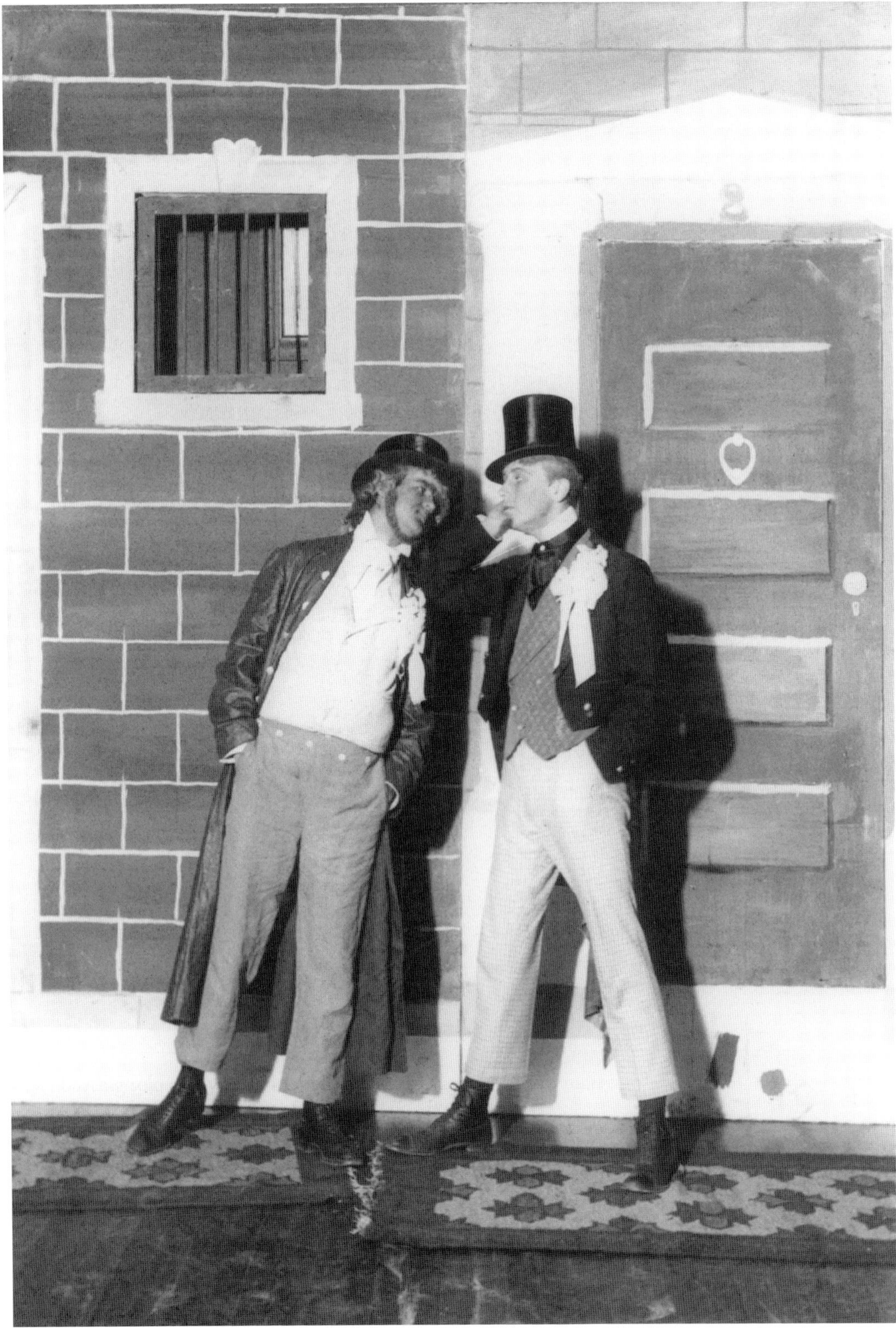

FDR had asked to borrow some of his father's old clothes—top hat and tails—to add authenticity to his performance. His parents and Aunt Kassie came to see the performance, which was deemed a success. (February 22, 1900)

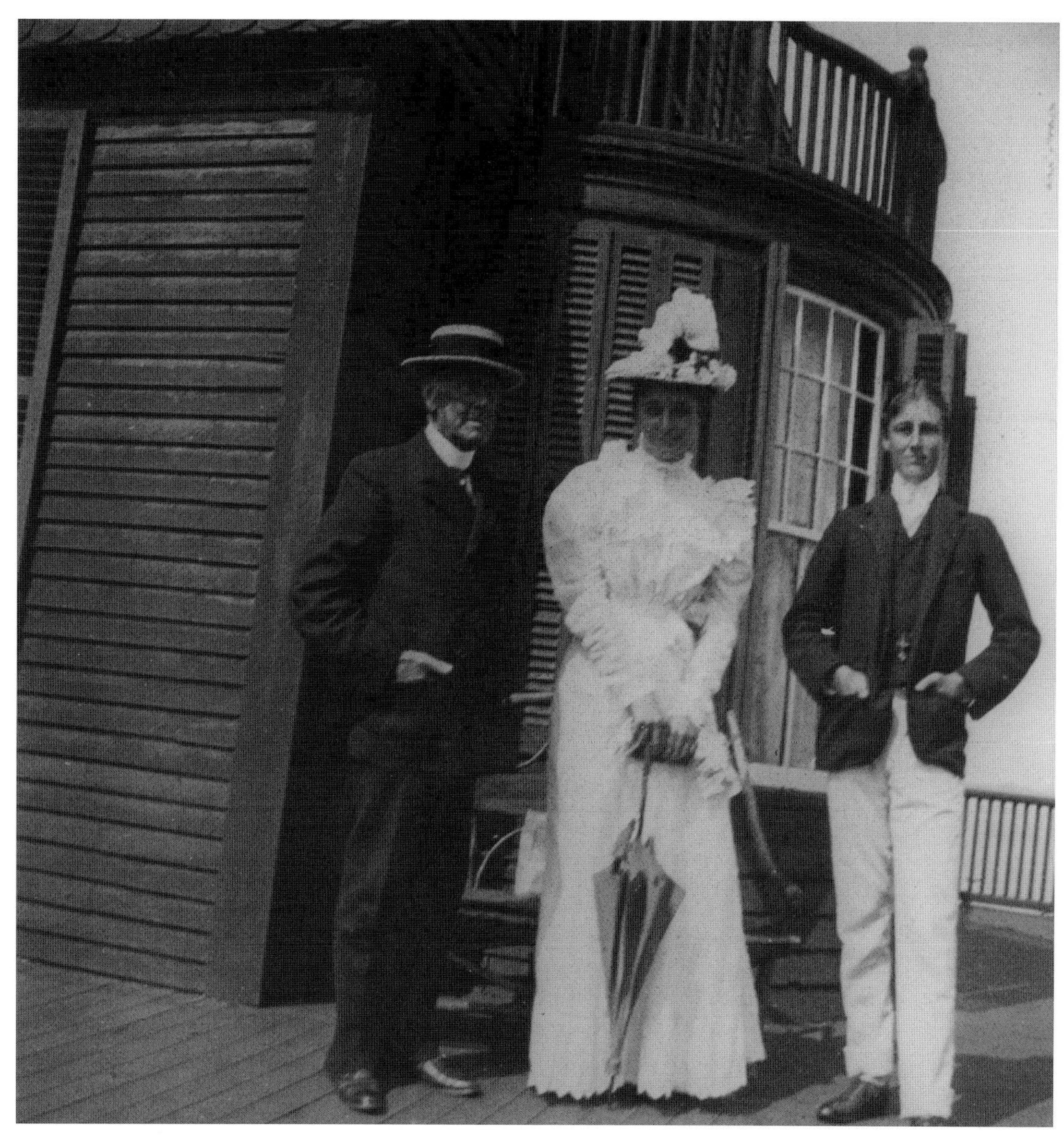

FDR, Mary Cochrane Rogers, and his father in Campobello. New Hampshirite Rogers was an antiquarian and author. (August 1900)

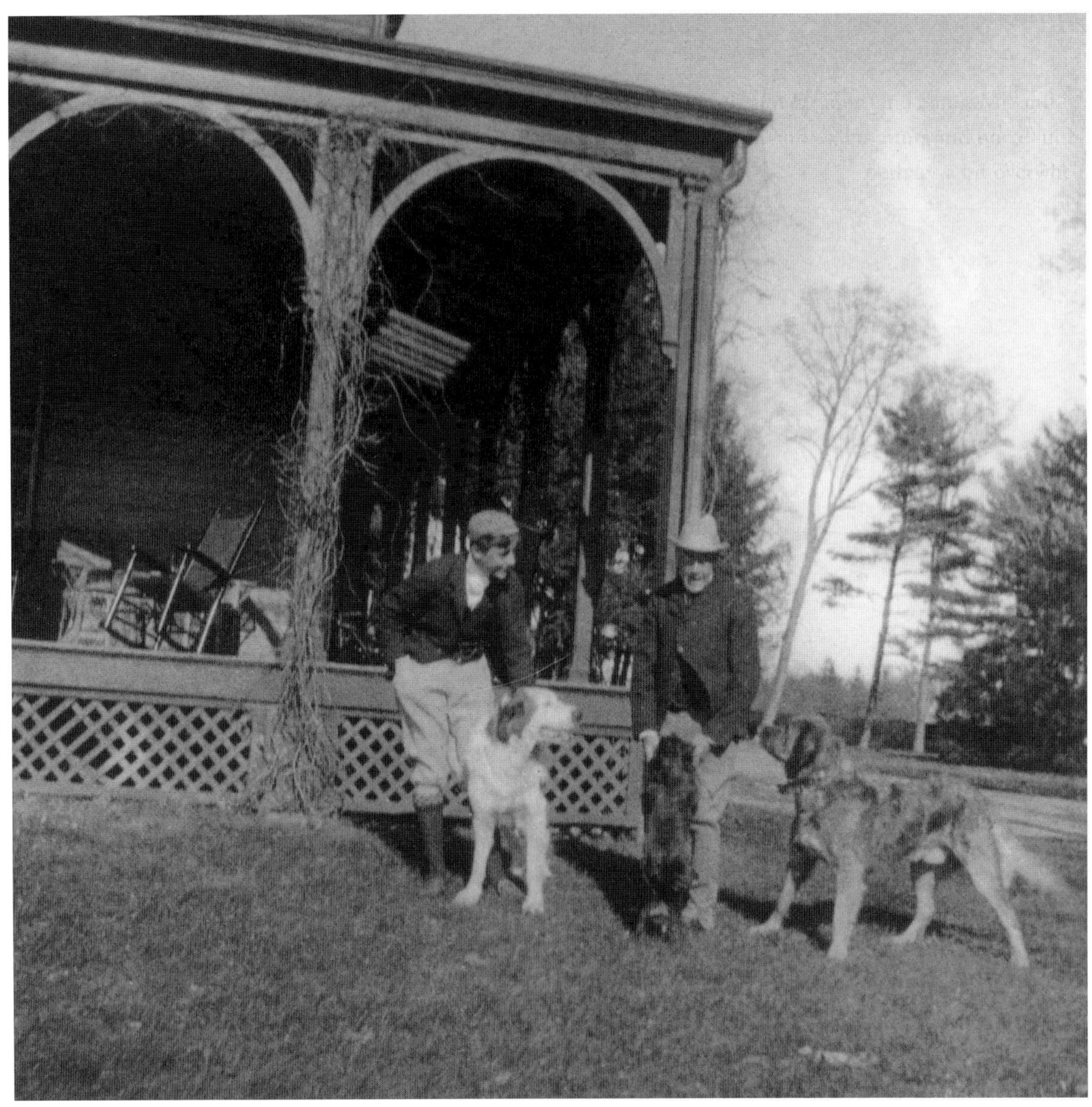

FDR, his father, and family dogs. This is one of the last photographs of Franklin and his father. FDR had graduated from Groton and entered Harvard. His father's fragile health had waxed and waned throughout the year, and he died December 8, 1900, seventy-two years old. Both sons, FDR and Rosy, were at his bedside; FDR would stay to console his mother until the new year. (November 1900)

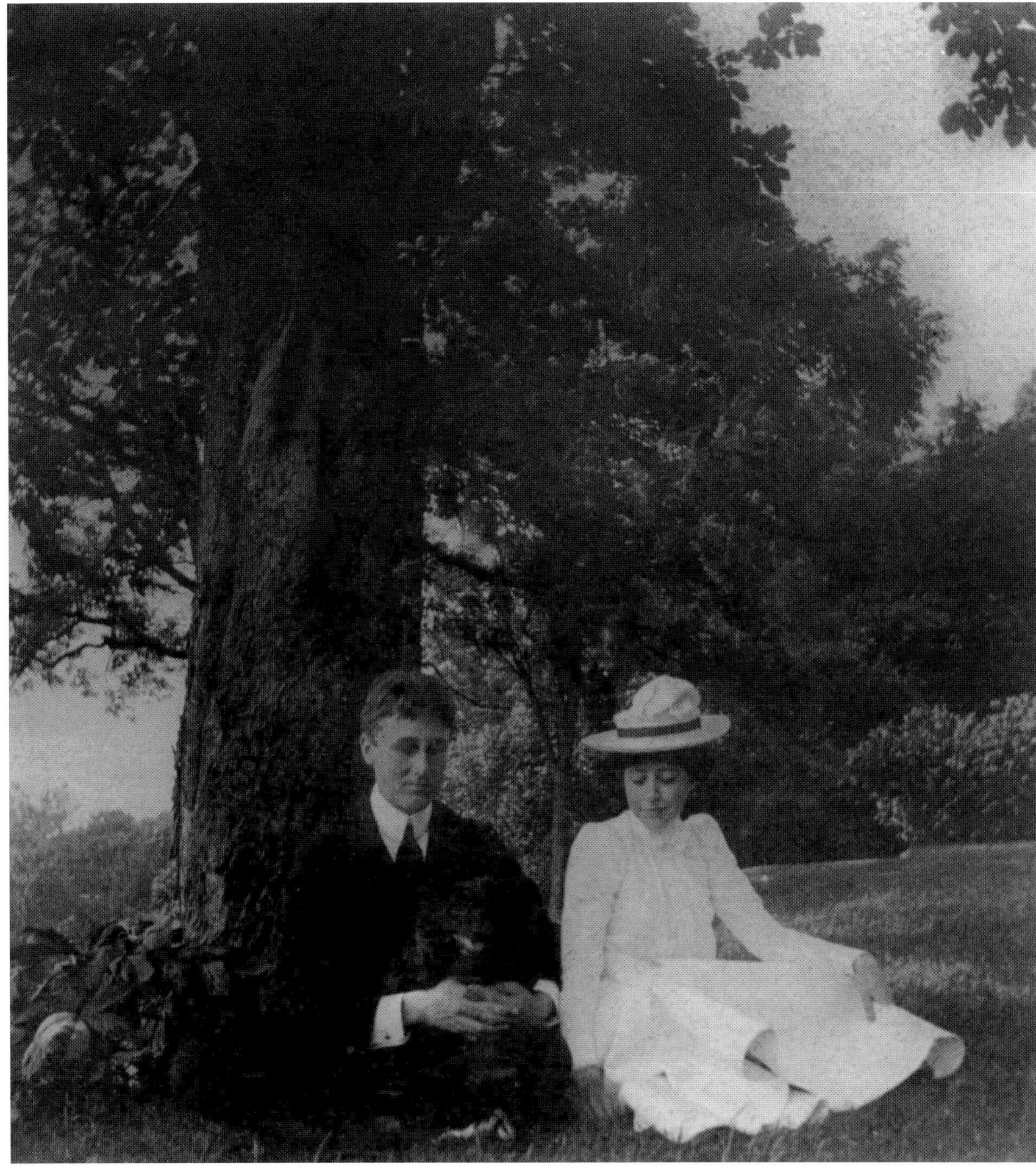

FDR and Helen R. Roosevelt and one of the family dogs in Hyde Park enjoying the fine spring weather. In 1904 Helen would marry Theodore Douglas Robinson, Teddy Roosevelt's nephew and son of his sister Corinne. Helen bridged the two branches of the Roosevelt family—the Republicans of Oyster Bay and the Democrats of Hyde Park—having been a frequent visitor to the TR White House. Theodore Robinson served in the Republican administration of Coolidge as Assistant Secretary of the Navy. Helen died in 1962. (1901)

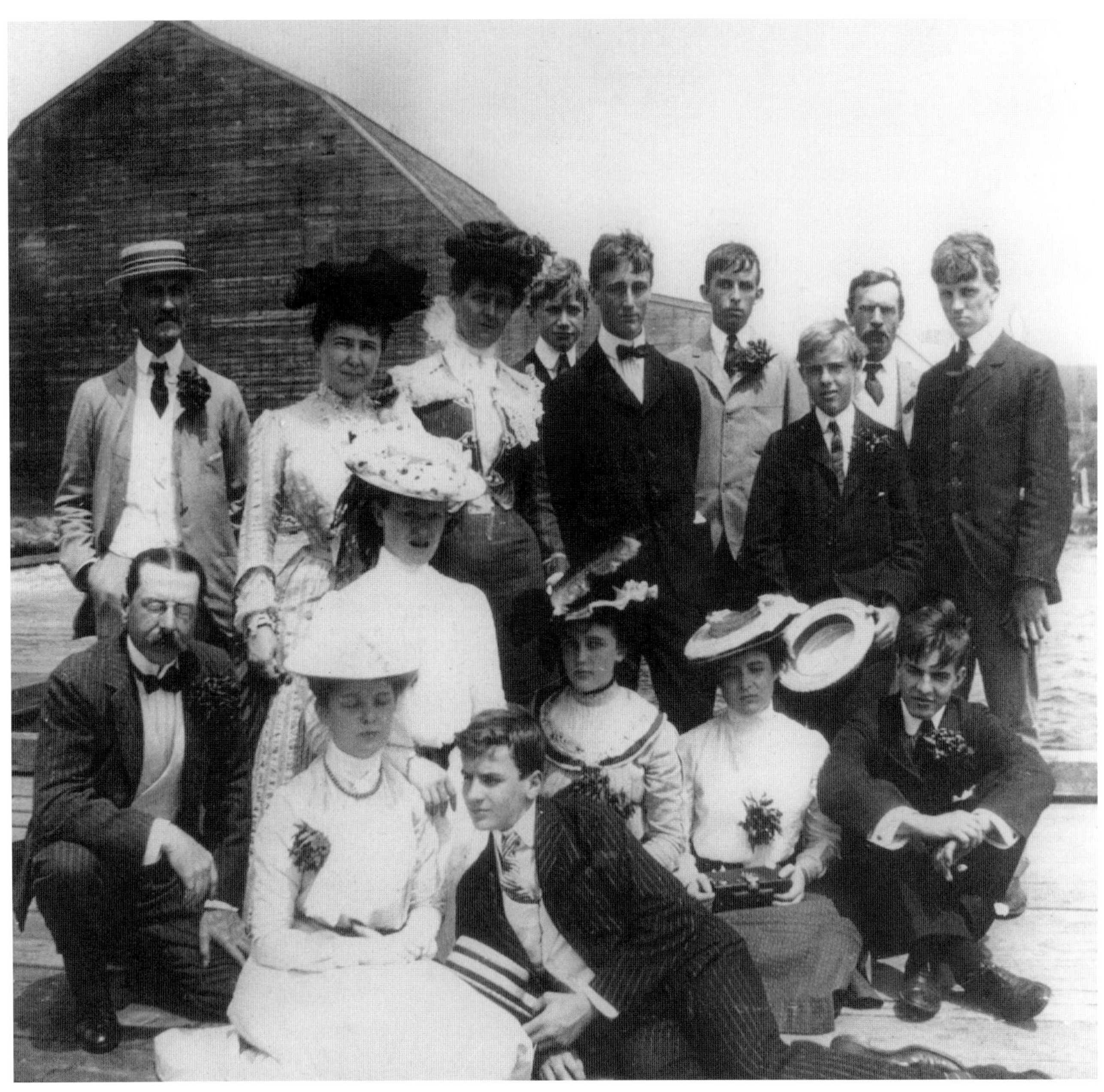

FDR, fifth from left, at Muriel Delano Robbins' 18th birthday party in New London, Connecticut. Muriel, whom FDR nicknamed "Moo," was the daughter of Aunt Kassie. She would marry Cyril Martineau in 1907. (1901)

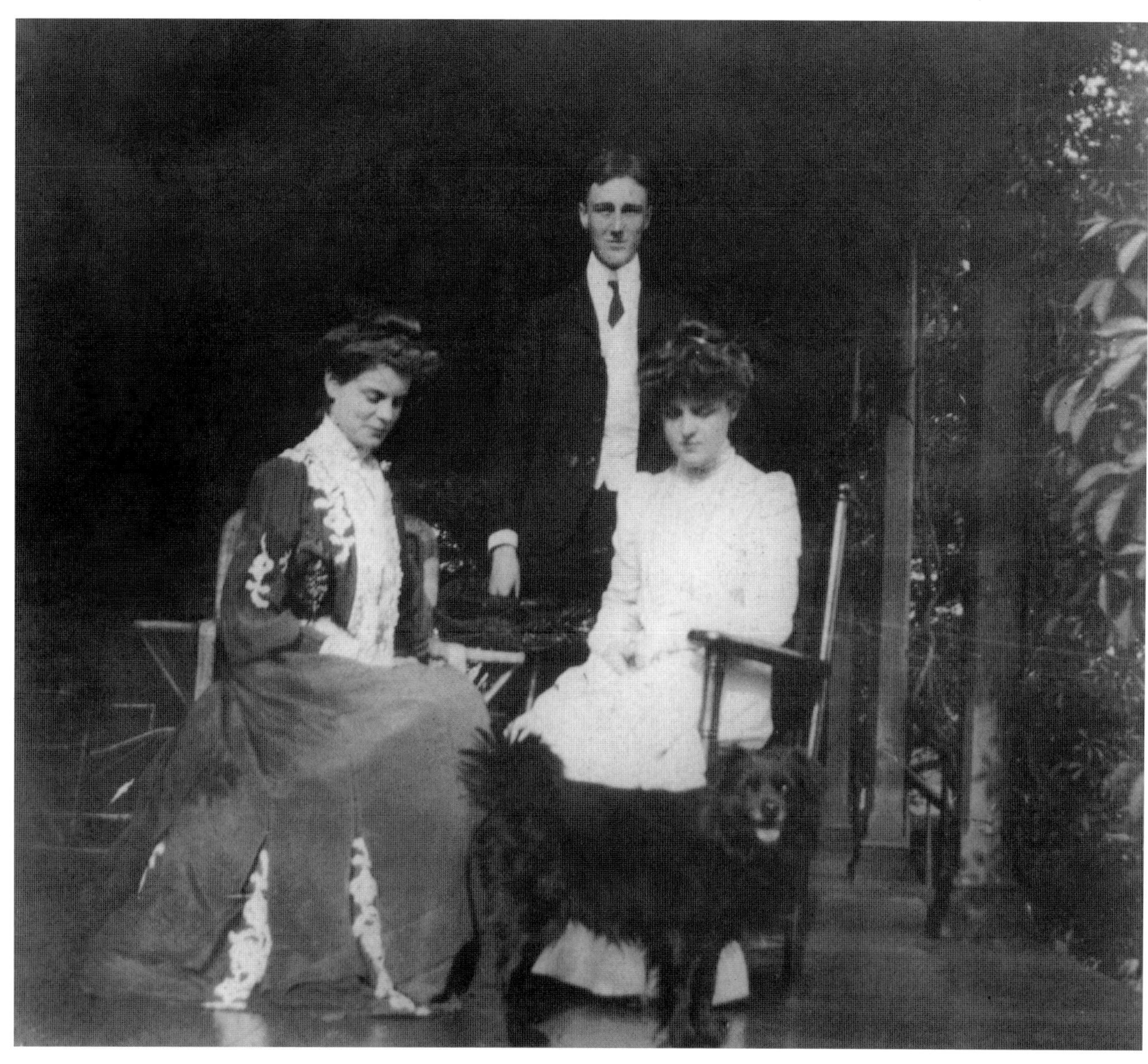

FDR, his mother, and an unidentified young lady in 1902. In that year, Franklin pursued Boston belle Alice Sohier, perhaps a bit too enthusiastically—in later years she recounted, "In a day and age when well brought-up young men were expected to keep their hands off the persons of young ladies from respectable families, Franklin had to be slapped—hard." (1902)

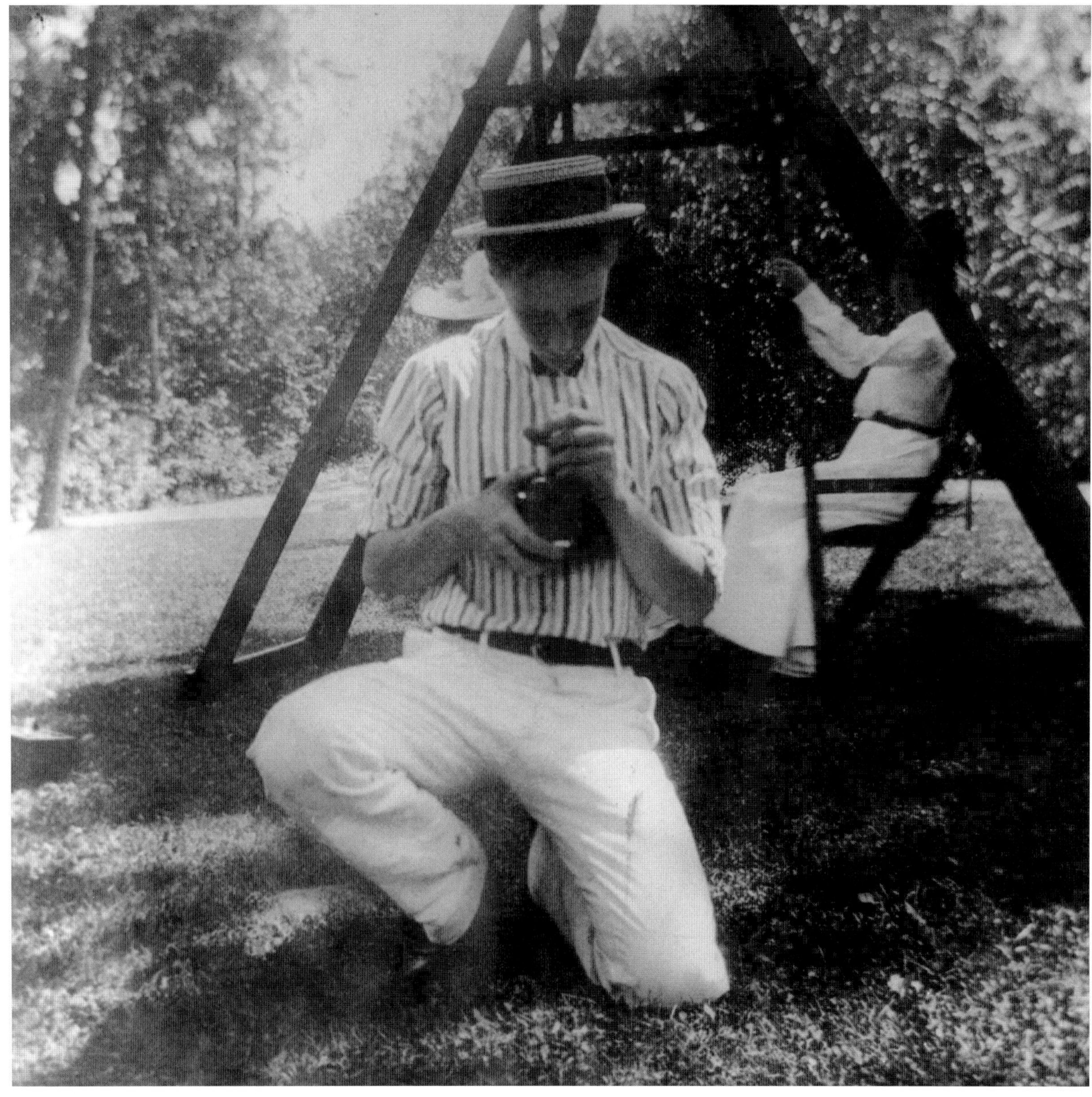

FDR in straw boater adjusting his camera at Barrytown, New York. Barrytown was the home of his great-uncle and namesake Franklin Hughes Delano (married to Laura Astor, whose father had given them this corner of the Rokeby estate). Just north of Rhinebeck, this property, Steen Valetje ("Stony Creek"), still stands and is known today as Mandara. (1902)

Formal portrait of FDR the collegian. He resembles his mother at a similar age, but his gaze is more reminiscent of the distant and abstracted look of his father. (1904)

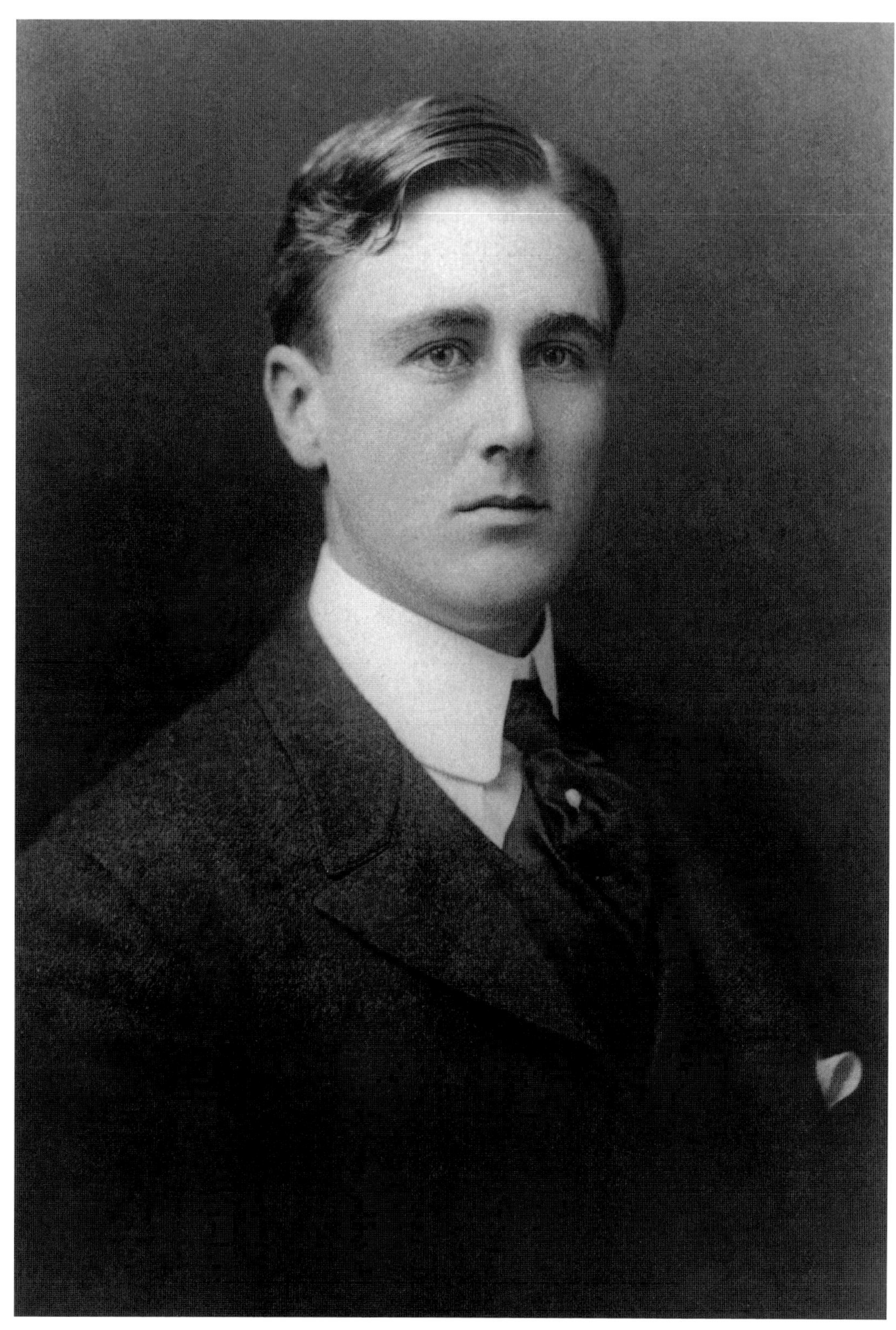

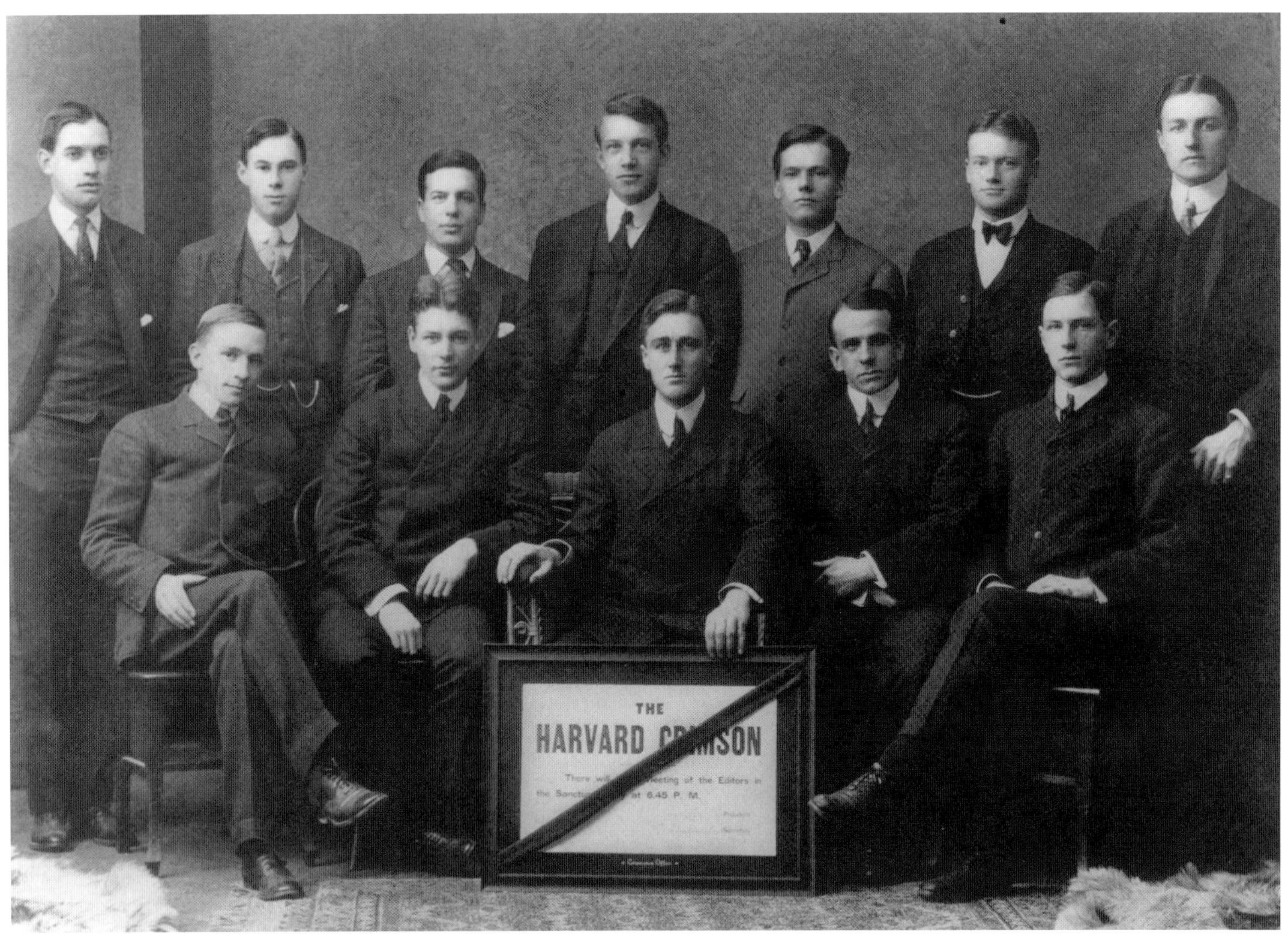

FDR at the center of things as president of the *Harvard Crimson.* In 1900 he'd written his parents that he was hoping to join the Crimson, and in 1901 he was writing that he worked three or four hours every day on newspaper assignments. His hard work paid off—he was elected Assistant Managing Editor, then President. (1904)

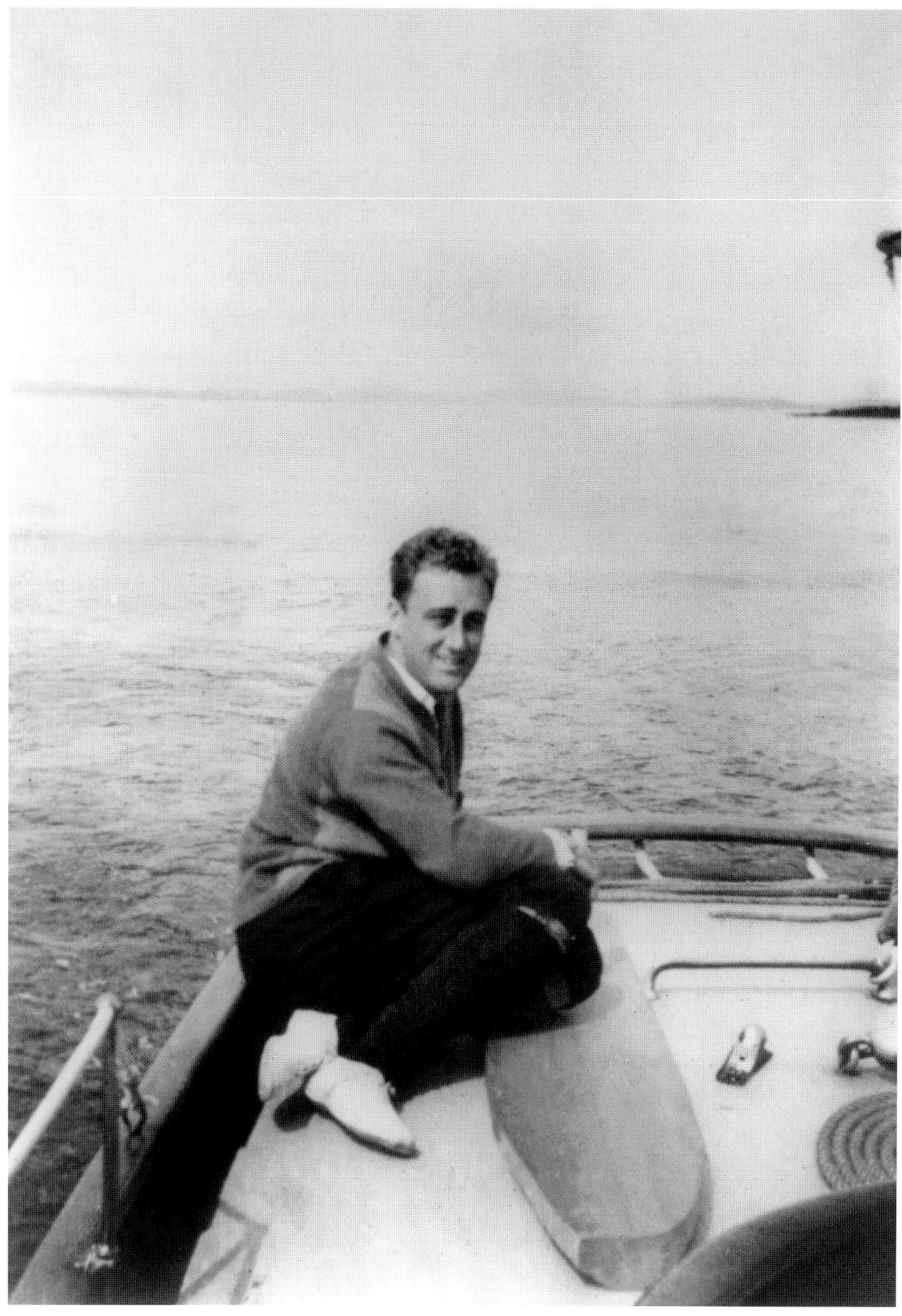

Yachting at Campobello. Uncharacteristically, FDR is simply at ease, not piloting. (1904)

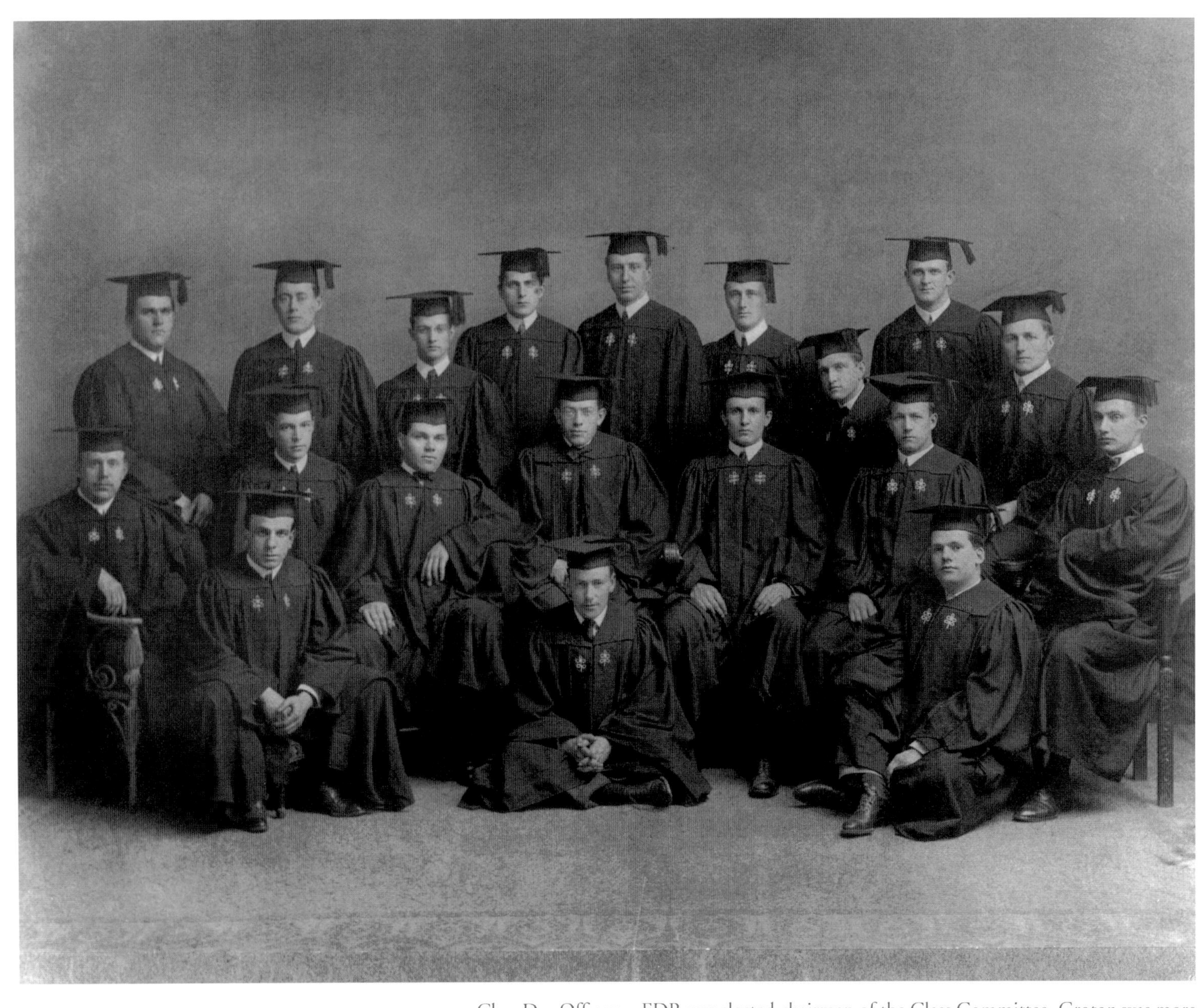

Class Day Officers—FDR was elected chairman of the Class Committee. Groton was more influential than Harvard in Franklin's education—much of his Harvard career was extracurricular, with clubs and the *Crimson,* although he did matriculate in three years. (1904)

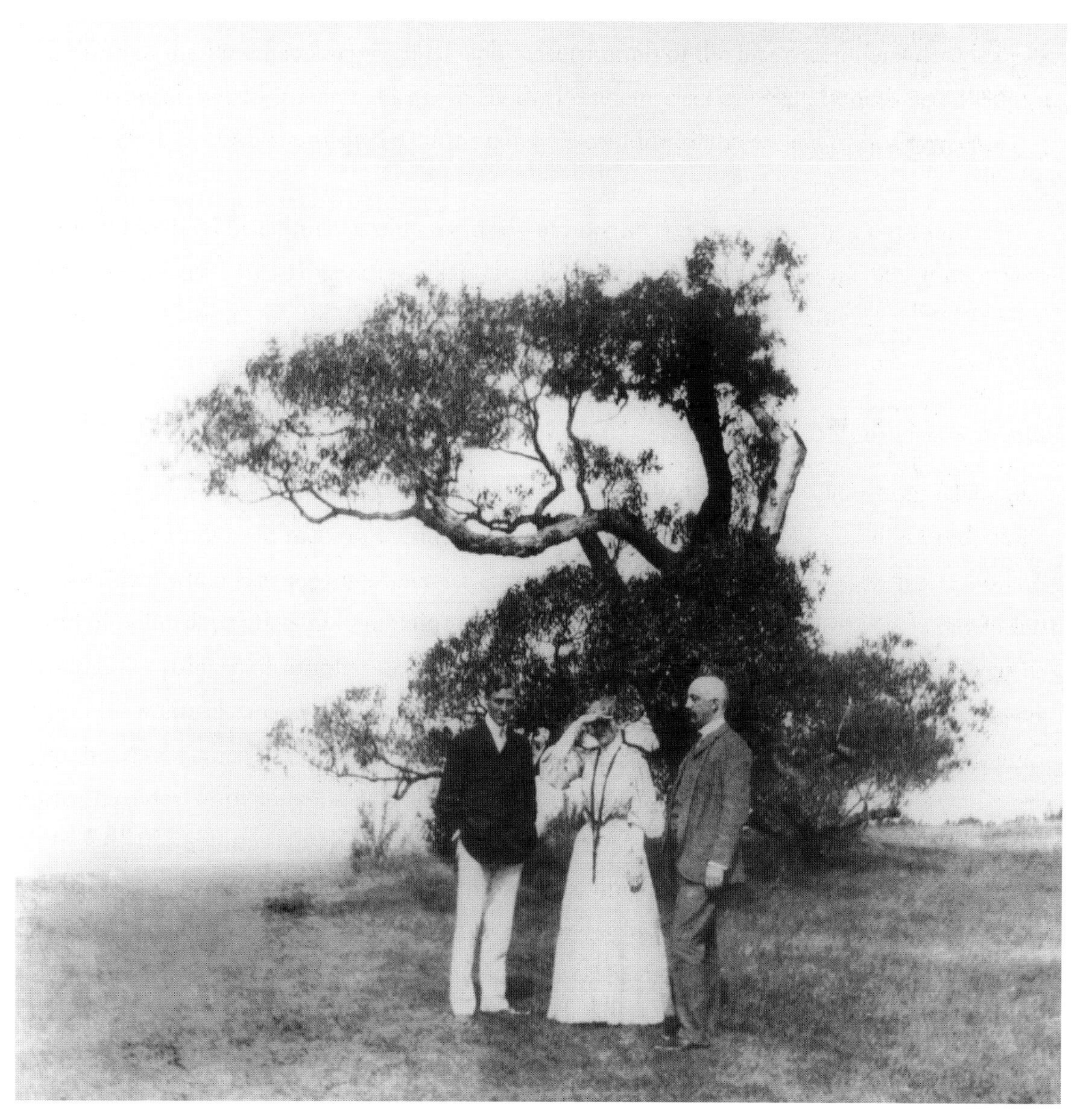

FDR with aunt and uncle, Mr. and Mrs. Paul Forbes, at the family retreat at Campobello. This would have been the first Campobello summer for his remarried Aunt Deborah ("Doe"). She had been married to her new husband's older brother William Howell Forbes and they had lived in the Delano home in Macao until his death in 1896. (1904)

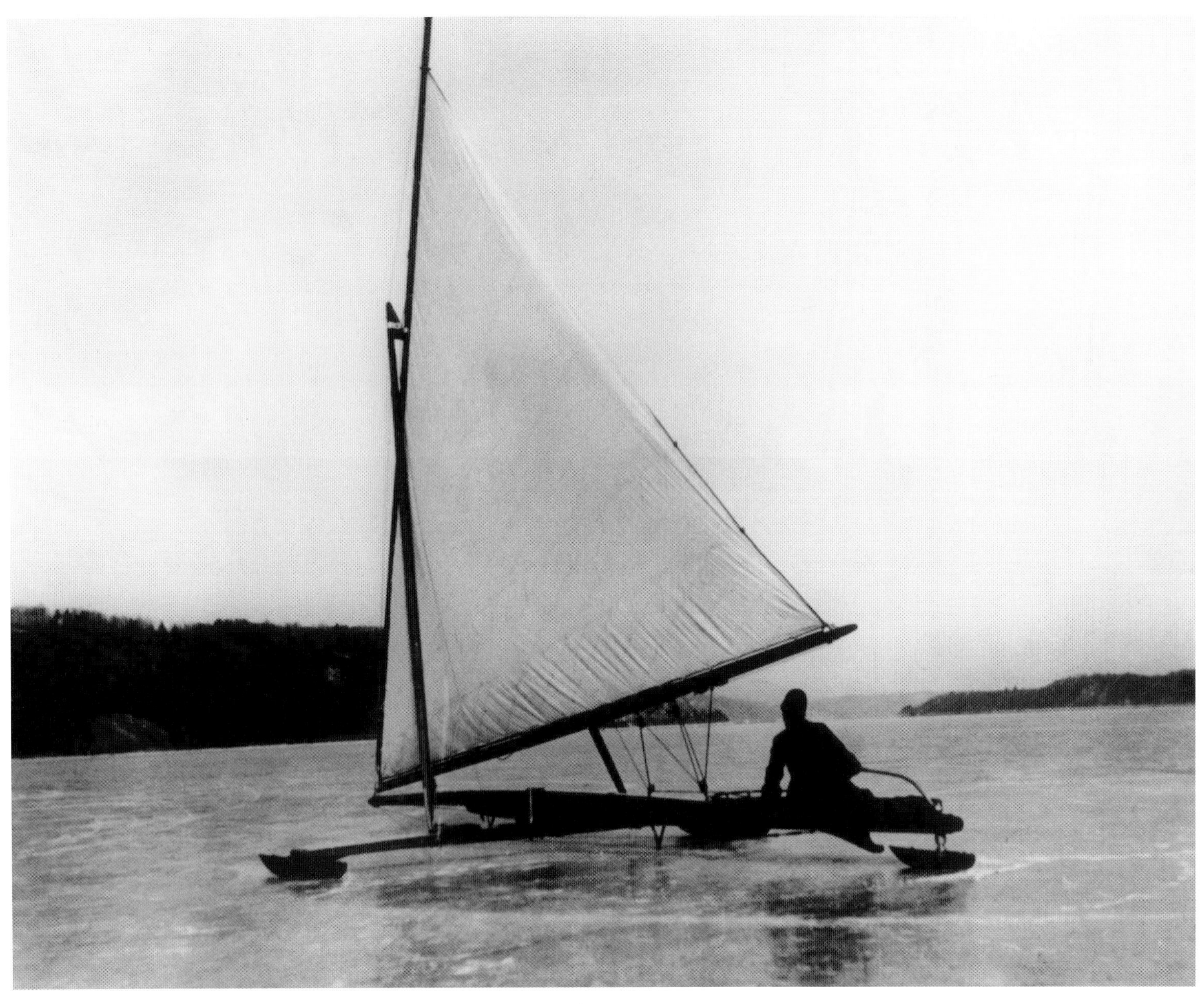

FDR boating solo at Hyde Park on the Hudson. He was soon to marry his cousin Eleanor and embark on a whole new life. (1905)

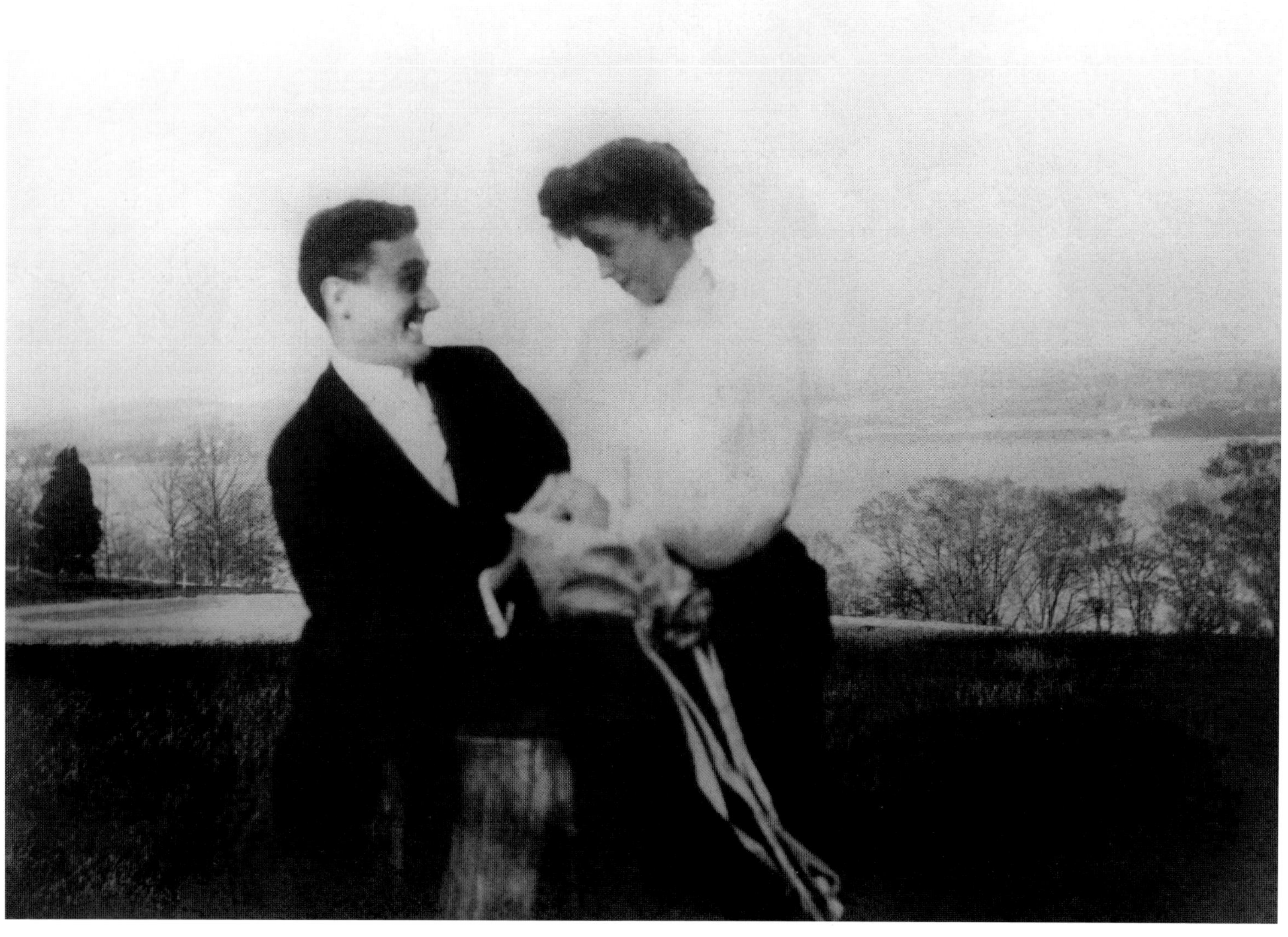

Charmingly candid photograph of the happy couple, FDR and Eleanor, at Newburgh, just downriver from the Roosevelt home, pictured here—perhaps the happiest picture of the couple. Uncle President Theodore Roosevelt stood in for Eleanor's deceased father, giving her away—and stealing the limelight, as was his wont. FDR and Eleanor were married in March, but they postponed their honeymoon until June so that he could finish that term at Columbia Law School. (May 7, 1905)

A Delano family gathering at Algonac with FDR and Eleanor (and Sara), Mr. and Mrs. Frederic Delano Hitch, Mr. and Mrs. Warren Delano III, and Mr. and Mrs. Paul Forbes, his aunts and uncles in Newburgh, New York. Eleanor looks perhaps a bit overwhelmed, or at least hemmed in. (1905)

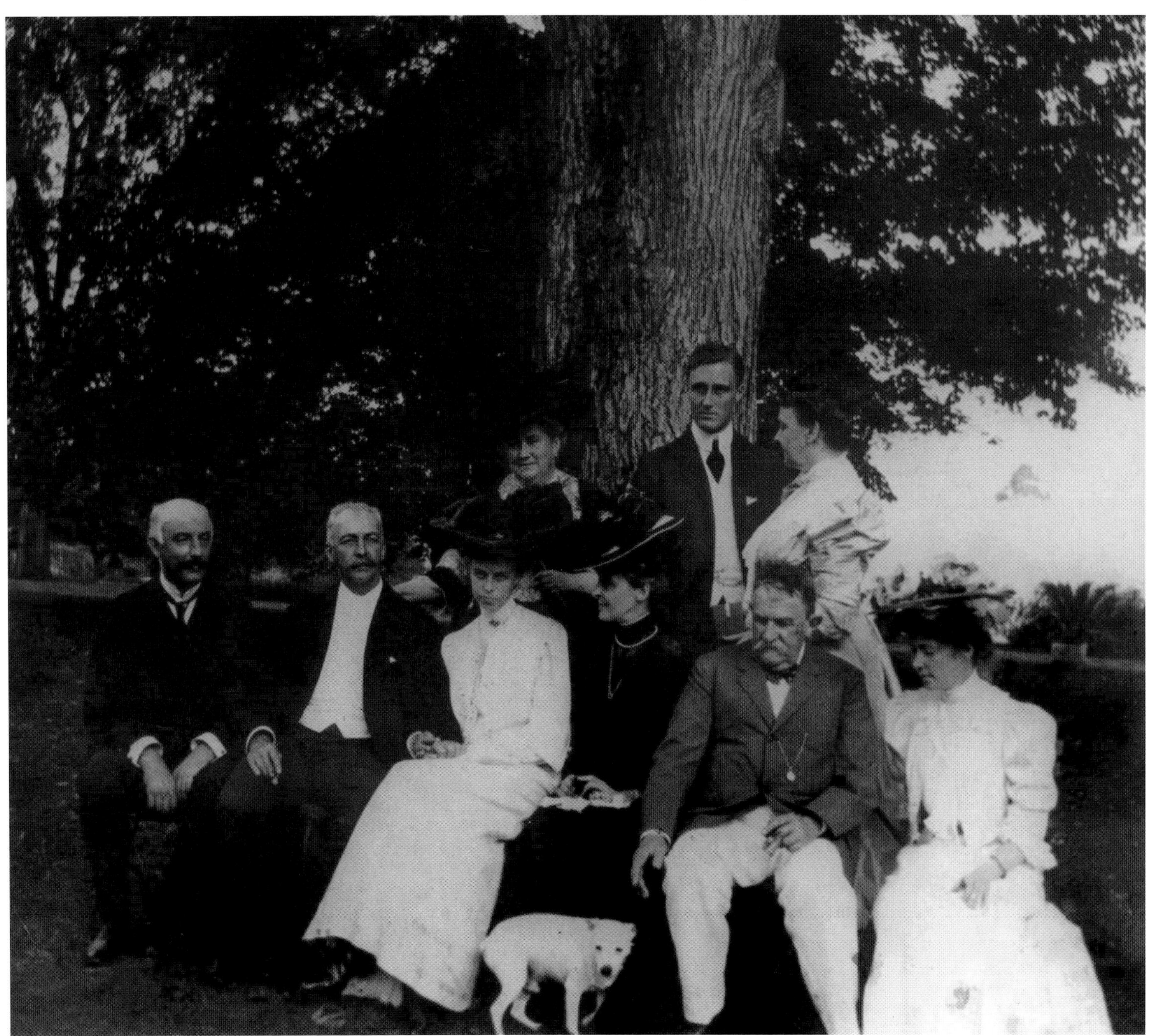

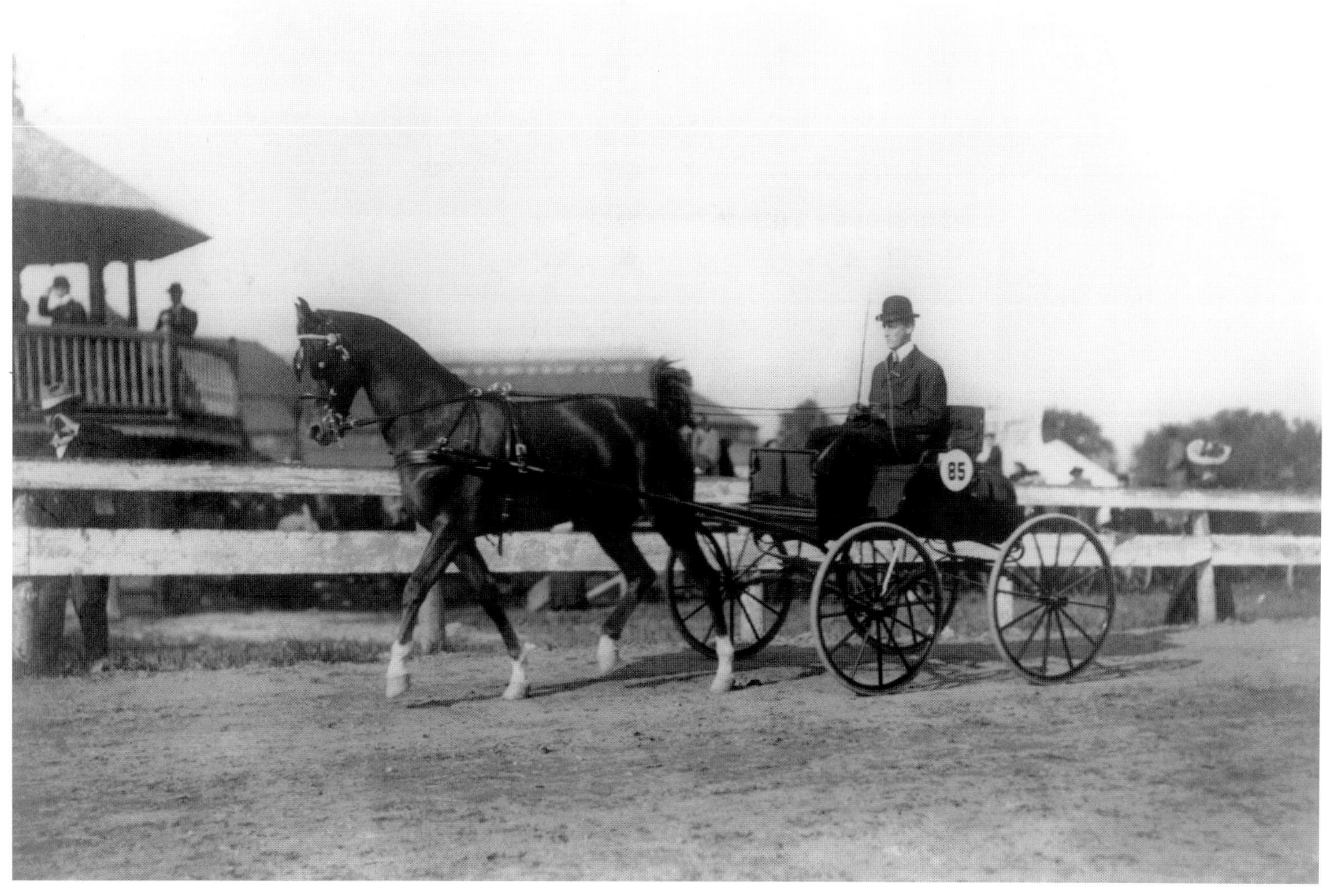

FDR driving a carriage at the Dutchess County Fair in Rhinebeck, New York. He had been given a Texas quarter horse. His uncle President Theodore Roosevelt had said "the Roosevelts are horse people," and his uncle Warren Delano was an avid horseman. Delano was killed by a train while on horseback in 1920 at Barrytown. (1905)

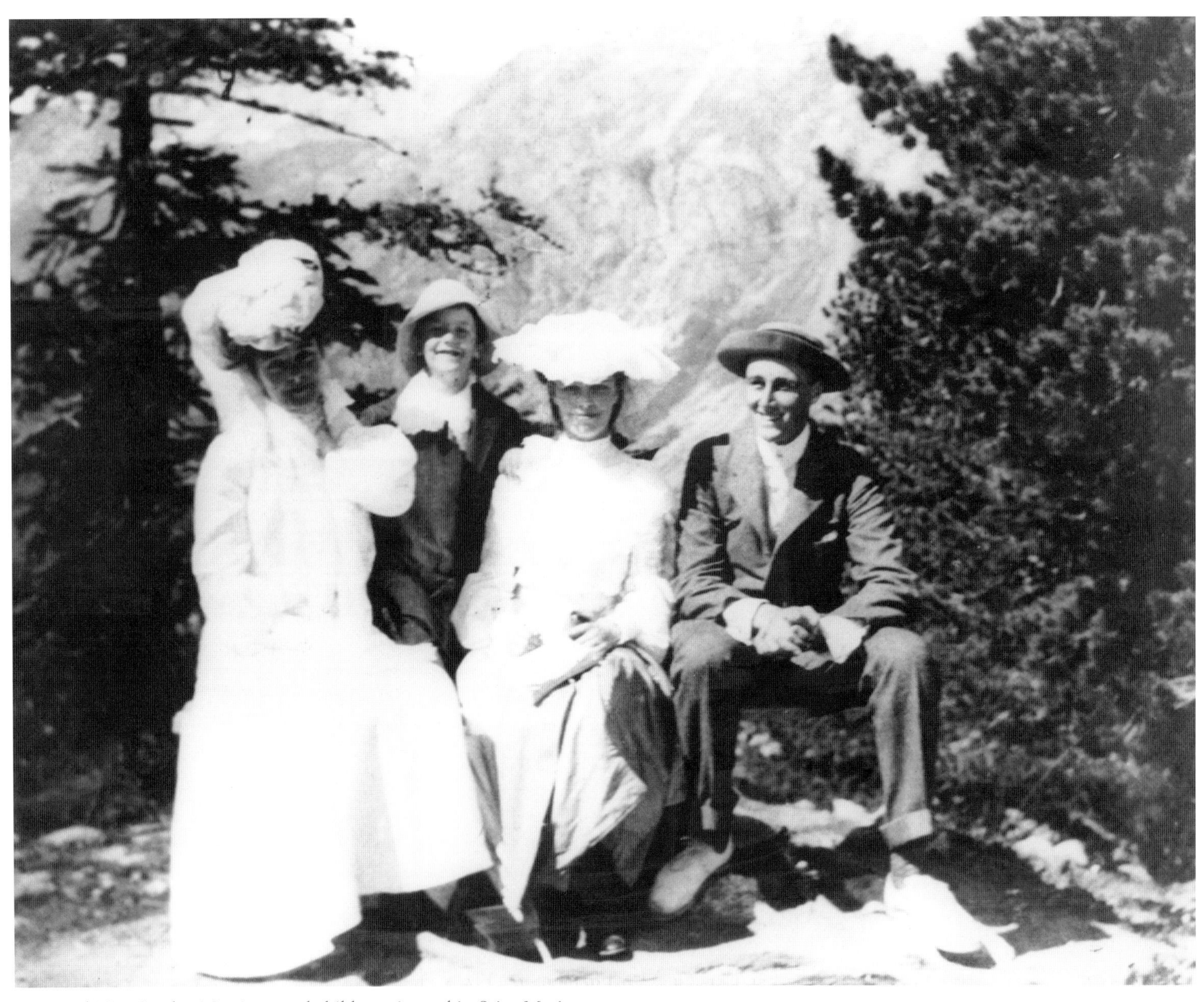

FDR and Mrs. Stanley Mortimer and children pictured in Saint Moritz, Switzerland. Mrs. Mortimer, Elizabeth Hall, Eleanor's "Aunt Tissie," was the sister of Mrs. Vincent Astor and Mrs. John Hay Whitney. (July 1905)

FDR with Sara Delano Roosevelt (to the left of center) in a group shot, at the wedding of Frances Pell to Sir Martin Archer-Shee. The wedding took place at Pellwood, her family home, in Highland Falls, the small village immediately adjacent West Point. The dashing major Martin Archer-Shee, future member of Parliament, had been in the 19th Hussars. The bride was the orphaned niece of J. Pierpont Morgan, who attended and gave her away. (October 14, 1905)

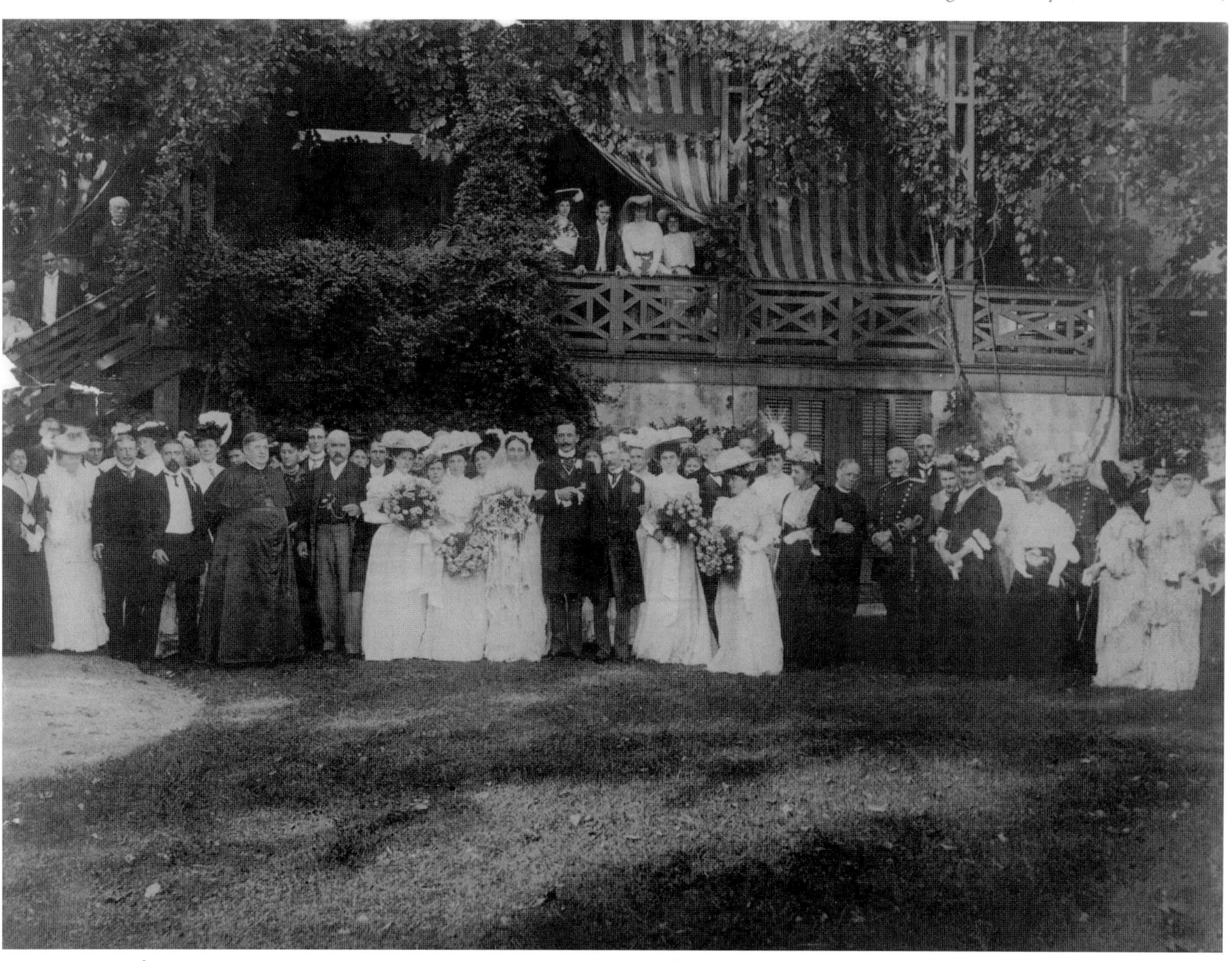

FDR and family at Campobello, picnicking at the seashore and skipping stones on the waves. (1906)

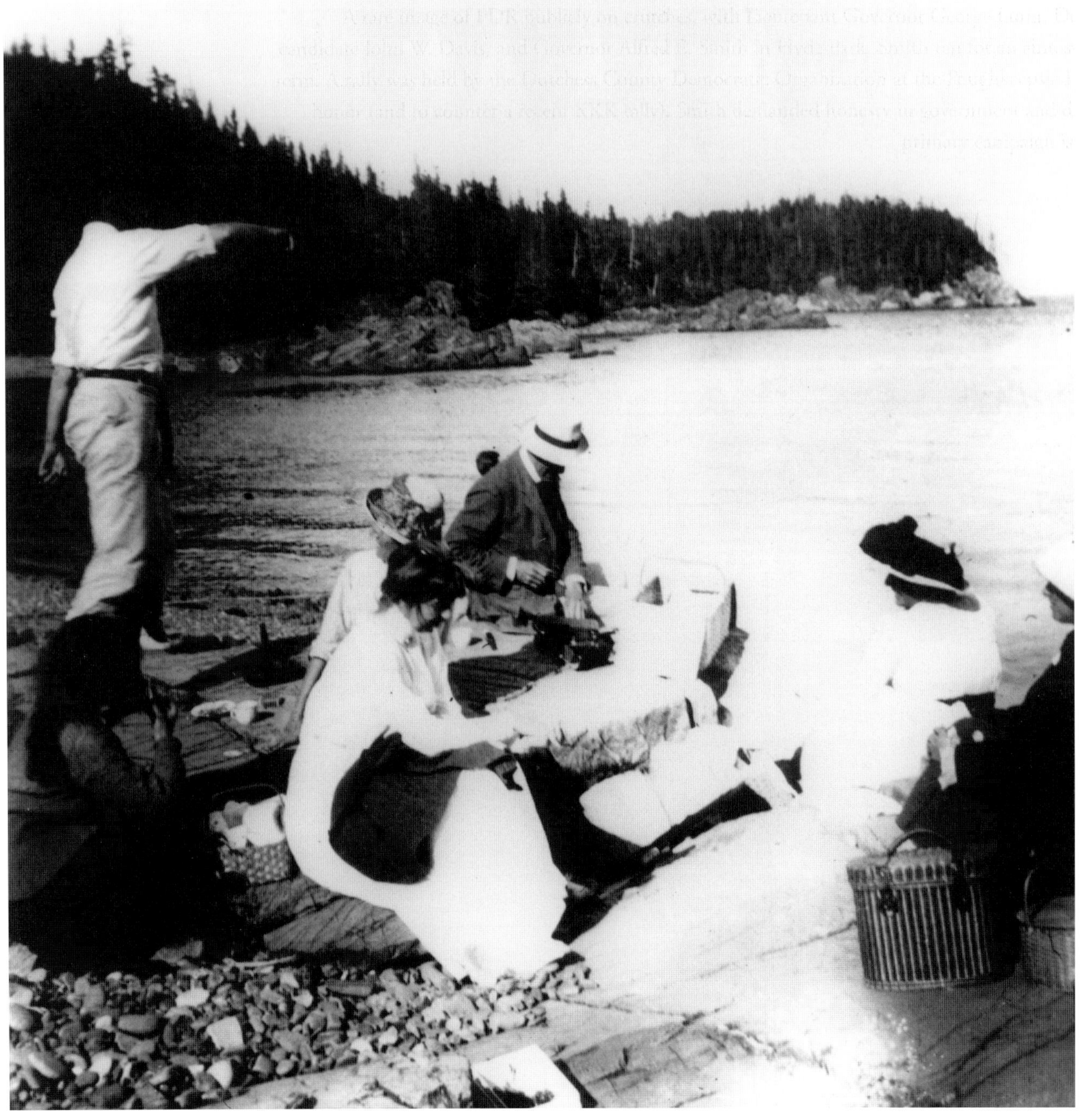

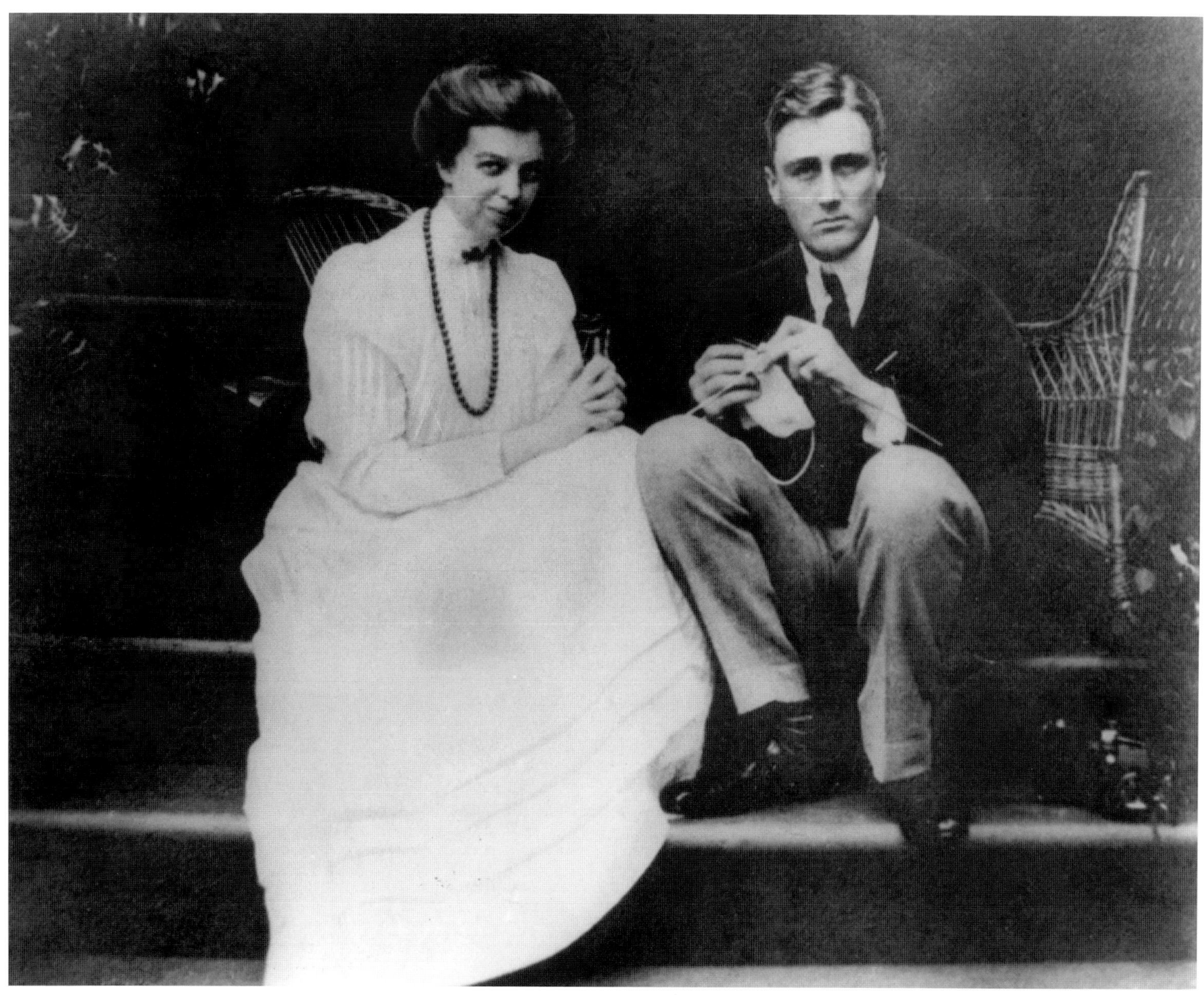

The newlyweds hard at work on the home front, with the hint of a smile on Eleanor's face. FDR is jokingly holding the knitting—which is perhaps something for their expected child? (1906)

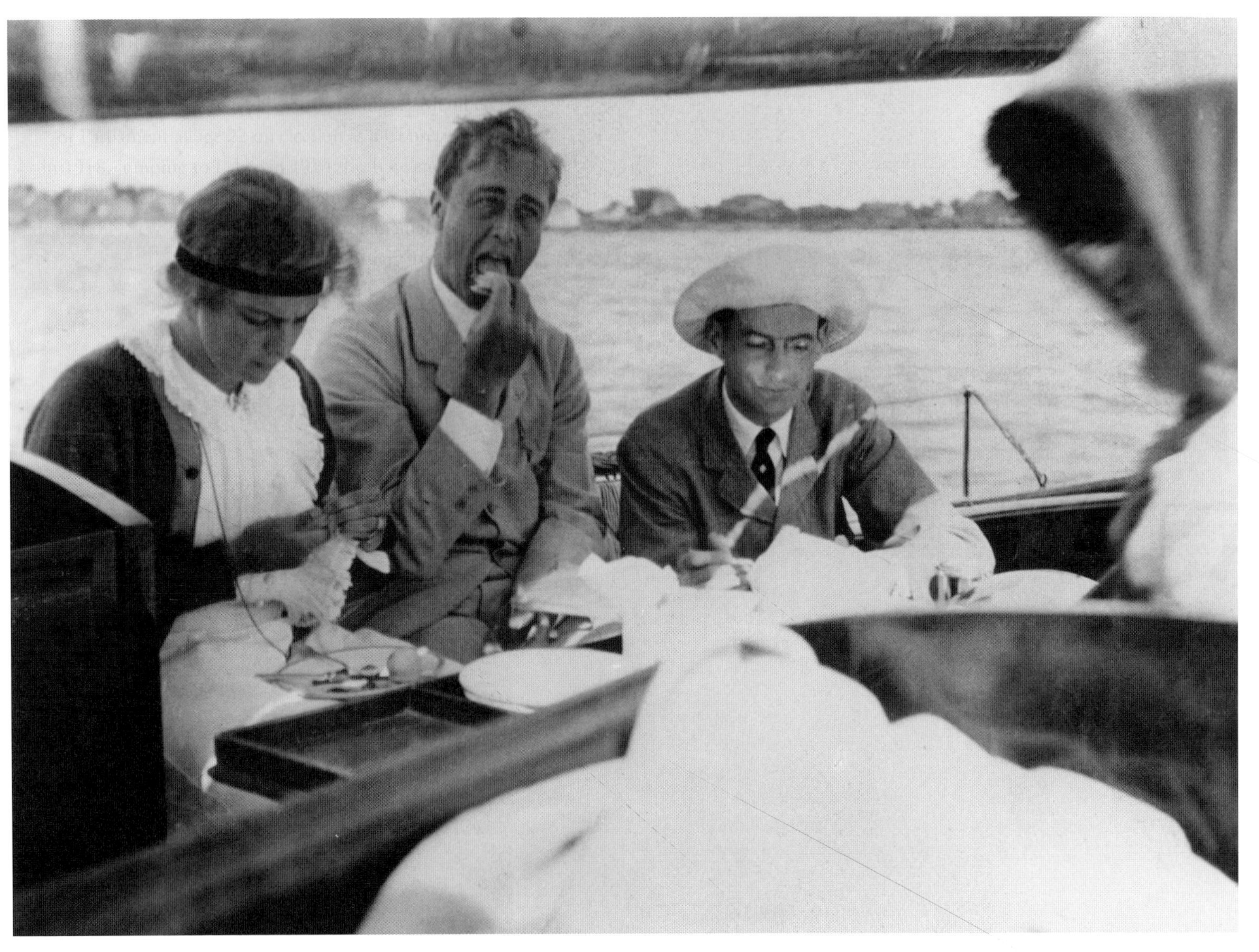

FDR with Frances Dana de Rham and her husband, Henry. Henry de Rham was a Harvard classmate of FDR's. Frances was granddaughter of two notables, Henry Wadsworth Longfellow and Richard H. Dana. (1906)

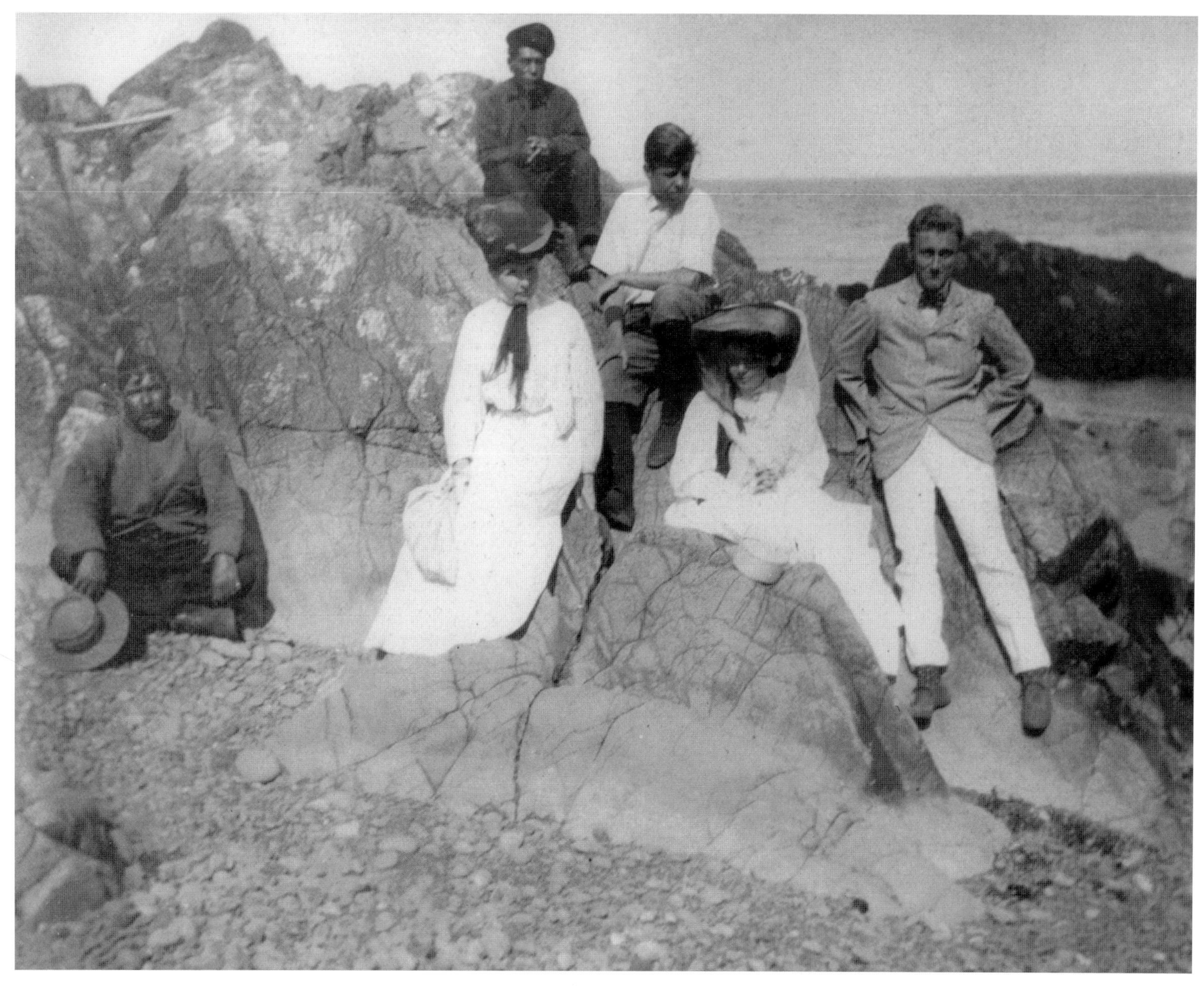

Family outing with cousin Sarah, G. (Gracie) Hall Roosevelt, Eleanor's brother, and Miss Spring, along with two locals, in Campobello. Hall would live with FDR and Eleanor when not at school, and he and FDR became fast friends. Miss Blanche Spring came to the Roosevelt's as nurse when Anna was born and returned for each new child. (1907)

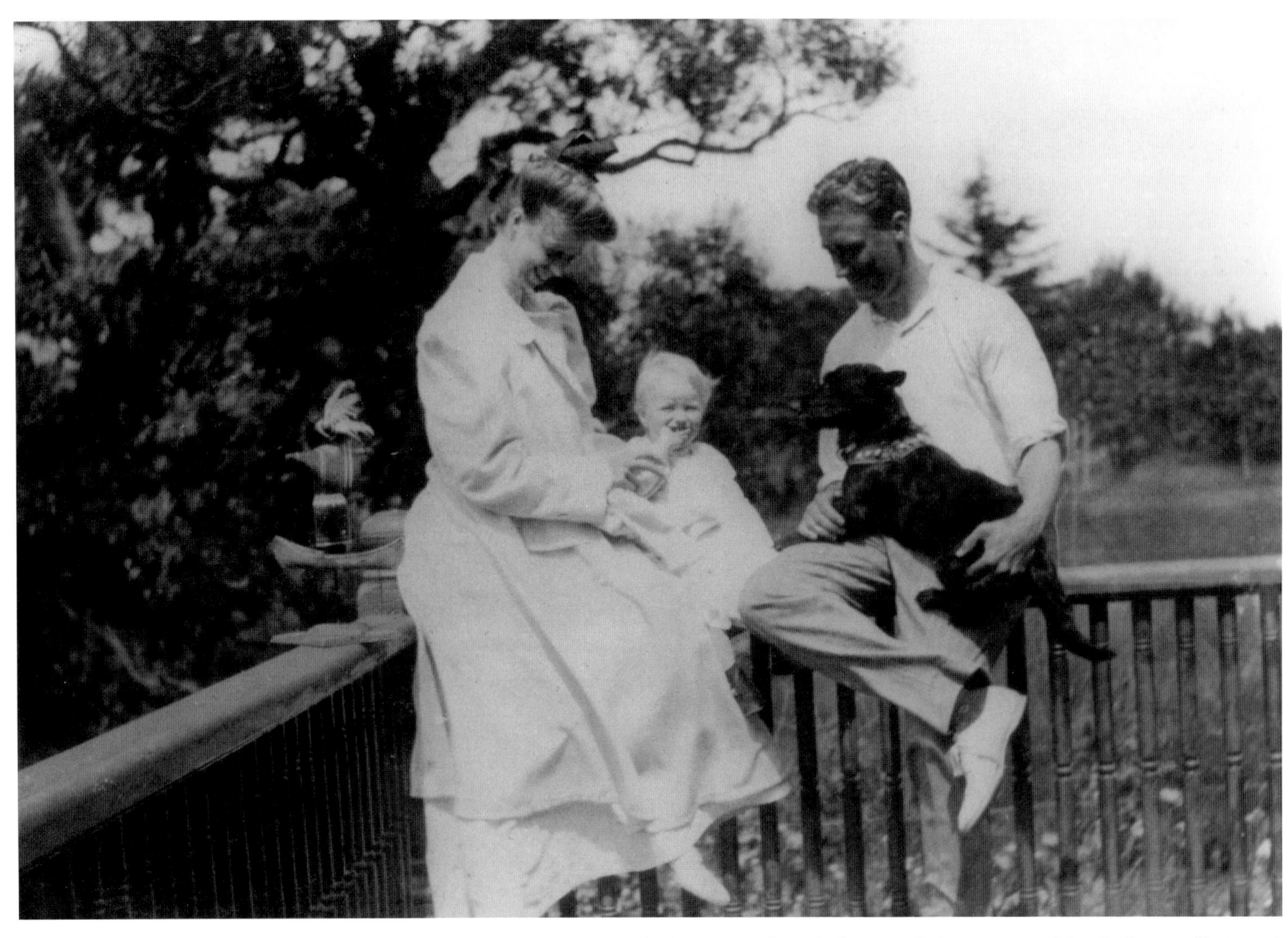

The happy couple with their new baby, Anna, and family dog, Duffy. (1907)

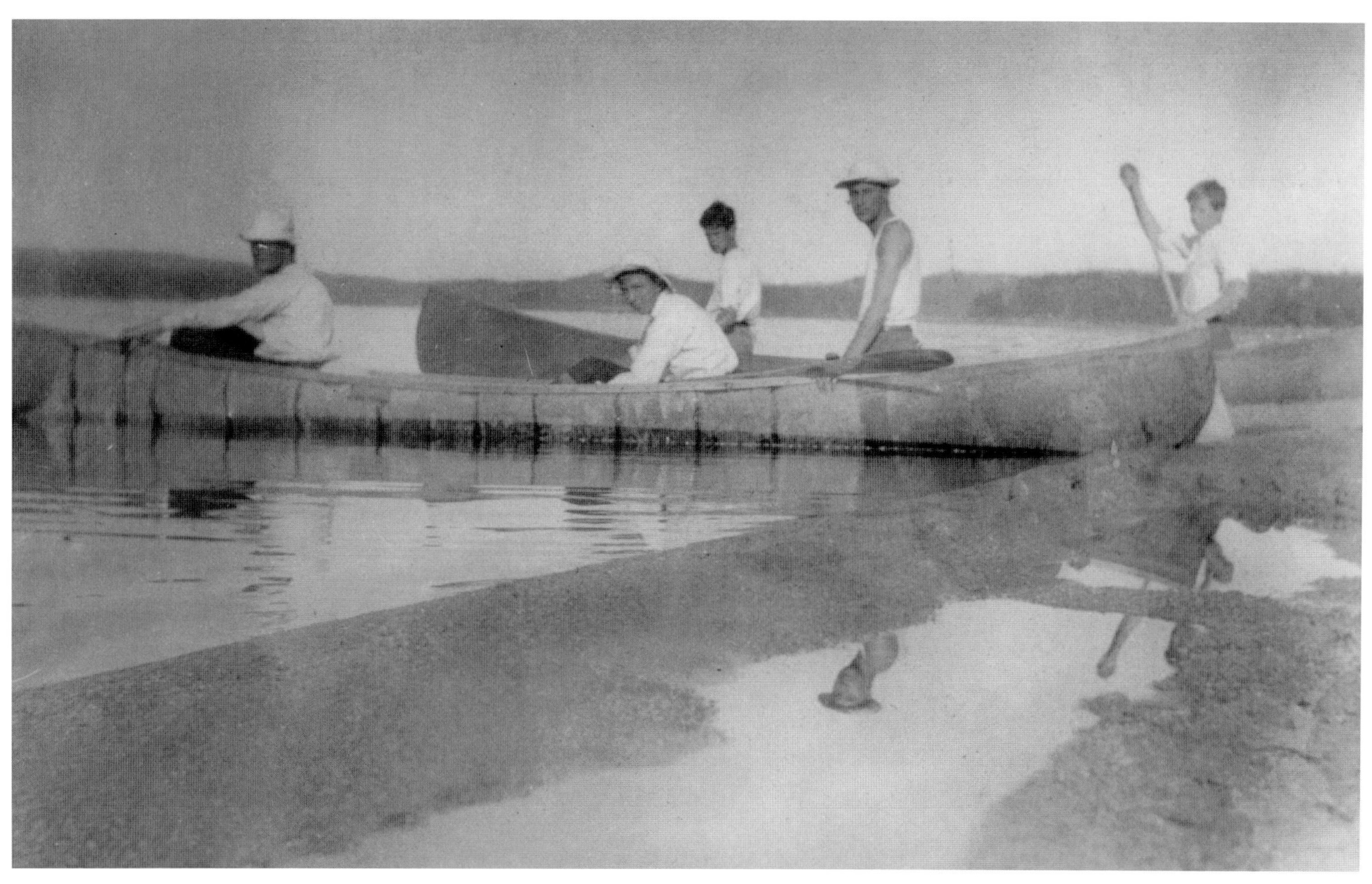

Canoeing at Campobello. An adventure begins. (1907)

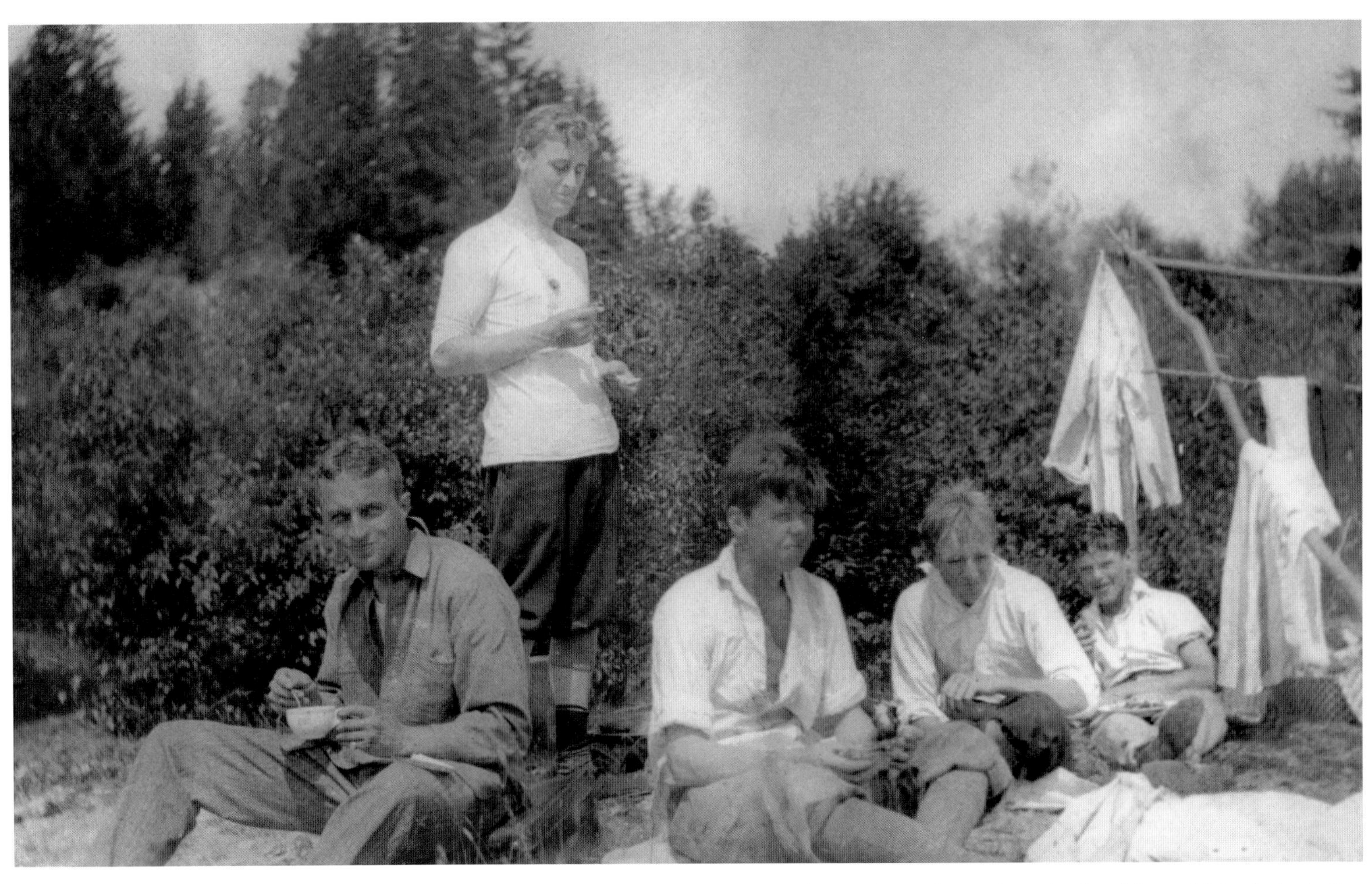

A camping and canoeing trip. Franklin and friends, including brother-in-law G. Hall Roosevelt, are roughing it. (1907)

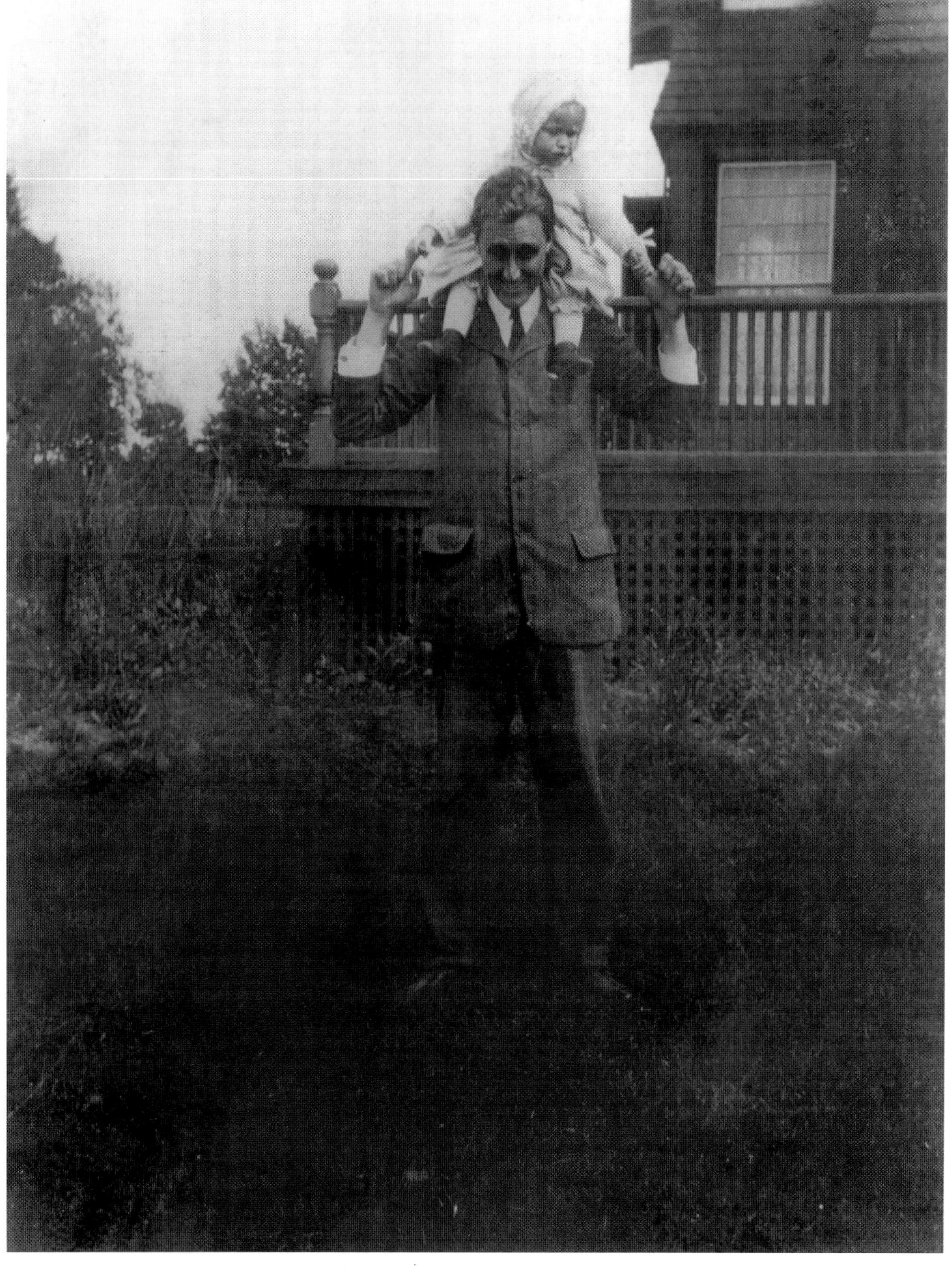

FDR giving his new baby daughter, Anna, a piggyback ride. Eleanor thought the sight quite amusing. (1907)

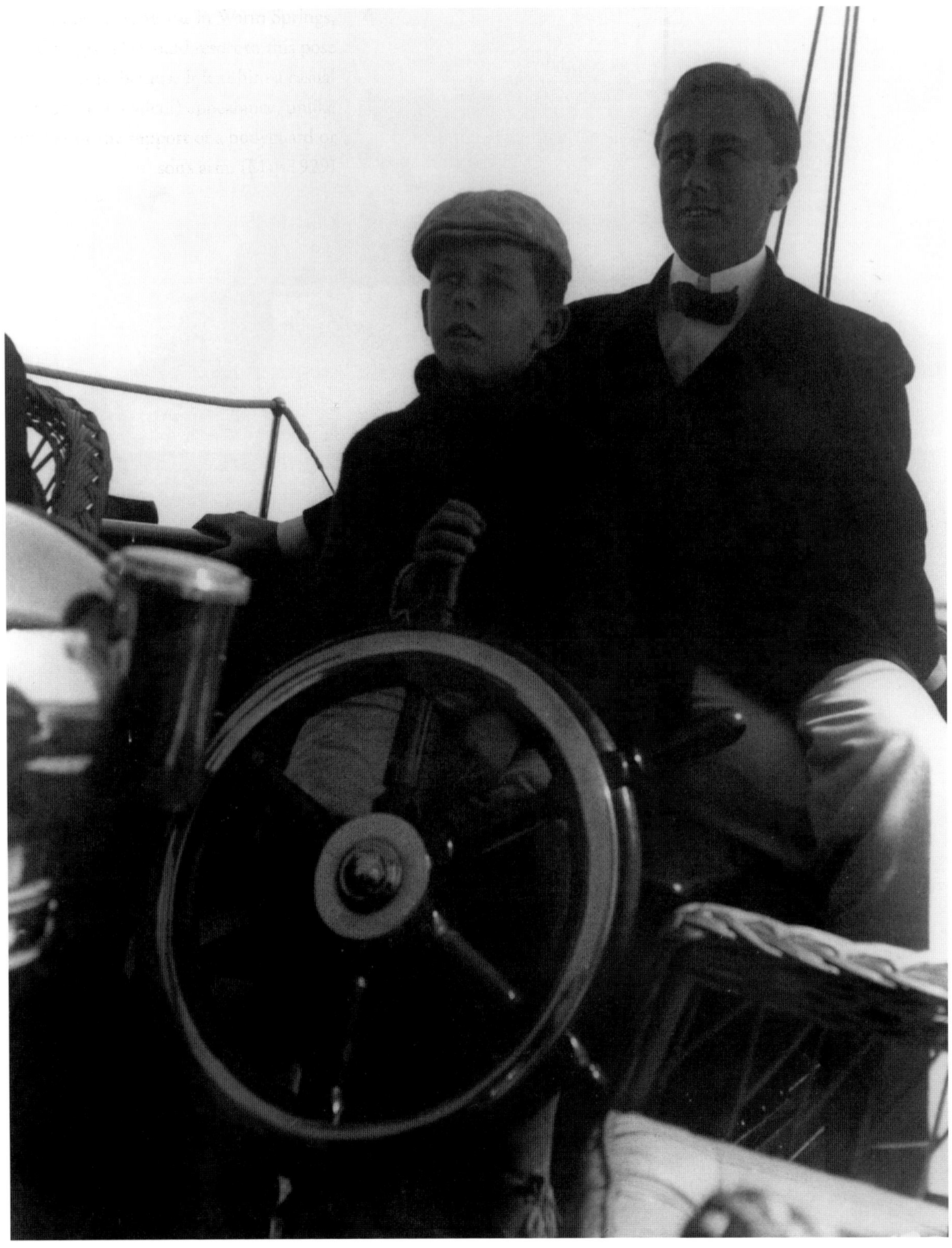

FDR watching over Gorham Hubbard piloting the Roosevelt family yacht at Campobello. Hubbard was the son and namesake of a Boston insurance broker and fellow Campobello enthusiast. (1908)

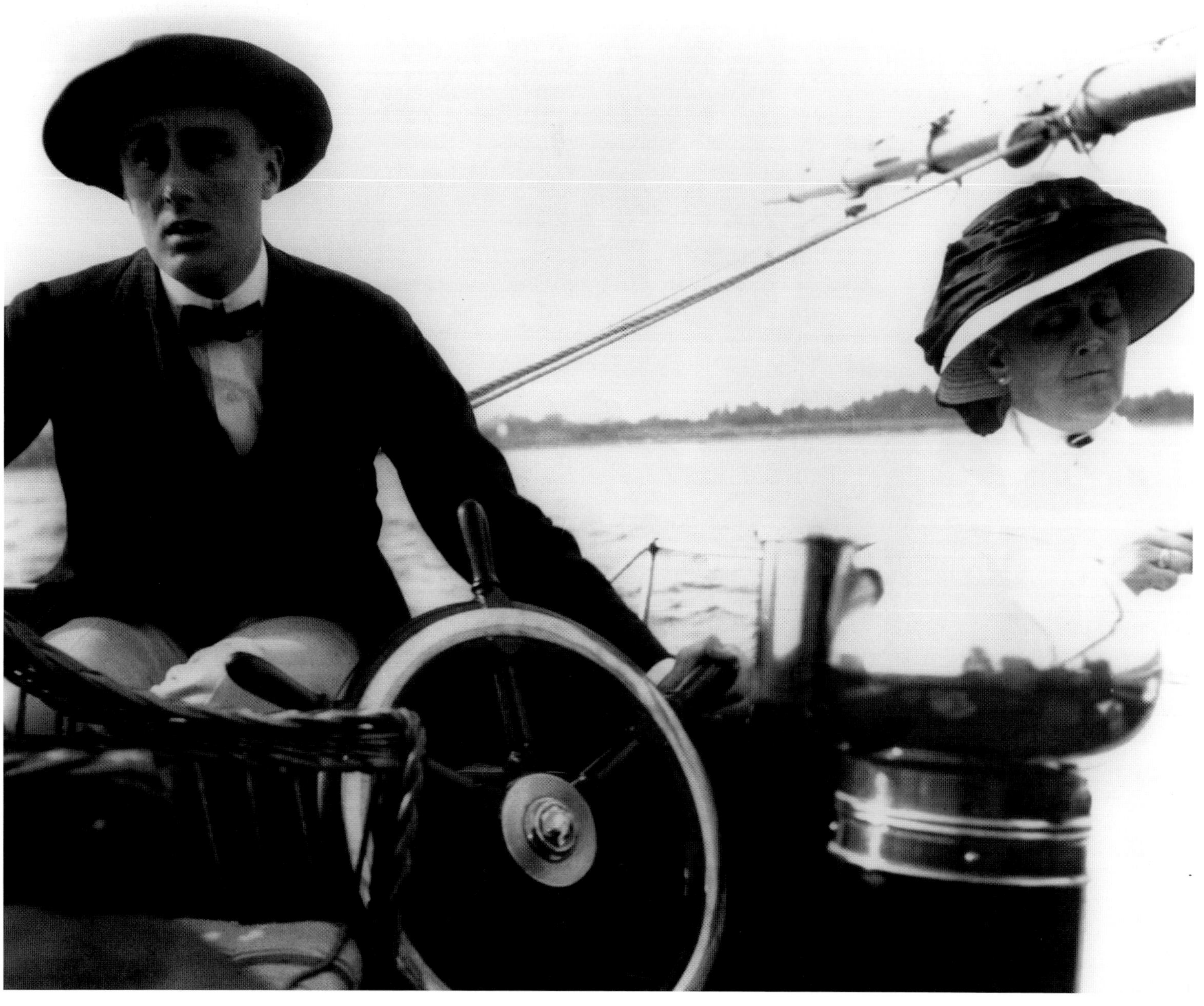

FDR and his mother at Campobello. He is piloting the family yacht in a more characteristic pose, with Sara serenely at his side. (1908)

FDR with Anna, on horseback in Hyde Park, New York. The many pictures of Franklin with Anna in these early years show him as a doting father. (September 1908)

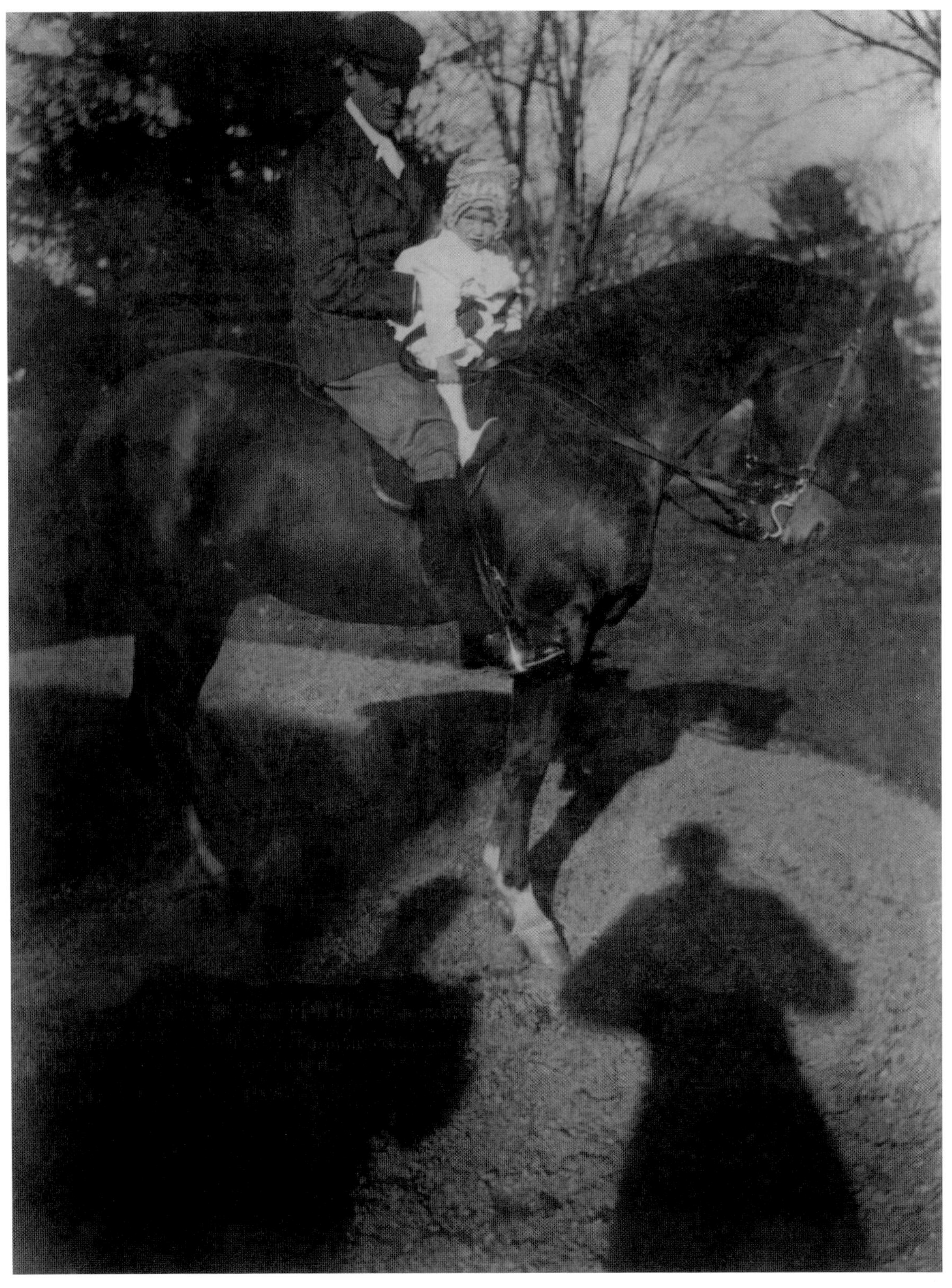

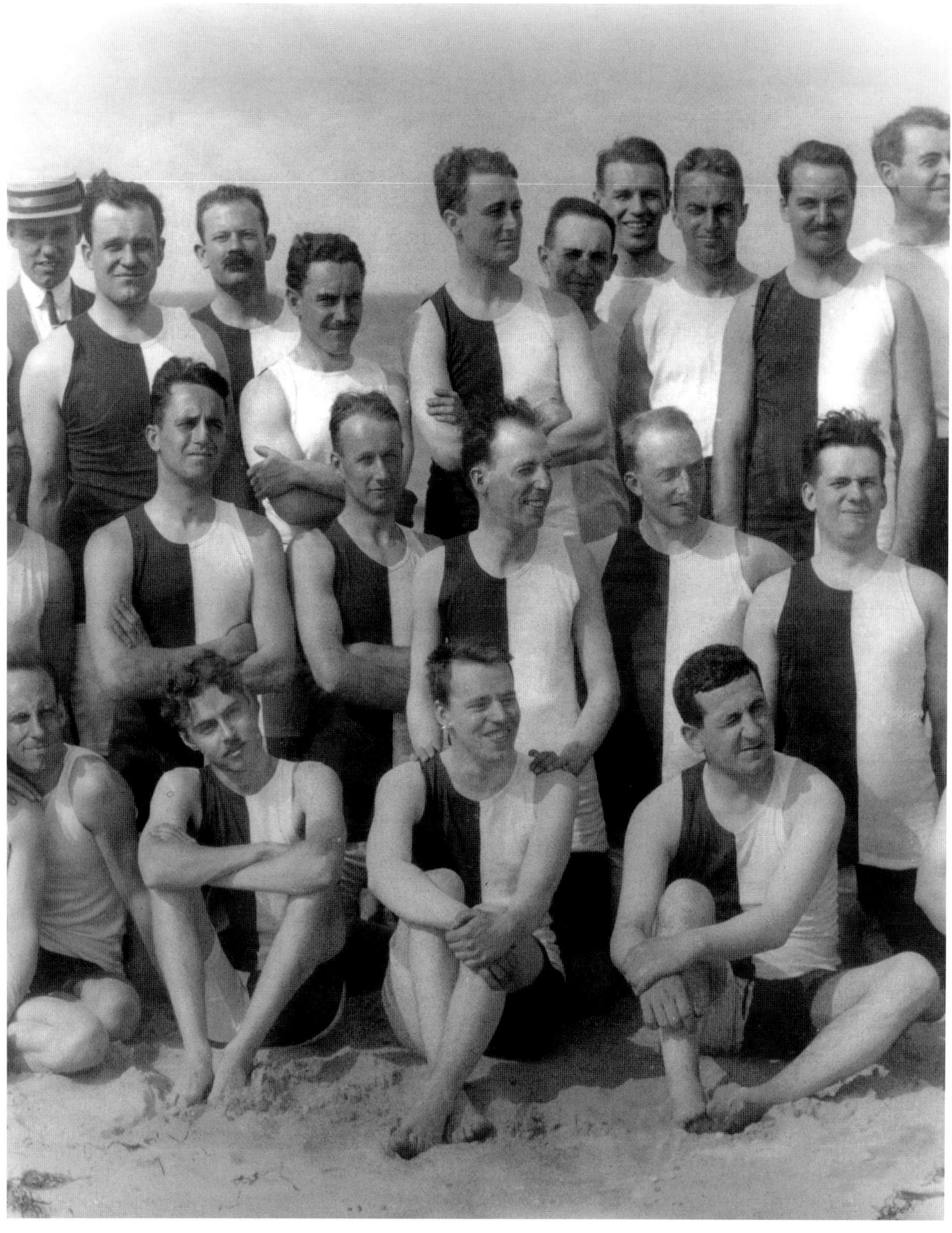

FDR in swimming costume, with Harvard class of 1904, from a group shot in Nantasket Beach, Hull, Massachusetts. In the early twentieth century, Nantasket Beach was a very popular tourist destination. Numerous Harvard classes held reunions there. (June 27, 1910)

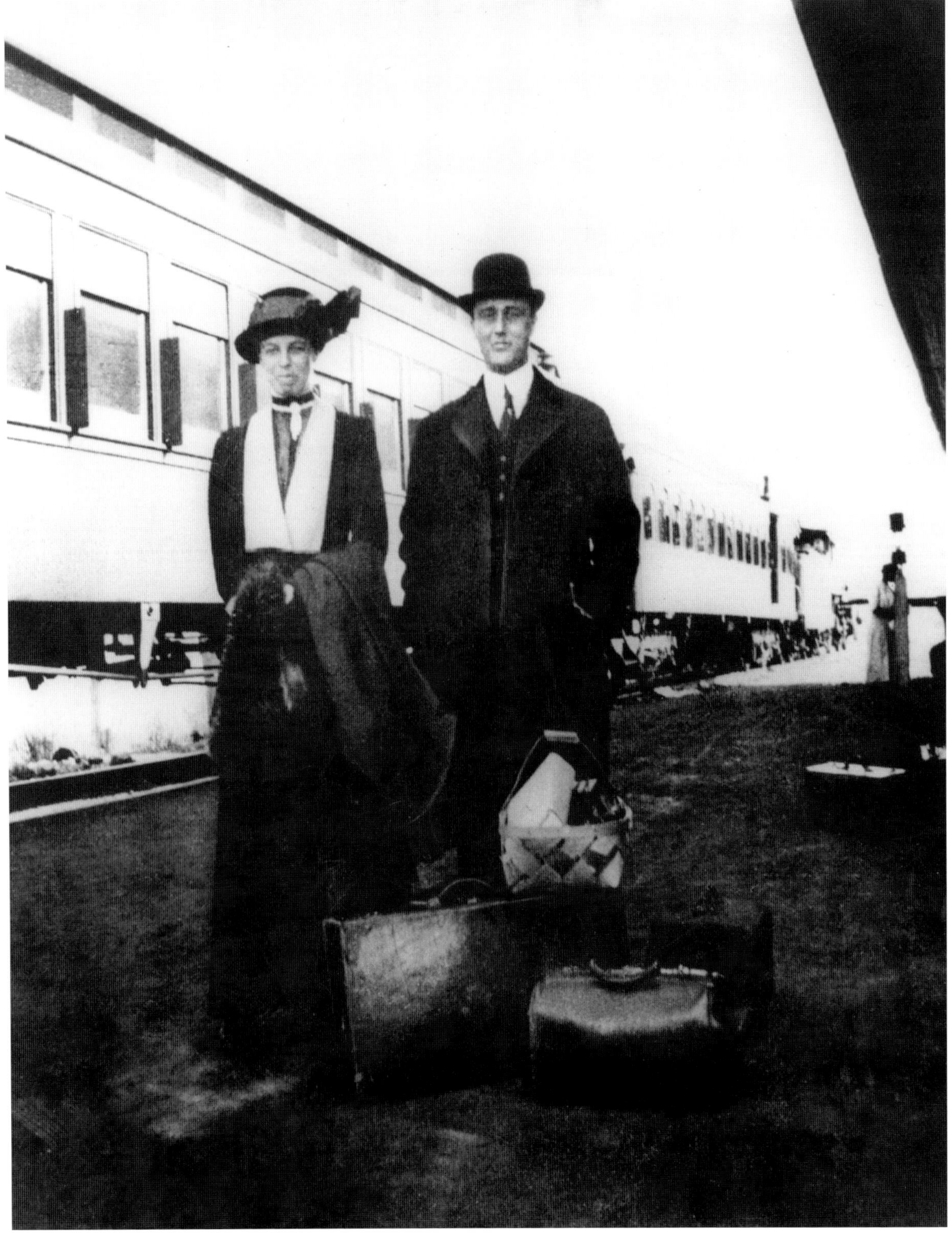

FDR and Eleanor waiting in Eastport, Maine, for the train to Campobello. They appear to be traveling light. (1910)

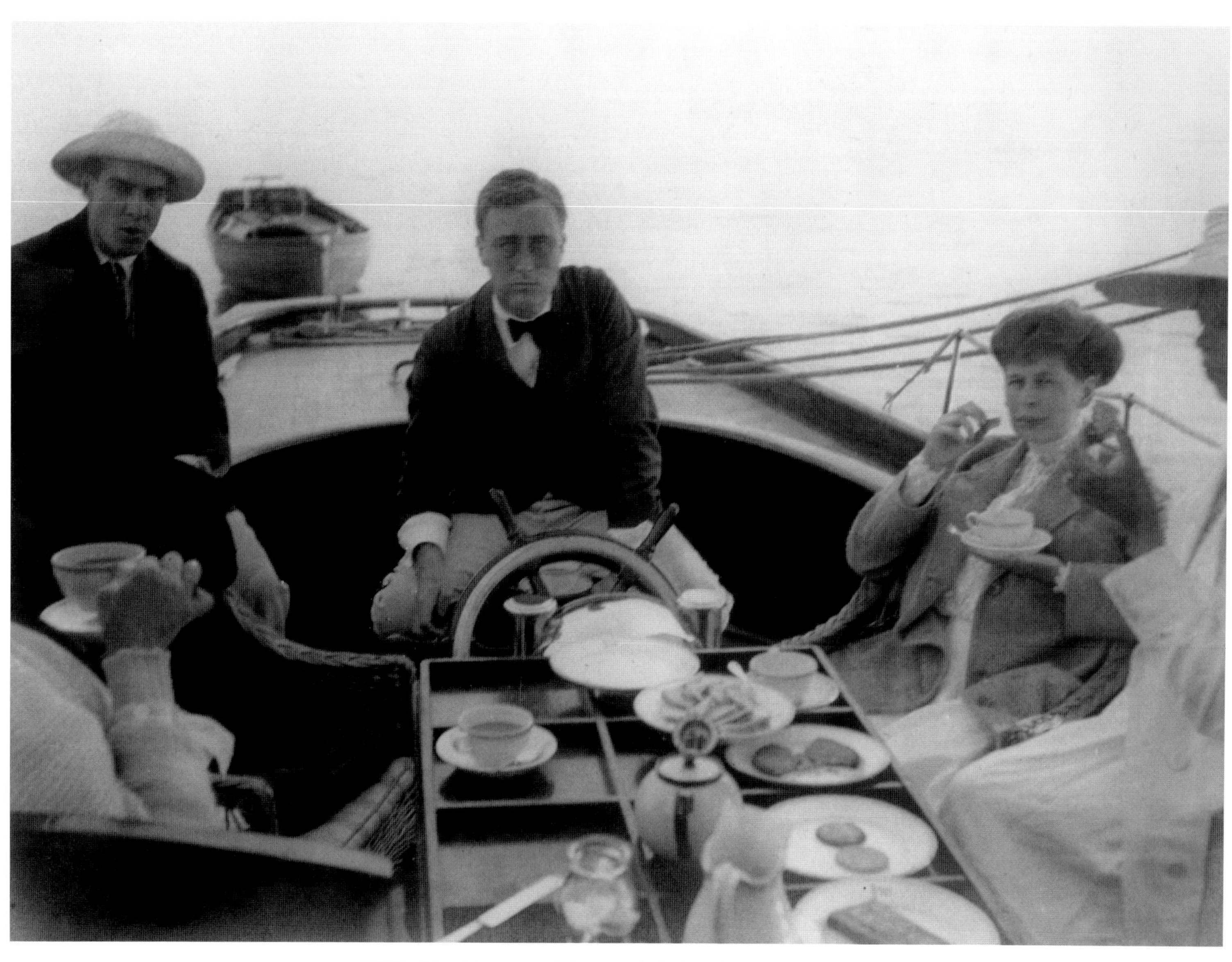

FDR taking his responsibilities at the helm of the family yacht quite seriously. Frances Dana de Rham, an early romantic interest, is on his left. Afternoon tea is in progress. (1910)

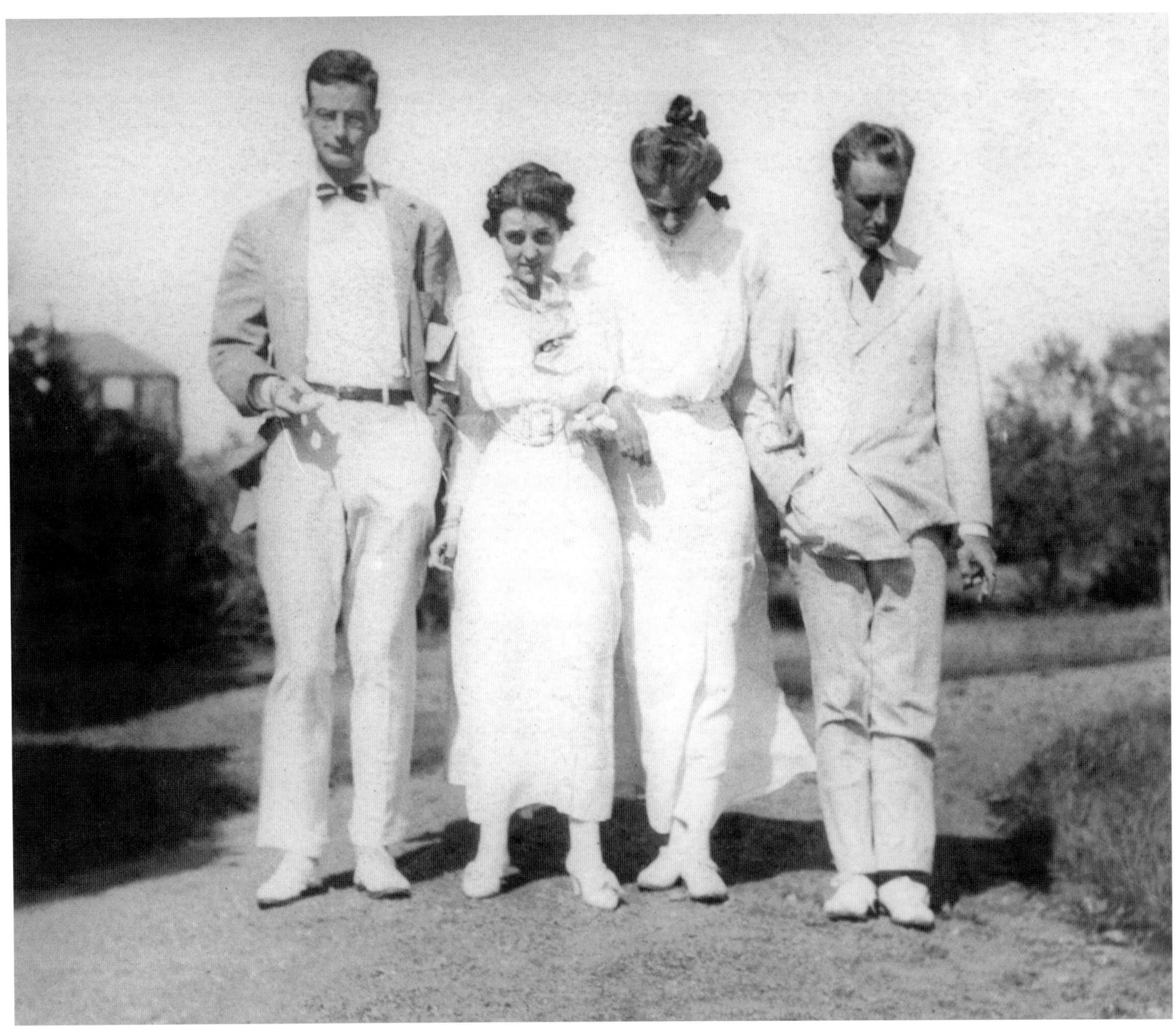

FDR, Eleanor, his aunt Laura F. Delano, and Harry S. Hooker at Campobello. Hooker was a law partner of FDR's. (1910)

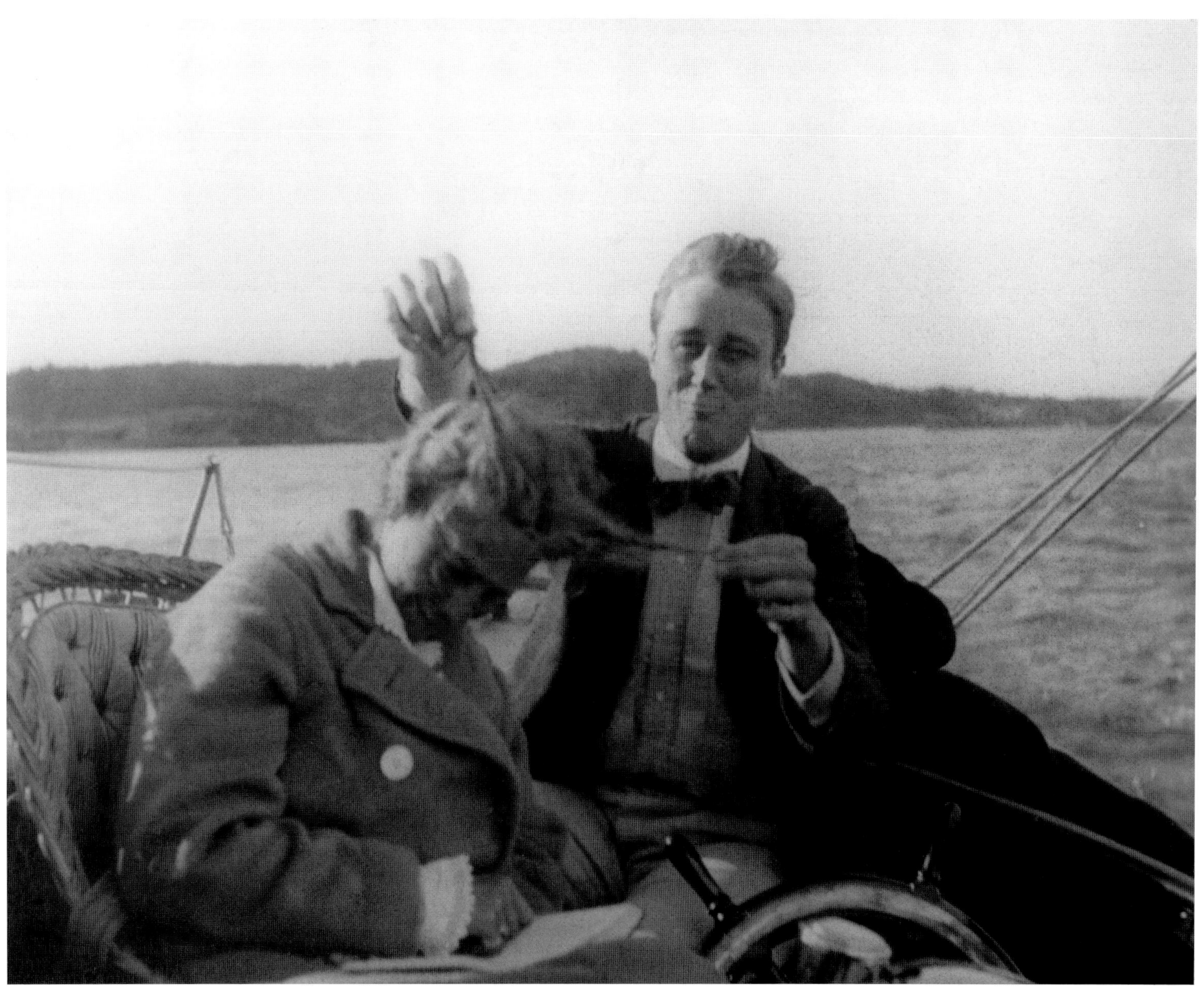

FDR teasing his cousin Jean Delano. The brisk wind has whipped her hair into disarray while she has been engrossed in the book she holds in her lap. Jean would marry George Edgell in 1914. (1910)

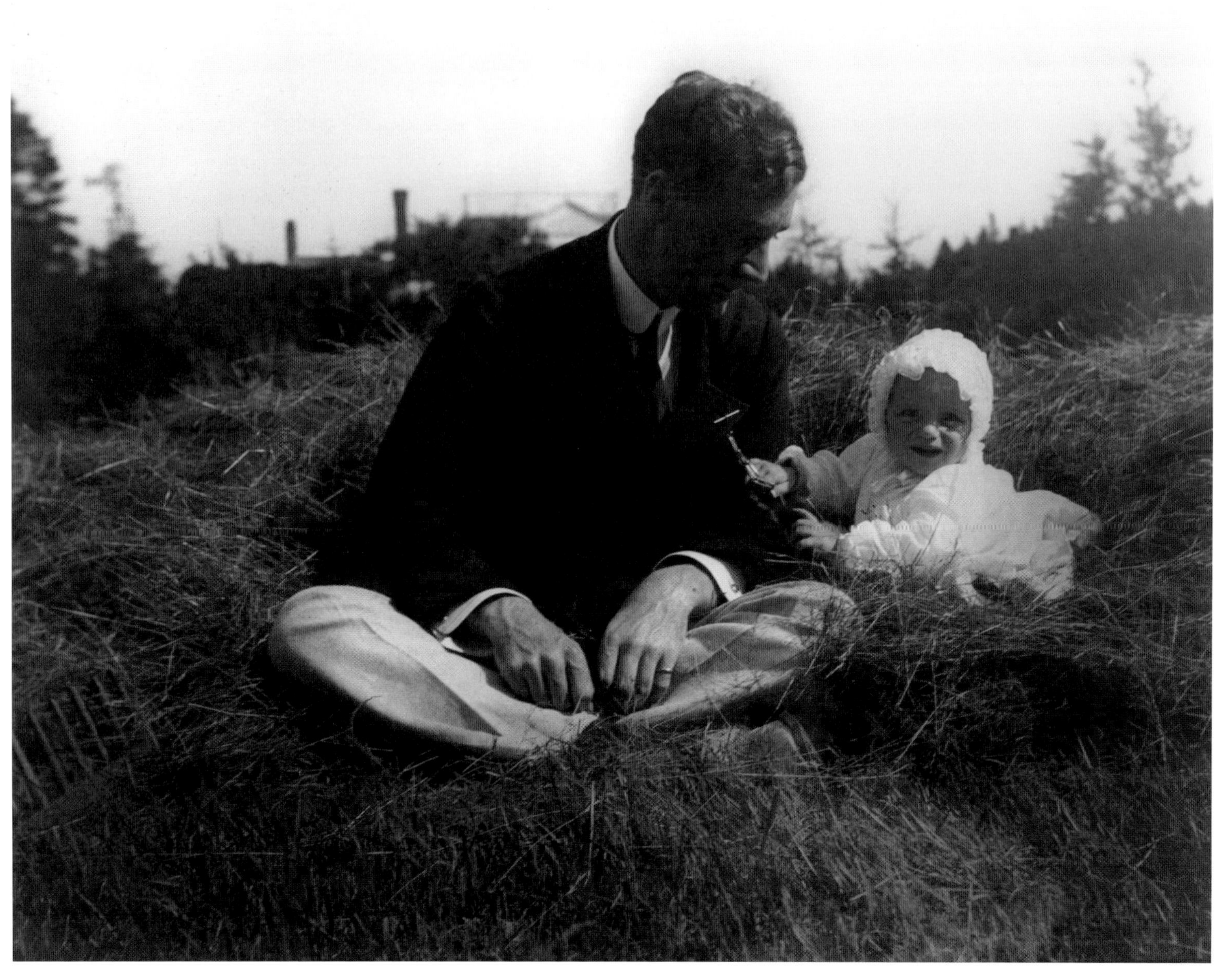

FDR and baby Elliott sitting in the hay at Campobello. Elliott, named after Eleanor's father, the younger brother of Teddy Roosevelt, was born in 1910. Franklin and Eleanor had lost one son, named FDR after his father, in 1909. (1911)

Political Man

(1911–1933)

With familial ties to the Astors, and positioned firmly among the Northeast elite, a life in politics would have been unthinkable but for Franklin's extraordinary downstate cousin Theodore Roosevelt. Theodore's mad rush to that very pinnacle of politics, the presidency of the United States, gave his more languid cousin a path to follow and a name on which to trade. He did and it served him well. Franklin, the Hyde Park Roosevelt, went into politics as a Democrat, something his Oyster Bay cousins could never forgive. Beyond simple admiration of his cousin's political skill, if not political party, Franklin became closely tied to his downstate cousins when he married Teddy's niece Eleanor in 1905, a marriage which produced five children and gave FDR in later years a political ally and stand-in.

Franklin began his political career locally, as had his cousin. Local in Franklin's case was a seat for Dutchess County in the state legislature. He met political mentor Henry Louis Howe in 1912, and the team that Howe created would help propel FDR to the highest political heights. His ambition led him to a misstep, and in 1914 he badly lost being nominated for the Senate. Soon recovering, he was off to Washington, following his cousin's footsteps and becoming assistant Secretary of the Navy. He had always had a seagoing nature, having been brought up on long ocean voyages and summer sailing at Campobello, New Brunswick. His amiable nature, good looks, and name brought him to the vice-presidential spot on the Democratic ticket in 1920, but the ticket, with James M. Cox, was soundly defeated and Roosevelt returned to his home state. The vice-presidency wasn't to be this Roosevelt's route to the White House.

The next were years of wilderness. In 1921 Roosevelt was struck with what was then diagnosed as polio (analysis of his symptoms now supports a diagnosis of Guillain-Barre Syndrome). Roosevelt struggled against the resulting paralysis for the rest of his life, for years convinced he might be able to walk again. The grit and determination he demonstrated to soldier on helped him overcome the "dilettante" image of his youth, however much he cloaked that resolve with an amiable exterior. These years in the desert would be ended by a triumphant return to politics, as Franklin was elected governor of New York in 1928.

In the campaign for the governorship, Roosevelt was almost overshadowed by the man he would be succeeding. Democrat Al Smith had run for the presidency, gaining the nomination but losing to Republican Herbert Hoover. Roosevelt, for his part, had kept the New York statehouse in Democratic hands. Smith, surprised by this unexpected turn of events, was reluctant to let go of power in Albany and perhaps might have even expected to continue to govern through a compliant Roosevelt. His hopes were dashed when Roosevelt brought in his own team.

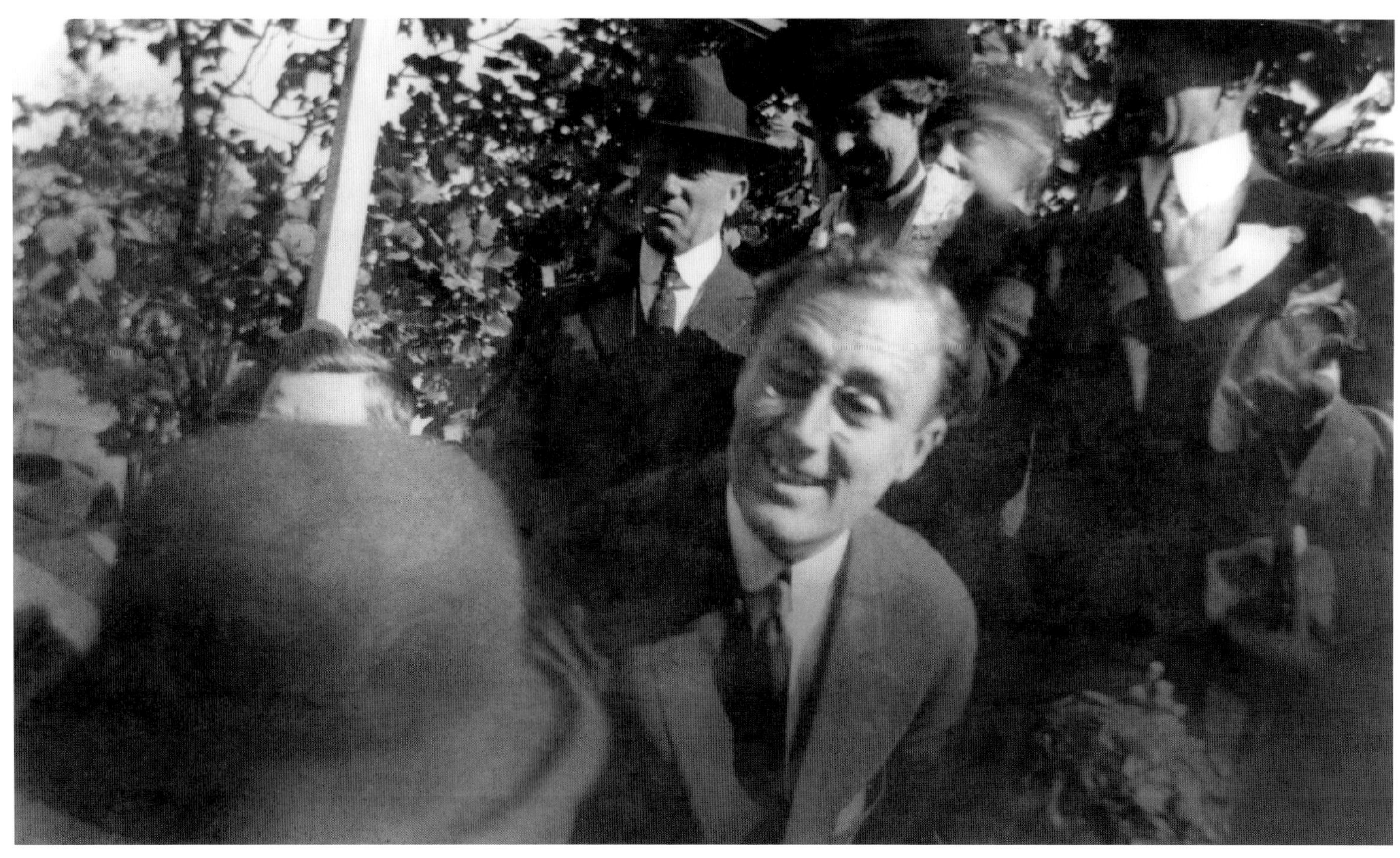

FDR electioneering in 1910. At his engaging best, he is appealing for votes to send him to Albany to the State Senate representing Dutchess County. (1910)

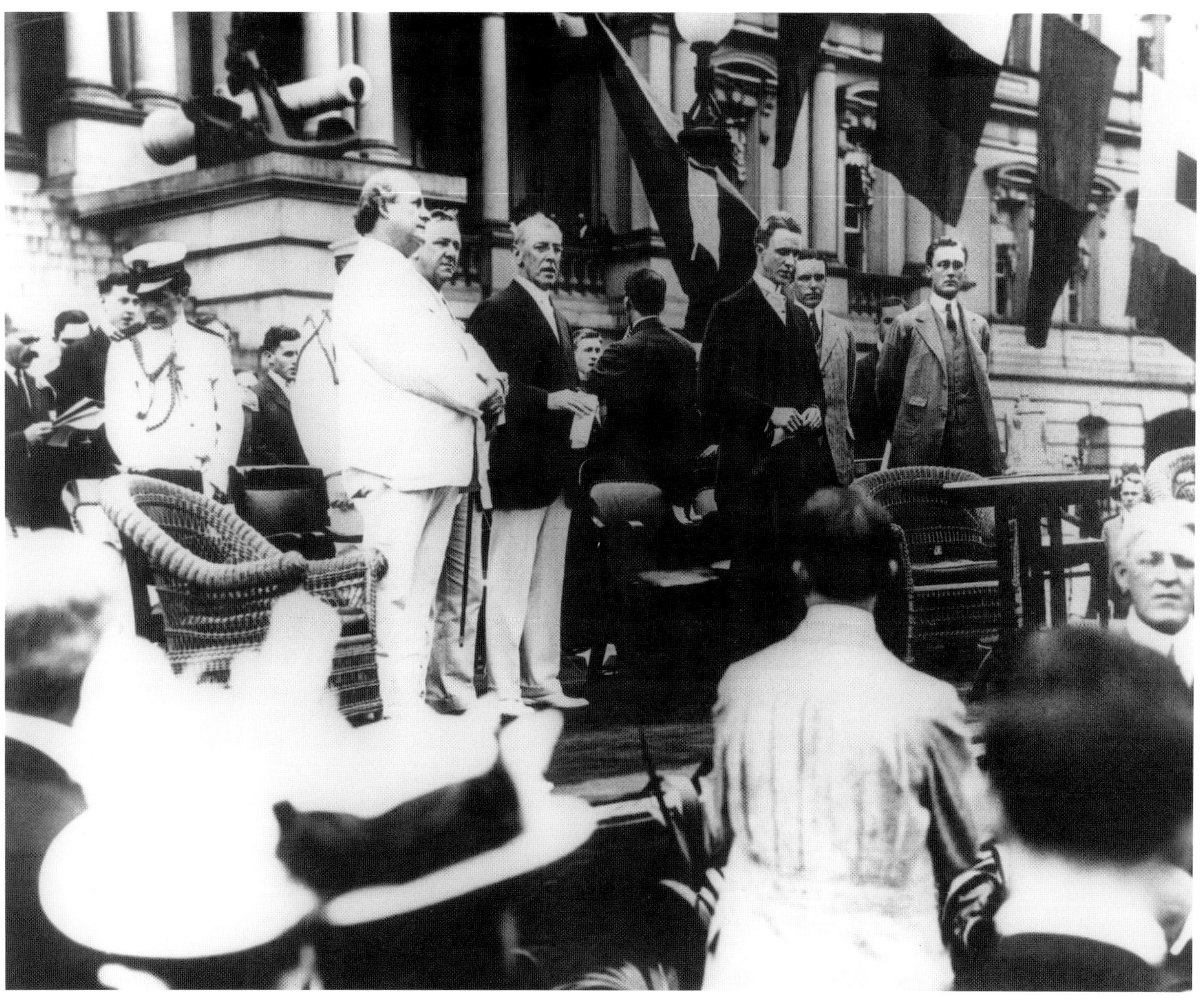

FDR, President Woodrow Wilson, Navy Secretary Josephus Daniels, Henry S. Breckinridge, Assistant Secretary of War, and Secretary of State William Jennings Bryan in front of the State, War, and Navy Building in Washington, D.C., on Flag Day, 1913. Bryan had orated "The American Flag and World Peace" earlier in the day but spoke only briefly here—this was the first celebration of Flag Day at State, War, and Navy. (June 14, 1913)

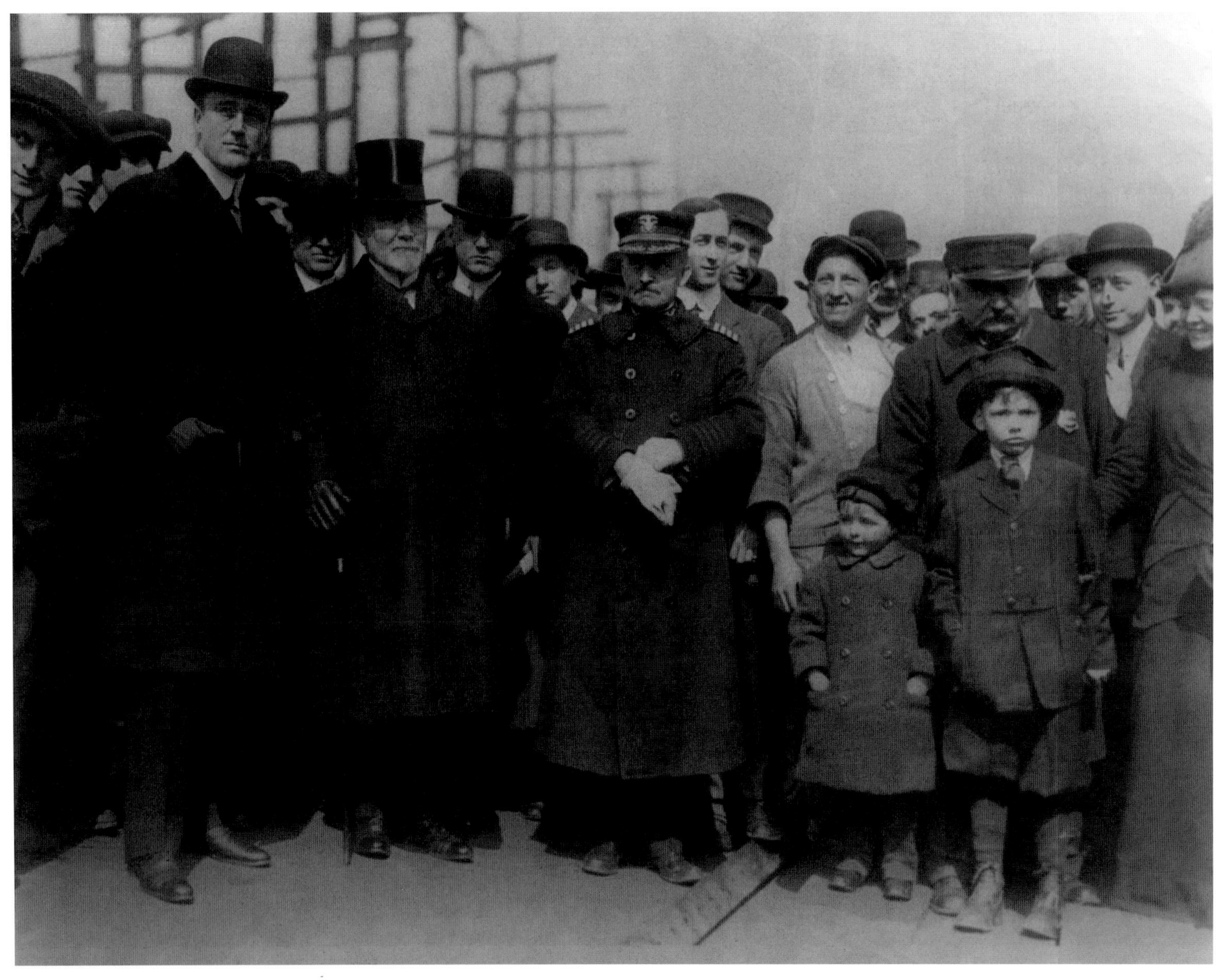

FDR and a crowd at Brooklyn Naval Yard. President Wilson is giving an address at the services commemorating those seventeen Navy men who lost their lives at Veracruz, Mexico, May 11, 1914. (1914)

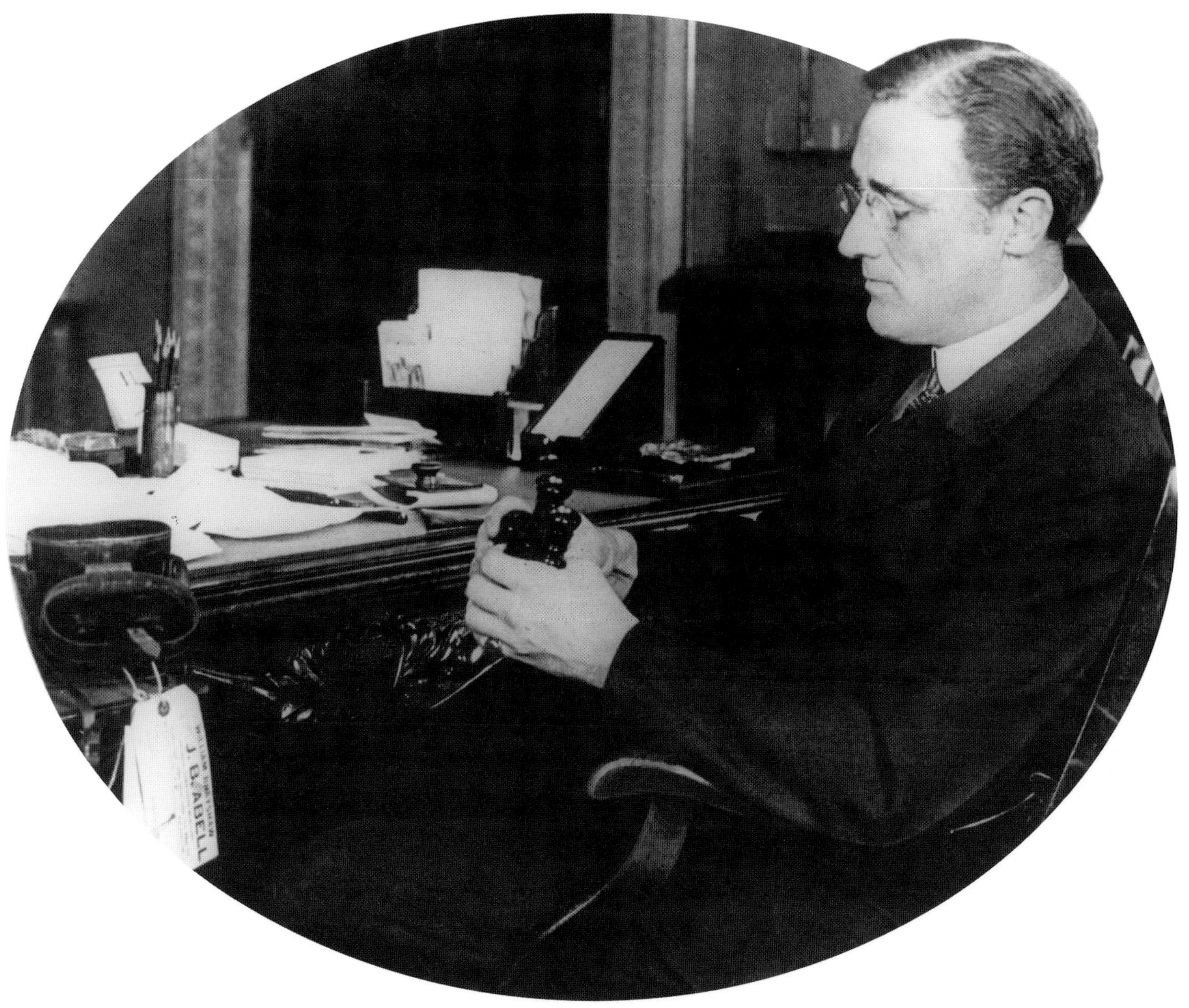

FDR at his desk as the Assistant Secretary of the Navy, an office his uncle Theodore Roosevelt had held and which TR's son Theodore, and cousins Theodore Robinson and Henry Latrobe Roosevelt, would hold in future administrations. Franklin is examining a pair of donated binoculars. To help locate German submarines, the Navy had put out a call for donations of binoculars, spyglasses, and telescopes—which it promised to tag and return. FDR did send out thank-you letters for the equipment for the "Eyes of the Navy," and the Navy indeed returned them at the end of the war, with letters of thanks from the assistant secretary. (1917)

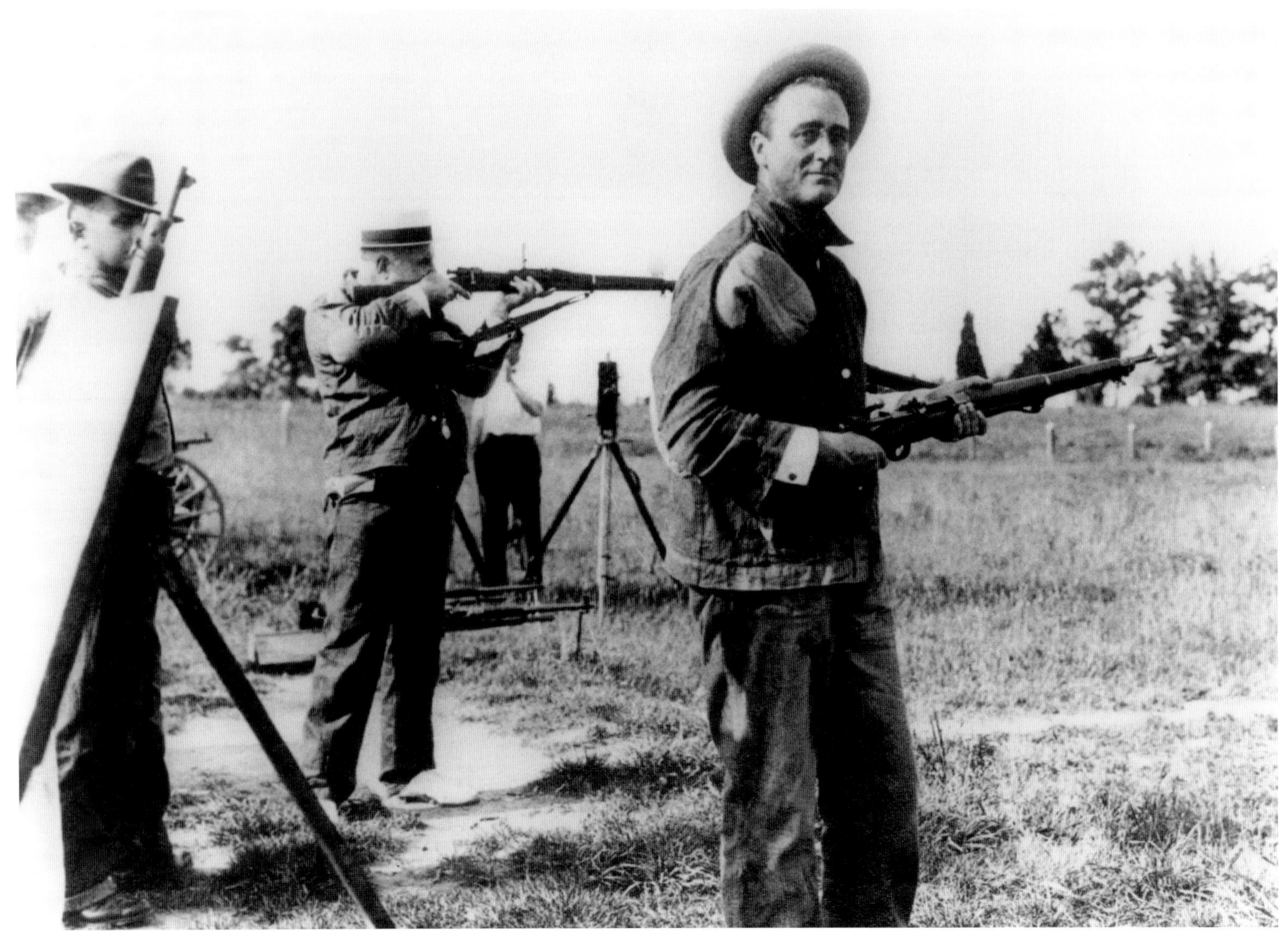

FDR shooting in Winthrop, Maryland. At the U.S. Marine Corps base at Winthrop, Marines were instructed in marksmanship. (1917)

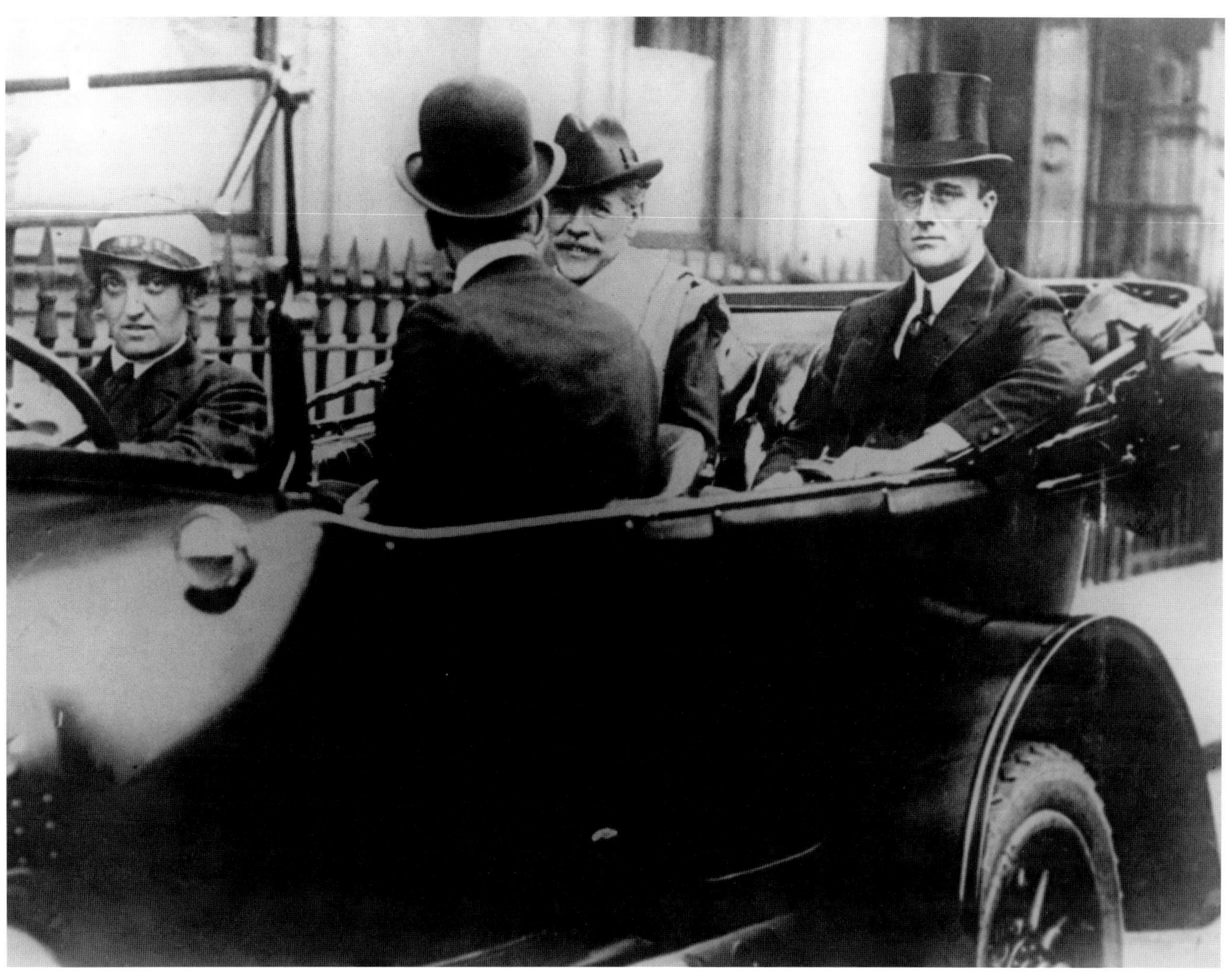

Franklin in top hat visiting London. He would meet with the King regarding the American Navy and its participation in Allied war efforts, culminating his talks with British naval officials. At this same time, news of his cousin Quentin Roosevelt's death in France was released. Twenty-year-old Quentin was shot down behind enemy lines and buried by the Germans. (July 29, 1918)

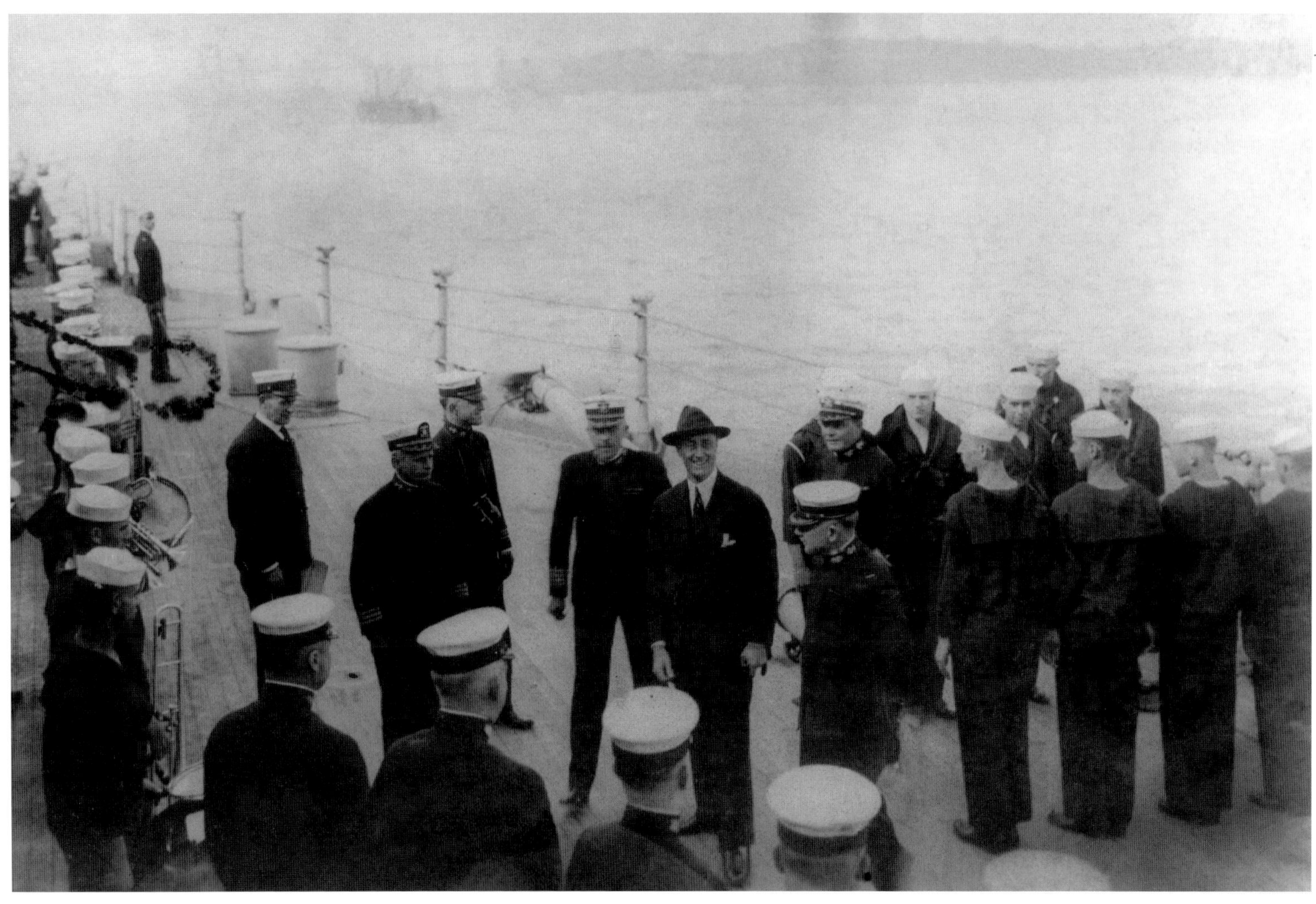

FDR as Assistant Secretary of the Navy arriving on the USS *Texas* in the Firth of Forth. In civilian garb, Franklin looks a bit out of place. "The Navy's work in this war, while not of a spectacular character, has been a most important one," said the *Washington Post*—which included mining the North Sea, building a pipeline across Scotland, and bombing German facilities in Belgium. FDR's was one of several VIP visits to the *Texas*—his was followed by that of Admiral Lord Jellicoe in September. (August 29, 1918)

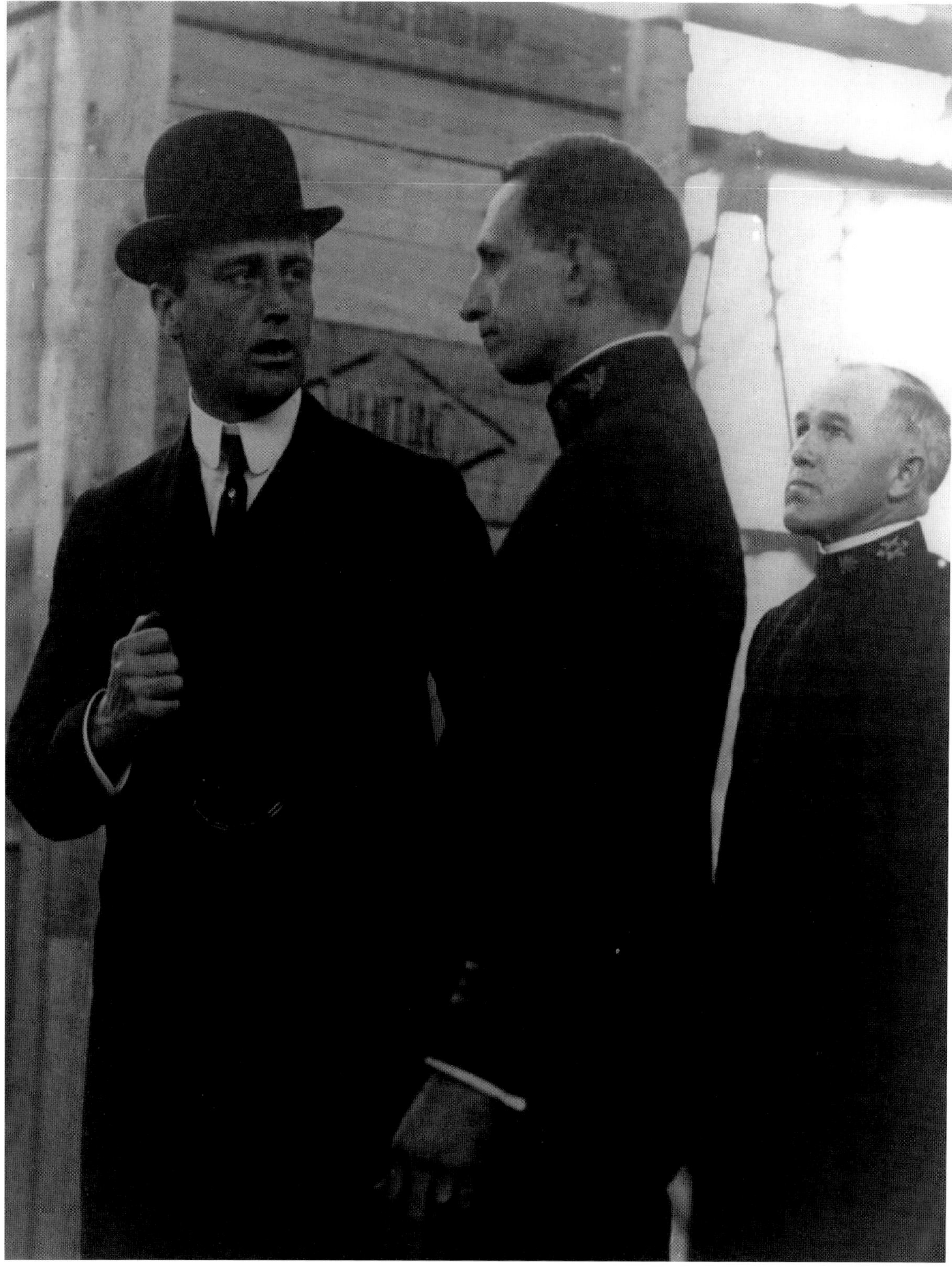

FDR in bowler at the Philadelphia Navy Yard. He was charged with resolving labor disputes and adjusting wage rates, through the Arsenal and Navy Yard Wage Commission, and succeeded at averting strikes. (October 1917)

The perfect family. This formal portrait of FDR, Eleanor, their five children, and his mother, Sara Delano Roosevelt, was taken during Franklin's tenure as Assistant Secretary of the Navy. Only the youngest child, son John, breaks pose and acknowledges the camera. (June 12, 1919)

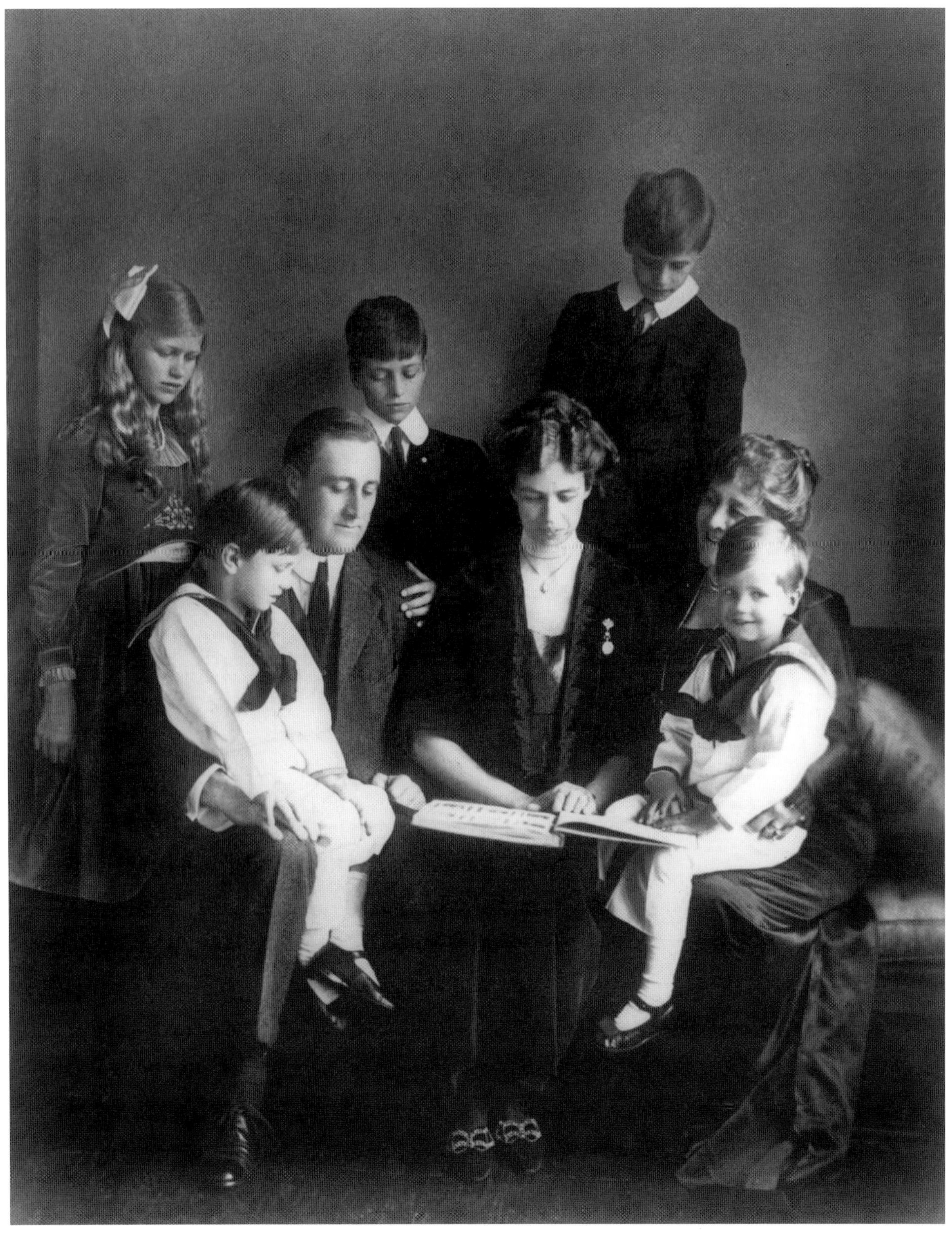

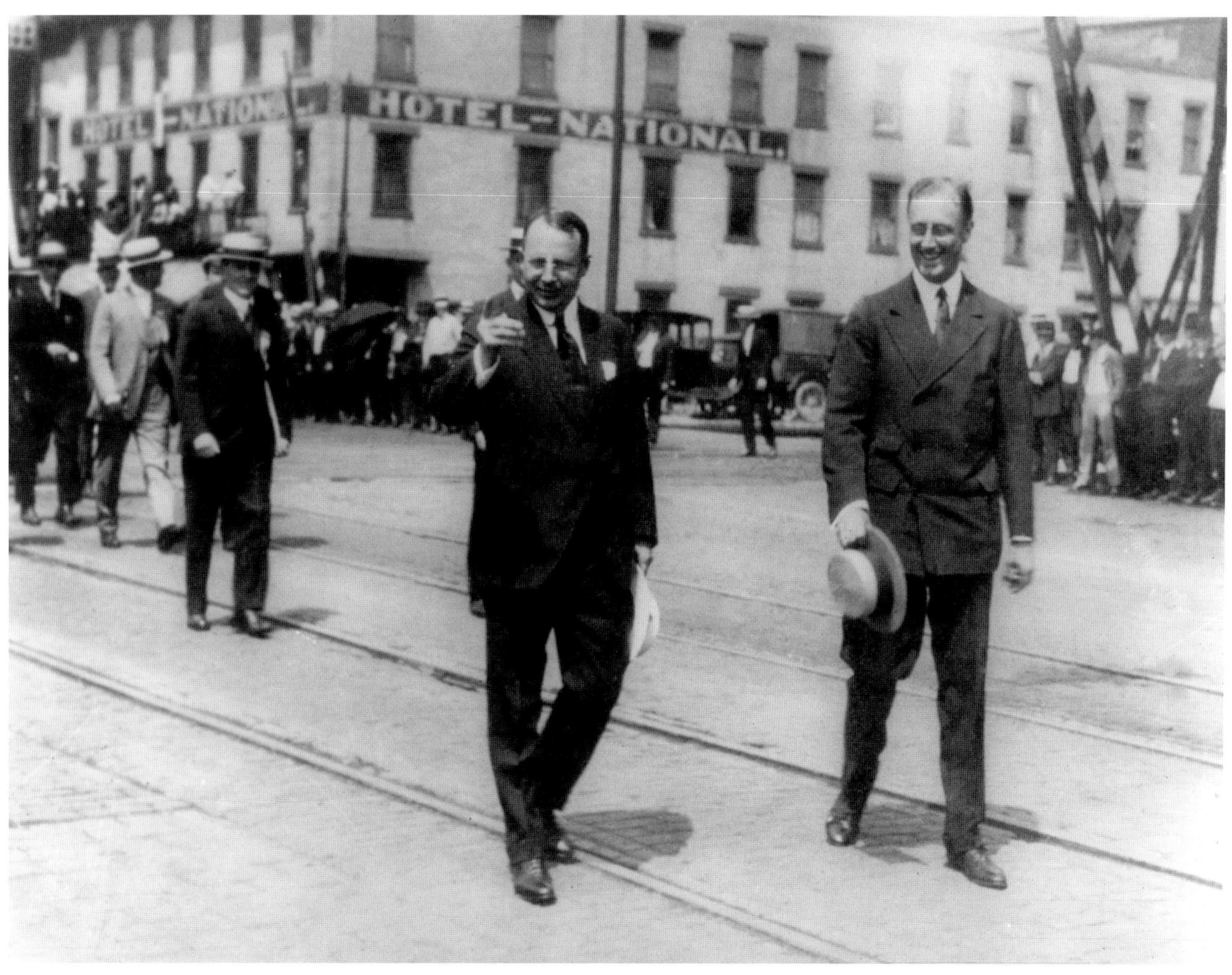

One of the most famous pictures of FDR, as vice-presidential candidate with James M. Cox campaigning in Dayton, Ohio, the day the ticket was announced. Franklin had turned in his resignation, ending almost eight years as Assistant Secretary of the Navy. They would be crushed by the Republican ticket in November. (August 7, 1920)

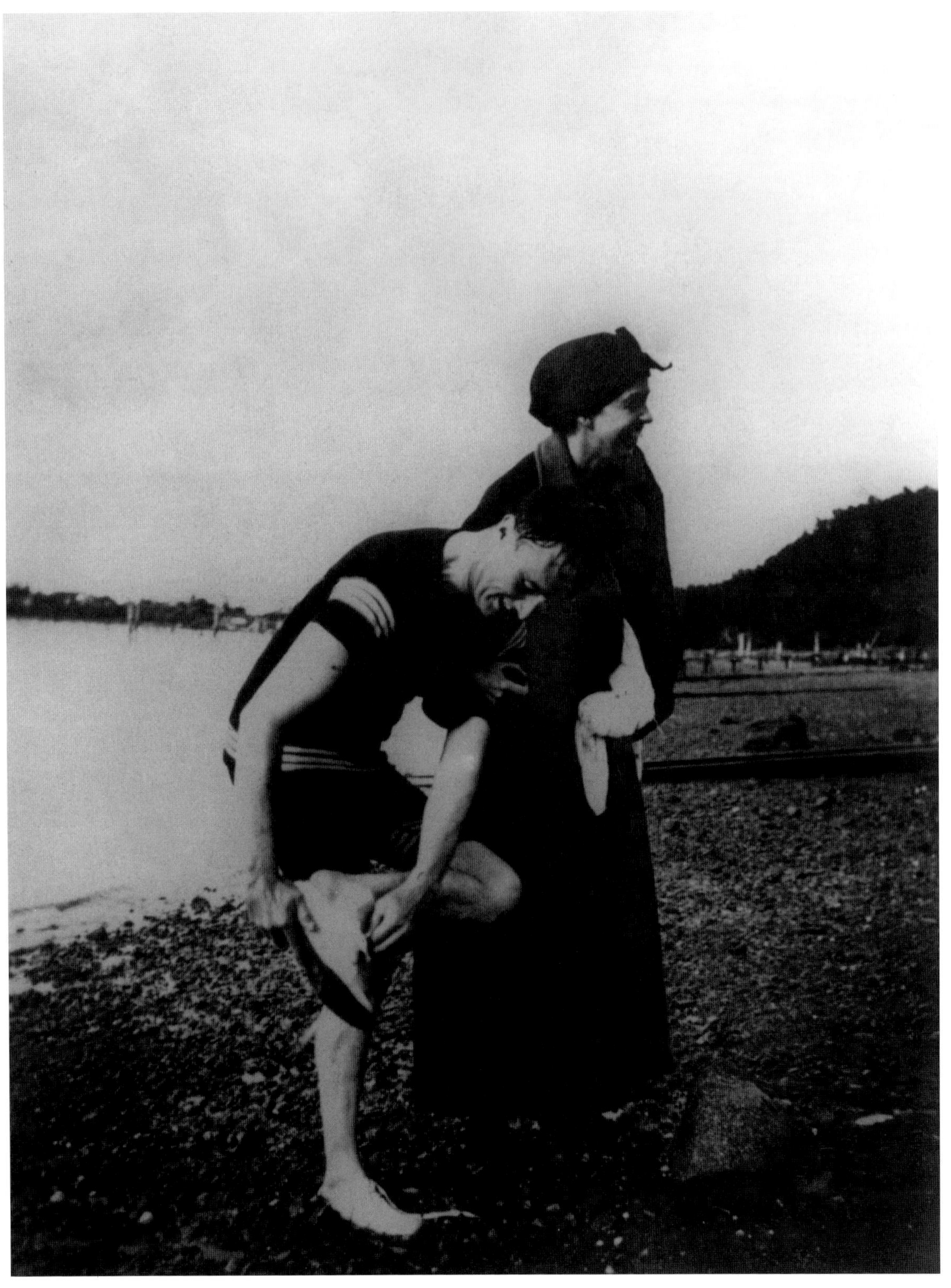

FDR and Eleanor at Campobello. Franklin took only a short break from the presidential campaign, merely a week at the end of July. (1920)

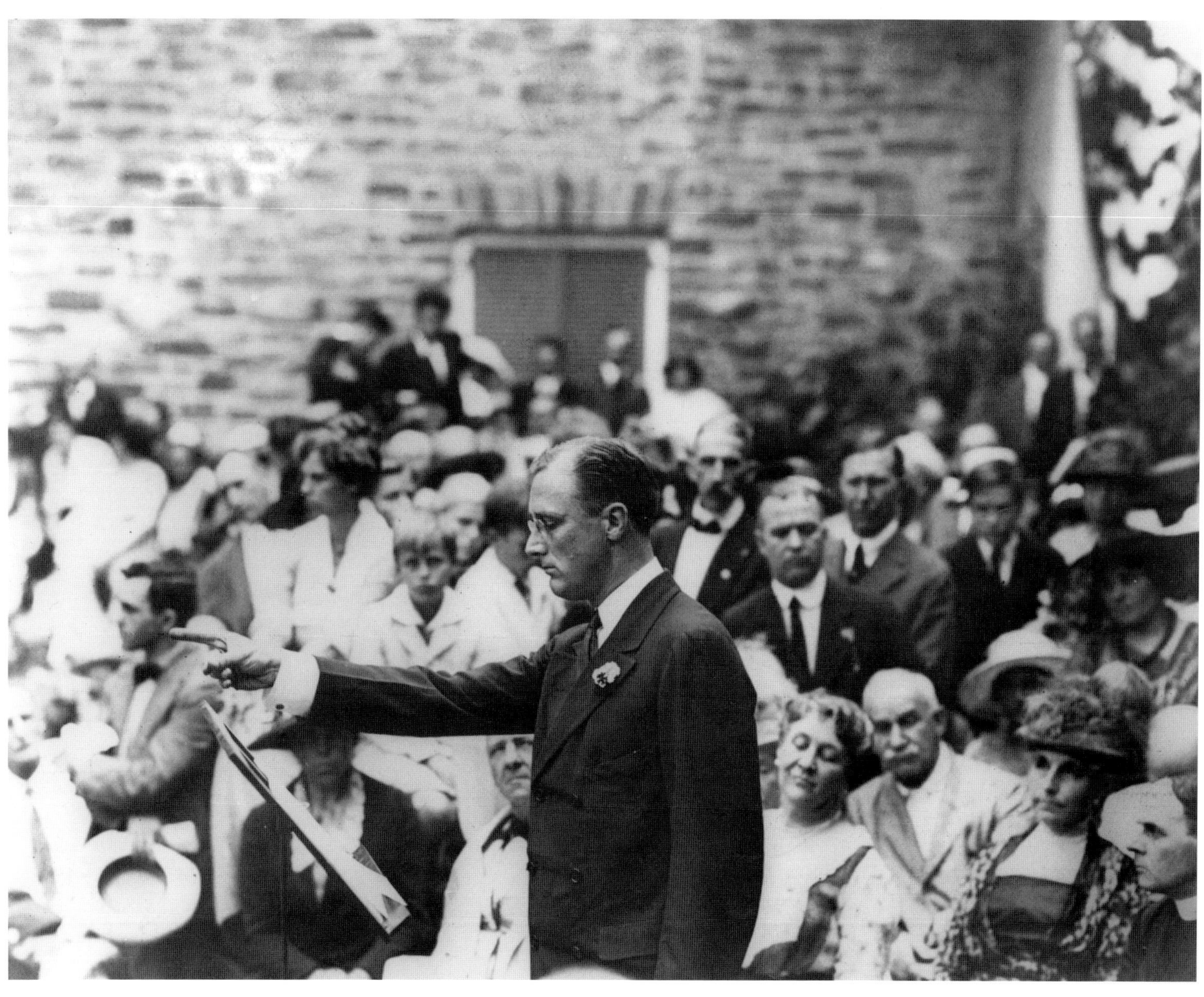

The candidate campaigning in Hyde Park, at his home Springwood. Plans were made to accommodate 10,000 supporters on the lawn. Here pictured, the audience, polite, but not receptive, listens. The speech, at 3,114 words, was the shortest of that year's acceptance speeches. FDR would never carry his home county in his political career. (August 9, 1920)

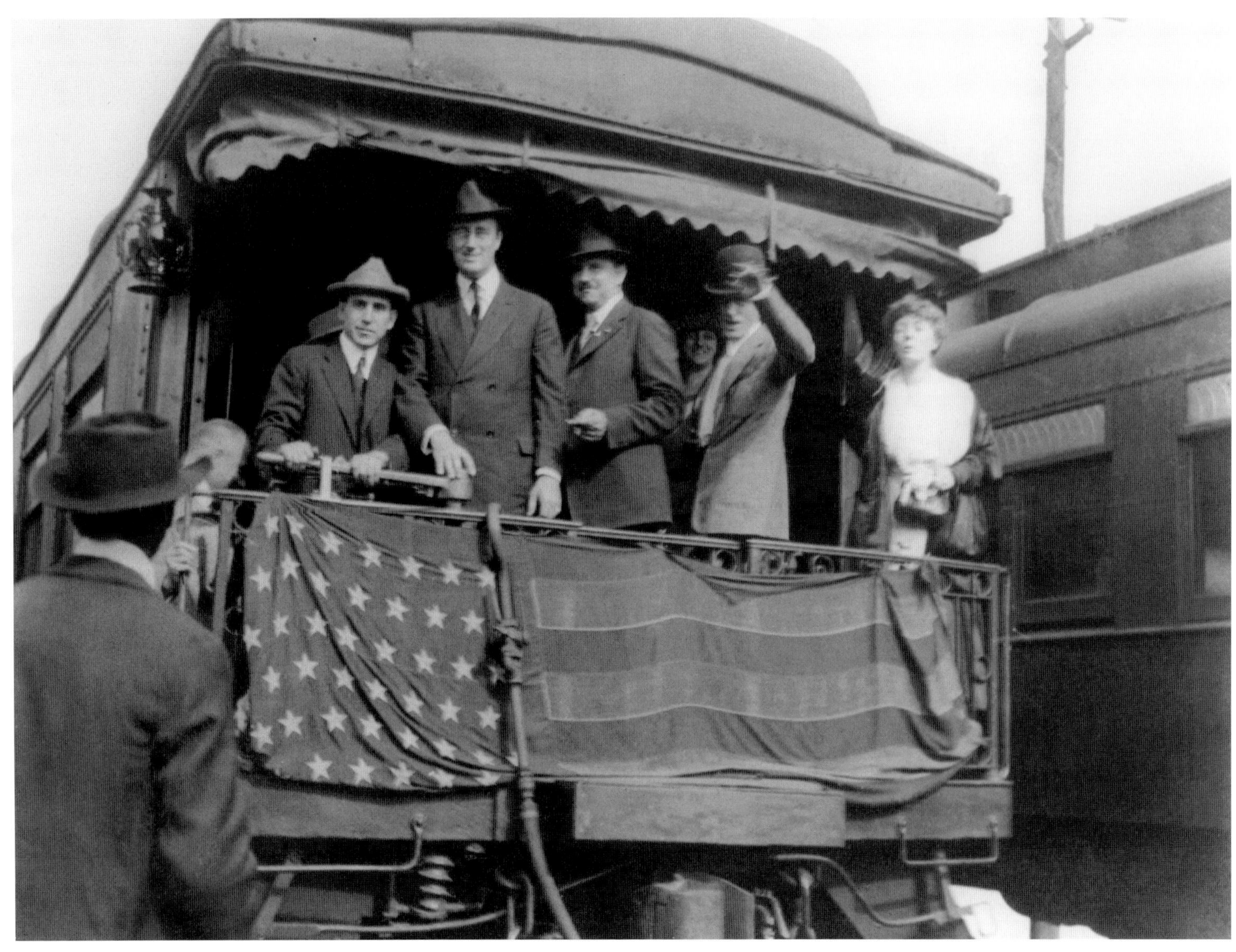

FDR on the stump as vice-presidential candidate, whistle-stop campaigning off the train, here in Morgantown, West Virginia. On this campaign tour, he challenged opponent Warren Harding's views on American entry into the League of Nations. (September 29, 1920)

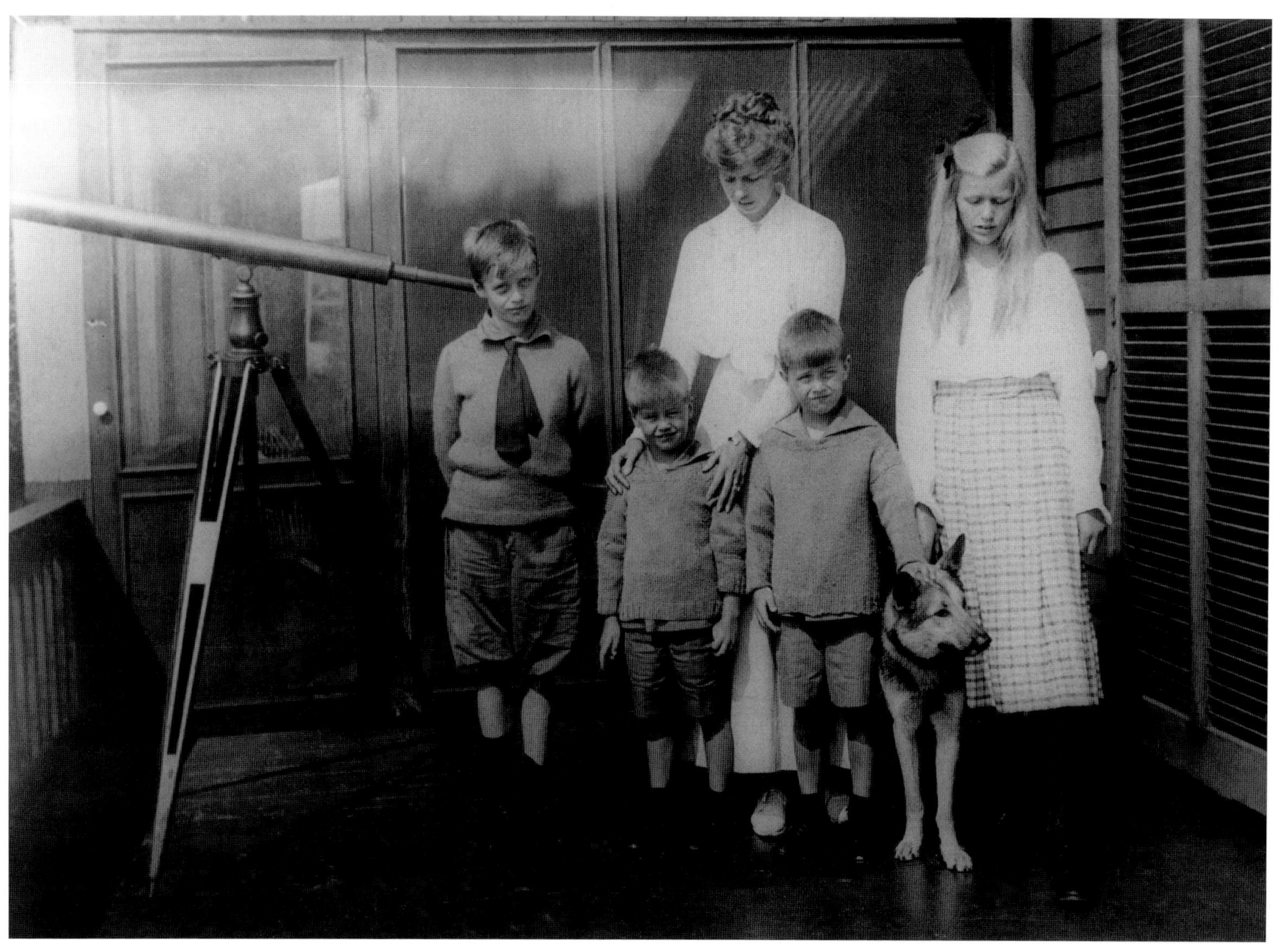

Eleanor and children Anna, Elliott, Franklin D., Jr., and John. Back at Campobello, they have with them a telescope and the family dog Chief. (1920)

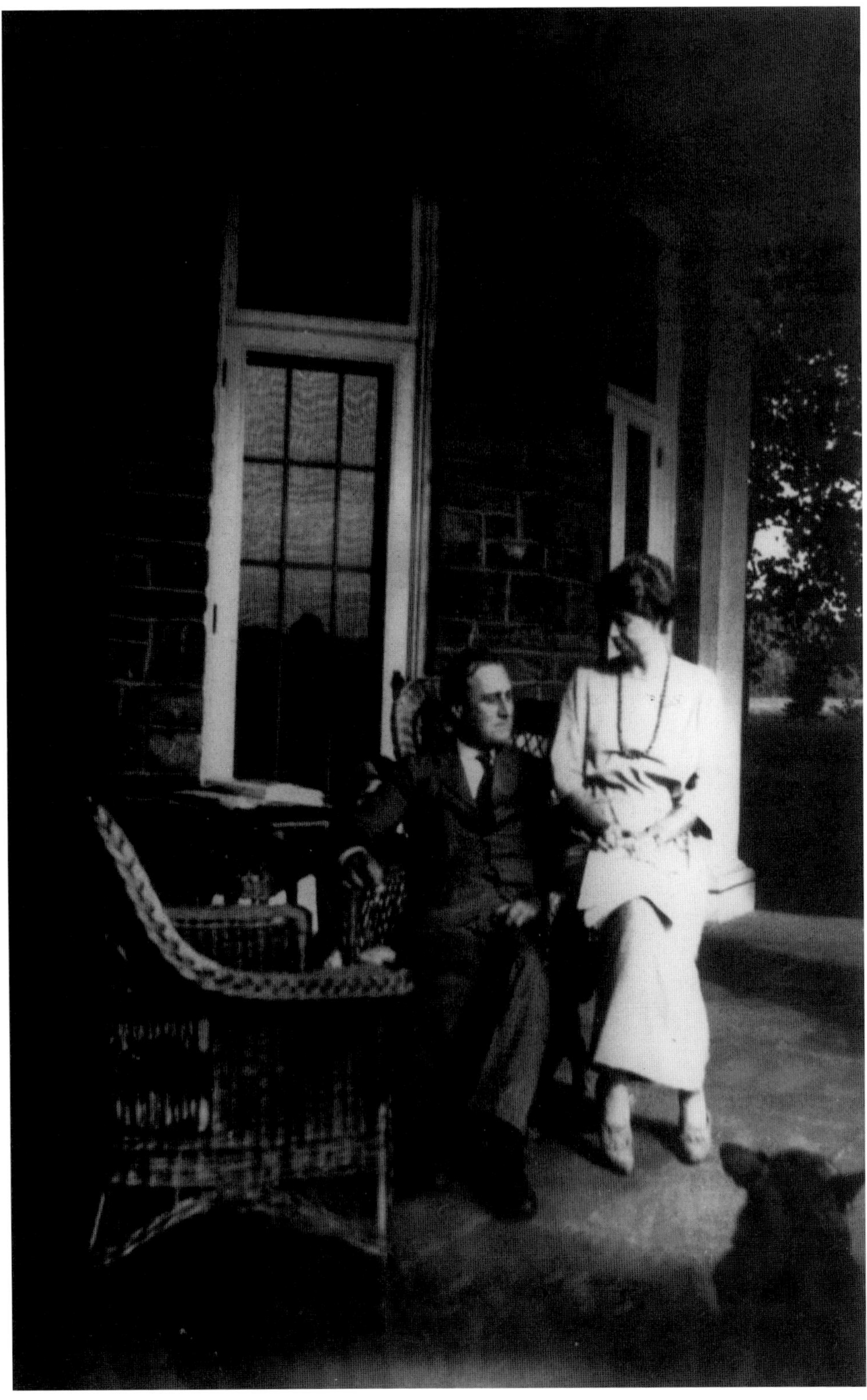

Franklin and Eleanor, an intimate portrait. (1922)

A formal portrait of FDR. (1924)

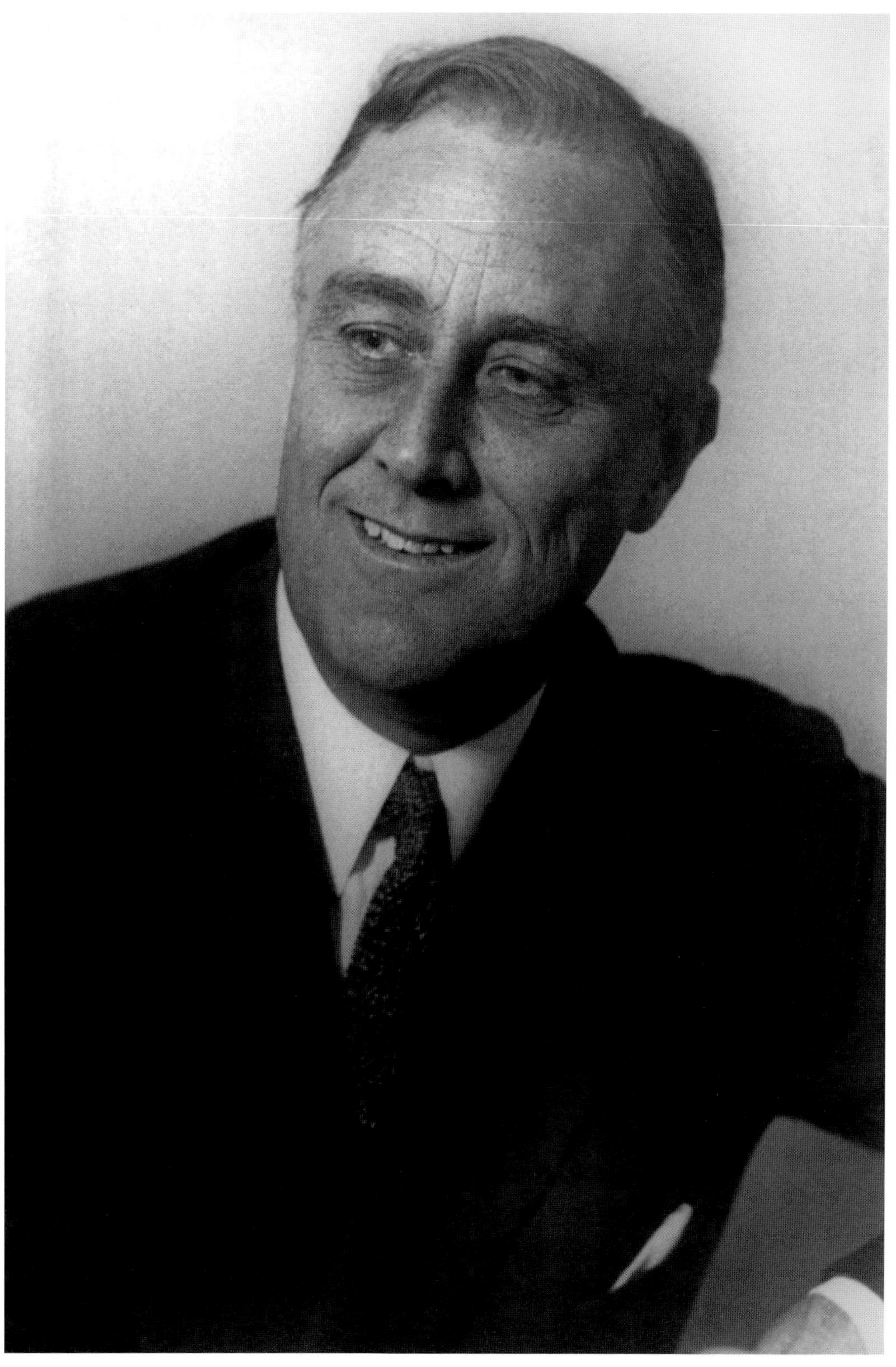

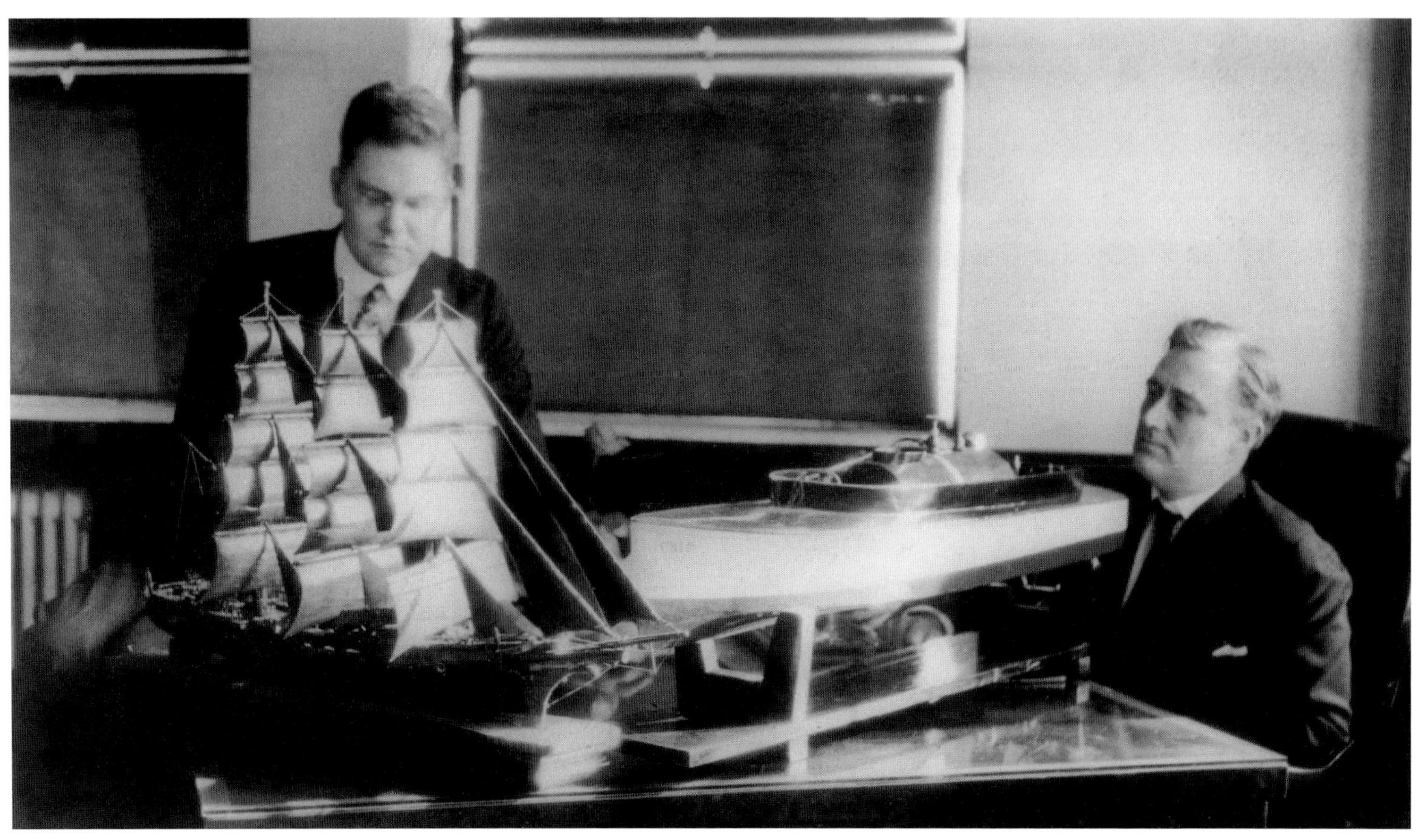

FDR and Dr. L. Etienne O'Brien with two model ships. At his death FDR left two hundred ship models (many of which had lined the walls of his office) as well as an enormous collection of prints and books. (January 24, 1924)

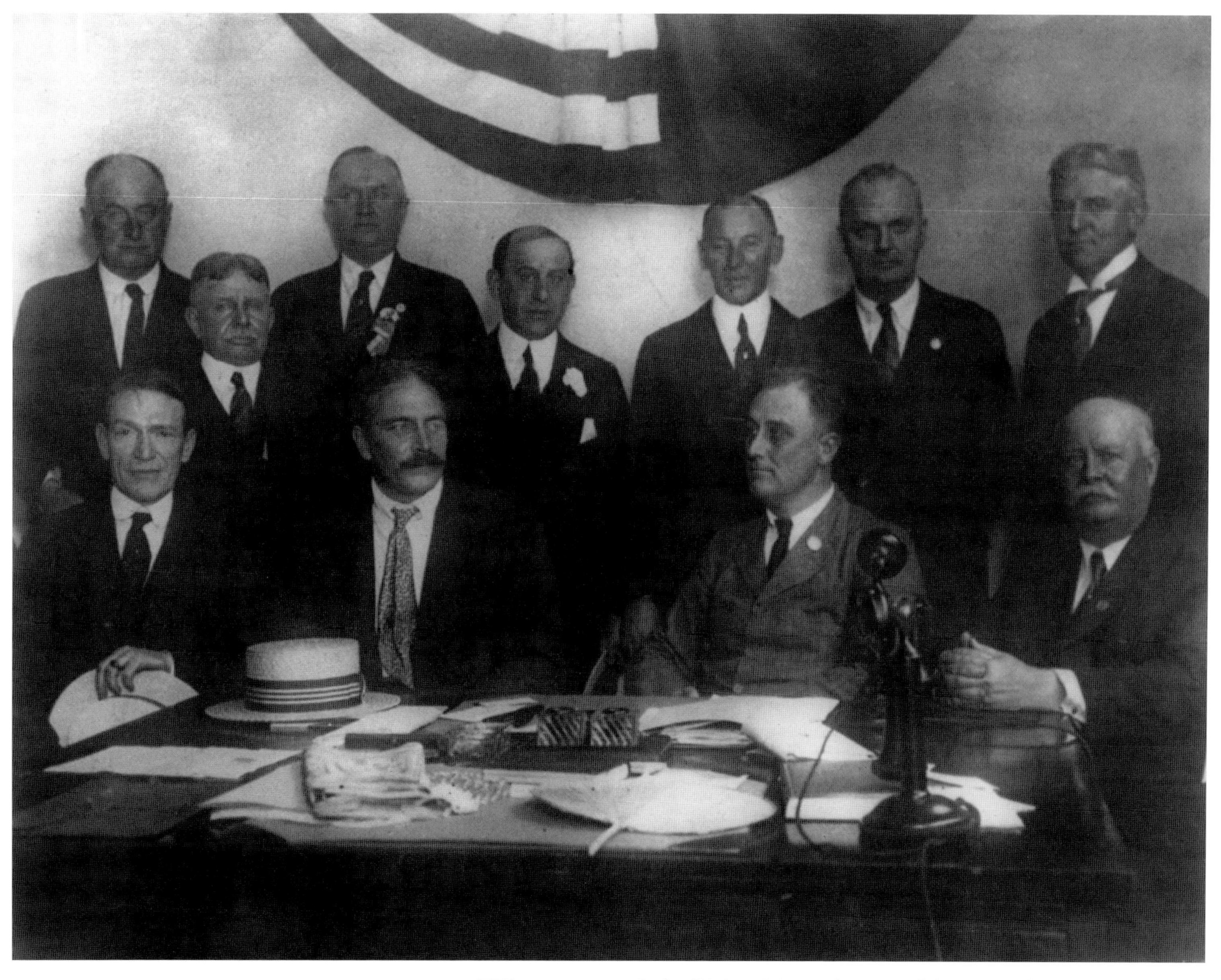

FDR among a crowd of politicians. He was chairman of the New York State Committee for the Nomination of Governor Alfred E. Smith. (1924)

A rare image of FDR publicly on crutches, with Lieutenant Governor George Lunn, Democratic presidential candidate John W. Davis, and Governor Alfred E. Smith in Hyde Park. Smith ran for an almost unprecedented third term. A rally was held by the Dutchess County Democratic Organization at the Poughkeepsie Driving Park in FDR's honor (and to counter a recent KKK rally). Smith demanded honesty in government and declared such to be the primary campaign issue. (August 7, 1924)

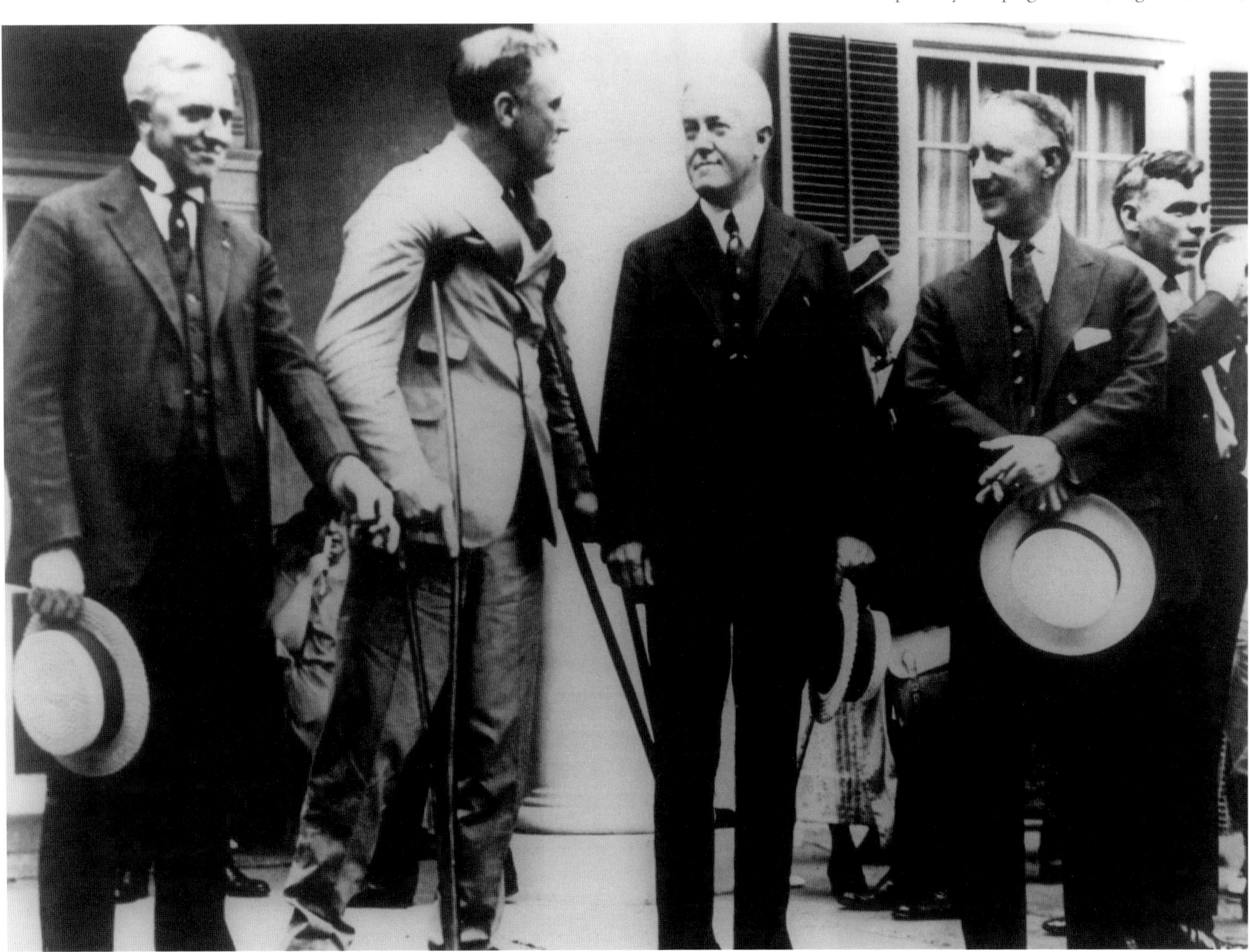

Franklin and the crew of his houseboat *Larooco* with a monstrous fish caught by his son Elliott, March 21, 1926. The jewfish (or goliath grouper) weighed well over 400 pounds and was 7 feet long. It would be one of the last adventures on the houseboat he and John Lawrence had purchased in 1924 (the name "Larooco" derived from Lawrence and Roosevelt). (1926)

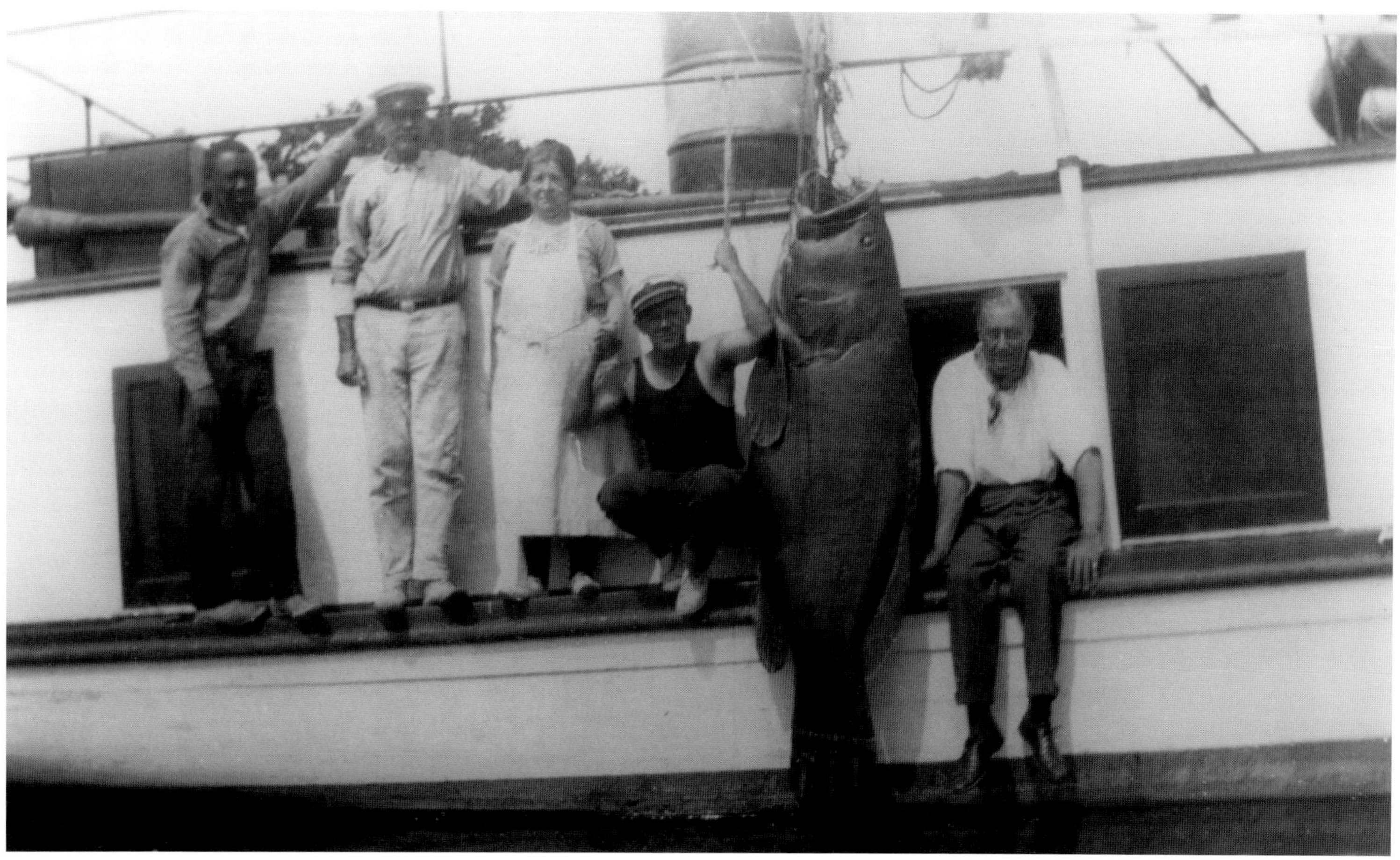

FDR and Cynthia Mosley, with fish caught by Franklin. The Mosleys, Oswald and Lady Cynthia, were friends and visited for a few days on this cruise in the houseboat *Larooco.* FDR found them to be a charming couple. The friendship would not survive the Mosleys' conversion from socialist to fascist. Oswald had been the youngest Member of Parliament at age 22 on election as a Conservative in 1918, jumping to Labor in 1924. Both he and Lady Cynthia would be elected to Parliament. In 1931, they formed the New Party and lost their parliamentary seats. (February 16, 1926)

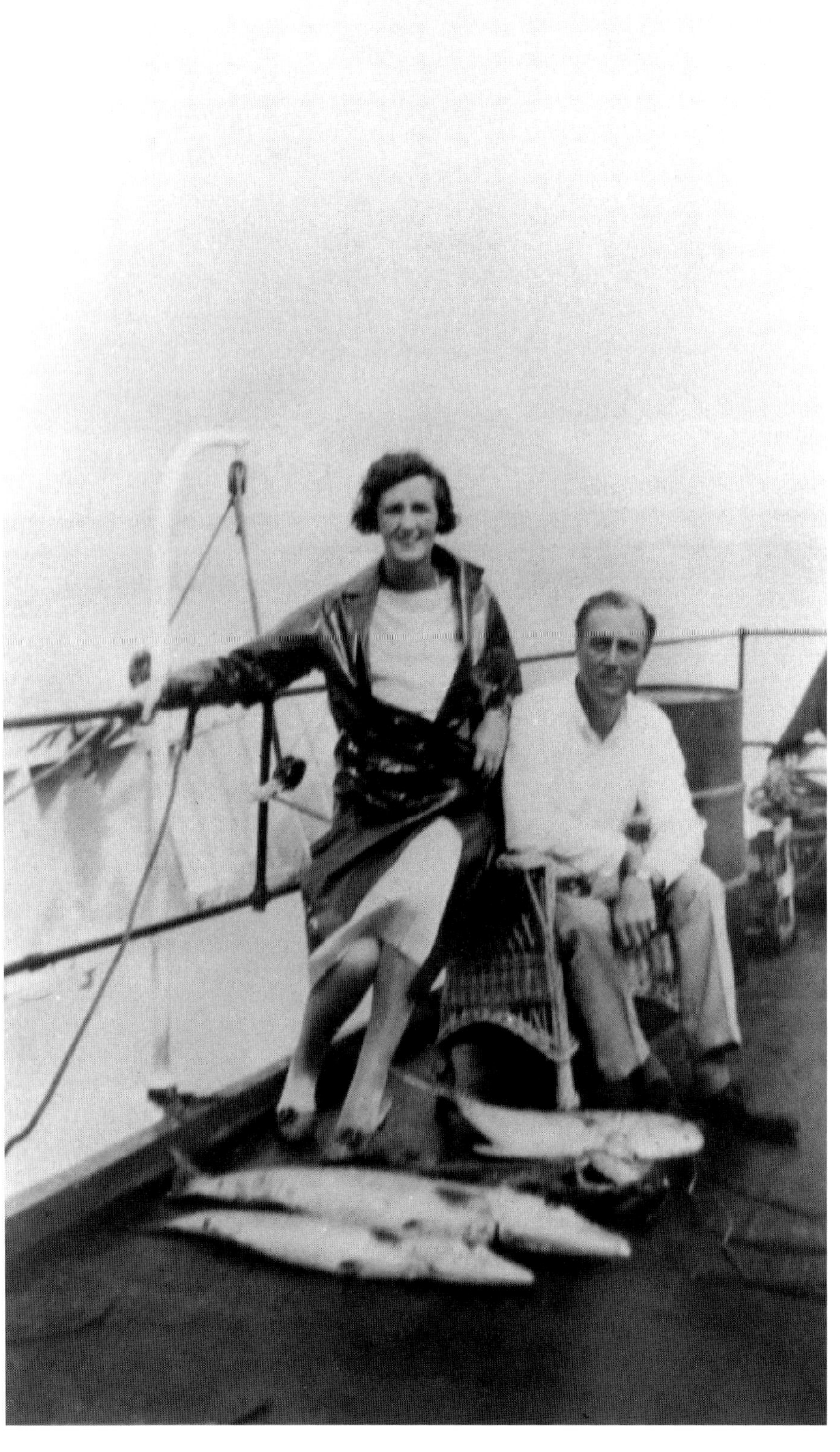

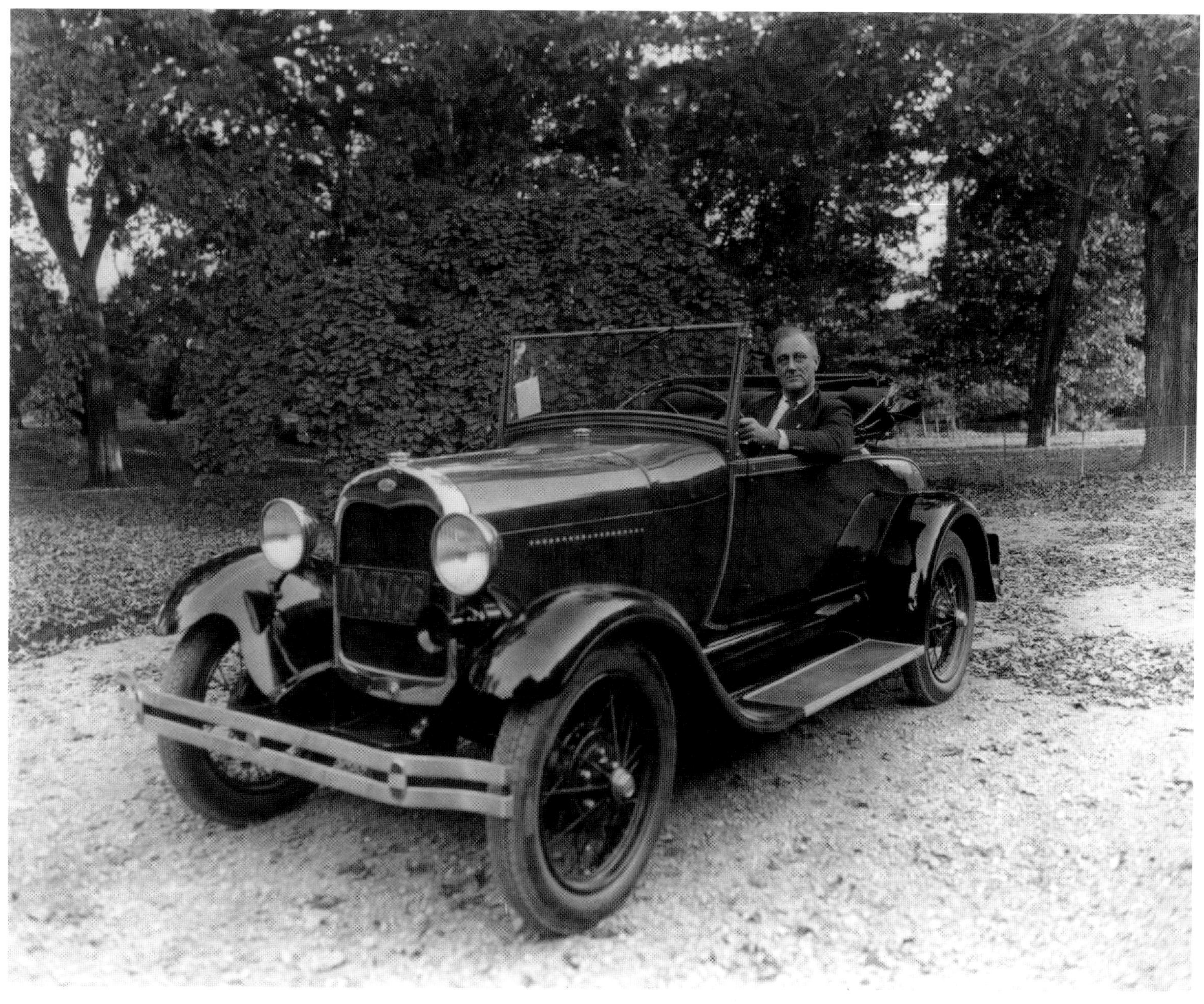

FDR at the wheel of his 1928 Model A Ford. Driving gave Franklin a freedom and mobility he otherwise lacked. His 1936 Ford is preserved to this day at the FDR Museum. (1928)

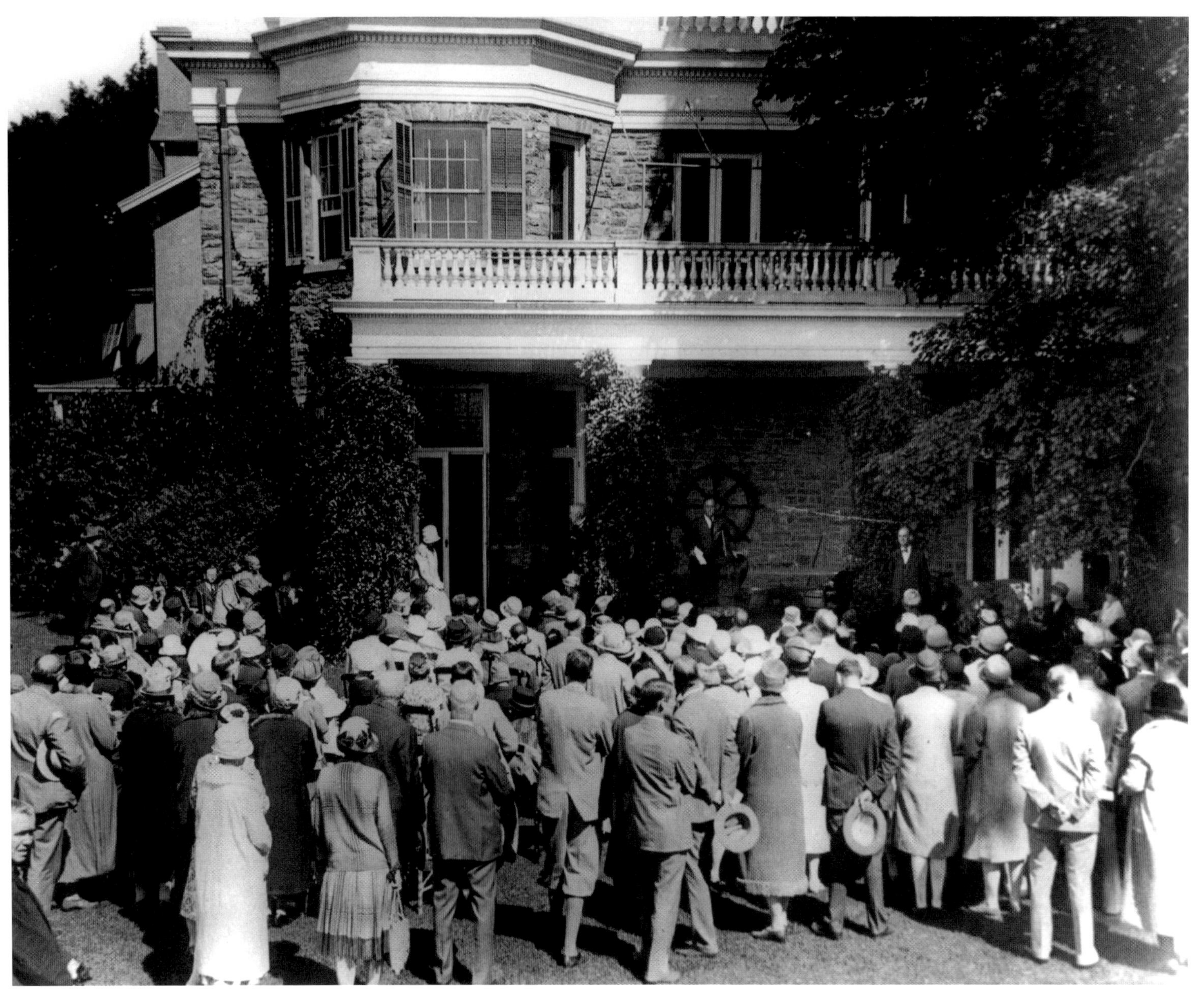

Franklin addressing a crowd at his home. (September 17, 1927)

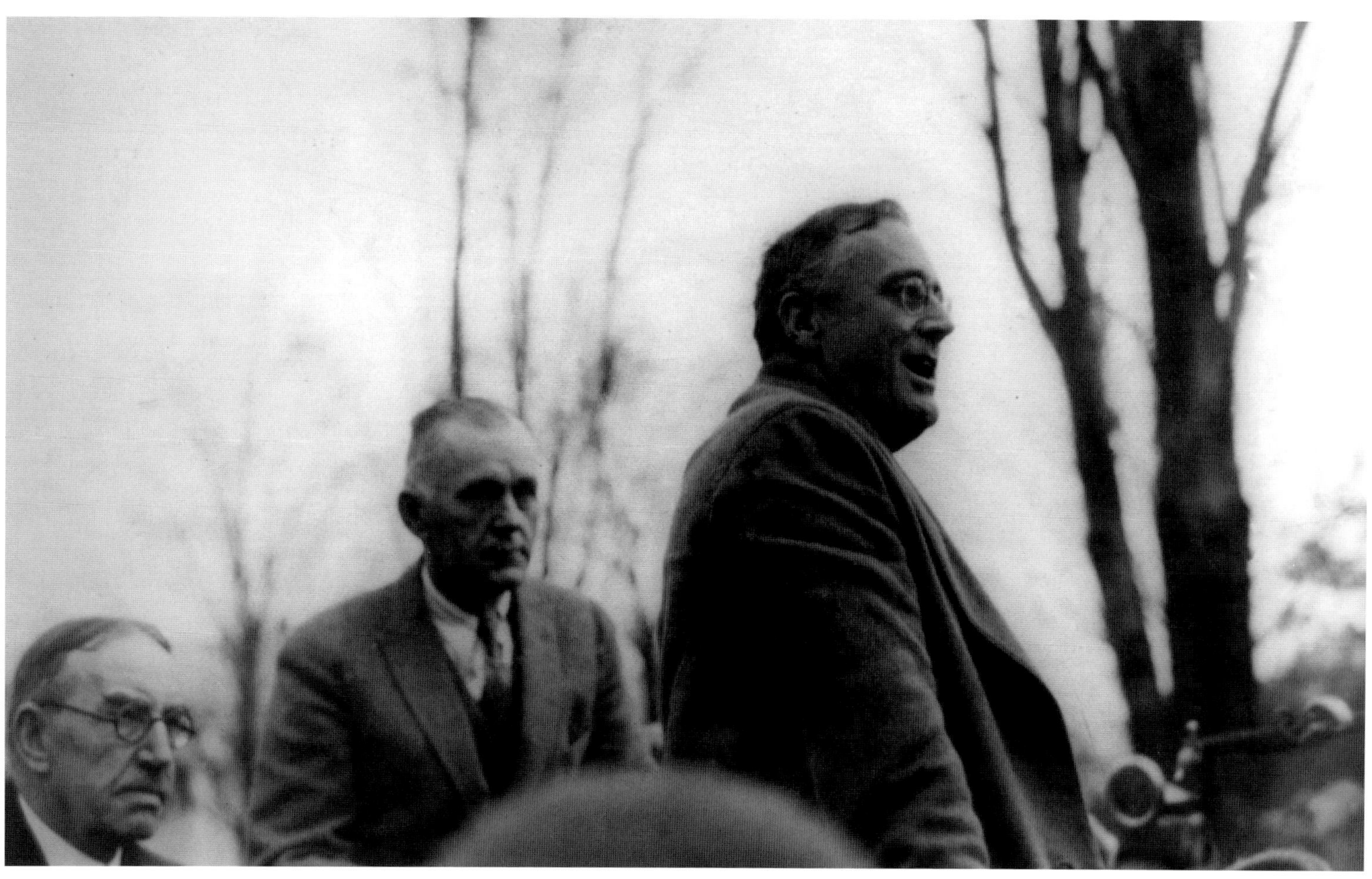

Franklin addressing a crowd in Olean. The New York gubernatorial candidate vigorously attacked the Republican presidential administration. FDR would narrowly win the governorship while Democratic candidate Alfred E. Smith was crushed by Herbert Hoover for the presidency. (October 19, 1928)

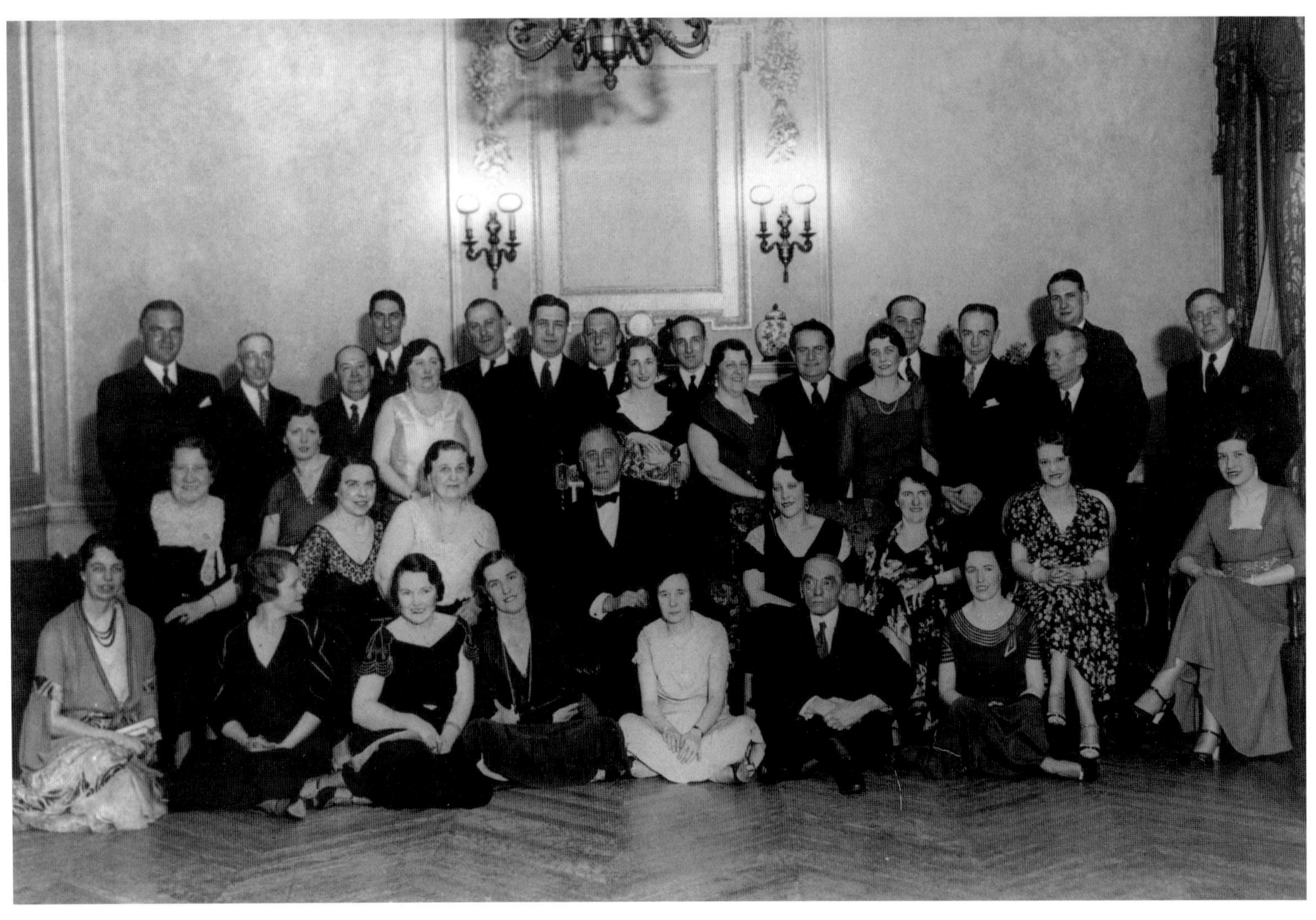

FDR, Eleanor Roosevelt, and Democratic Party workers in Albany, New York. (1928)

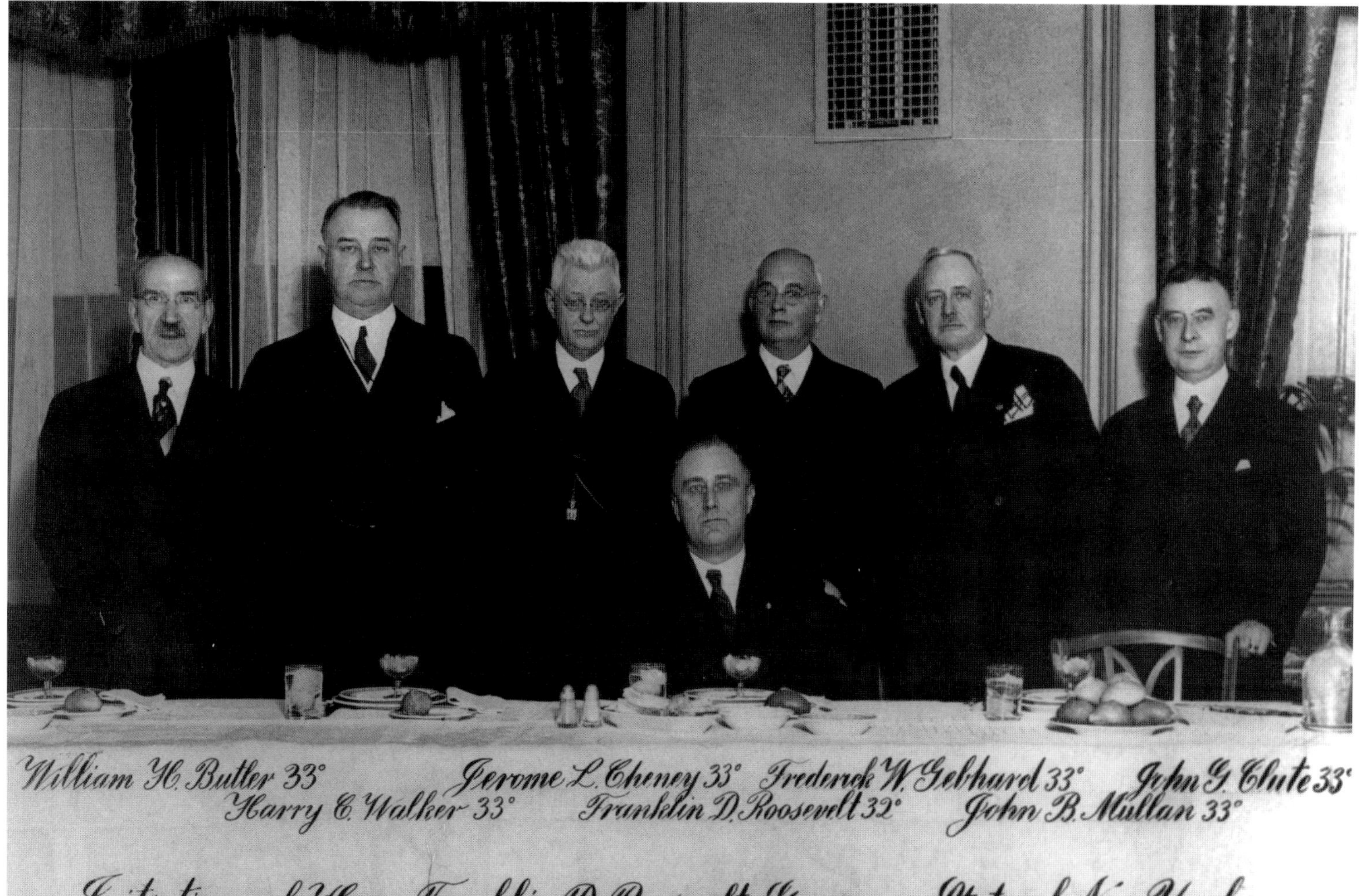

After winning the campaign to become governor of New York, FDR did typical political-social things. Here is his induction into Scottish Rite Freemasonry. (February 28, 1929)

FDR posing at his car in Warm Springs, Georgia. He would resort to this pose repeatedly, because it lent him a casual (and independent) appearance, unlike crutches or the support of a bodyguard or son's arm. (May 1929)

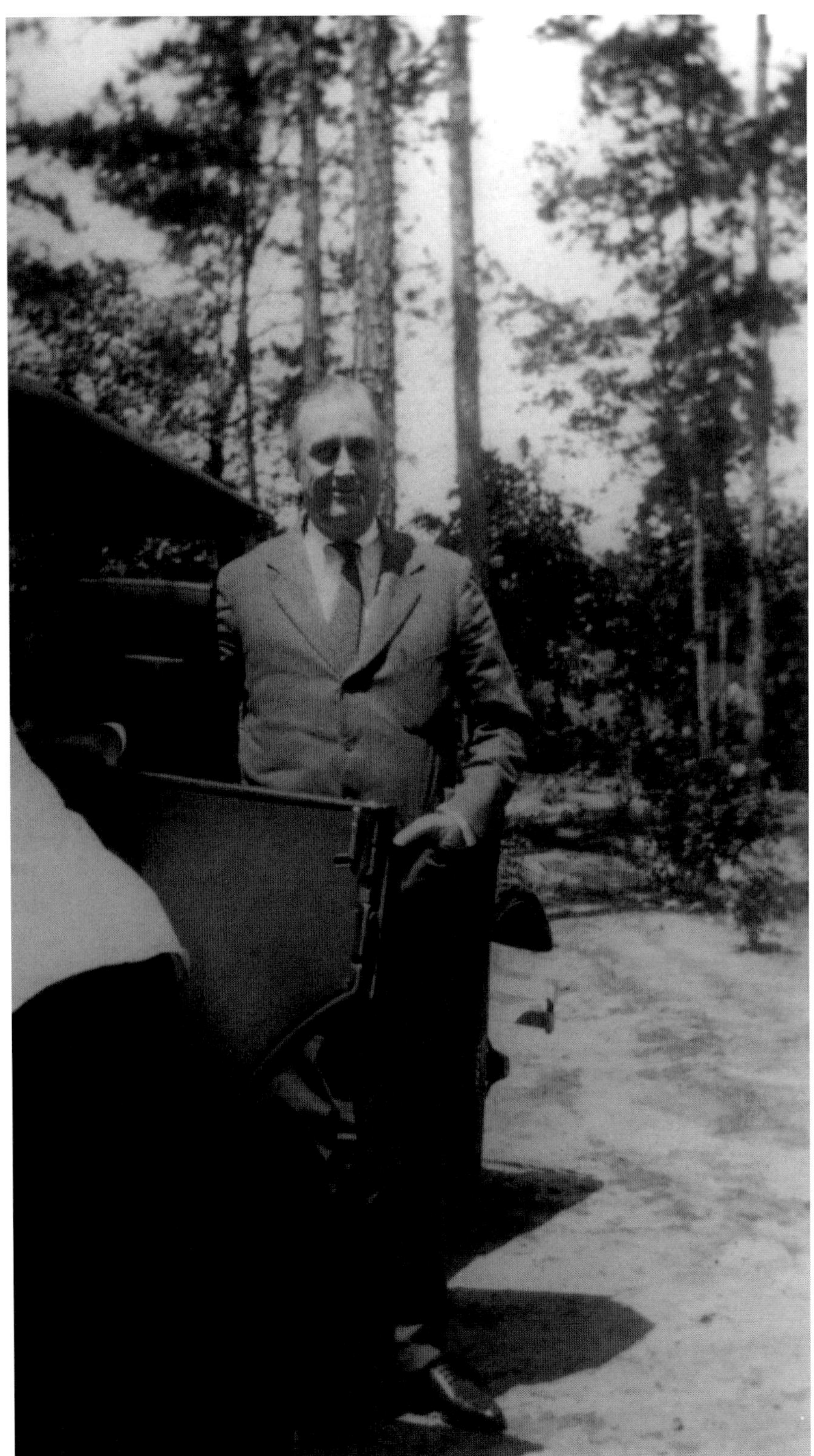

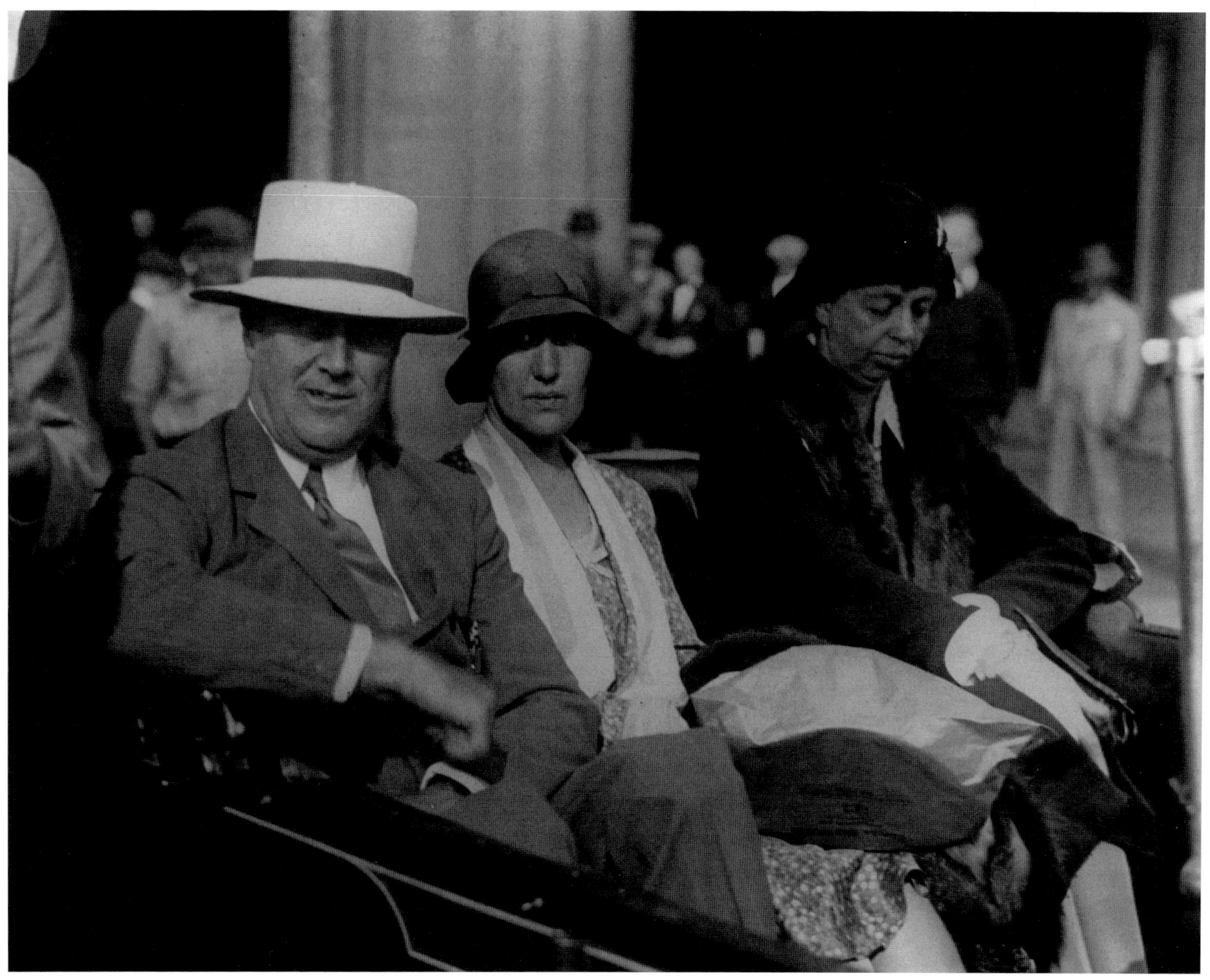

FDR, Missy LeHand, and Eleanor together. Marguerite LeHand ("Missy") was long a part of FDR's life, first hired as his secretary in 1920, following the defeat of the Democratic presidential ticket. Following his paralysis in 1921, Missy kept the Roosevelt household in Warm Springs whenever FDR went there to recuperate—Eleanor disliking it and avoiding the retreat as much as possible. LeHand did the same in Albany, with Eleanor teaching in New York City, and even the White House. She was part of Franklin's staff, managed his finances, and was valued for her opinions. (1929)

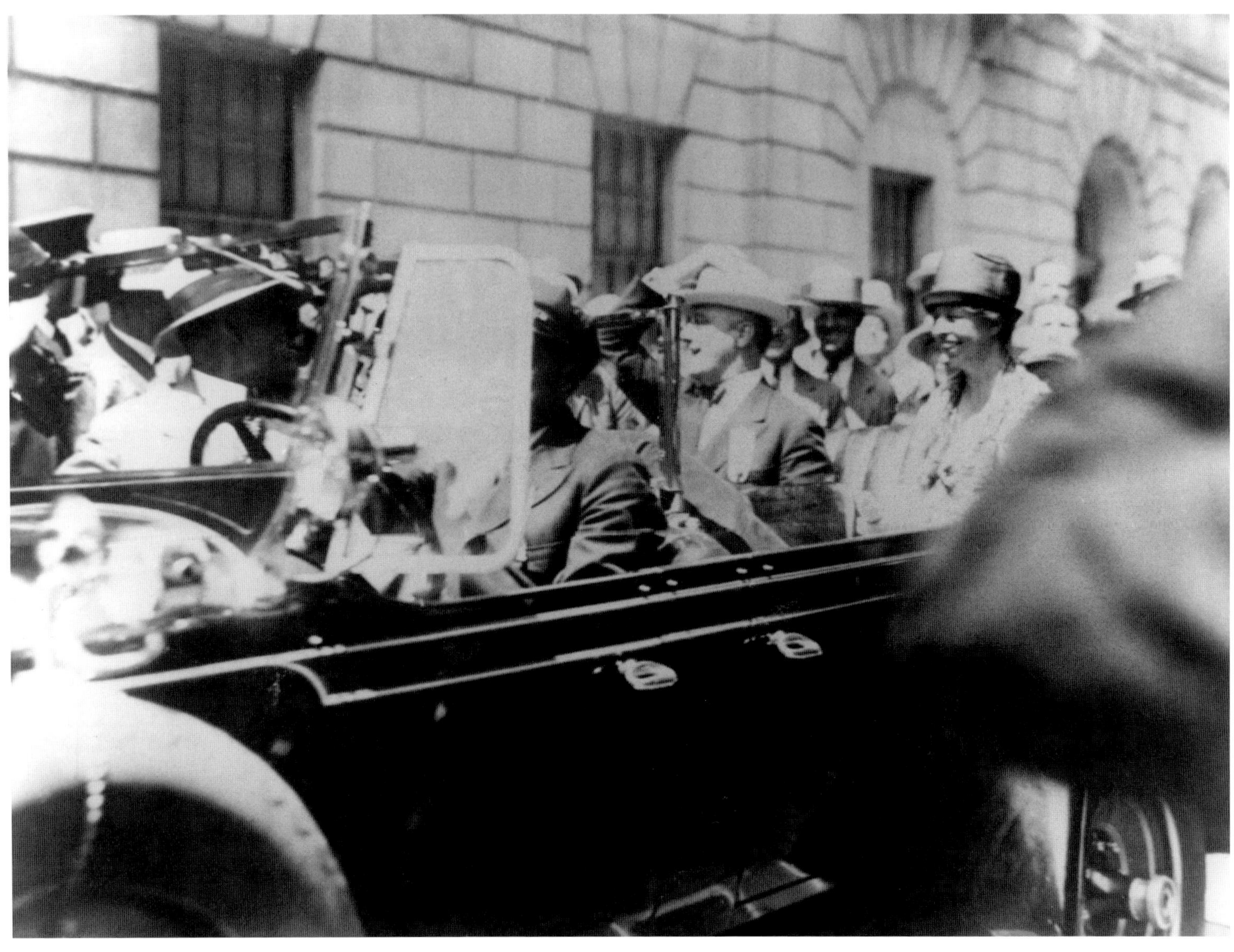

FDR and Eleanor celebrating in Peekskill. (July 4, 1929)

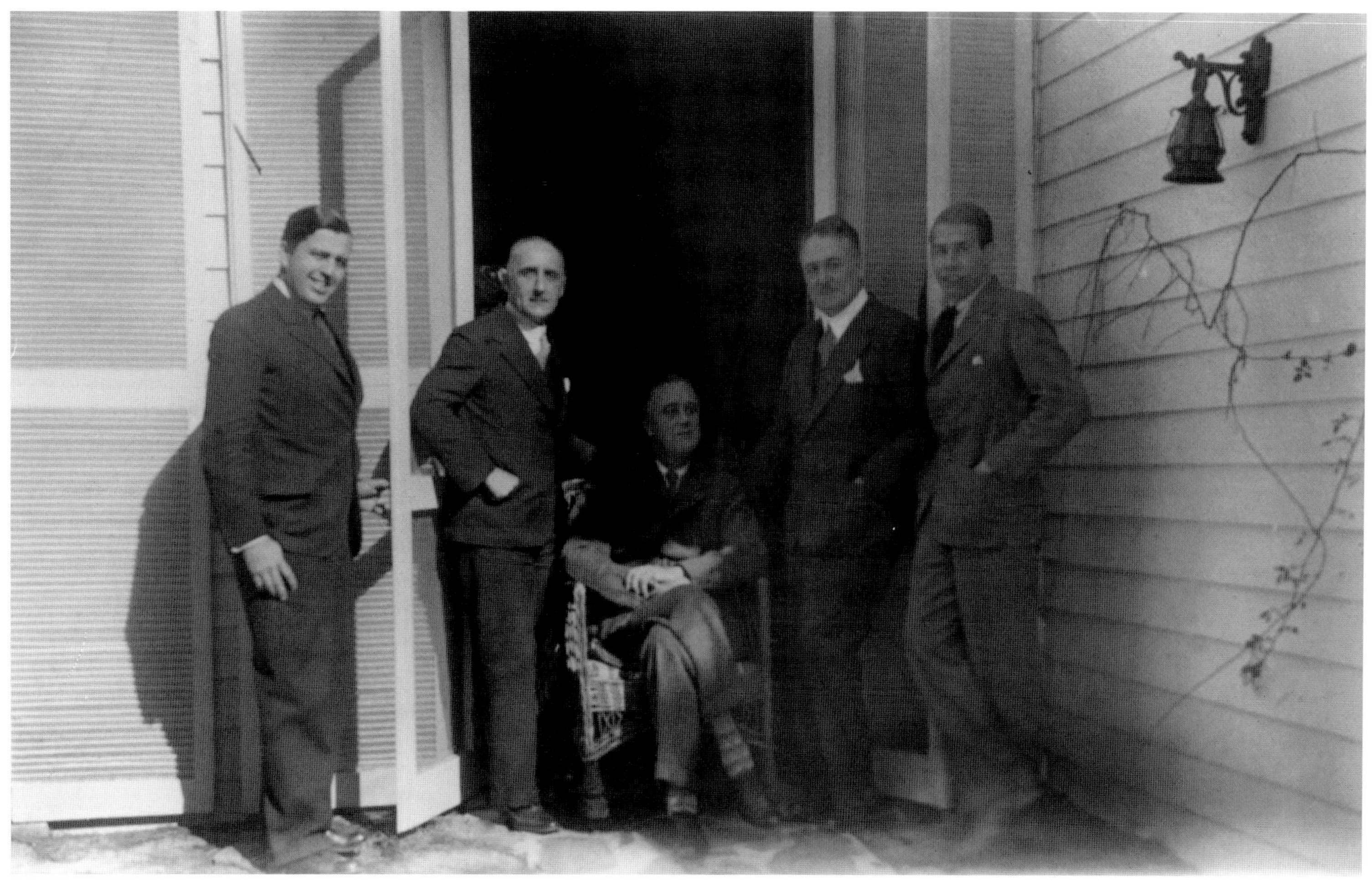

FDR, with medical advisors and consultants at Warm Springs, Georgia. Pictured are William Snyder, Oskar Baudisch, Paul Haertl (managing director of Bad-Kissingen spa), and Schoenborn. FDR spent one-third of his inheritance to purchase the facility and long maintained an involvement with the foundation he established to run it. (December 3, 1929)

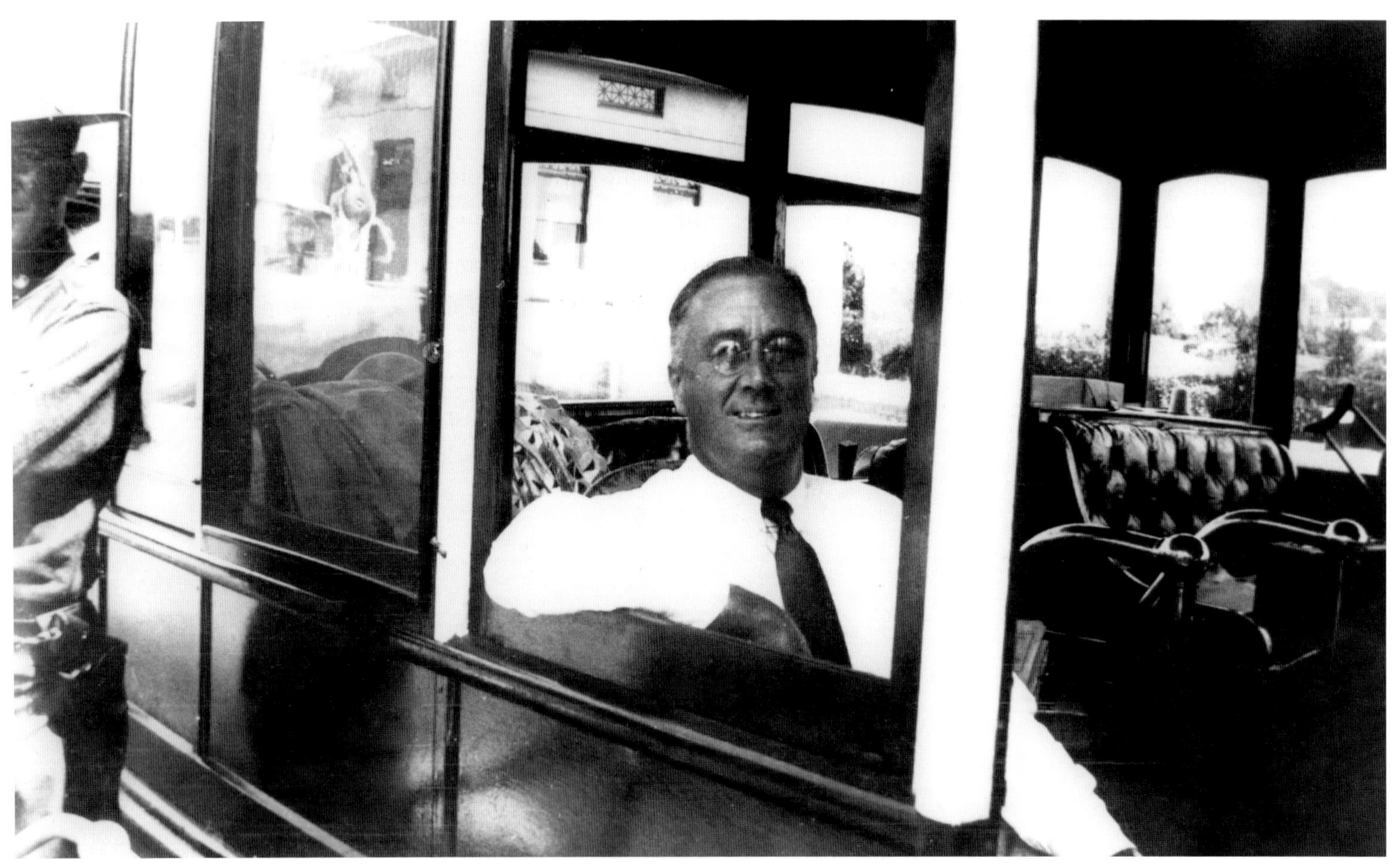

A jaunty FDR preparing to tour the state. In July 1929, FDR and colleagues toured state institutions in the western part of New York State on the state yacht *Inspector.* Here Eleanor played a vital role as his eyes and ears, visiting patients and inspecting the facilities. (July 1929)

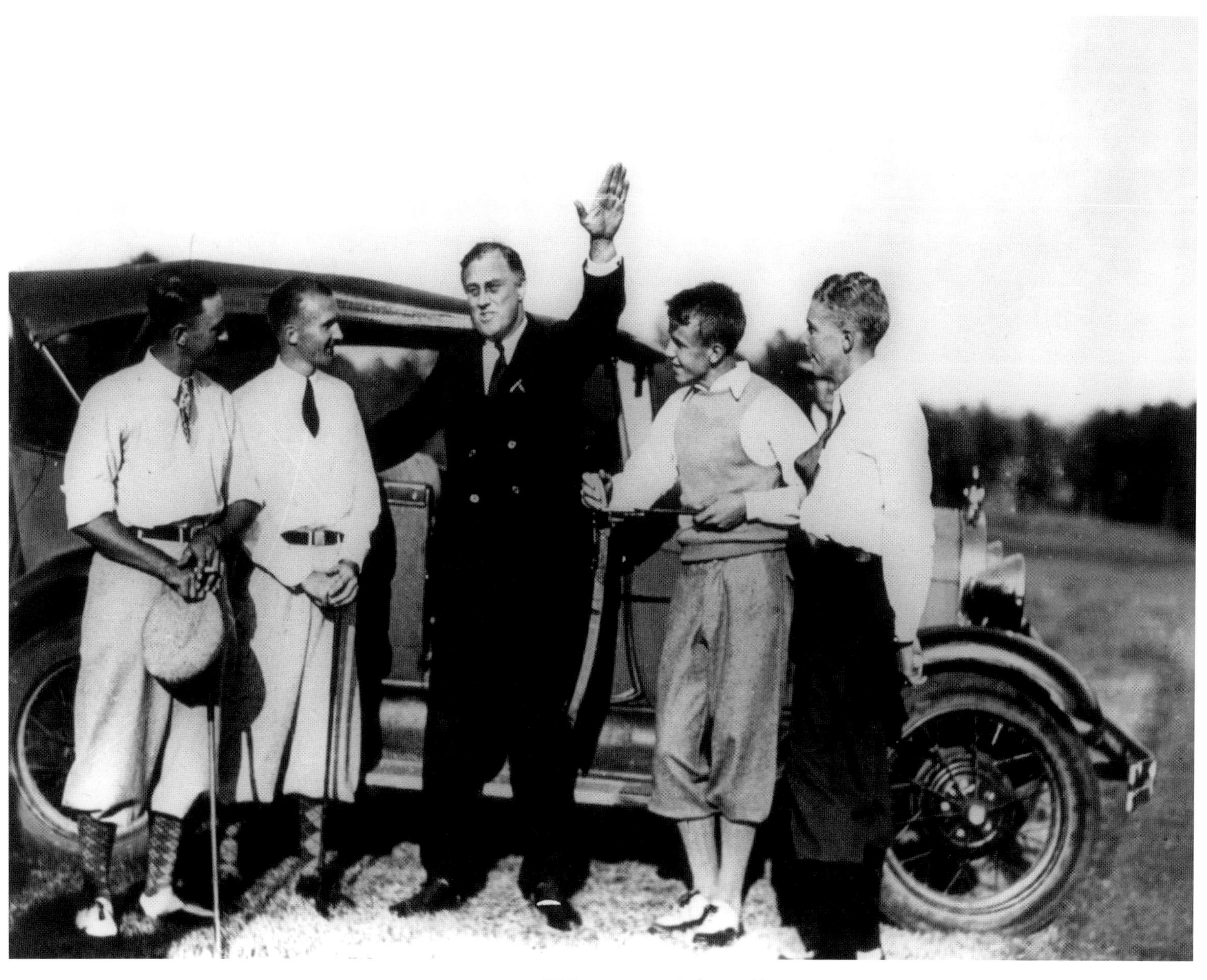

FDR waving, with four golfing compatriots at Warm Springs. For years after being stricken, FDR hoped and planned to return to one of his favorite sports, golf, but was never able to do so. (1930)

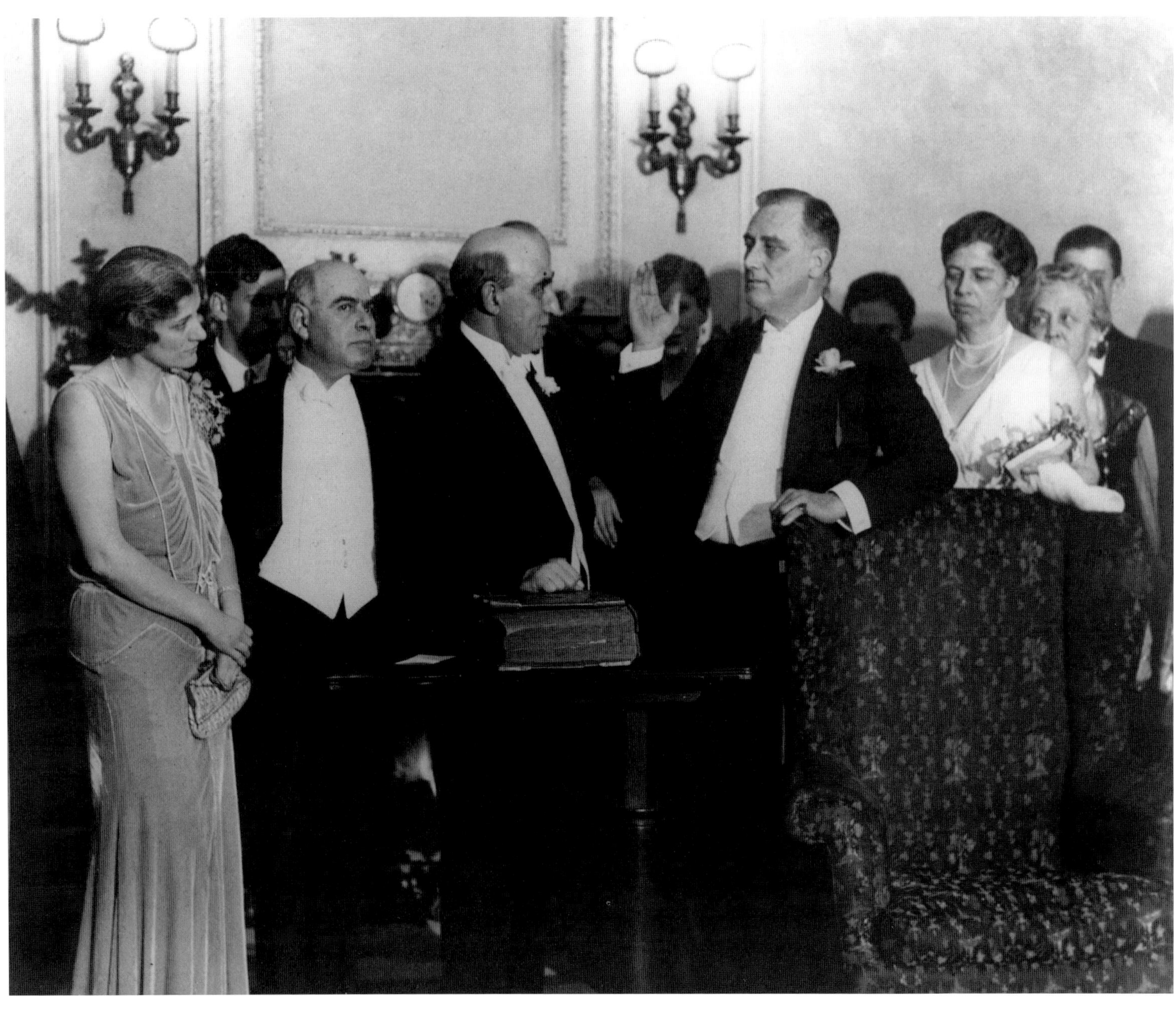

FDR, partly concealed by a rather large chair, taking the oath of office in Albany, to begin his second term as governor of New York. Pictured are Mrs. Lehman, Lieutenant Governor Herbert Lehman, Eleanor Roosevelt, Sara Delano Roosevelt (partly obscured), and Judge Irving Lehman administering the oath. Franklin took the oath on the 270-year-old Roosevelt family Bible. (December 31, 1930)

FDR, Eleanor, James, Anna, and Earl Miller at the gubernatorial inauguration in 1930. The ceremonies were simpler, cutting costs $17,000, which Franklin planned to apply to public works. (December 31, 1930)

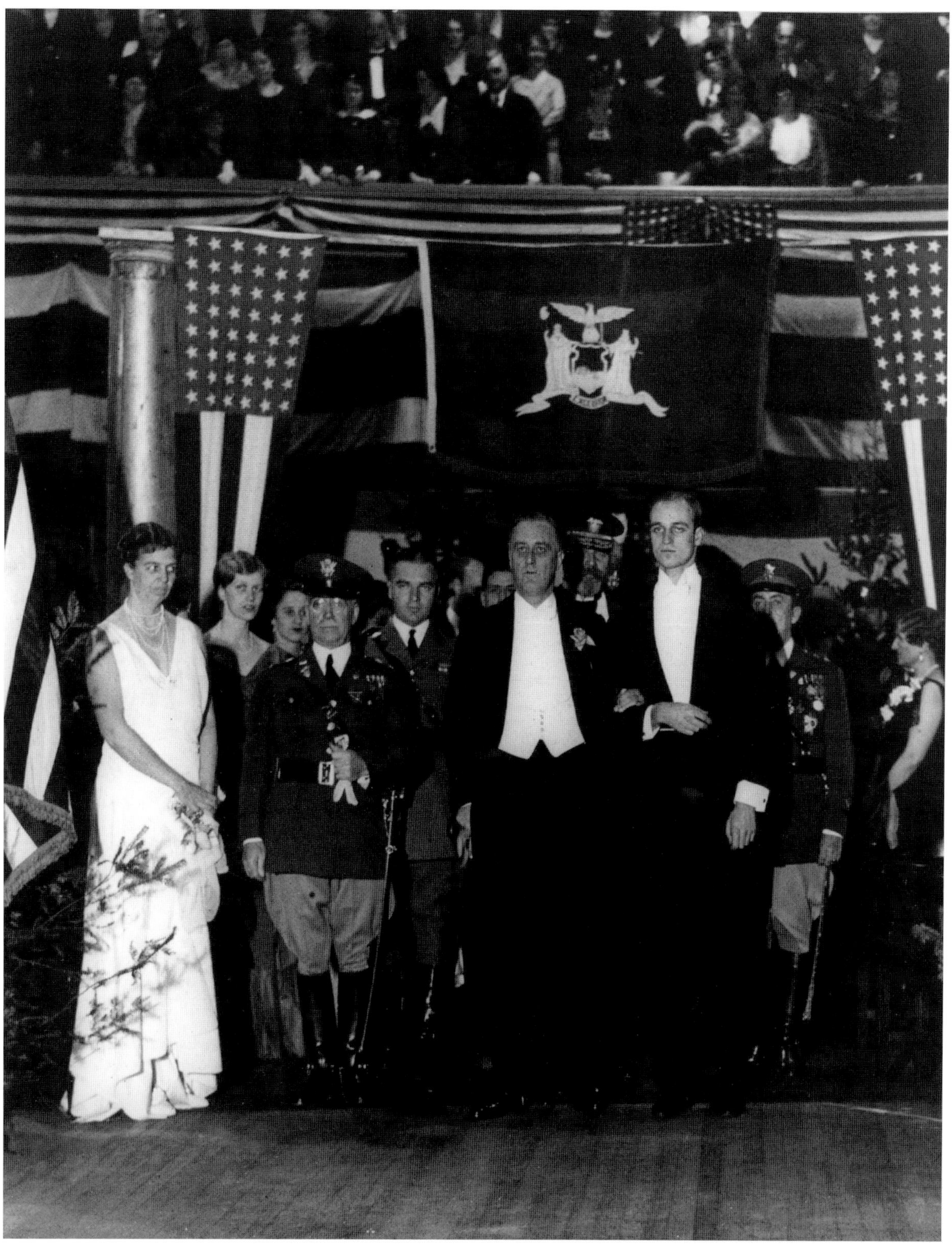

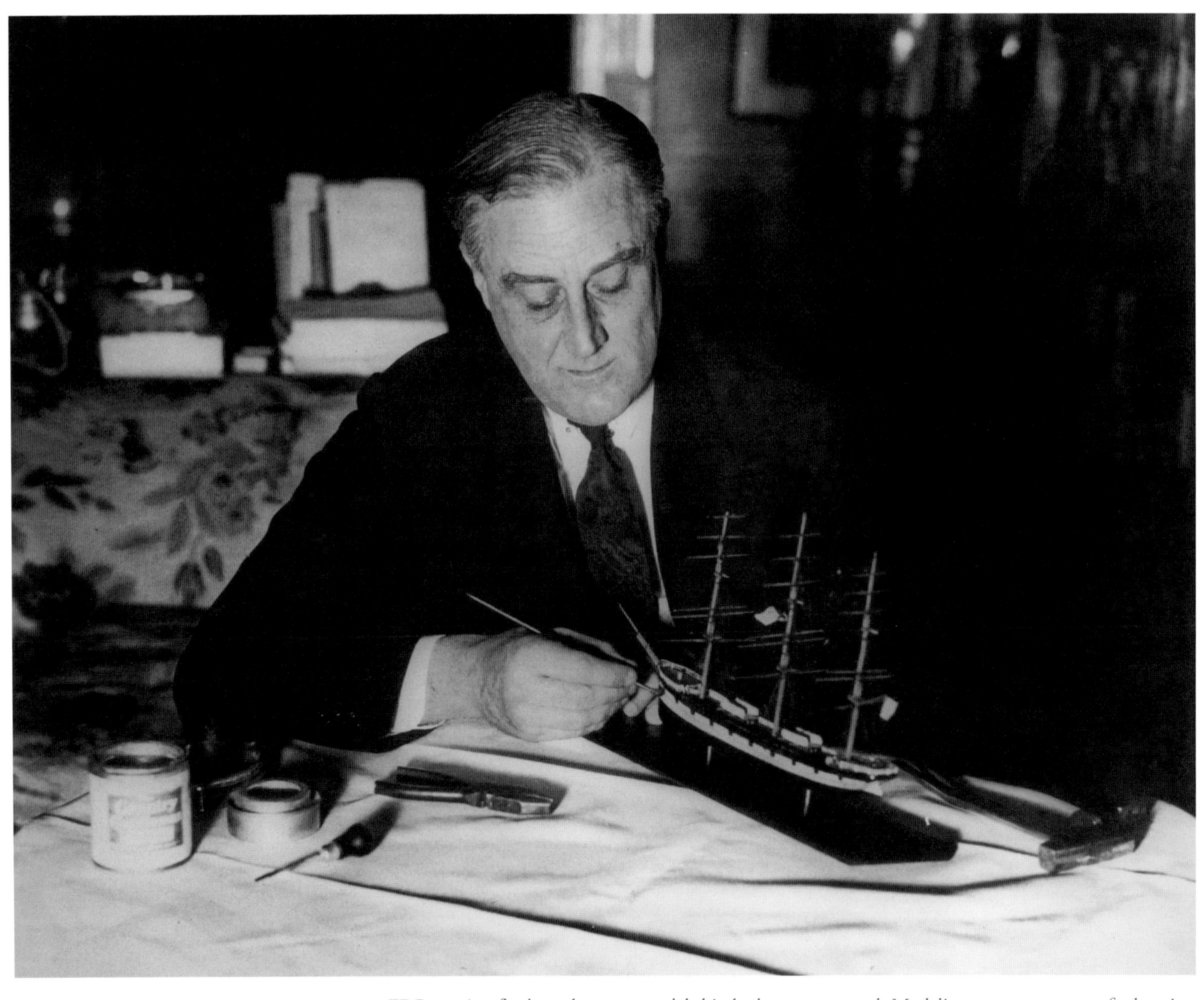

FDR putting final touches on a model ship he has constructed. Modeling was one means of relaxation from gubernatorial duties. (1930)

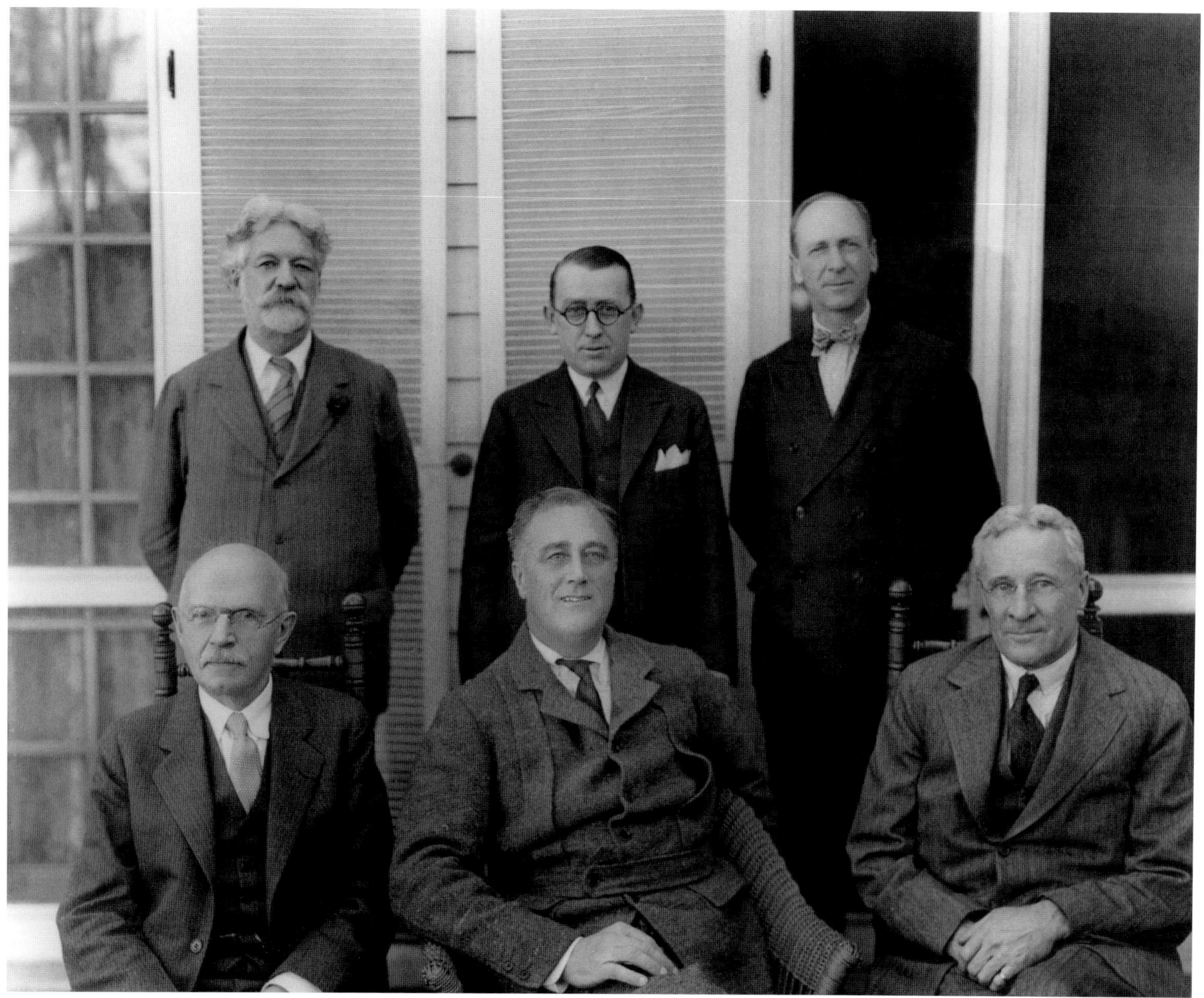

FDR and five colleagues, including George Foster Peabody. After a stunning reelection victory as governor of New York, Franklin went to Warm Springs where he "tried somewhat in vain to get a little holiday," as he wrote with chagrin to Senator Thomas Walsh. (1930)

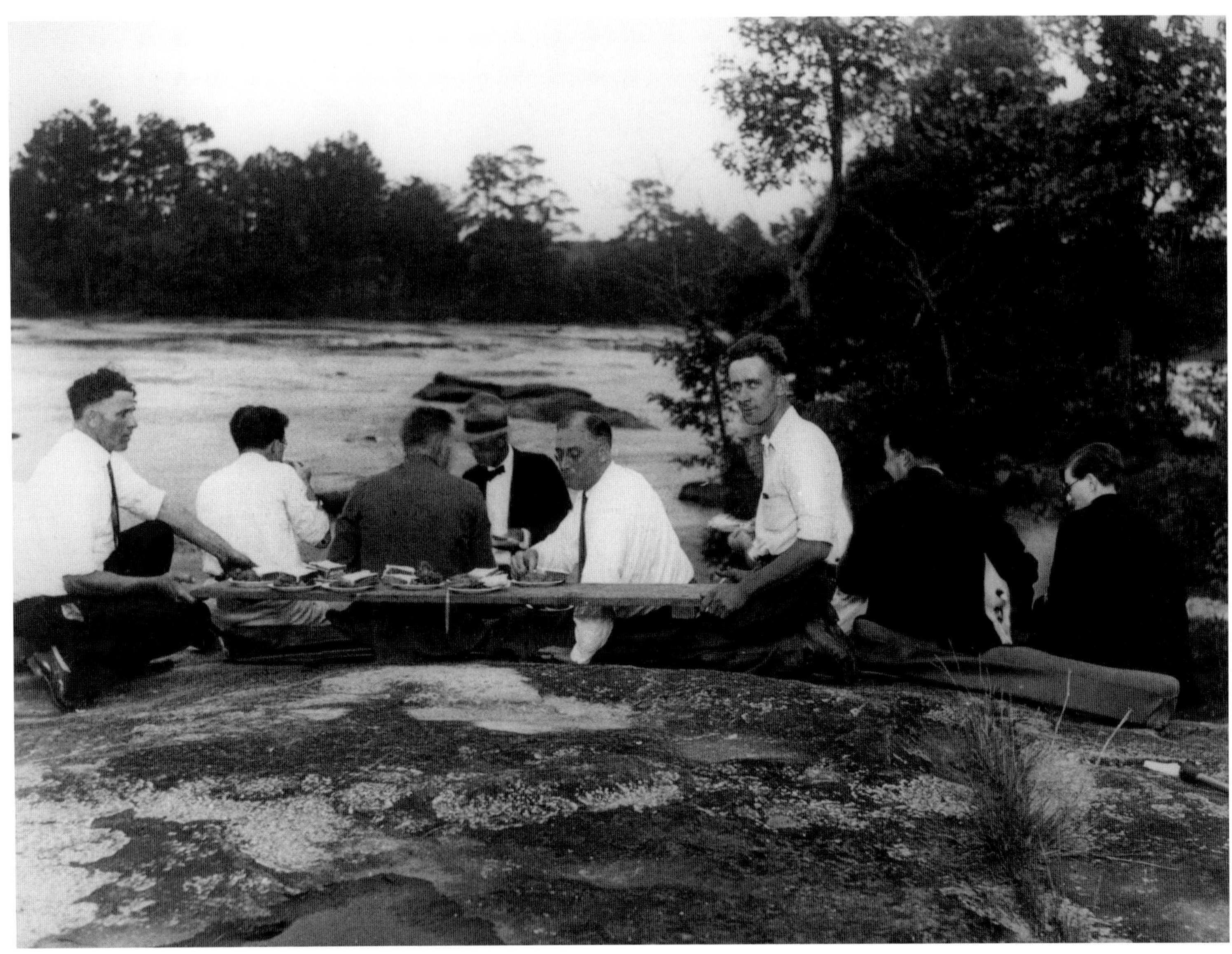

FDR in Warm Springs. He spent much of that May in Warm Springs, returning to New York for his son James' wedding to Betsy Cushing, then returning to Albany. Despite the bucolic setting, FDR spent much of his time here doing business. (May 1930)

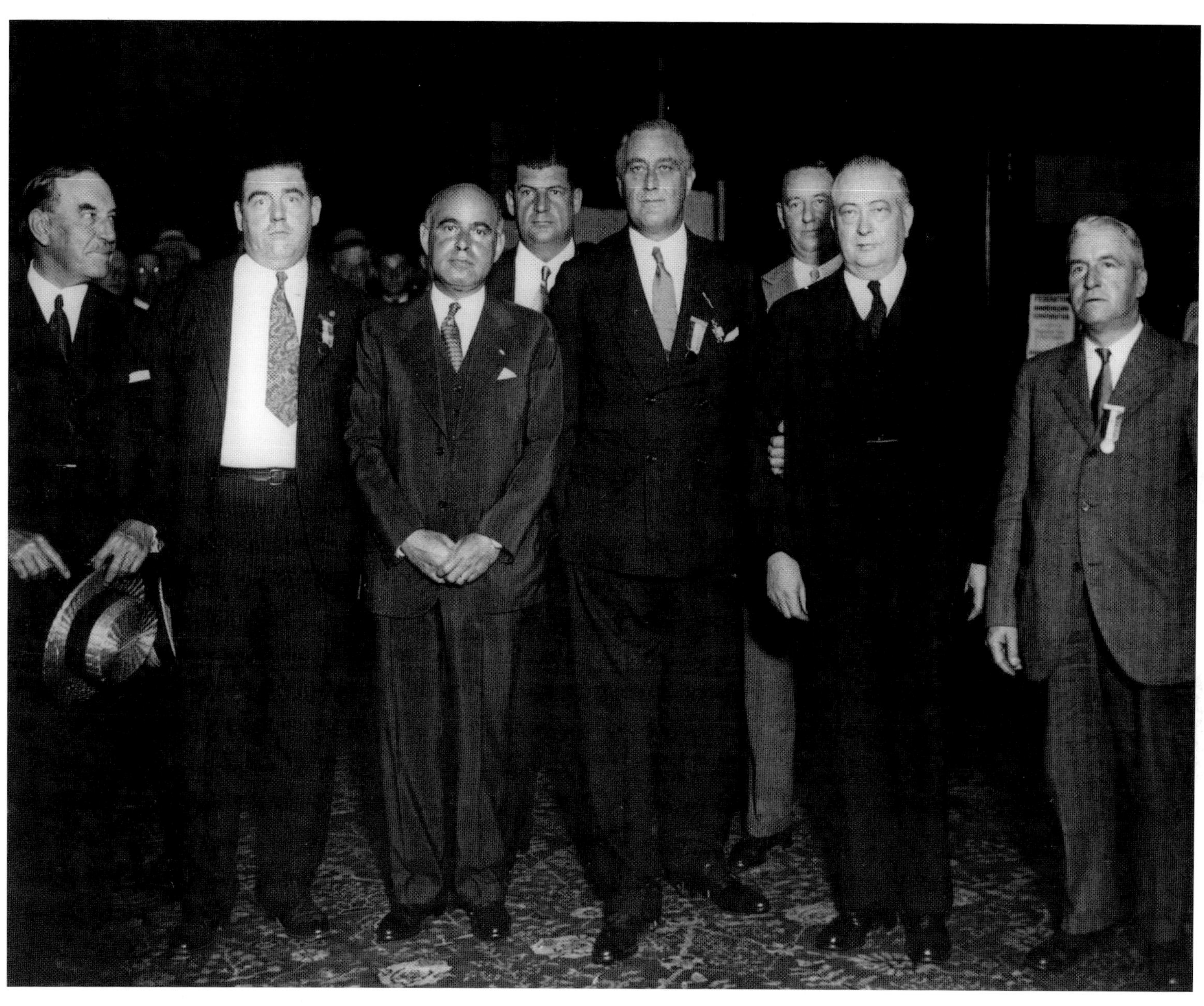

FDR and seven Democratic Party colleagues, including Herbert Lehman. (1930)

FDR and Eleanor with their youngest child, fourteen-year-old son John in Albany. (1930)

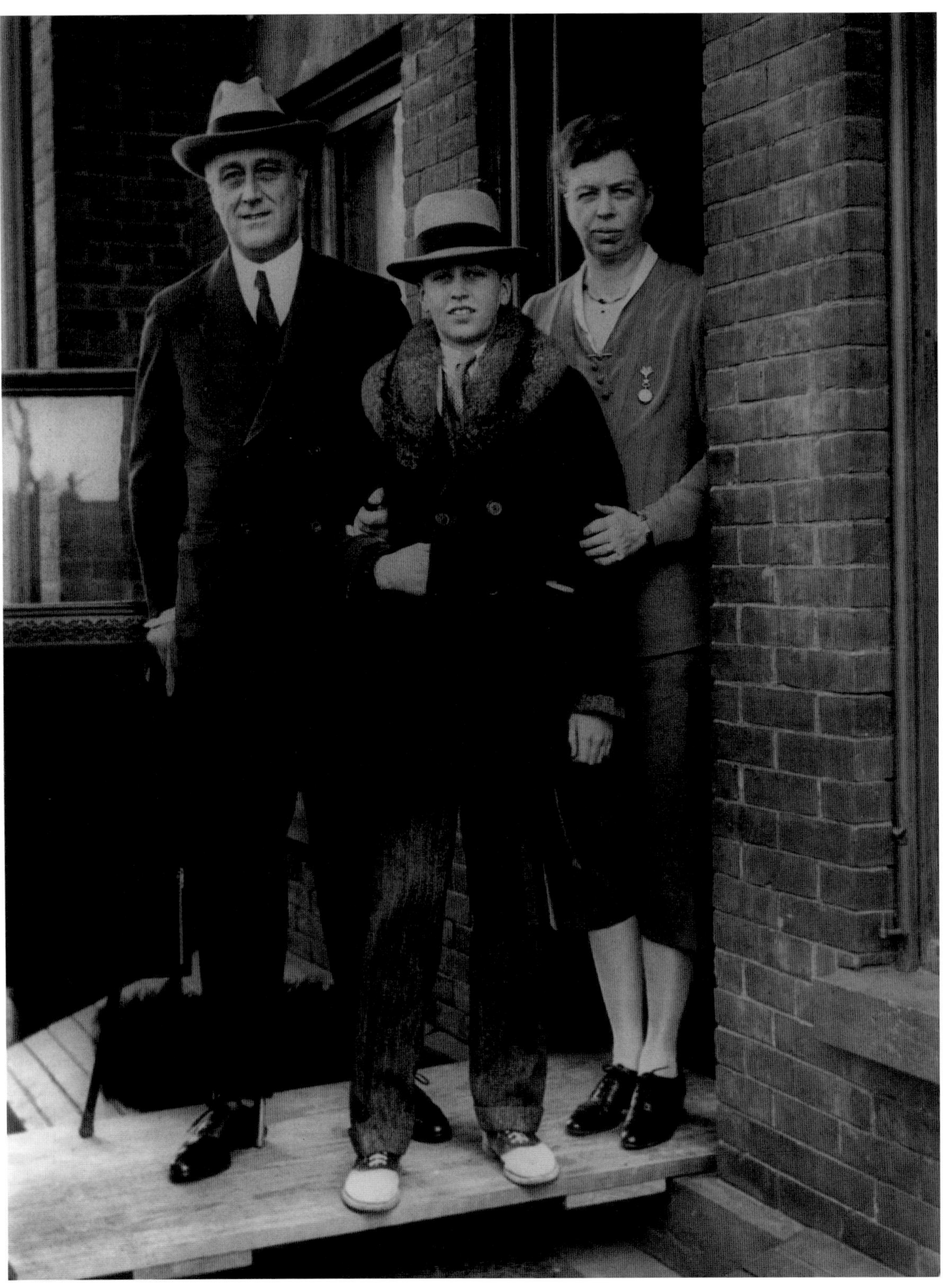

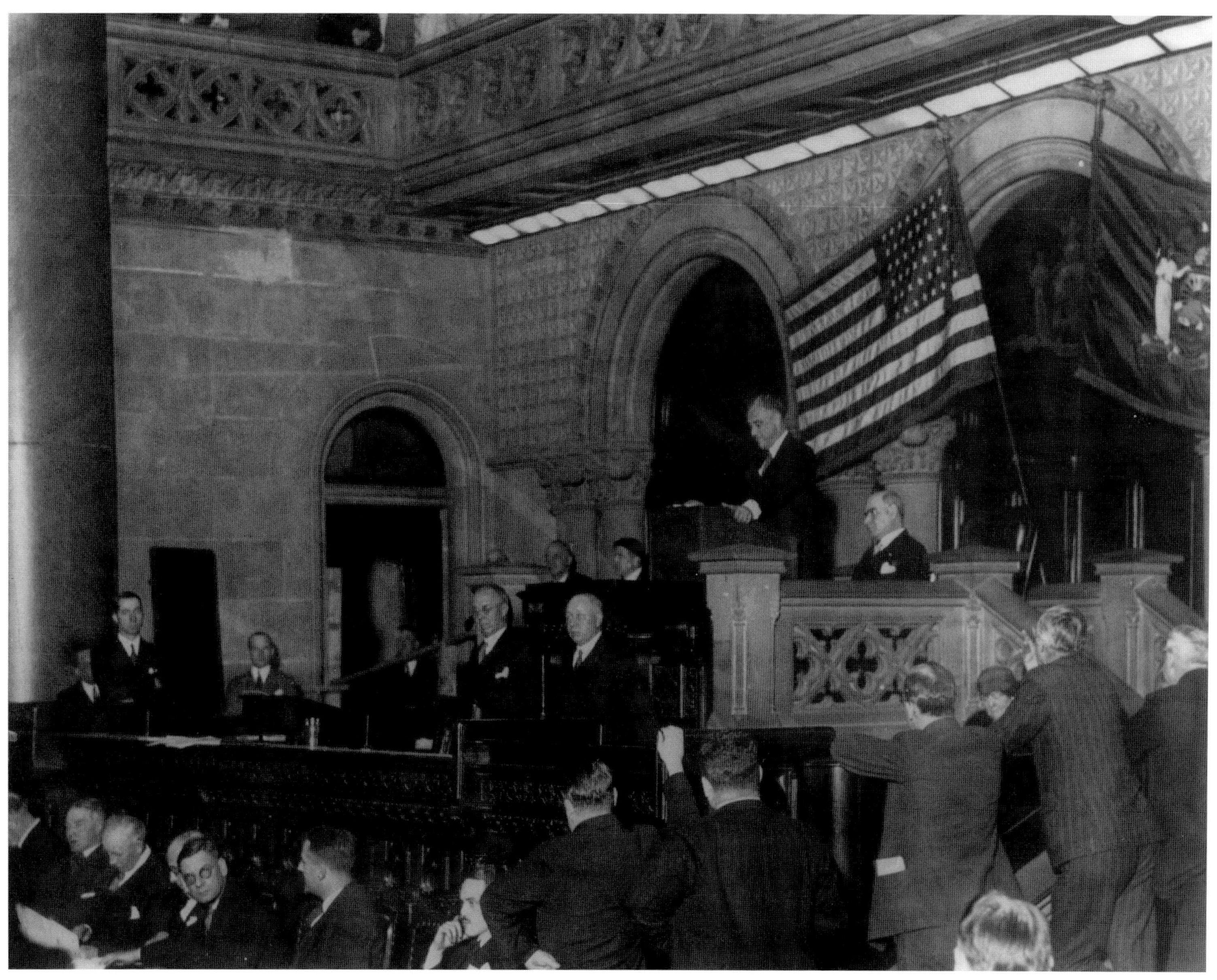

FDR addressing the New York State Assembly. To open a new legislative session, Governor Smith had started the tradition of the governor's annual address. Franklin's message focused on prison reform in response to recent prison riots, but was subject to sharp debate among Republican opponents. (1930)

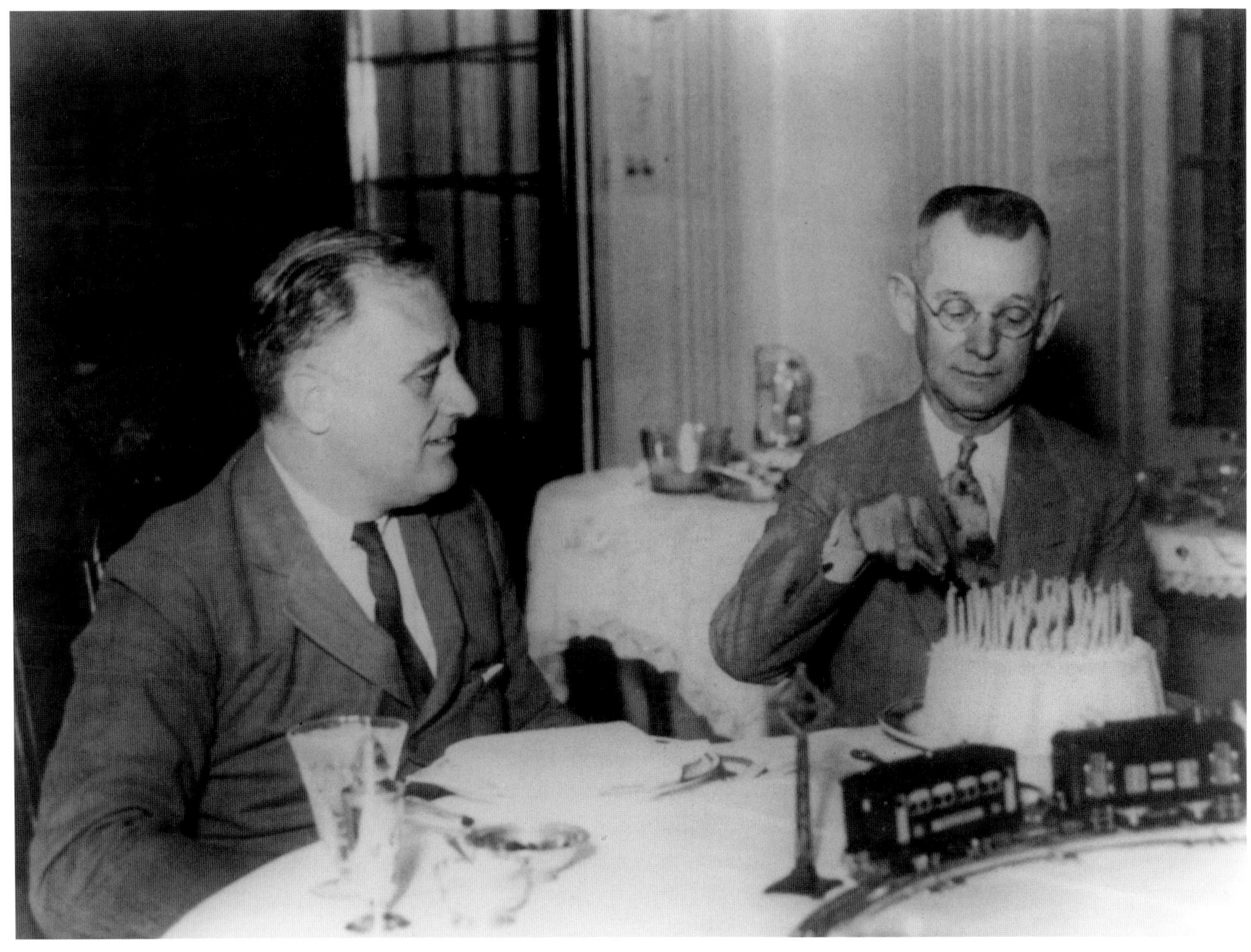

FDR celebrating. He had made a big splash at the National Governor's Association Conference in French Lick, Indiana. His assigned topic was "Land Utilization and State Planning" but included a much broader (and campaign-like) appeal: "The ultimate answer is that government, both State and National, must accept the responsibility of doing what it can do . . . [such] as a scientific tariff aimed primarily to create a movement of world commodities . . . a better thought-out taxation system . . . a plan to cut the excessive cost of local government . . . [and] the extension of the principle of insurance." Soon newspapers around the nation would be supporting his presidential bid. (June 8, 1931)

President

(1933–1945)

As the national economy crashed and the Republican administration seemed bereft of ideas on how to prompt a quick recovery, eyes turned for an alternative, as they often had, to the governor of New York. New York's governorship was a traditional stepping stone to the presidency, and its current occupant had won in 1928 despite the Republican tide which swamped the Democratic presidential ticket, and had won a record-breaking reelection victory two years later. FDR had been on a presidential trajectory since the Wilson administration, touched by the fire of his uncle's political brilliance and spurred by his political advisors including Louis Howe.

FDR puzzled contemporaries and has puzzled historians. He was a fierce partisan, but he was no ideologue. He was a man who saw goals that needed accomplishing and he was far less concerned about some of the niceties of getting there. He had some fixed ideas, such as reforming the electric power distribution system, but mostly he was compelled by situation, and the situation in 1932 was dire. He was an accomplished politician, with the skill to concentrate on whomever he was talking with at the time. His agreeable manner misled people to believe that he shared their ideals or beliefs, and they would inevitably be disappointed when that proved not to be the case.

When he assumed the presidency he faced tremendous challenges. The American economic system was experiencing a crisis. He had successfully eluded President Hoover's post-election, pre-inaugural attempts to either co-opt or preempt him, but he was not above making use of mechanisms Hoover had already begun to deploy to stabilize the economy. Hoover had a political tin ear—rather than call the economic crisis a "panic" as had been traditional, Hoover had chosen "depression"—hardly a reassuring word. FDR's first action, in contrast, revealed his rhetorical skill—he declared a bank "holiday."

FDR brought a cheerful confidence with him to the presidency, along with a reassuring determination and an almost ironic energy—he was constantly traveling to Hyde Park or Warm Springs, or taking an ocean fishing vacation, or making a political trip. Perhaps this partly derived from his disability and need to overcome it. The public knew FDR had had polio, but though it was hinted at by publications like *Time,* they were never shown the extent of his disability. His determination and confidence, political skill and gravitas brought him to the presidency and helped sustain him through its most difficult passages.

The first one hundred days of his first term were the most successful. His "New Deal" set a trajectory for his terms in office and for American polity to this day. Congress approved a wide variety of economic reconstruction spending measures and agencies that FDR's team devised. Perhaps his was a patrician response to a capitalist crisis—FDR has been excoriated by the left as the savior of American capitalism and by the right as its destroyer—or perhaps it was simply his way to get something done. Whatever the case, resistance grew as time passed. Parts of the New Deal were repealed, and as the economic crisis ebbed the political urgency to "do something" subsided. Yet FDR was reelected an unprecedented three times (each by successively narrower margins). Ultimately, economic recovery remained elusive and the coming of war trumped his New Deal programs. The economy had to move to a war footing, as America threw its vast resources into the titanic struggle to defeat the Axis powers.

These two struggles, one for economic recovery from the Great Depression, one for military victory in World War II, dominate FDR's presidency. The war would transform the national economy out of all earlier conceptions, as it would the politics of the world. The circumstances surrounding these struggles and what Franklin Delano Roosevelt did to overcome them make FDR one of the most significant of American presidents.

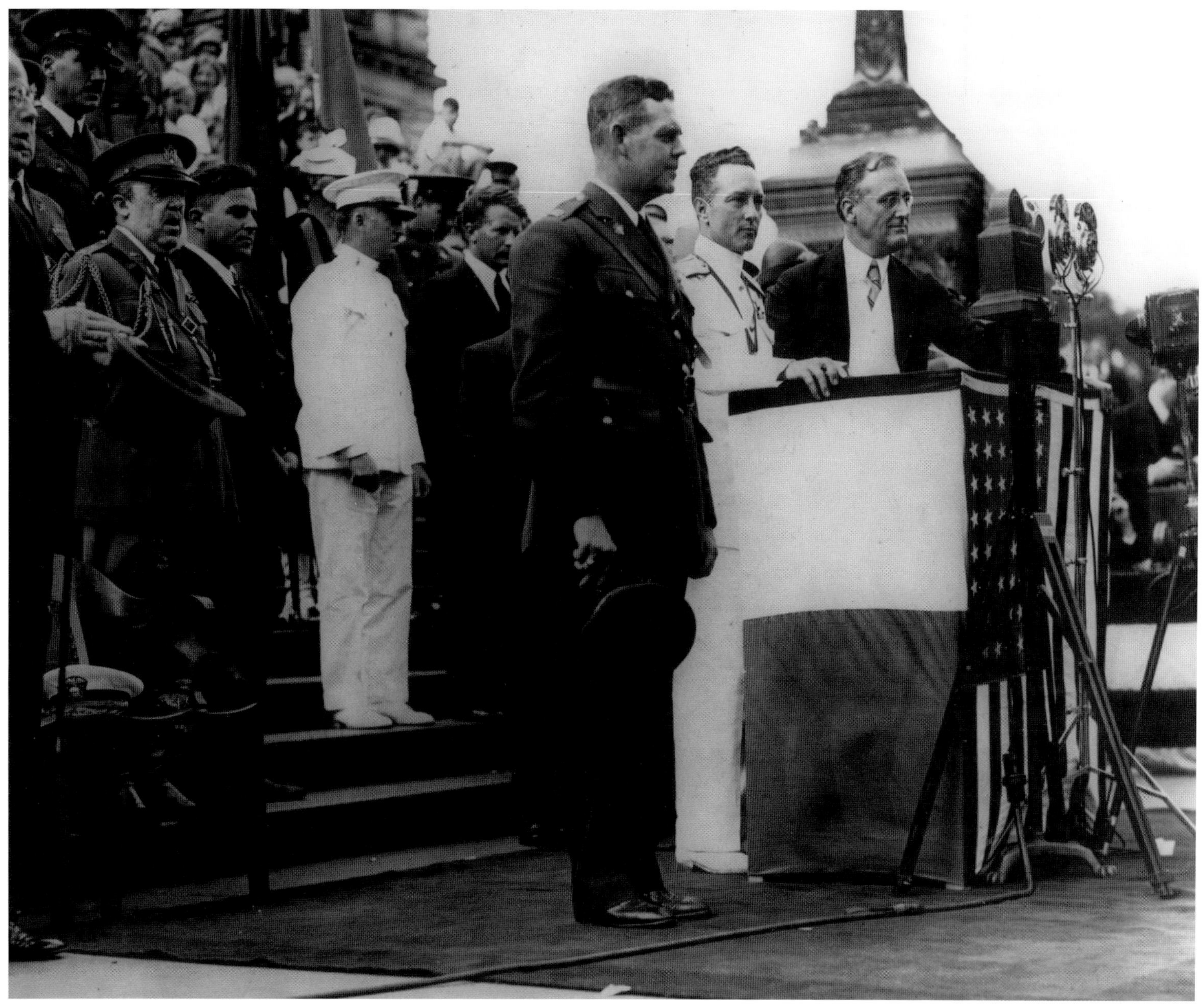

FDR at the ceremony honoring Admiral Richard Byrd. Crowds of thousands choked Albany streets as Byrd wended his way from the waterfront where the destroyer landed him to the state capitol where FDR awaited. The two men had known each other from FDR's days as Assistant Secretary of the Navy. (June 24, 1930)

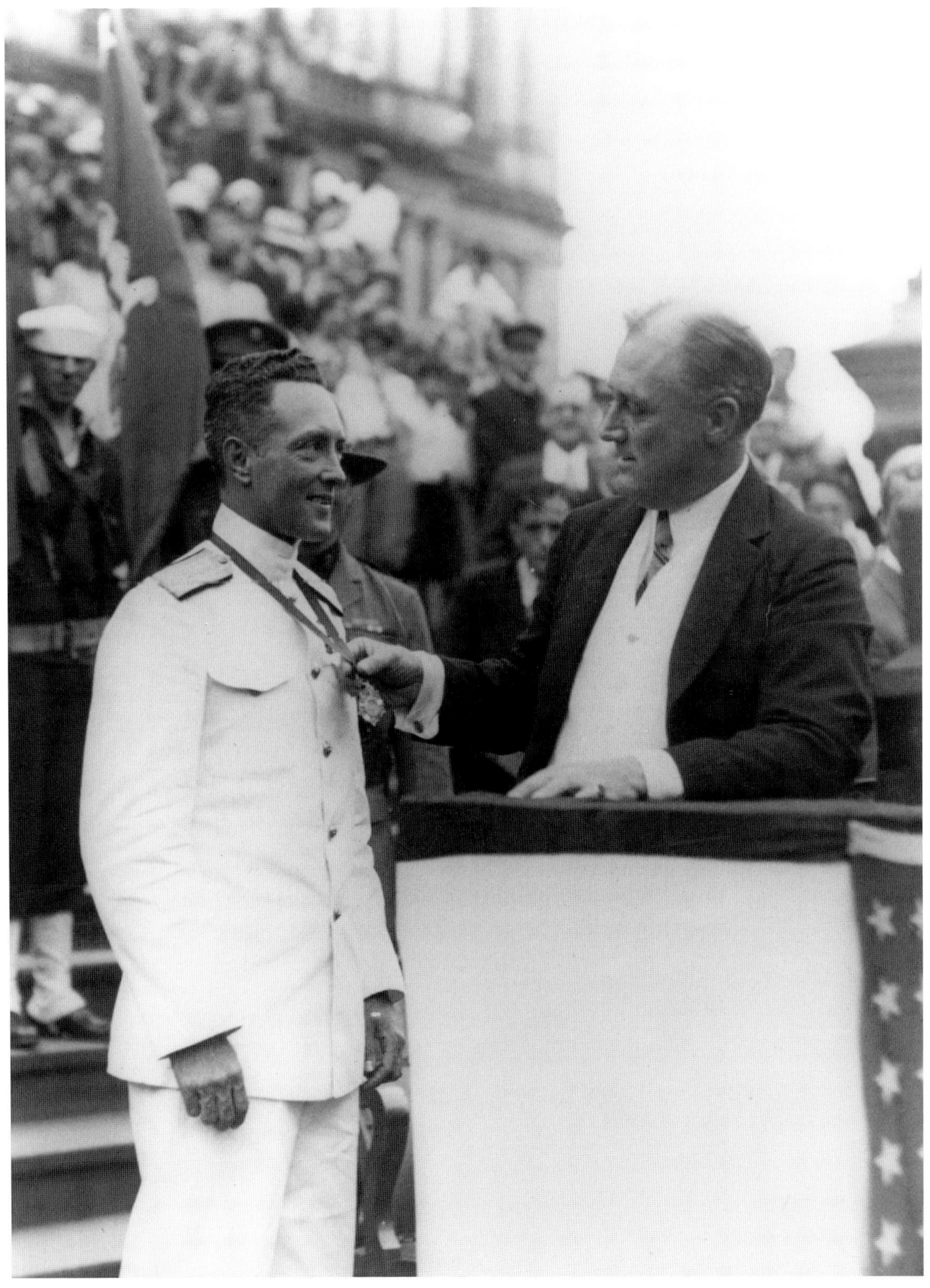

FDR at the ceremony with Admiral Byrd. He is inspecting the Distinguished Service Medal of the State of New York awarded the explorer. Byrd had just returned from one of his historic explorations of Antarctica. (June 24, 1930)

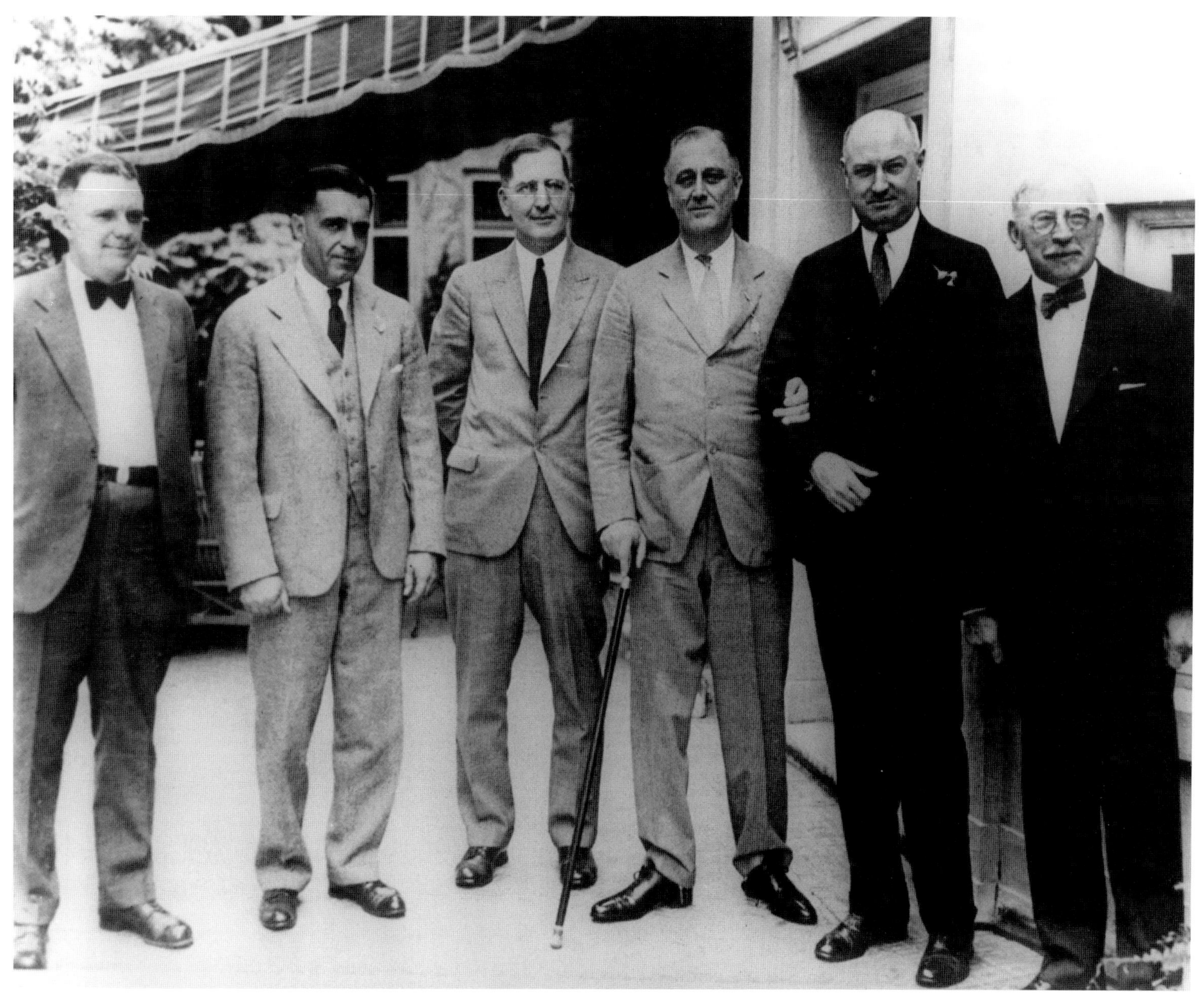

FDR, James Farley, H. Morgenthau, Jr., and colleagues in Albany. Morgenthau was appointed in December 1930 as State Conservation Commissioner, an important patronage post. (1930)

FDR laying the cornerstone in Hudson, New York, for the Firemen's Home of the State of New York. This was a brief interlude as he started his vigorous campaign for reelection as governor against Charles H. Tuttle, New York City district attorney. FDR won a smashing victory over Tuttle, a victory that also crowned him front-runner for the presidential nomination. (October 13, 1930)

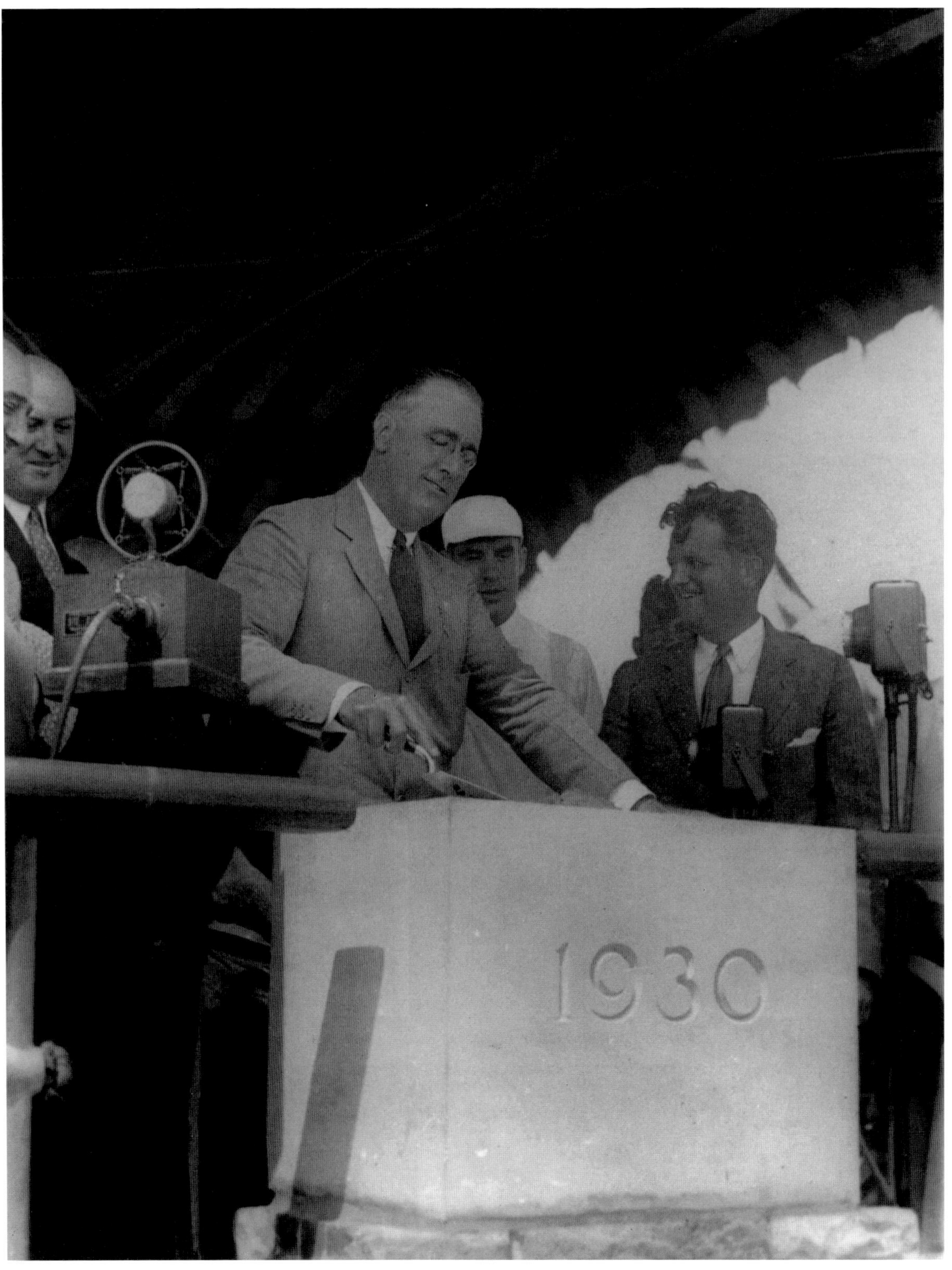

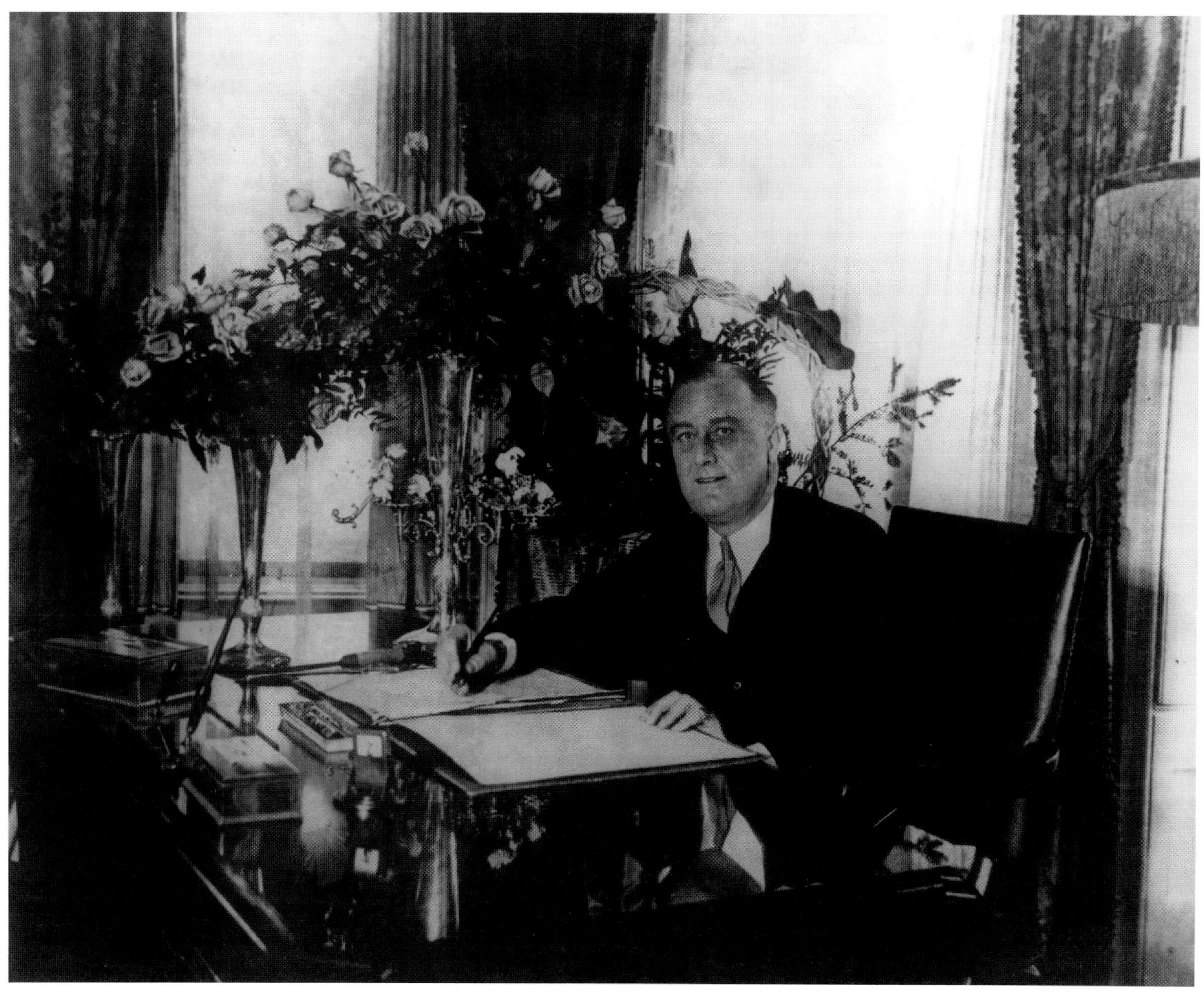

FDR poses at his gubernatorial desk in Albany for a formal, inauguration photograph.
(January 1, 1931)

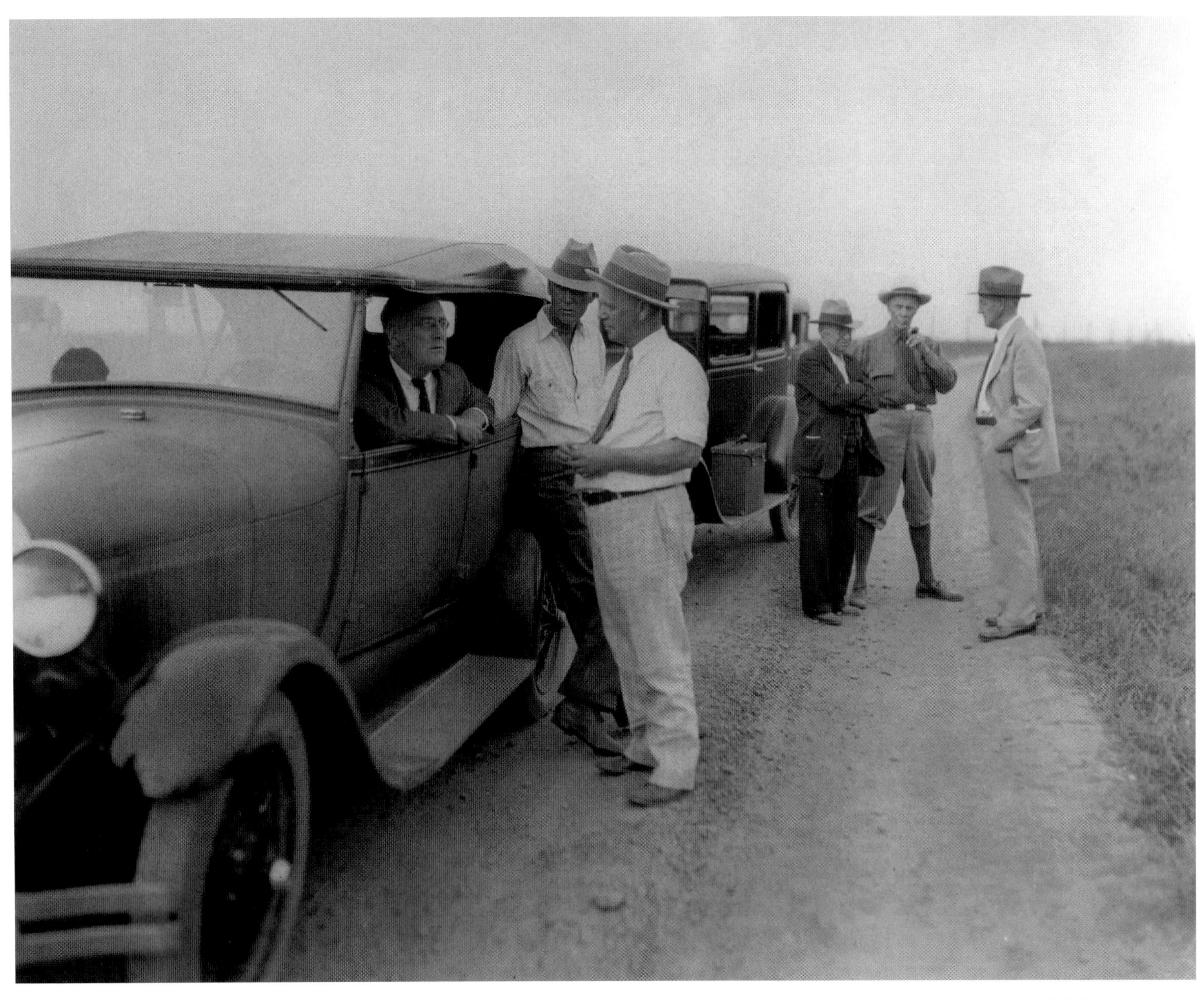

FDR at roadside, Otis Moore, and Ed Doyle, among others, in Warm Springs, Georgia. Ed Doyle served as FDR's local contact. Otis Moore farmed the land FDR owned, until it was transferred to the Warm Springs Foundation. (1931)

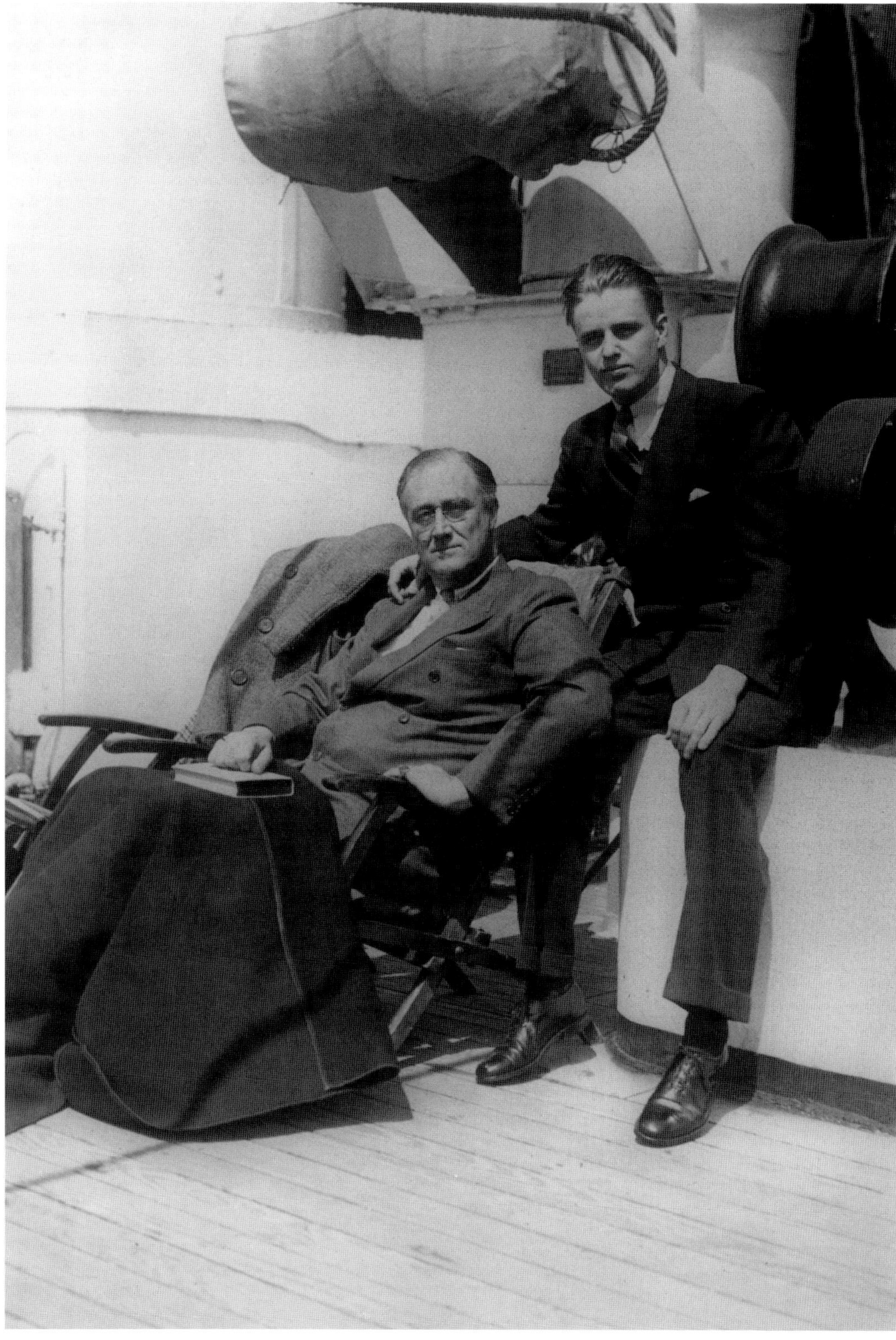

FDR with his son Elliott onboard the S.S. *Aquitania.* This was Elliott's first trip outside the country. In his book *The Roosevelts of Hyde Park,* Elliott recounts how flirtatious his father was and how they were both pursuing the same not-yet-twenty girl. (May 11, 1931)

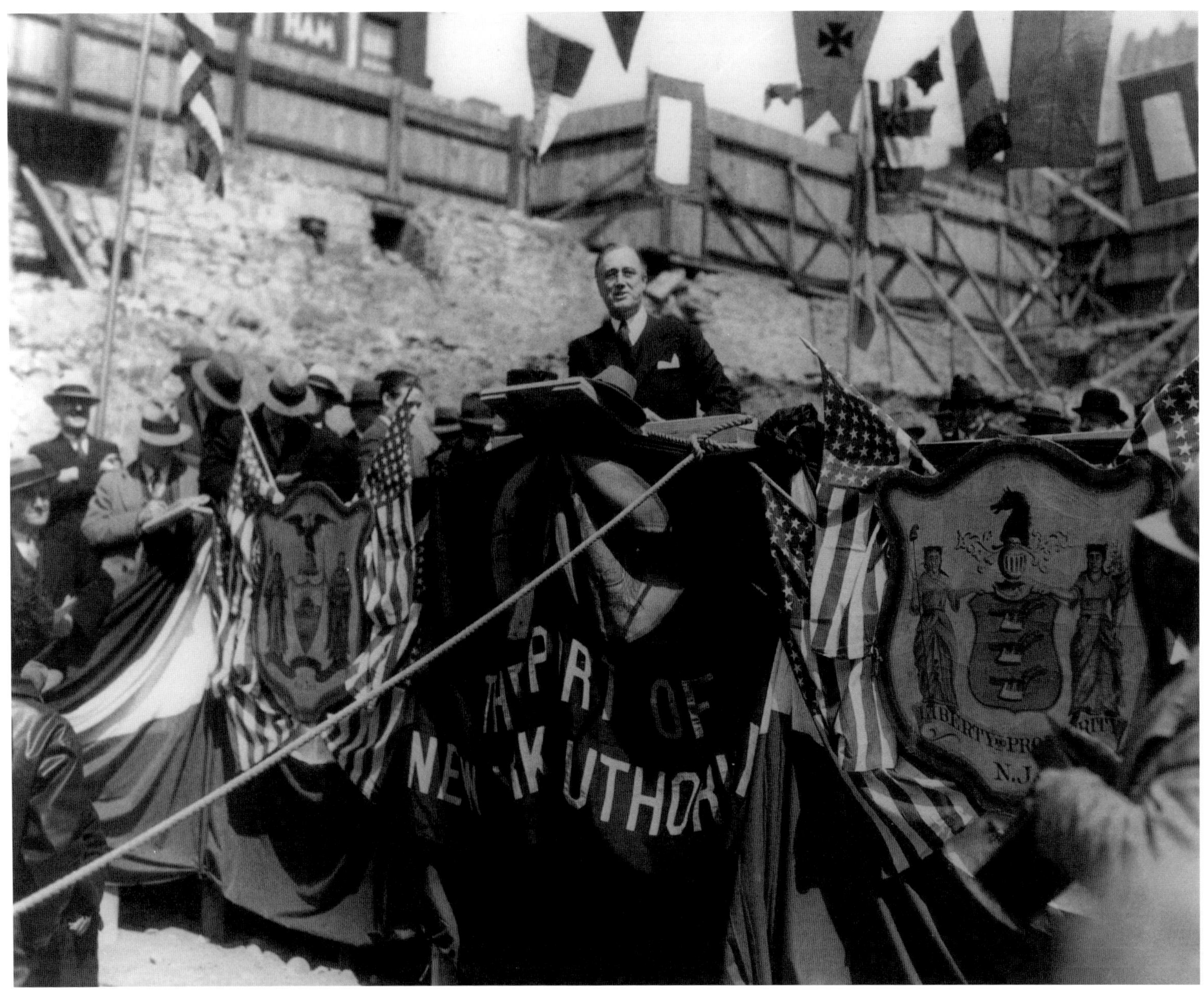

FDR at a Port Authority of New York groundbreaking. Former governor Smith was present too—as a Port Authority commissioner. This was the tenth anniversary of the founding of the authority and its most significant project to date. (April 30, 1931)

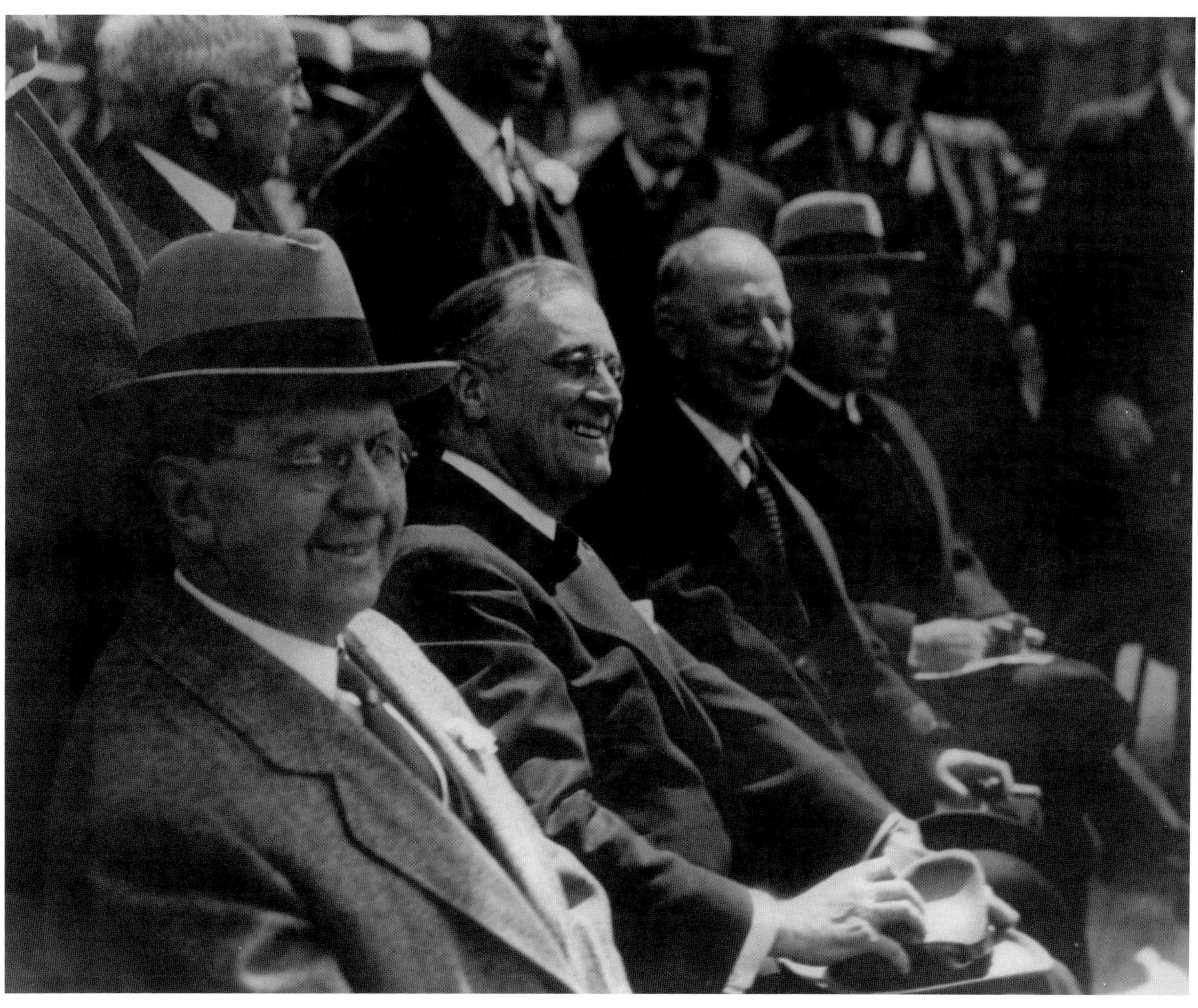

FDR, with his trademark grin, at the Port of New York Authority groundbreaking. Later that day he would attack the Hoover administration as "reactionary" at the Young Men's Democratic Club banquet. (April 30, 1931)

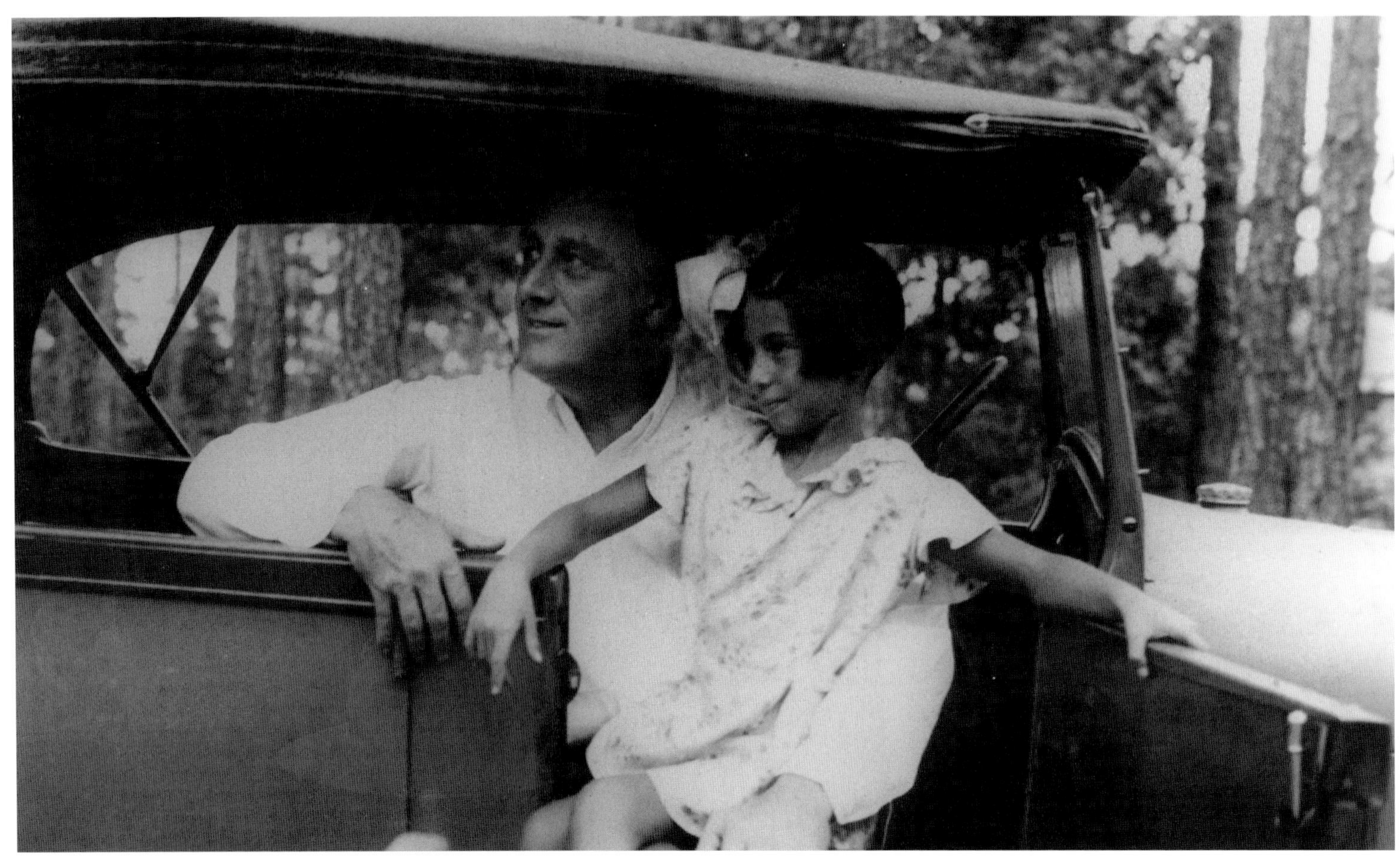

FDR with the young Harriet Golden in Warm Springs, Georgia. Franklin sits at the wheel of his roadster, specially equipped with hand controls, allowing him an unprecedented mobility and freedom. (1931)

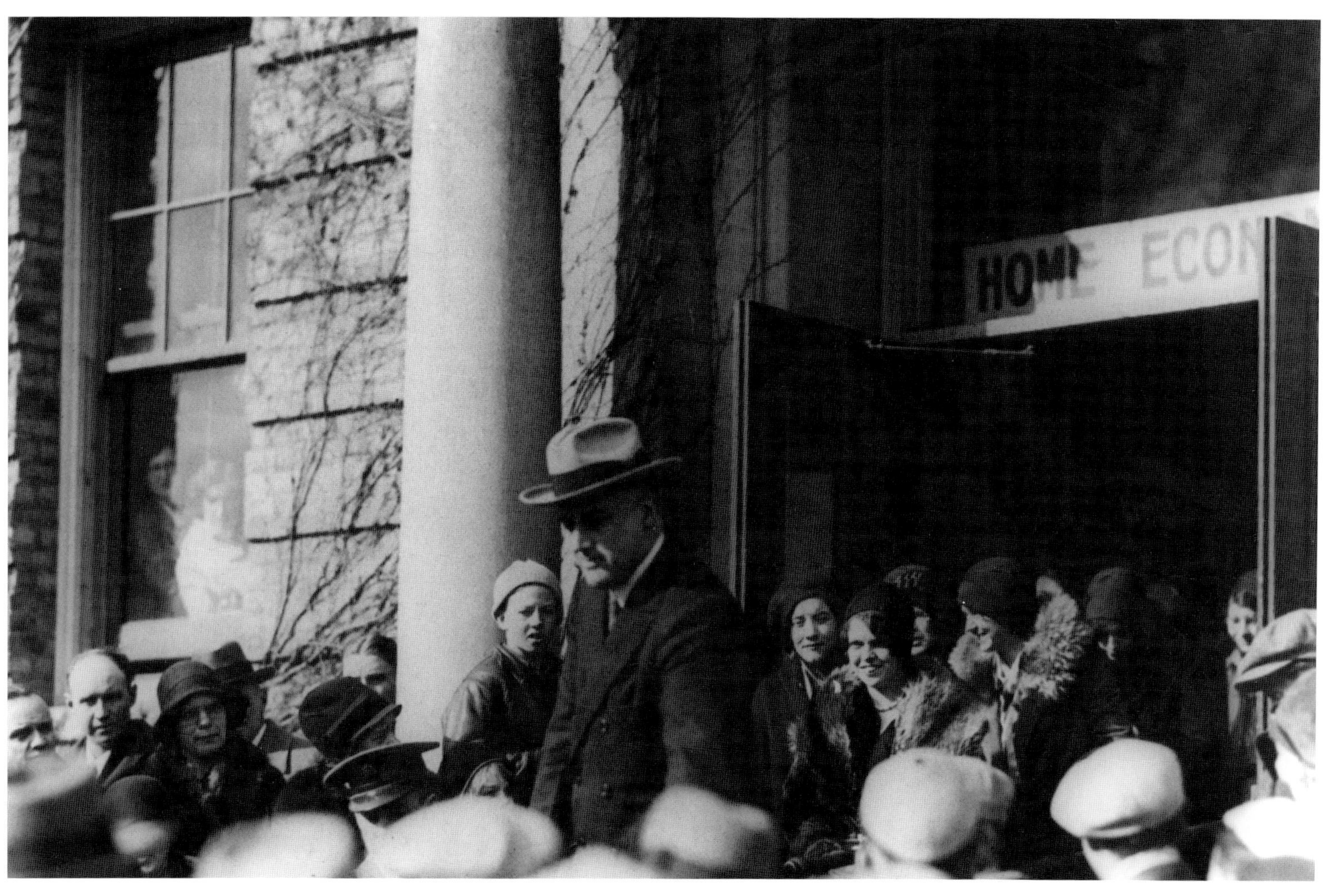

FDR greeting crowds in Ithaca, New York. The next day the *Ithaca Journal-News* reported why FDR was in town: The city might be the site of a new state tuberculosis hospital. He had also come to attend the 14th annual American Country Life Conference at Cornell University. (August 19, 1931)

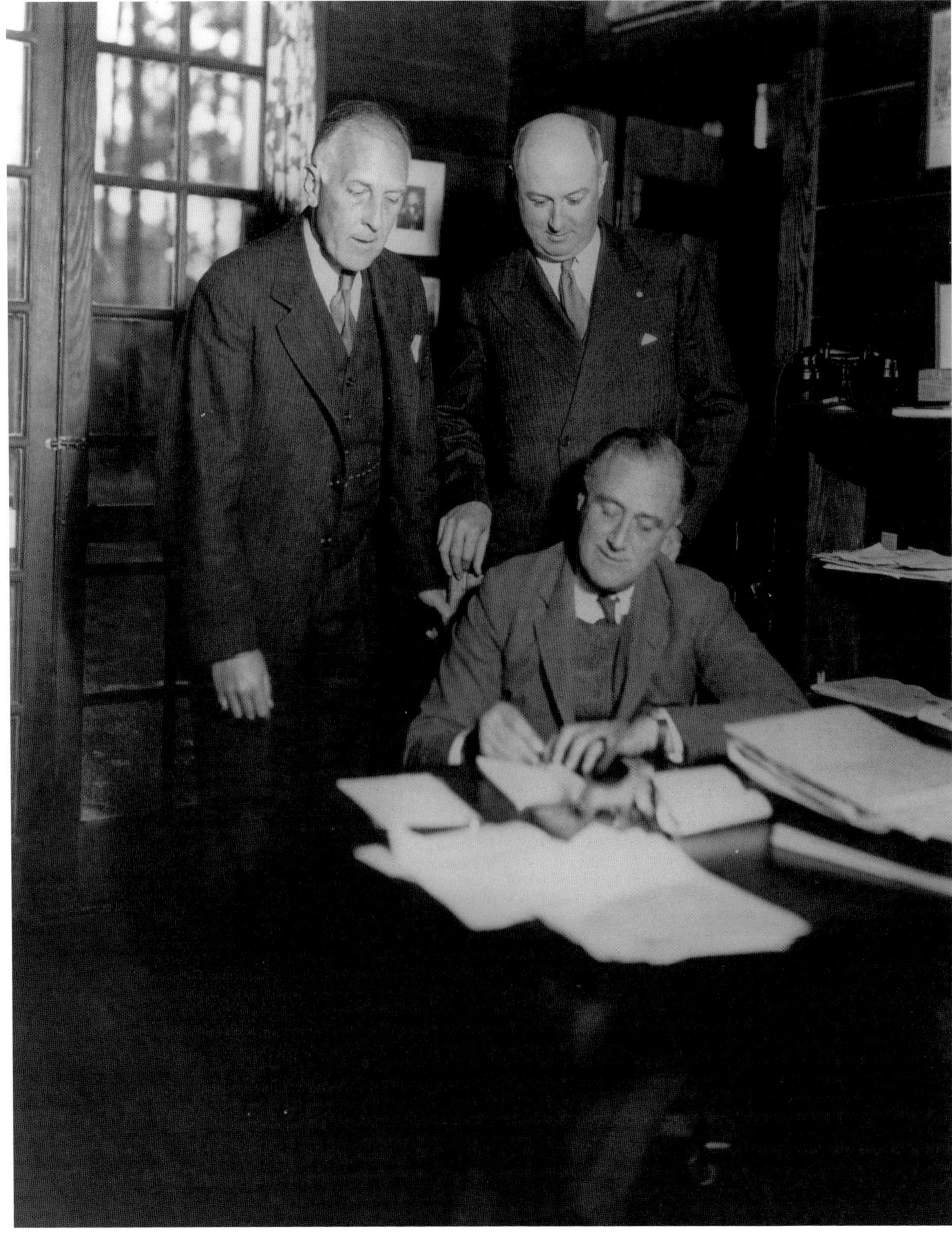

FDR signing, with James Farley and Charles Richard Crane looking over his shoulder. Crane was a wealthy Arabist and may have had a distinct influence on FDR's approach to Palestinian and Jewish affairs. He had served on the Root commission to Moscow in 1918 and the King-Crane commission to Turkey in 1919. (December 7, 1931)

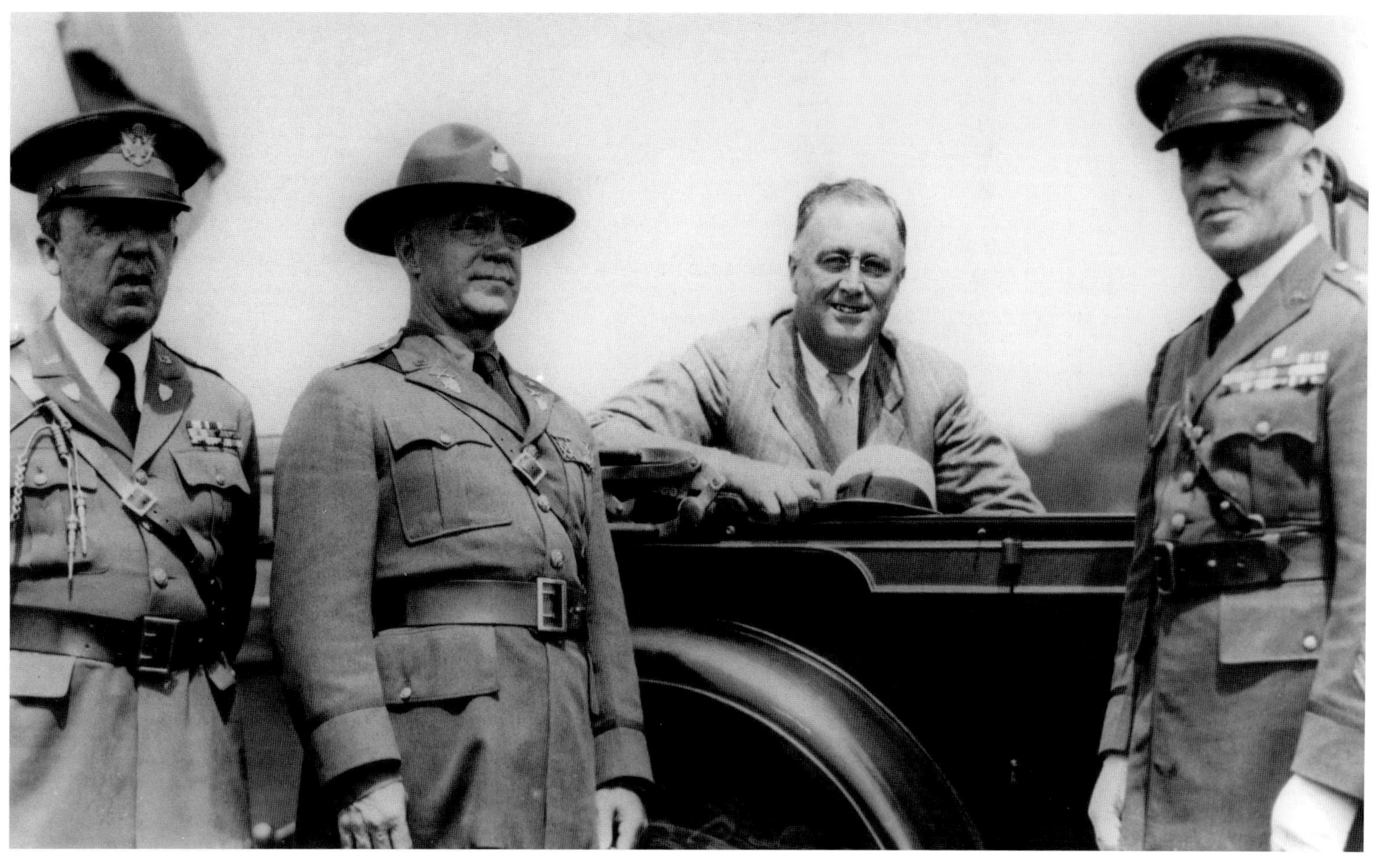

FDR with military aides, Major General William N. Haskell, New York National Guard, and Rear Admiral William B. Franklin, Naval Militia. (1932)

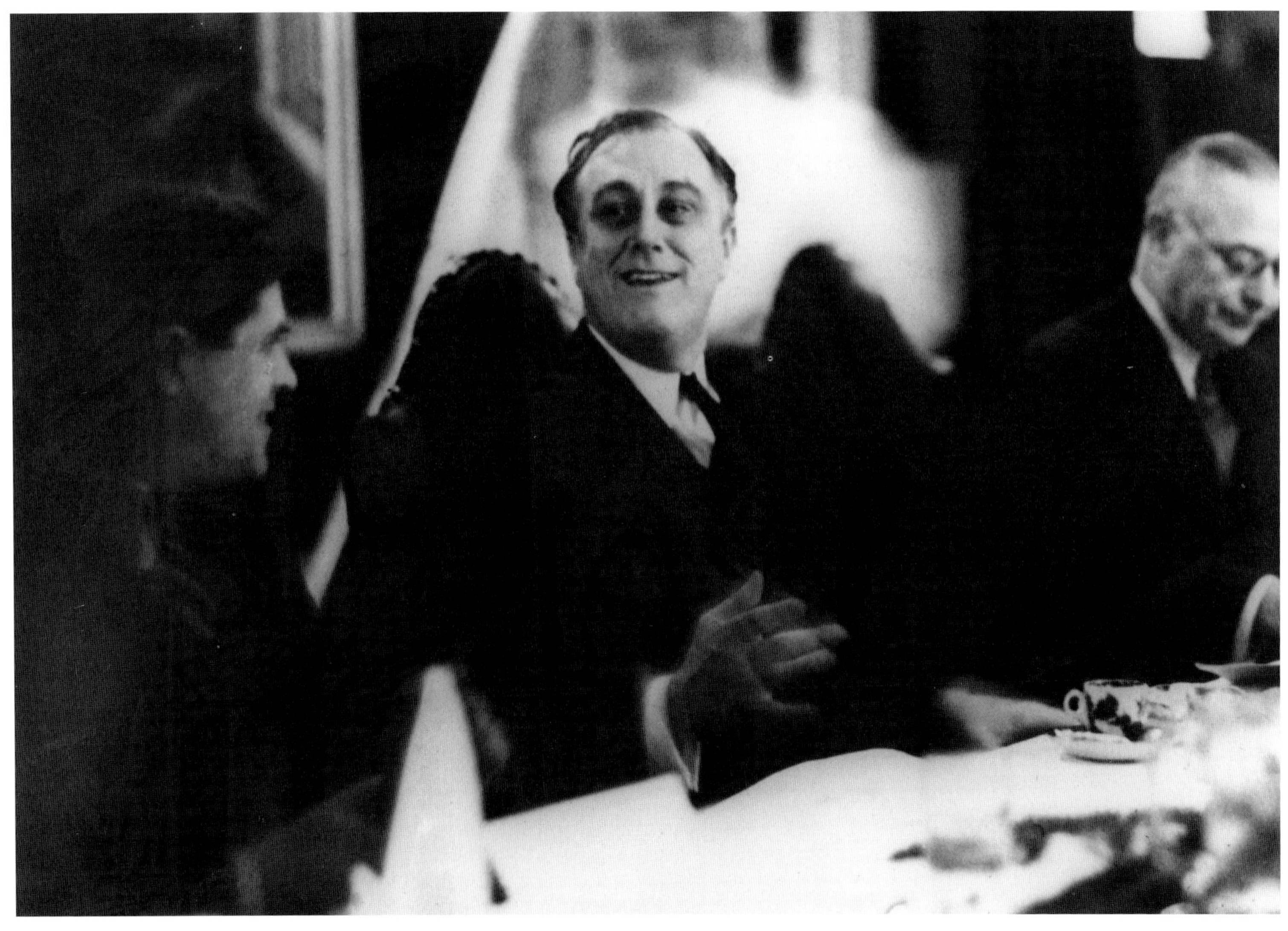

Vincent Astor was one of the northeastern elite FDR recruited to supplement his official espionage sources. Astor reported back to FDR and to the Office of Naval Intelligence information he gathered as he sailed in his yacht *Nourmahal.* Later he became the Area Controller for intelligence activities in New York. Ill health and the start of World War II sidelined Astor's activities. (April 8, 1932)

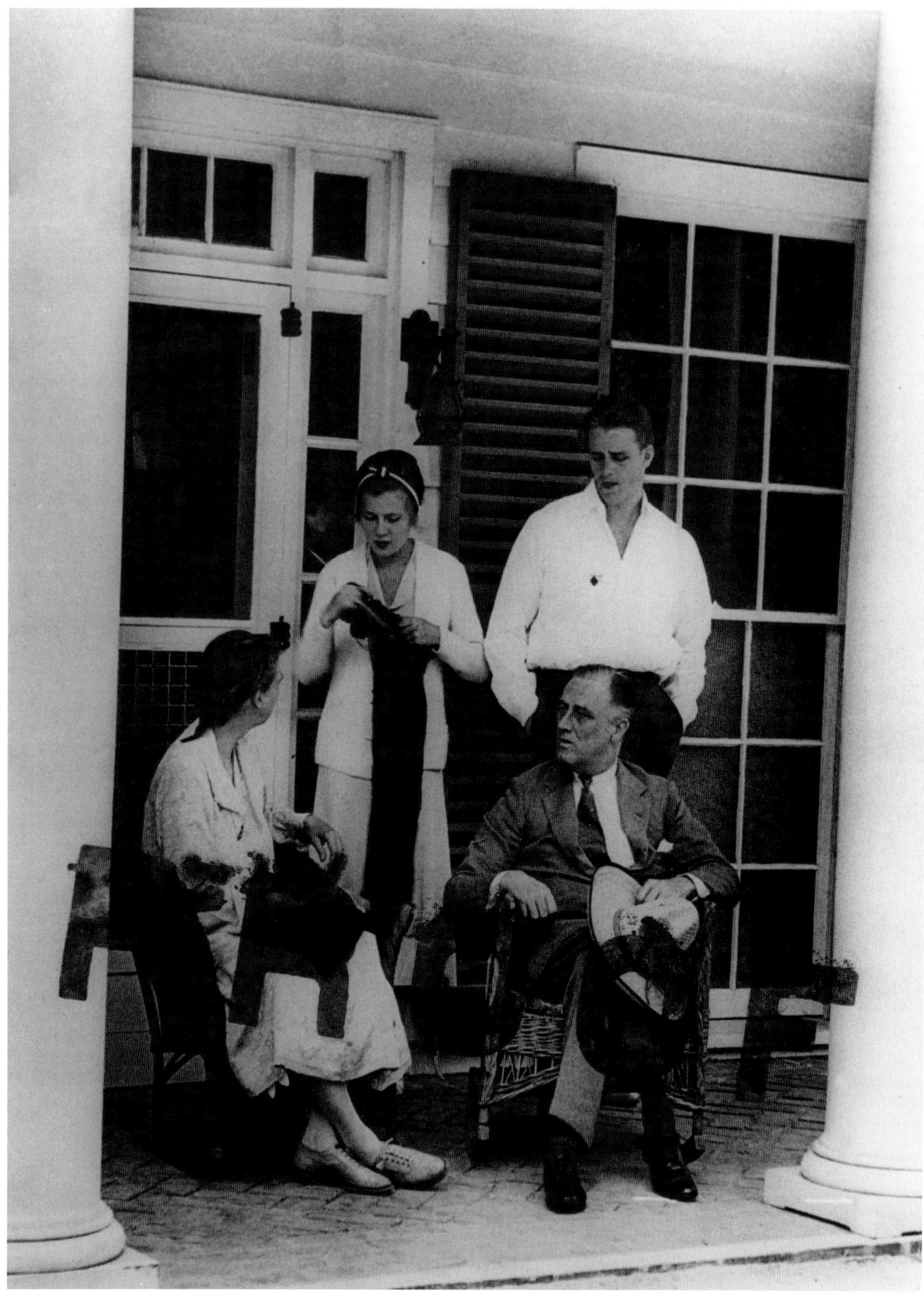

FDR and Eleanor, with Elliott and wife in Warm Springs, Georgia, at Franklin's new cottage retreat. FDR had a simple cottage built overlooking a wooded, deep ravine. Moving into the cottage May 1, 1932, he invited all the "residents of Warm Springs" and all "the patients, employees, and cottagers" to a housewarming party, on May 5. After the presidential election, the cottage was nicknamed "the Little White House." (May 7, 1932)

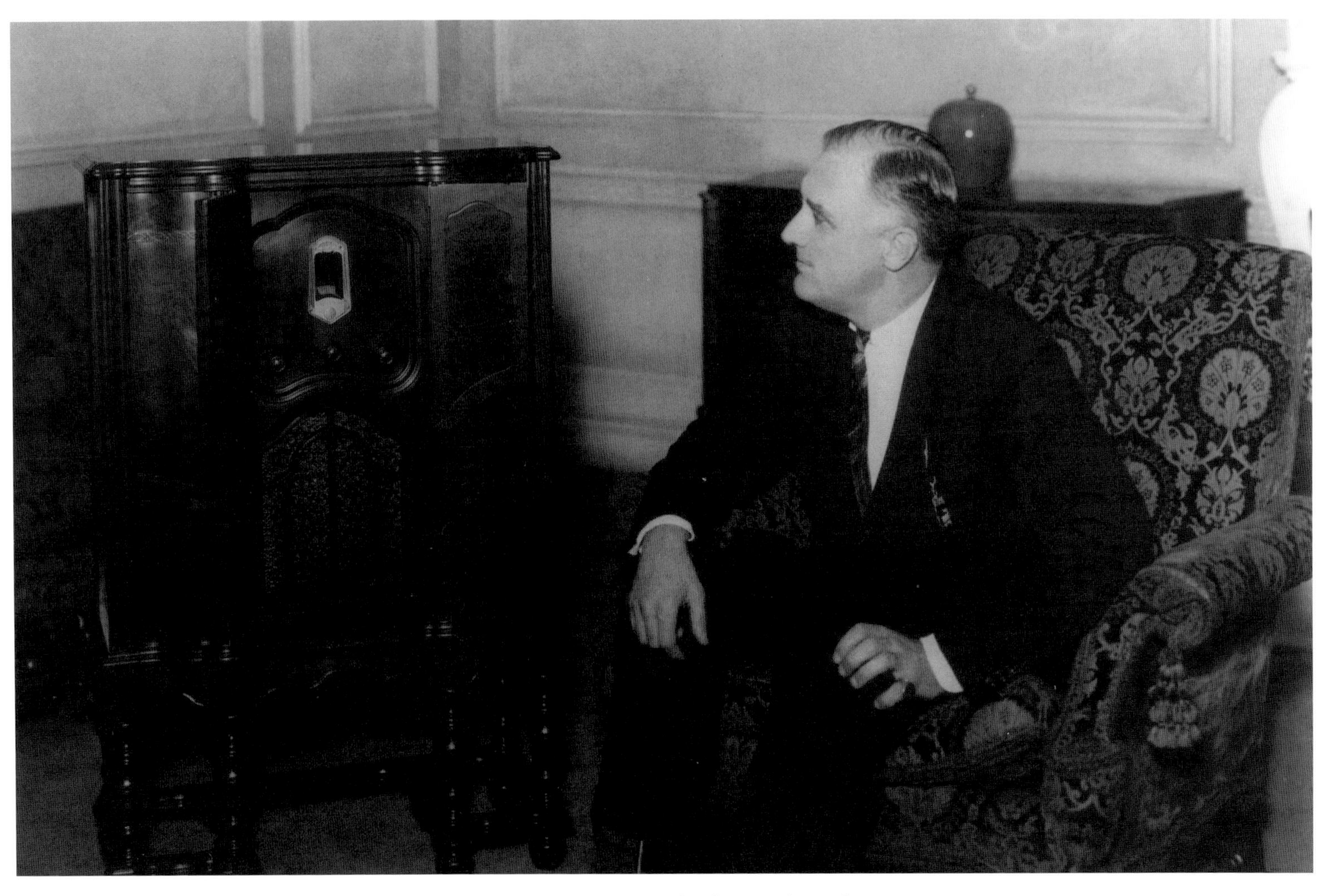

FDR listening to the radio for news of his nomination to the Democratic ticket for President of the United States. (July 1, 1932)

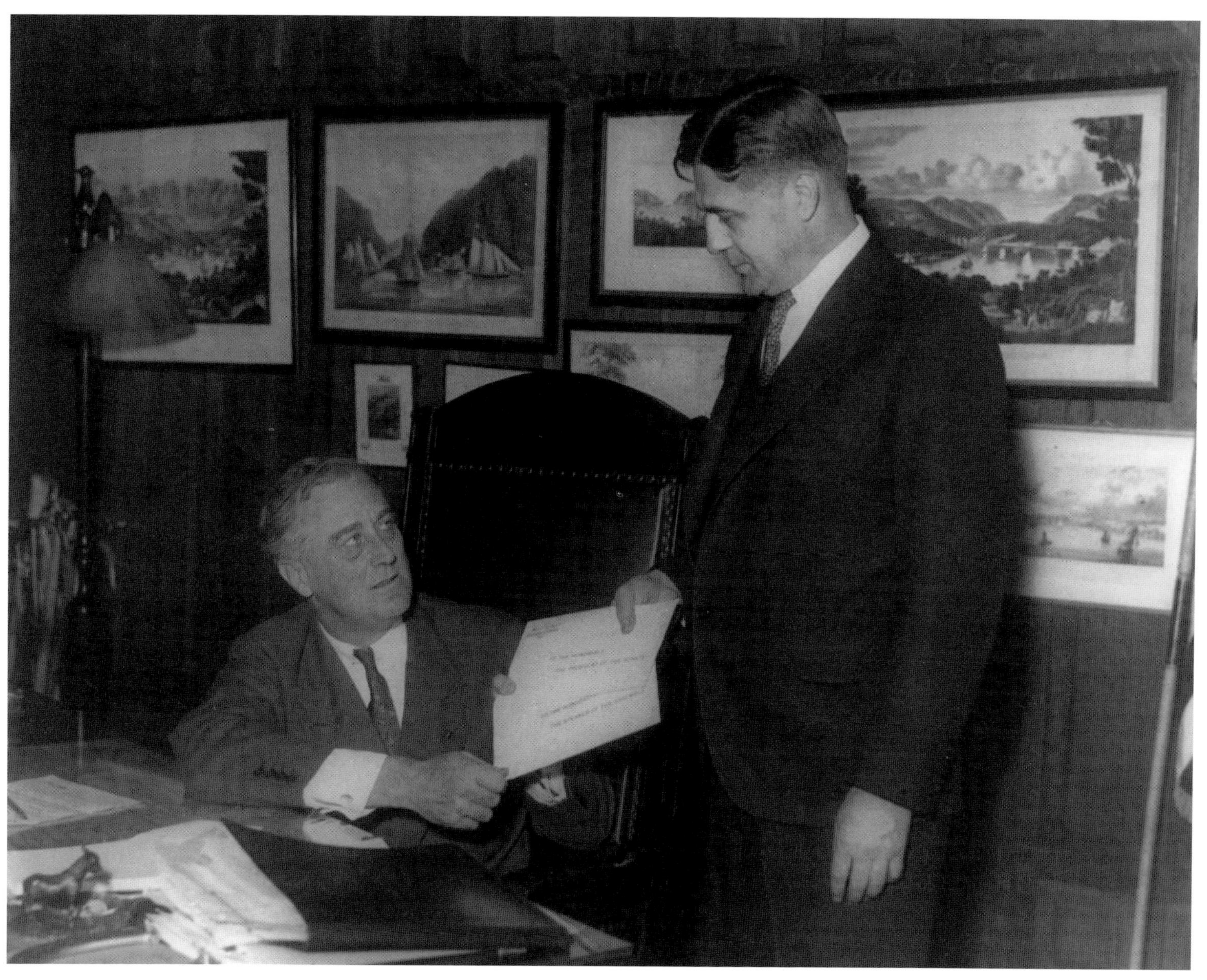

FDR receiving the start of a flood of congratulatory telegrams following his nomination on the Democratic presidential ticket. (1932)

A formal portrait of FDR, inscribed "At Albany." Telegrams congratulating him on his nomination for president are filling his desk. (1932)

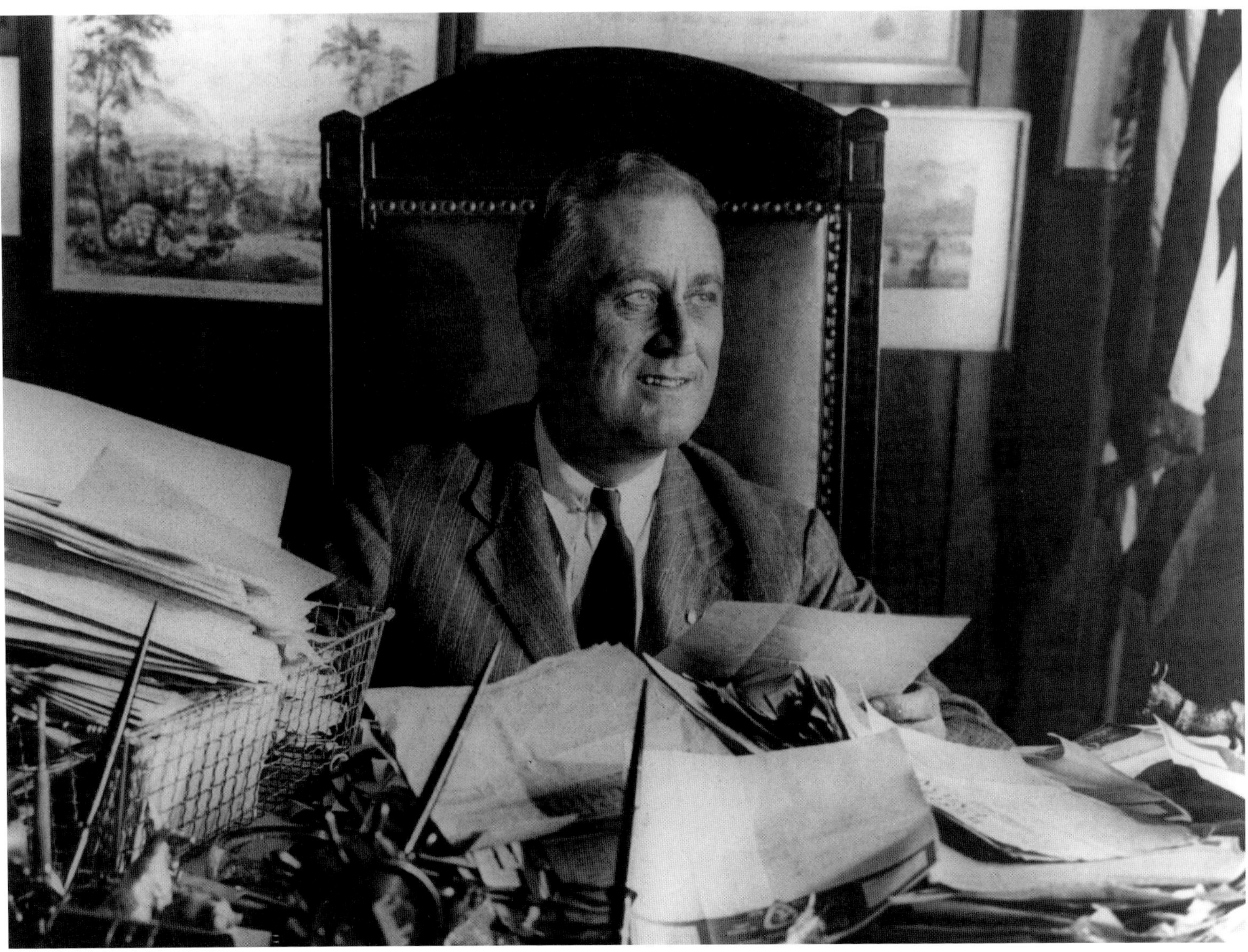

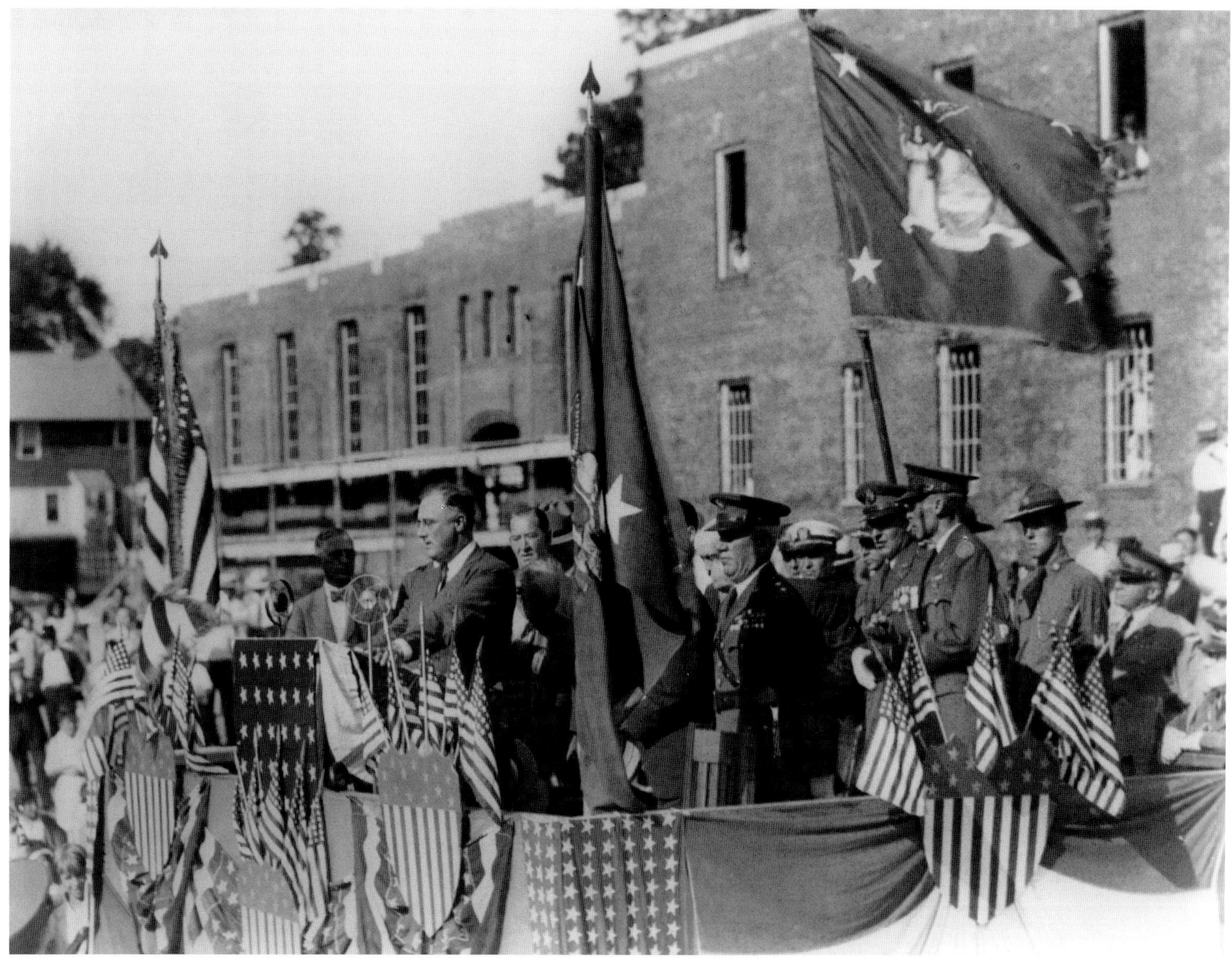

FDR on the stump in Peekskill. He met up with Senator John Nance Garner (and Sam Rayburn), observed a cornerstone-laying, had dinner at the Roosevelt home in Hyde Park, and drove to Albany. This was the first meeting of the running mates in two years. (August 14, 1932)

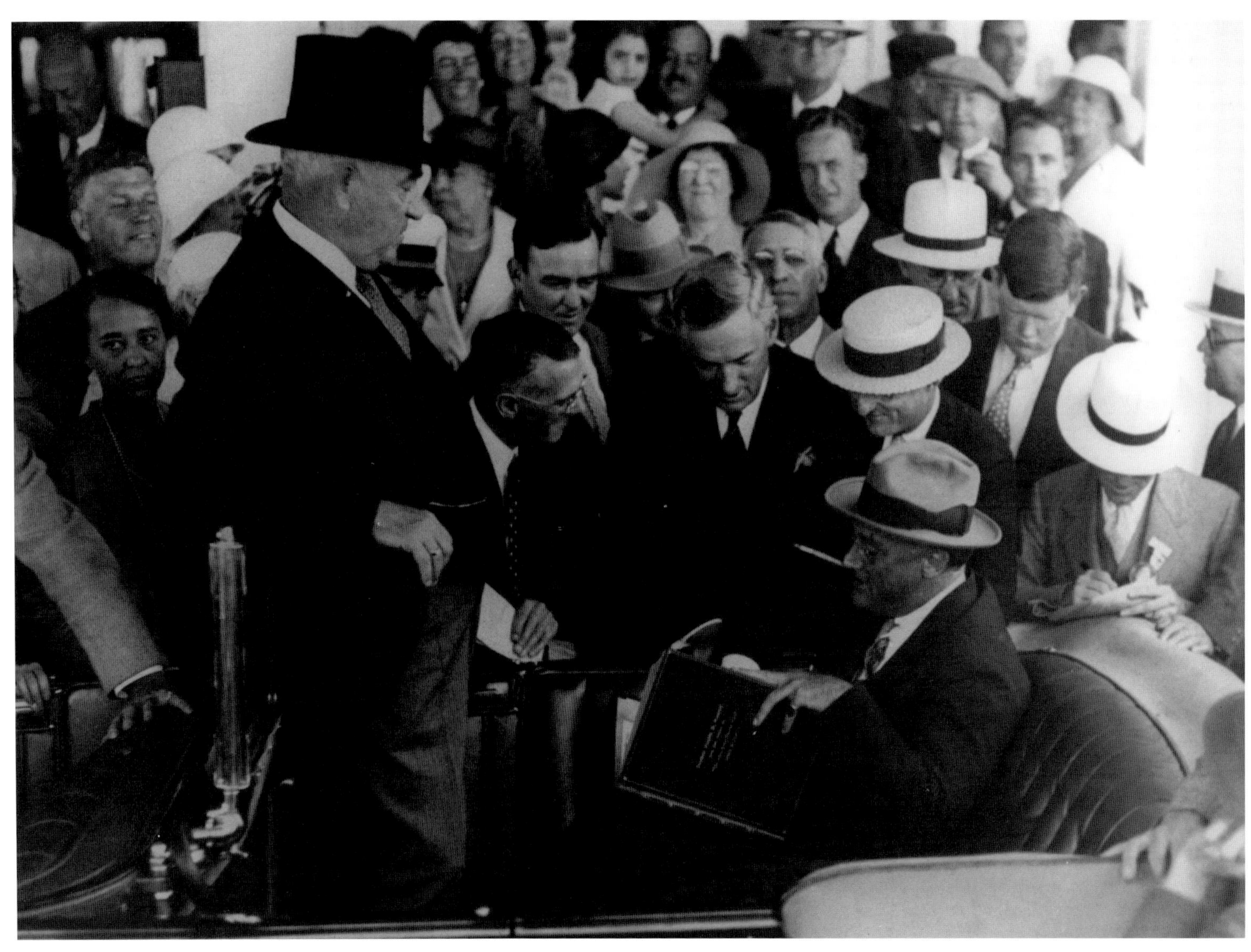

FDR in Hampton Beach, New Hampshire. His son James had a summer cottage nearby, so Roosevelt opened his presidential campaign here Sunday, July 17, 1932. Roosevelt arrived in an open touring car with the mayor, Fernando Hartford. Mayor Hartford was in frock coat and shiny silk hat, outshining the guest of honor, who wore an unpressed business suit and a battered gray fedora, as recounted by newspaper columnist James W. Tucker. (July 17, 1932)

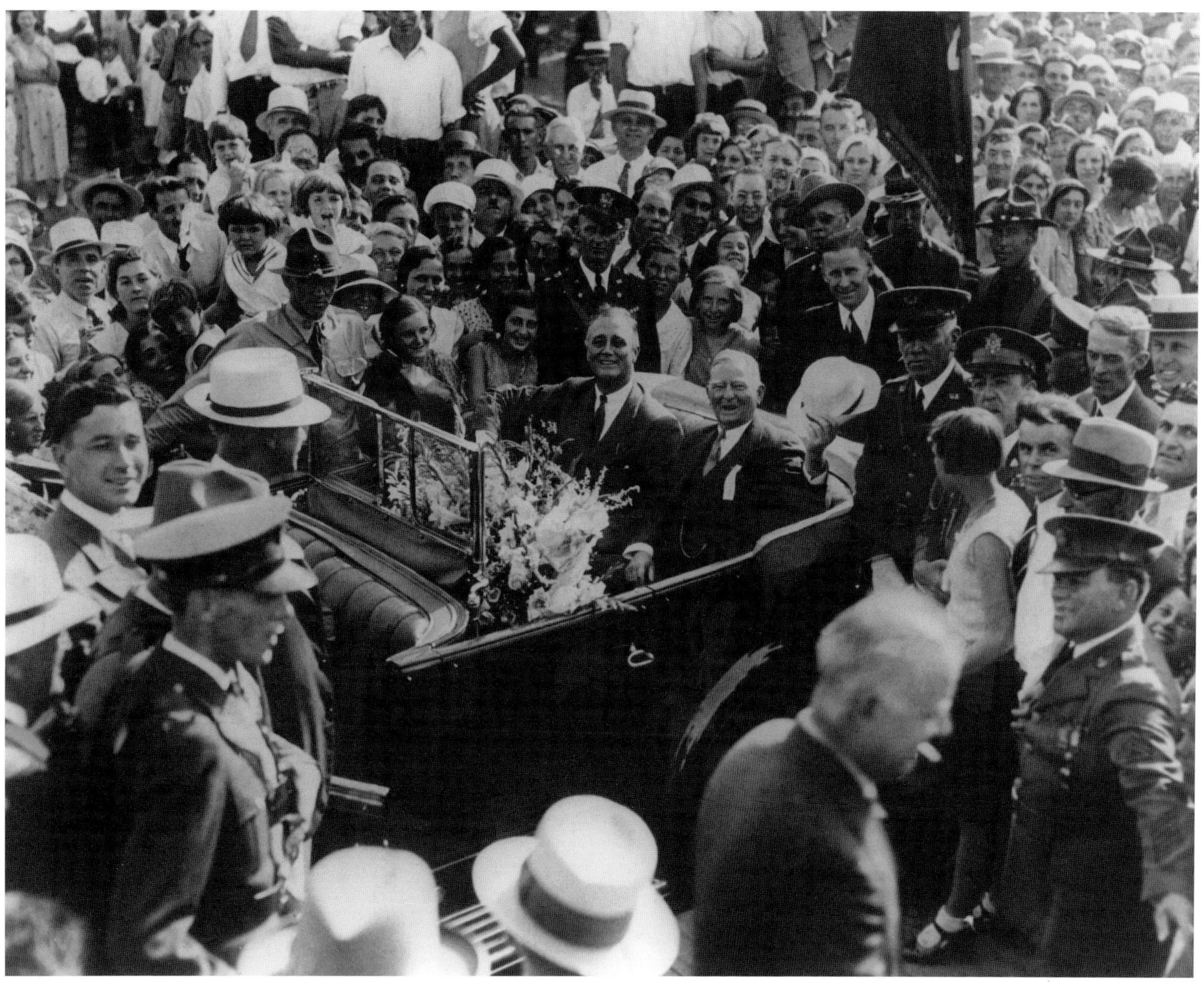

FDR in a car with vice-presidential candidate John Nance Garner, campaigning in Peekskill, New York, not far from FDR's Hyde Park home. As noted by *Time,* "Governor Roosevelt and Speaker Garner met for the first time since their nomination. Speaker: 'Hello, Governor.' Governor: 'Hello, Jack. How's my teammate?' Speaker: 'I'm fine. Jiminy, you look as though you'd been training for a prizefight.'" Garner would serve as FDR's vice-president for two terms, then run against him for the top line on the ticket. (August 14, 1932)

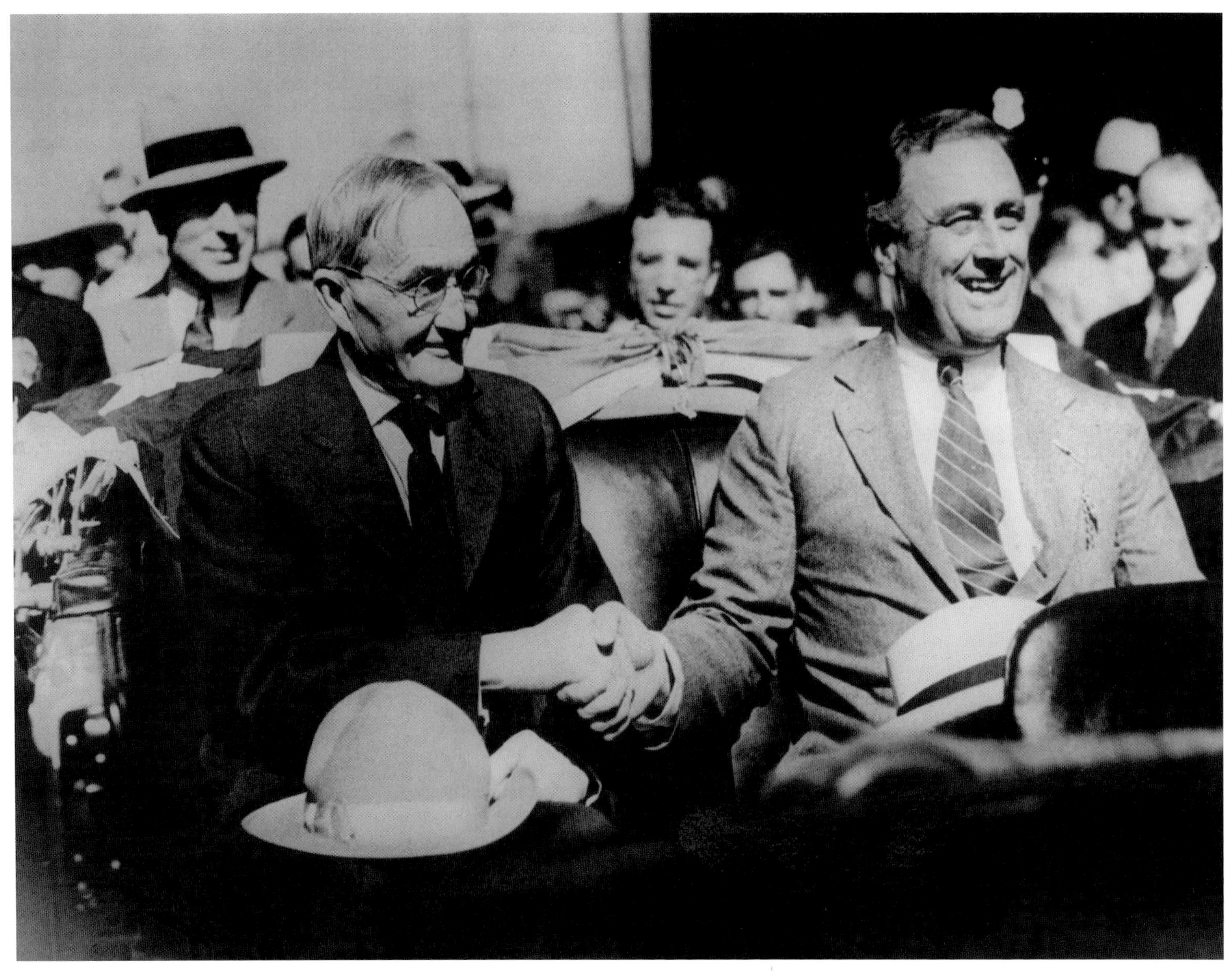

A cheerful FDR shaking hands with Governor William H. Adams in Denver. FDR had just come from the cheers of crowds in Topeka, where he proposed "national planning in agriculture" and castigated the failure of the Hoover administration's farm relief efforts. Yet in Denver he said, "I am having a hard time to make the press and people of the country understand this is not a campaign trip." He was feted by the governor, escorted in an open car in a parade through Denver from the train station to the Brown Palace Hotel, where from the balcony he addressed the crowd. (September 15, 1932)

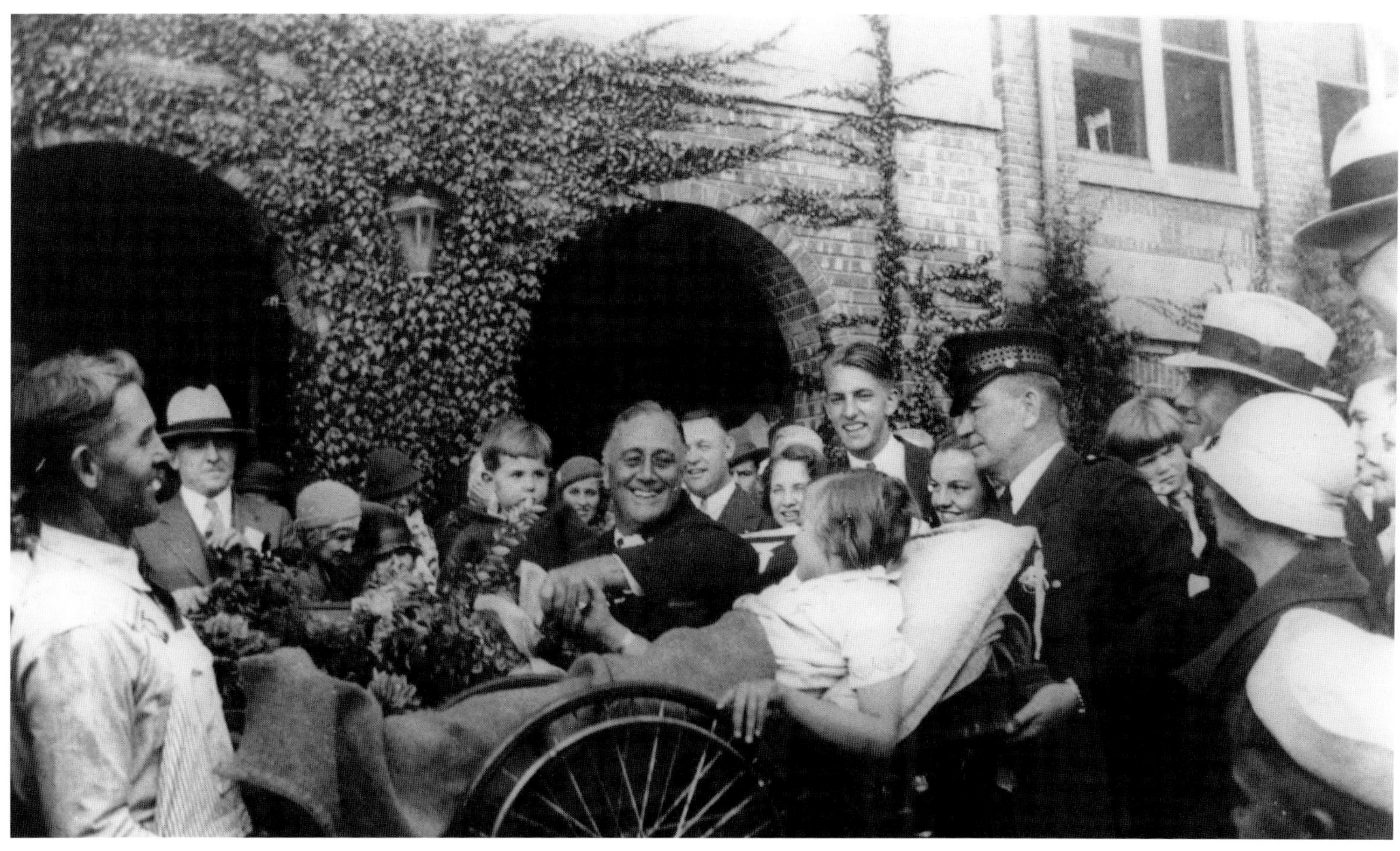

FDR in Seattle greeting patient Melody Bresina on the campaign trail. *Time* reported, "Visiting a hospital for crippled children, lame Governor Roosevelt sympathized: 'It's a little difficult for me to stand on my feet, too.'" His reception in Seattle was enthusiastic, where he promoted his program of "a new deal."

"Governor Roosevelt got his first red-hot reception at Seattle. From 75,000 throats roared forth a boisterous welcome as he rode through the streets with Mayor John Dore, nominal Republican, who declared, 'President Hoover is a menace'." (September 22, 1932)

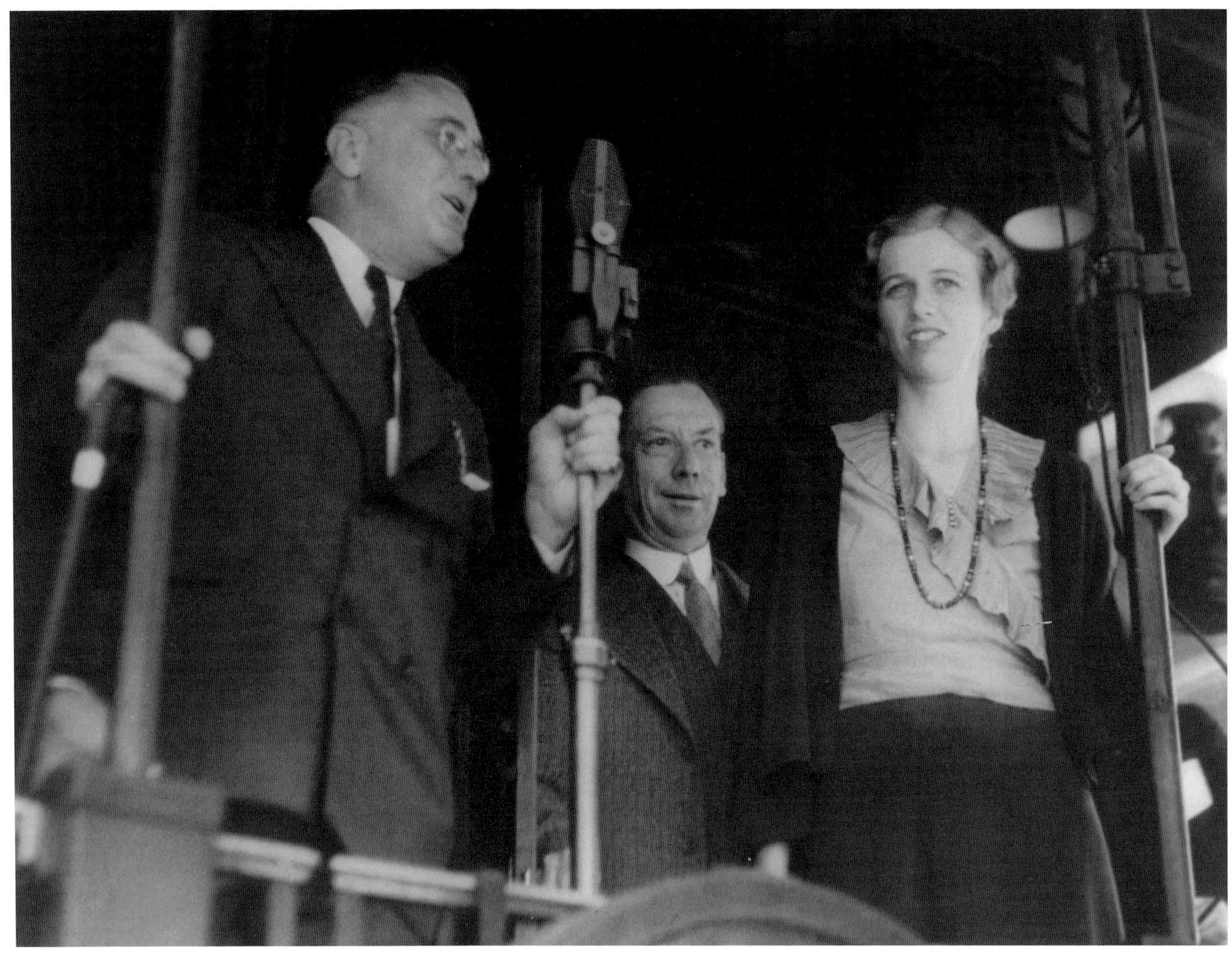

FDR, Judge Francis Carr, and the Roosevelts' daughter, Anna, in Redding, California. The day before, Franklin had given what has gone down as the "Portland Speech" on Public Utilities and Development of Hydro-Electric Power. "I have come, not primarily to speak but, rather, to hear; not to teach, but to learn. I want to hear of your problems, to understand them and to consider them as they bear on the larger scene of national interest.

"I have strengthened the belief that I have had for a long time and that I have constantly set forth in my speeches and papers in my work as Governor of the State of New York, that the question of power, of electrical development and distribution, is primarily a national problem. . . . I therefore lay down the following principle: That where a community—a city or county or a district—is not satisfied with the service rendered or the rates charged by the private utility, it has the undeniable basic right, as one of its functions of Government, one of its functions of home rule, to set up, after a fair referendum to its voters has been had, its own governmentally owned and operated service." (September 22, 1932)

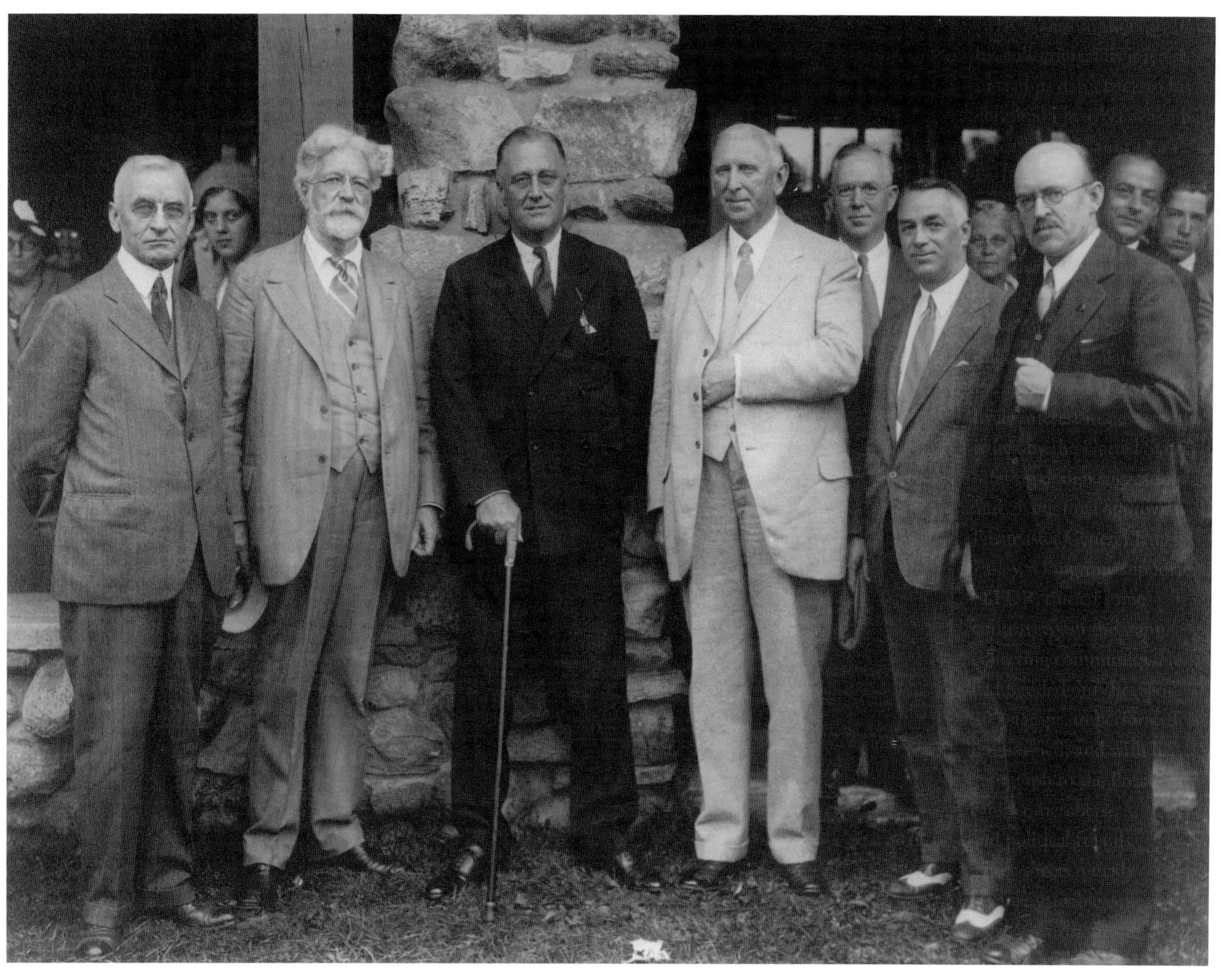

FDR with a group including George Foster Peabody. It was Peabody's estate at Warm Springs, Georgia, where Roosevelt recuperated soon after he contracted (what was considered to be) polio. Roosevelt purchased the site in 1924 and founded the Roosevelt Warm Springs Institute for Rehabilitation. (1932)

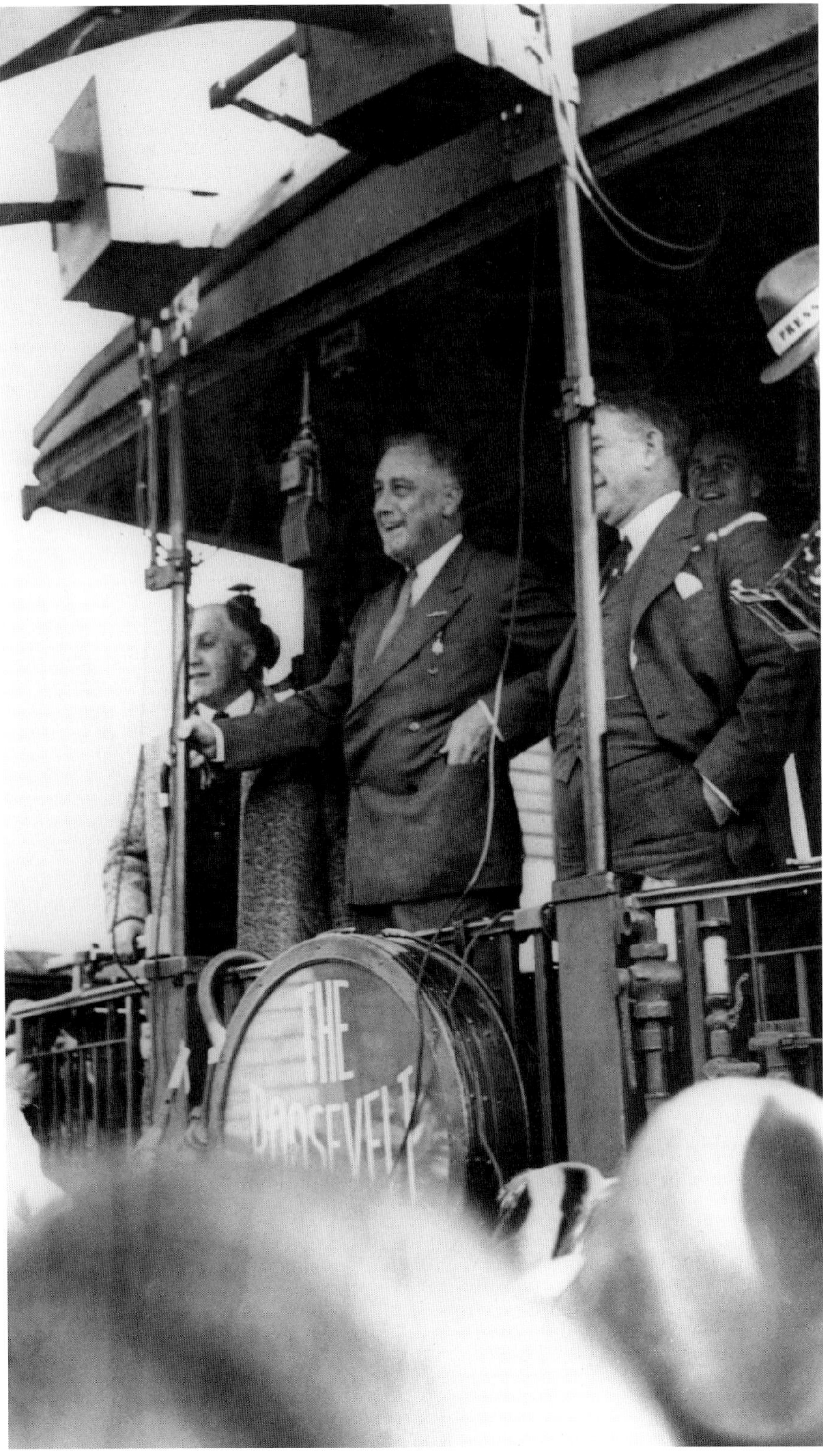

FDR on the stump in New Albany, Indiana, en route to Louisville from St. Louis. A crowd has gathered around the train in New Albany, directly across the river from Louisville, to listen to FDR speak extemporaneously. In Louisville he would quote the old song "hard times have come a knocking at the door" with the crowd-pleasing refrain "the sun shines bright on my old Kentucky home!" (October 22, 1932)

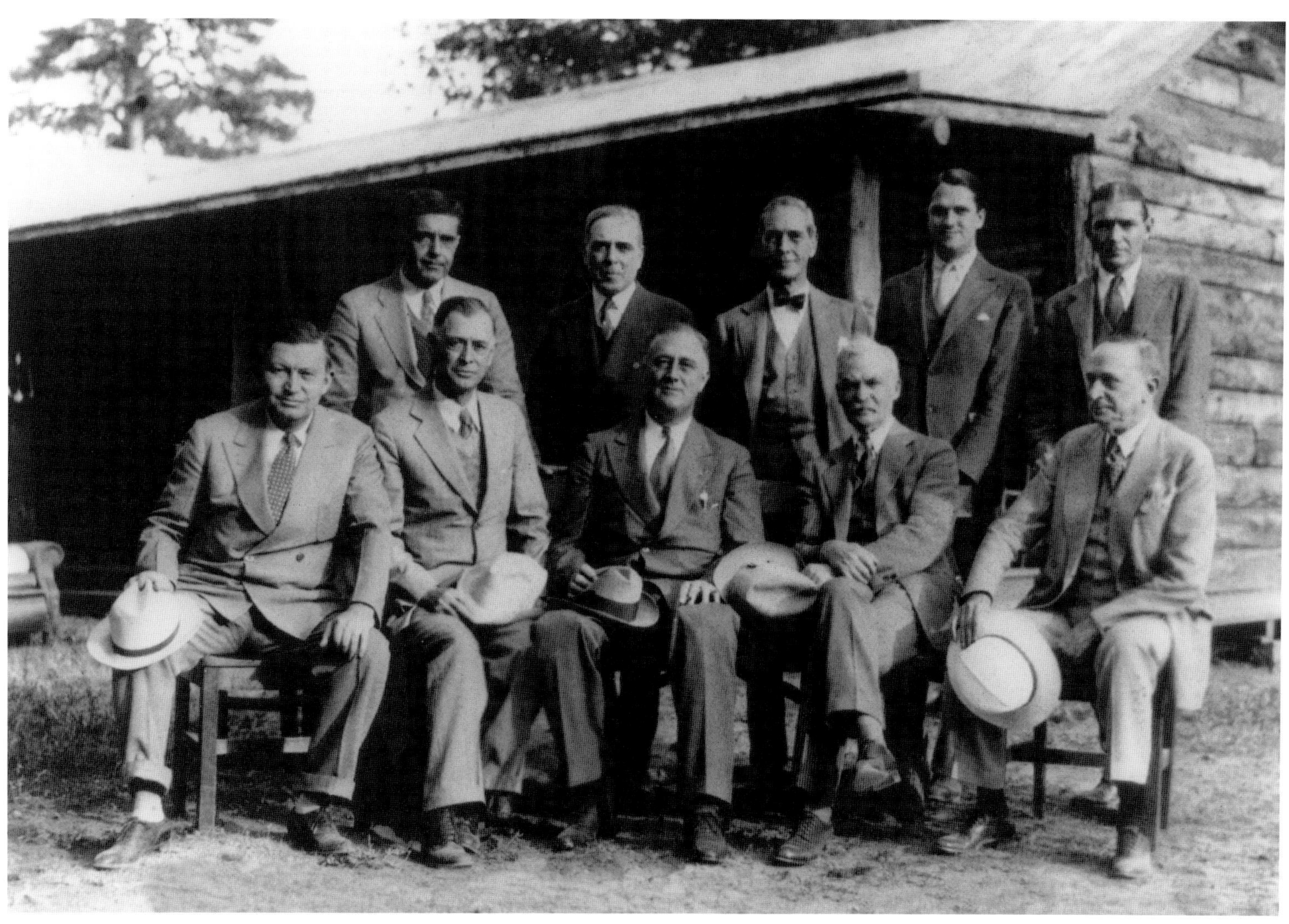

FDR at Greenway (Double X) Ranch, Arizona. Mrs. Isabella Greenway had close connections with Roosevelt—serving as bridesmaid for Eleanor Roosevelt and seconding Roosevelt's nomination in Chicago. She would win a special election to fill the congressional seat of Lewis Douglas and join Roosevelt in Washington. The group includes Senator Thomas J. Walsh (D) of Montana, C. C. Pettijohn, General Counsel of MPAA, Senator Key Pittman (D) of Nevada, Senator John S. Cohen (D) of Georgia, Judge Robert Marx, founder of Disabled American Veterans, J. Bruce Kremer, delegate to the Democratic National Committee, Breckinridge Long, W. F. Githens, and Senator Carl T. Hayden (D) of Arizona. (September 26, 1932)

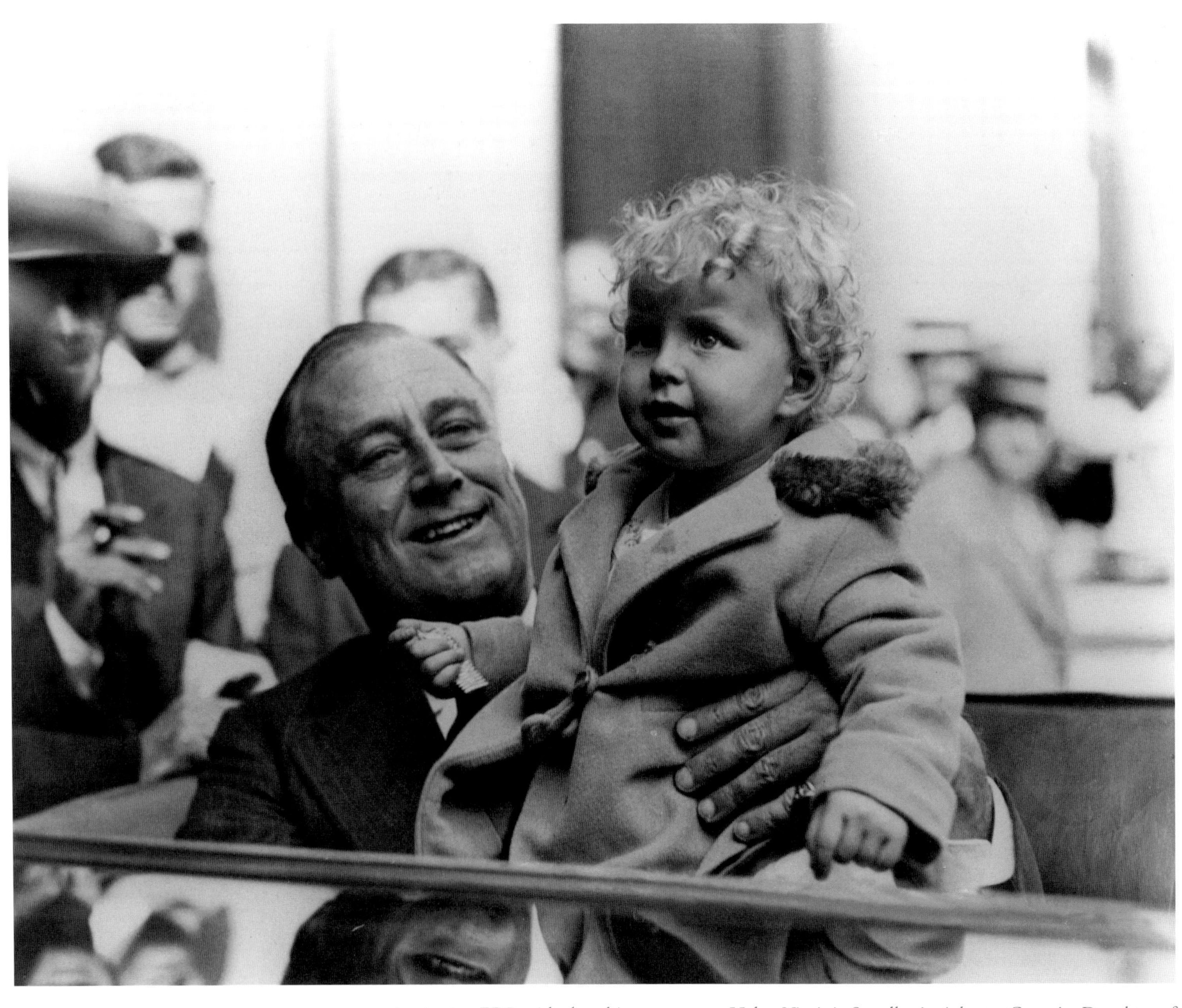

A grinning FDR with cherubic supporter—Helen Virginia Sewell—in Atlanta, Georgia. Daughter of prominent businessman Robert Anderson Sewell, precocious little Helen would be playing the harp at the White House in a few years. (October 23, 1932)

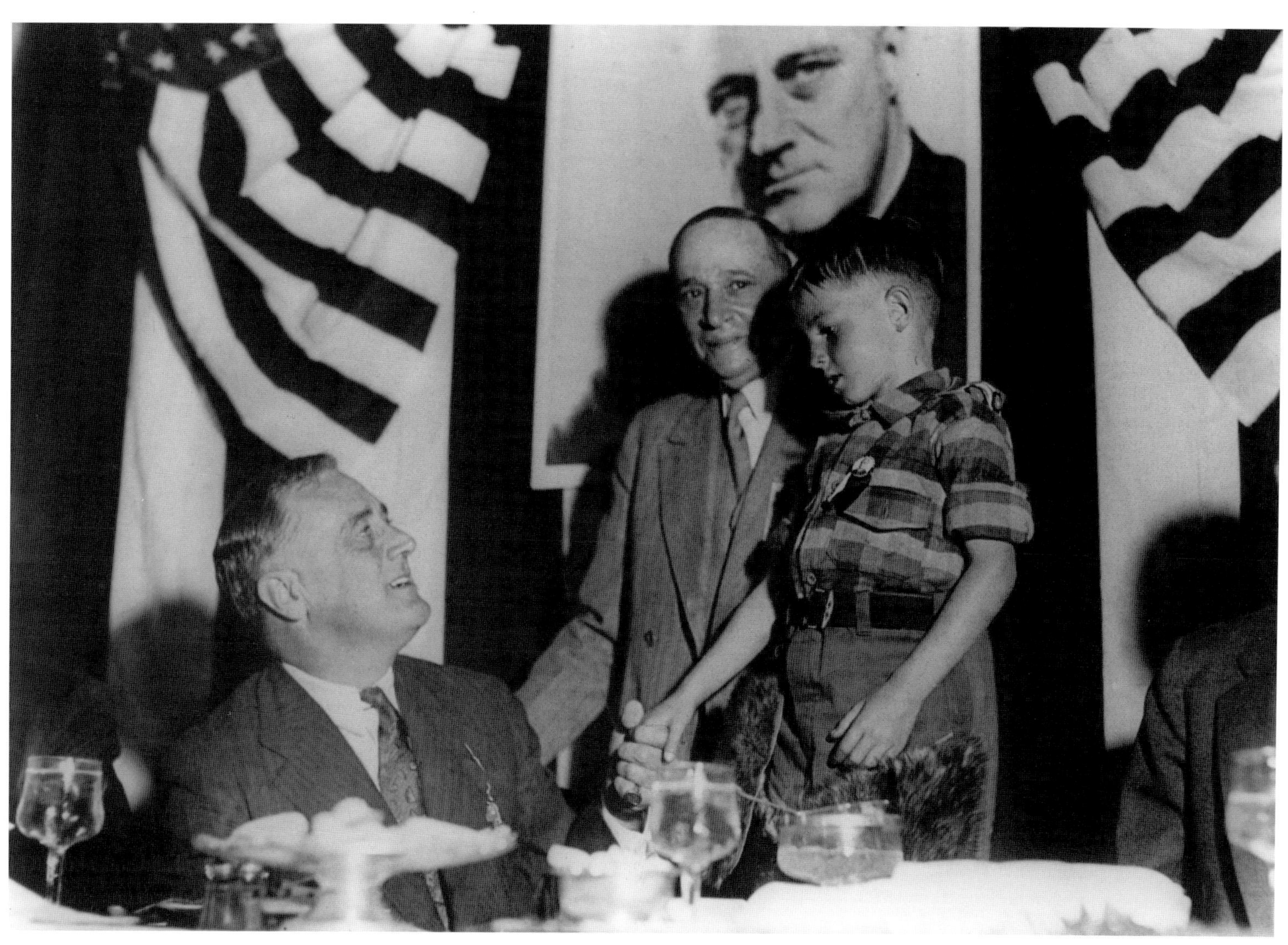

FDR shaking hands with supporter Toby Cook in Atlanta, Georgia. The youth rode 210 miles on his pony to greet FDR. (October 24, 1932)

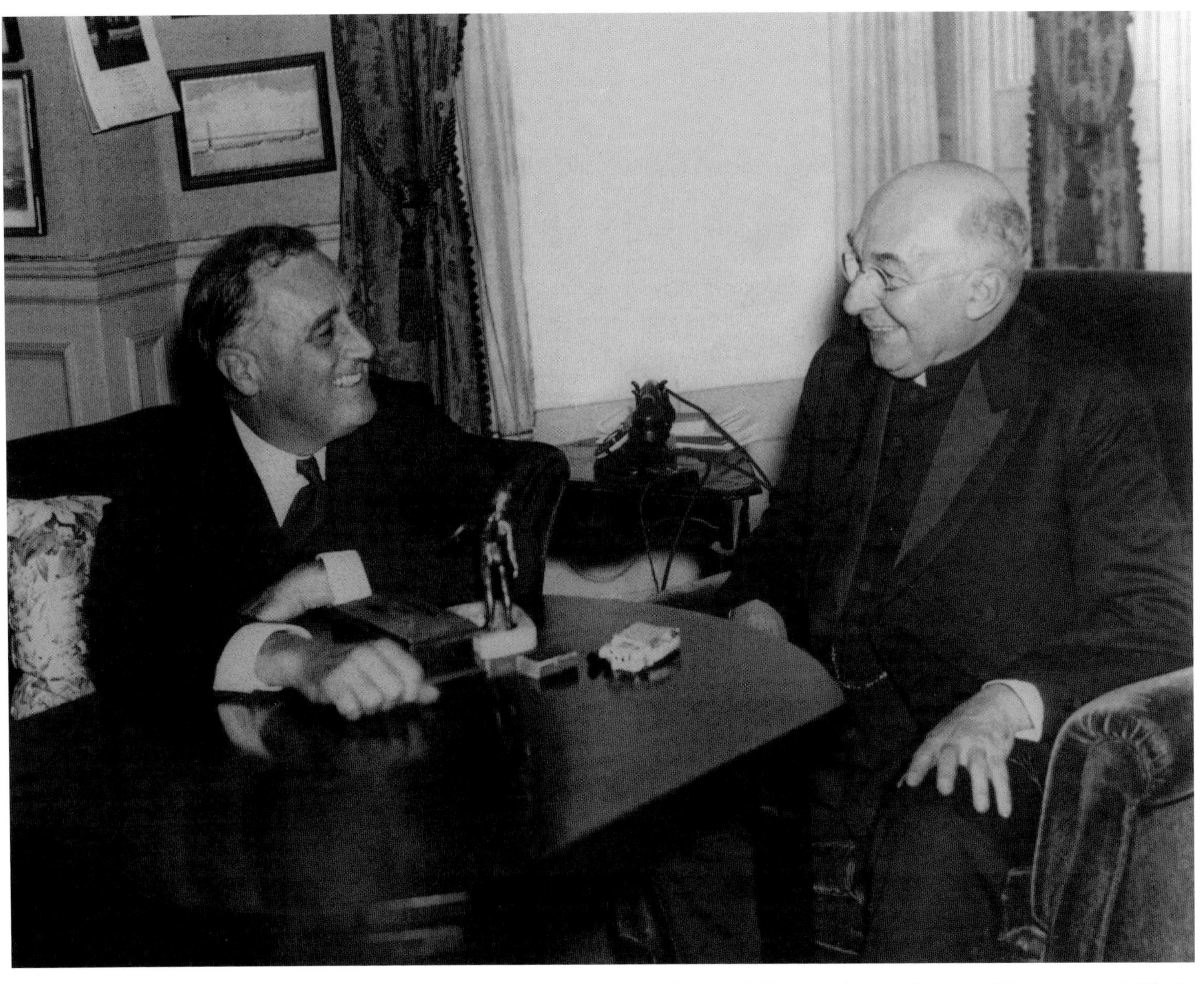

FDR and George Cardinal Mundelein, Archbishop of Chicago, who signed a copy of this photograph "To the President of the U.S. with grateful appreciation of one of the most pleasant visits I have ever had. And with best wishes for four happy and most successful years." (November 18, 1932)

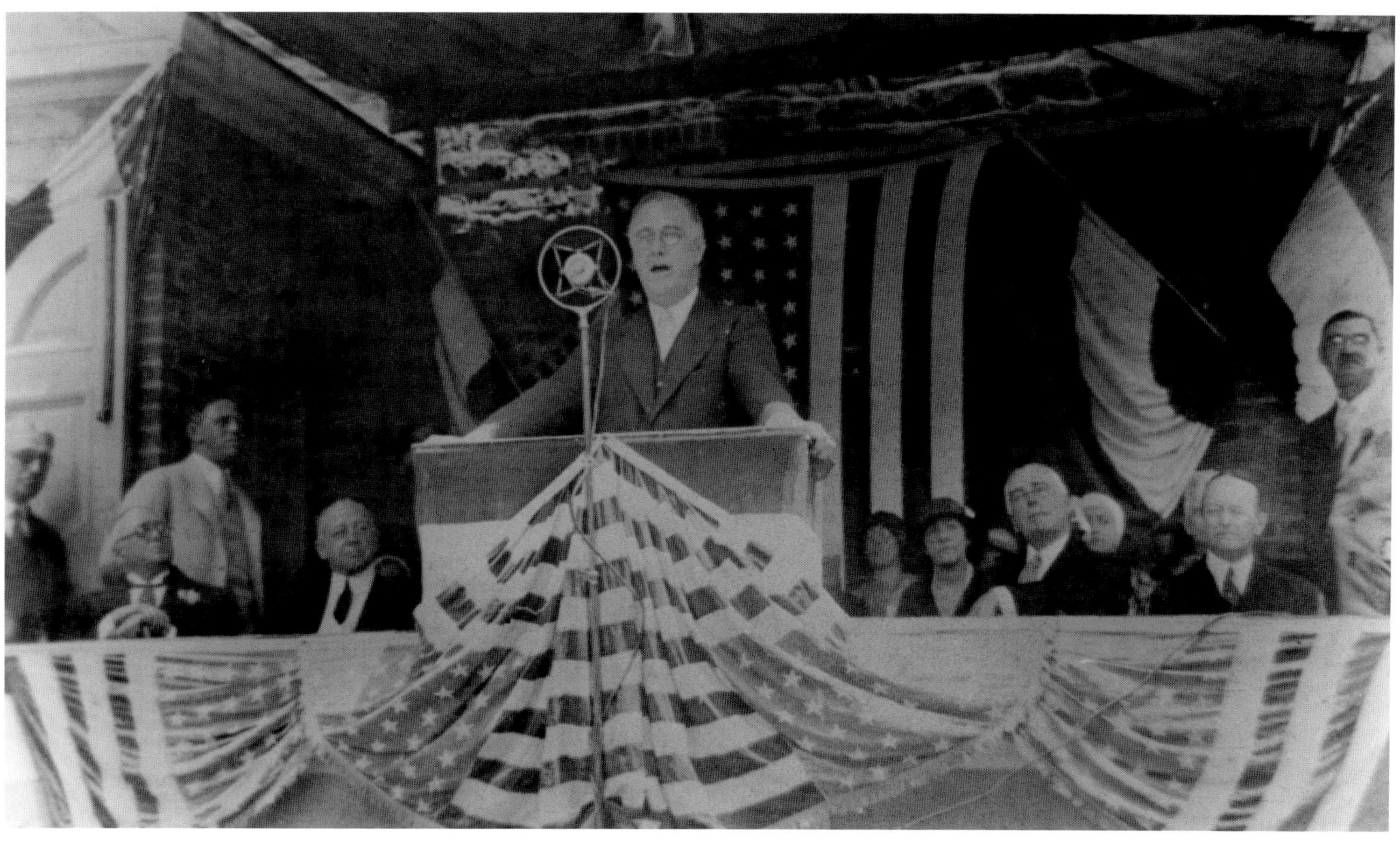

FDR speaking on the campaign trail. Despite the difficulties, he would always speak standing up, not from his wheelchair. (1932)

FDR at work in Albany. This photograph shows him without his leg braces. (1932)

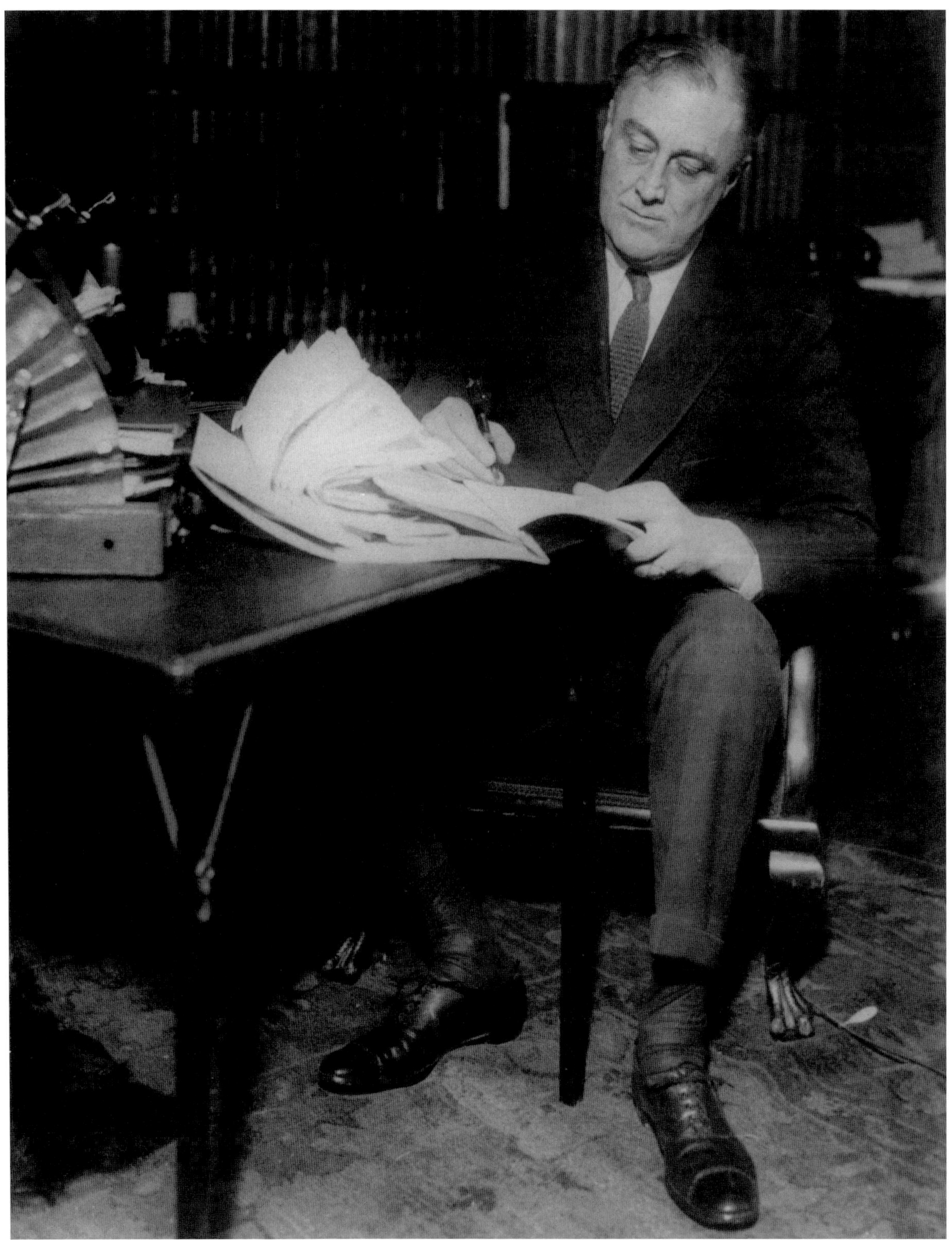

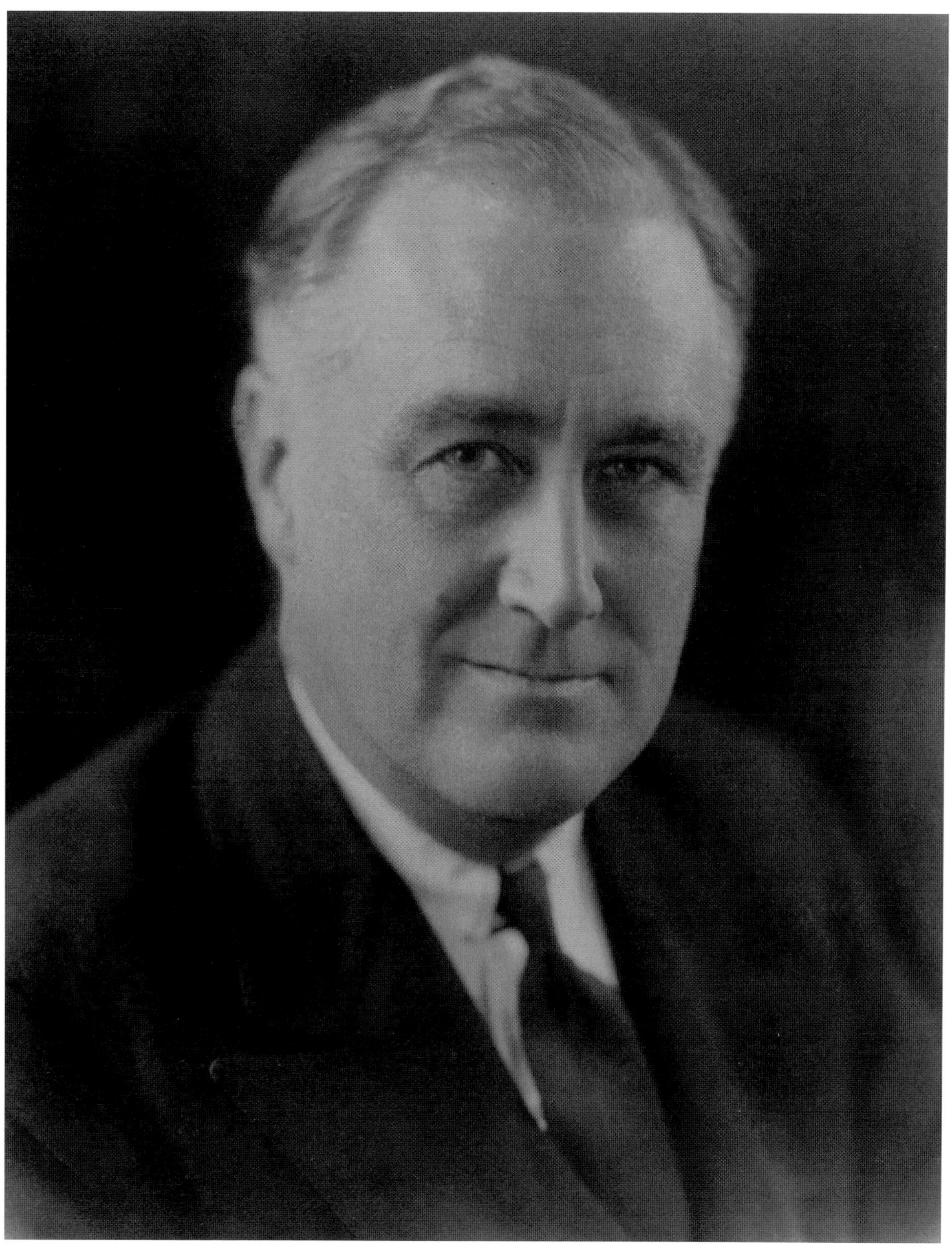

Official portrait of the new president. FDR has left off his glasses to make clear and serious eye-contact with the camera and the viewer. His smile exudes a sober confidence—if broader, it might have seemed too casual for the daunting tasks facing the new President. This is one of the first of many such portraits of FDR, but probably the most engaging. (1933)

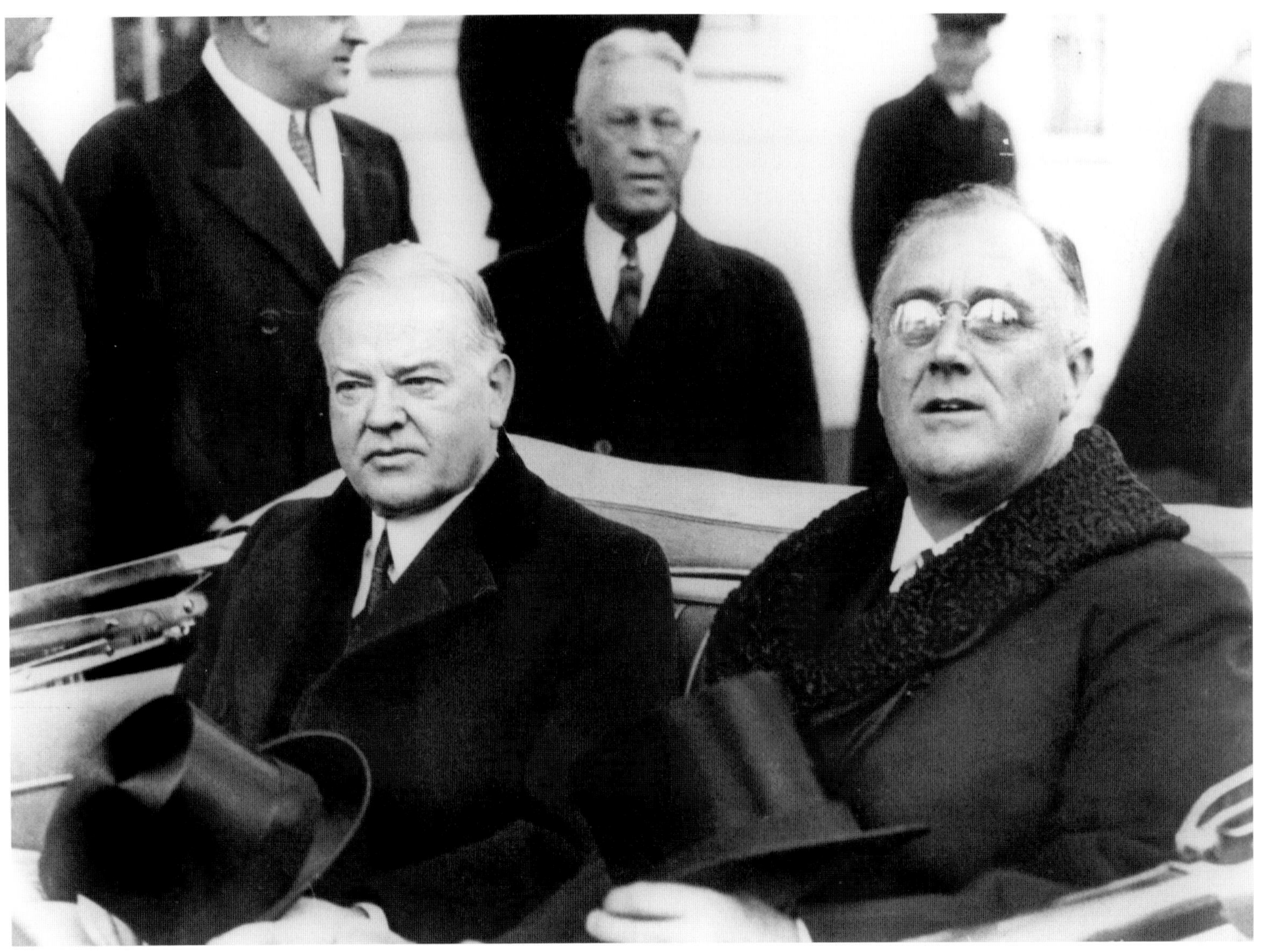

FDR and outgoing President Hoover on inauguration day, March 4, 1933. Hoover and FDR had a long history, even friendship, both having served in the Wilson administration back in 1917. Roosevelt even proposed drafting Hoover in 1920, perhaps with the prospect of a Hoover-Roosevelt ticket, but Hoover made it clear he was Republican. Here in 1933, Hoover was unhappy with FDR. In the four months between the November election and the March inauguration, Hoover had tried unsuccessfully to co-opt FDR and his political and economic program. Instead, FDR left Hoover in the dark, not revealing any of his plans until the explosion of new programs in the First Hundred Days. (March 4, 1933)

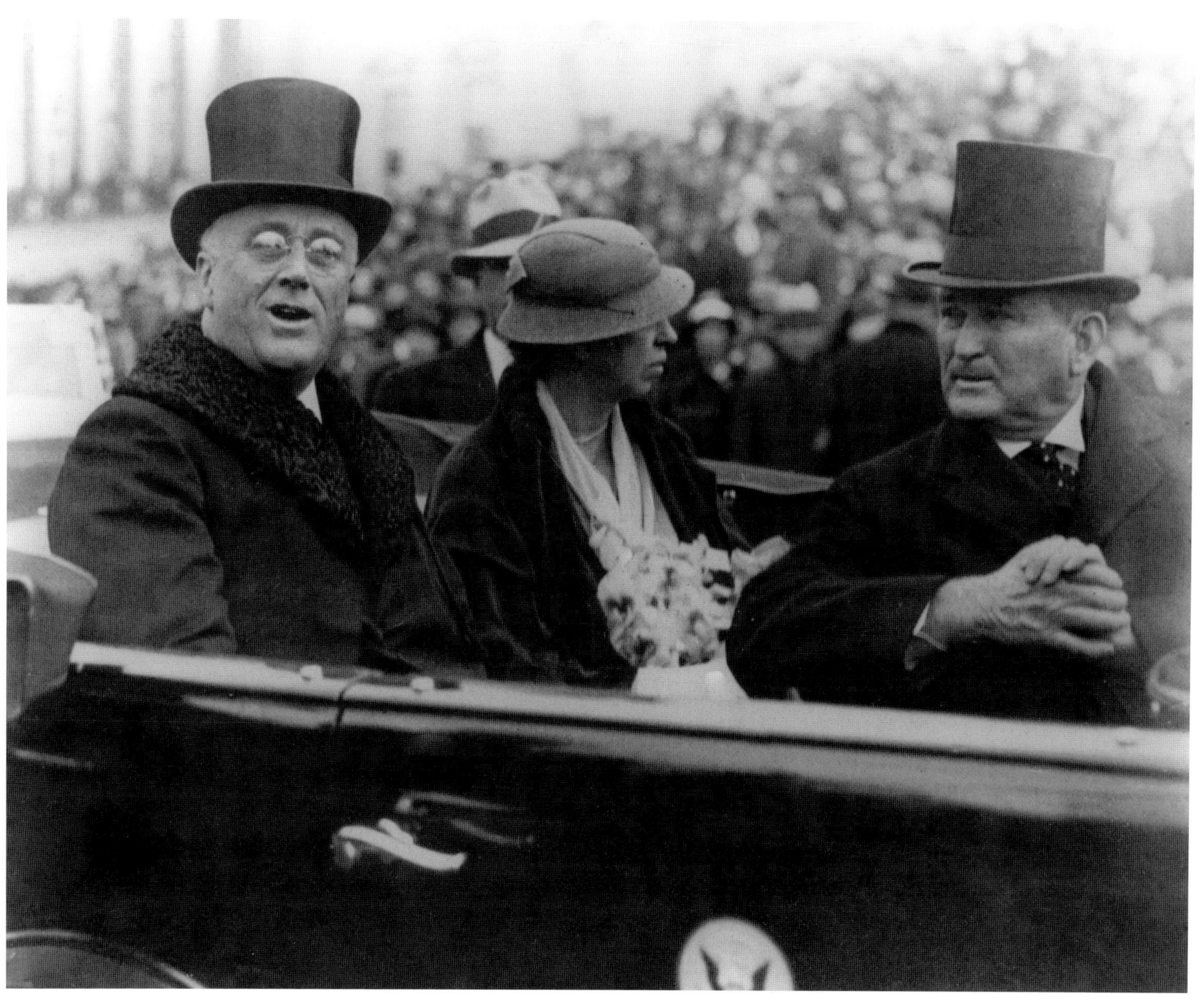

FDR, Eleanor, and the new Senate Majority Leader, Joseph Robinson, at FDR's inauguration as President of the United States. They are riding back from the Capitol to the White House. (March 4, 1933)

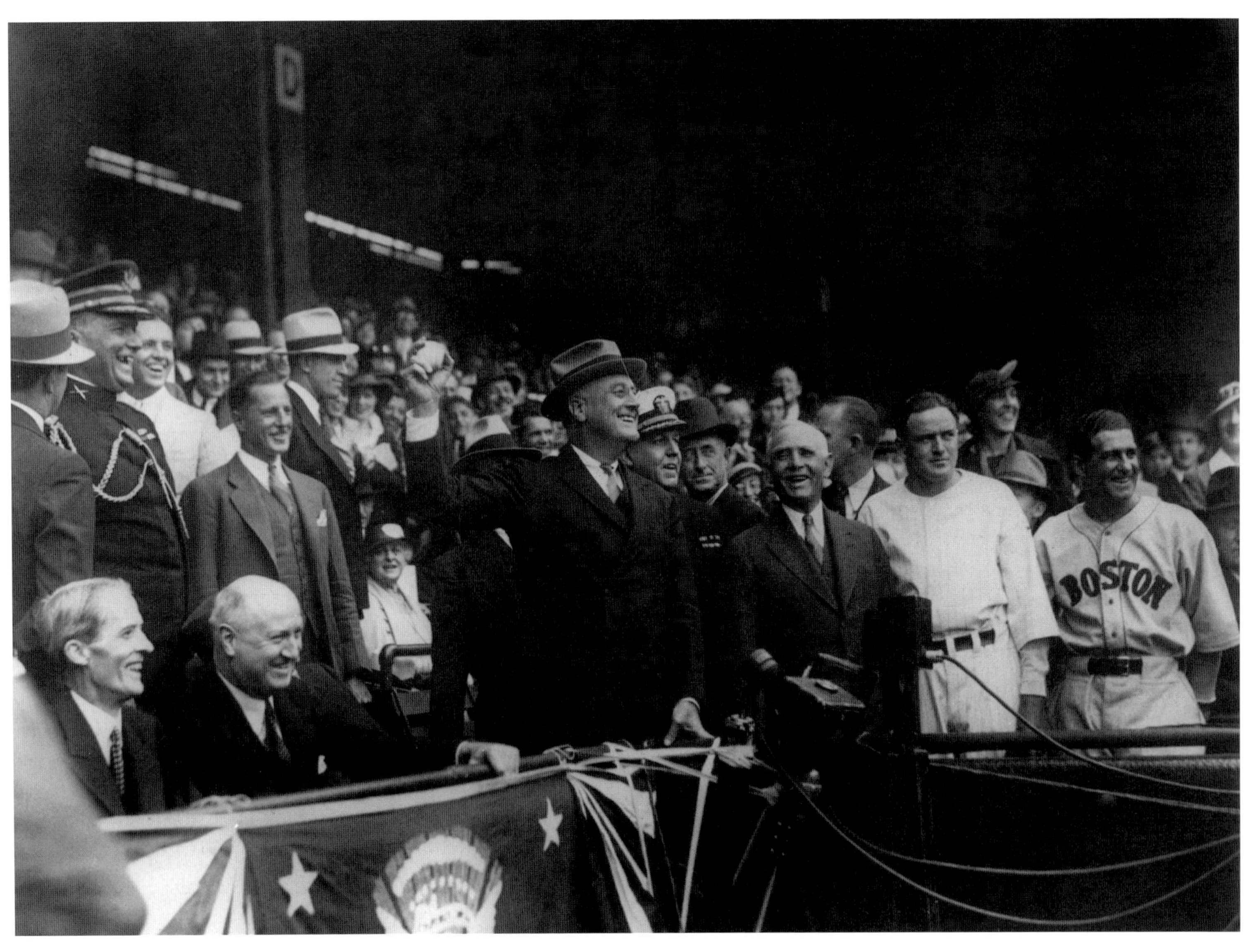

FDR throwing out the first ball at the Washington Nationals versus Boston Red Sox game at Griffith Stadium. He threw out more ceremonial pitches than any other president, every April from 1933 through 1941 (except 1939). The Nationals' record was split: of the games for which FDR threw the first pitch, they won four, lost four. (April 24, 1934)

The newly inaugurated President and First Lady Eleanor Roosevelt at home in the White House. It would be his official home for the rest of his life, yet his wanderlust and sea-loving nature would take him virtually around the world—to five of the seven continents and many countries. (1933)

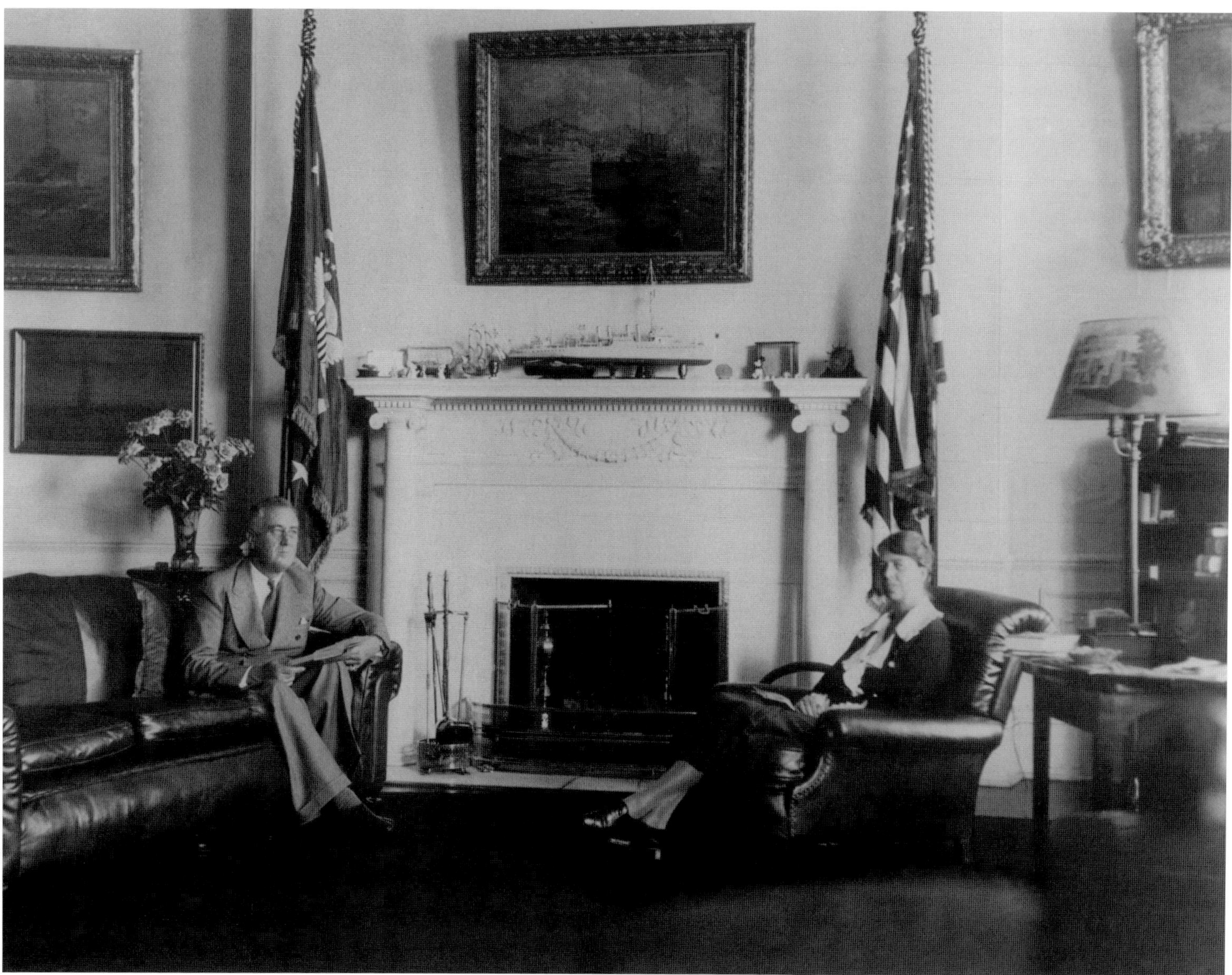

FDR poses with his mother, Sara Delano Roosevelt, at home in Hyde Park. Even before he took office, FDR declared that Krum Elbow, Hyde Park, his birthplace, would be his summer White House (it turned out that he retreated to Warm Springs more often). (1933)

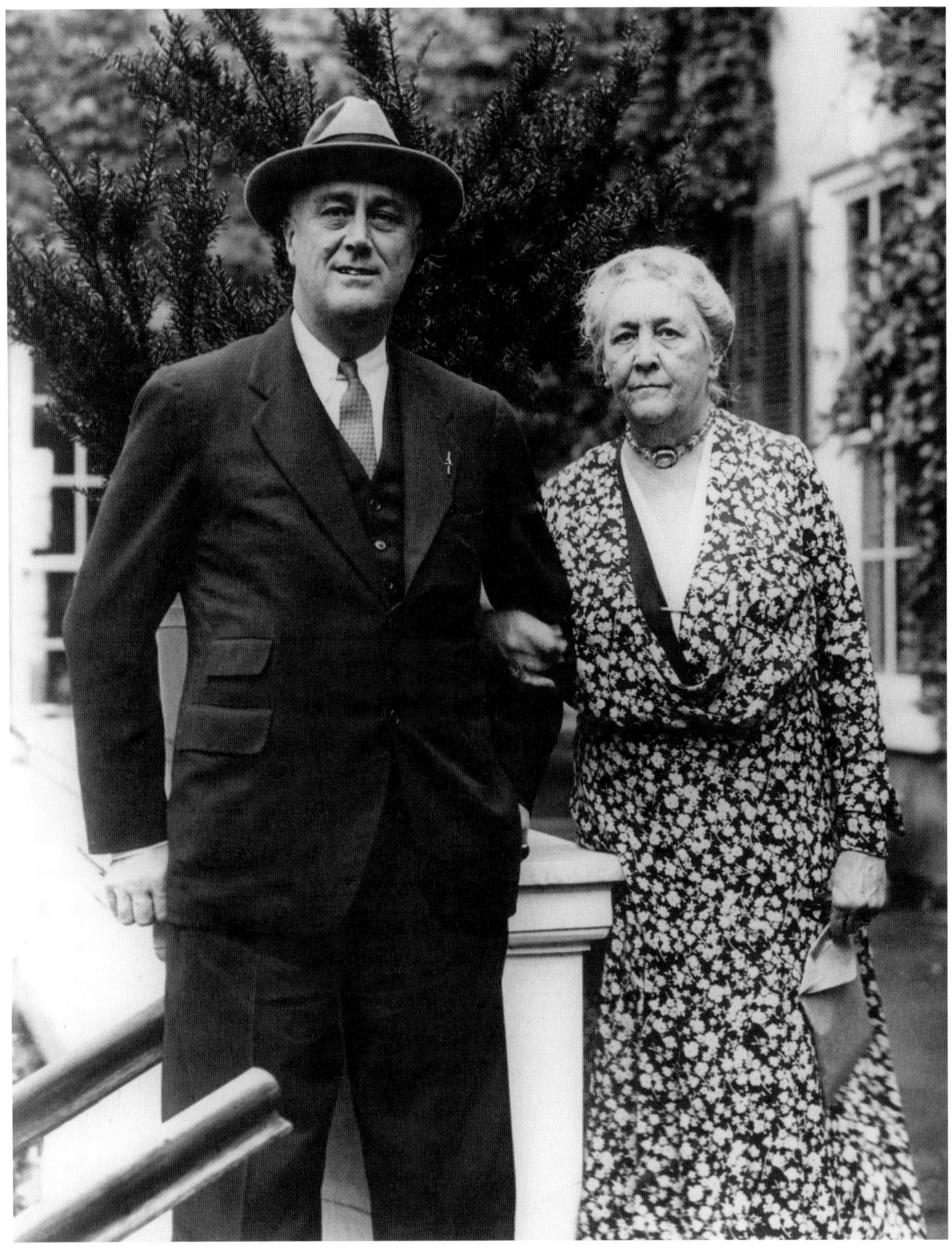

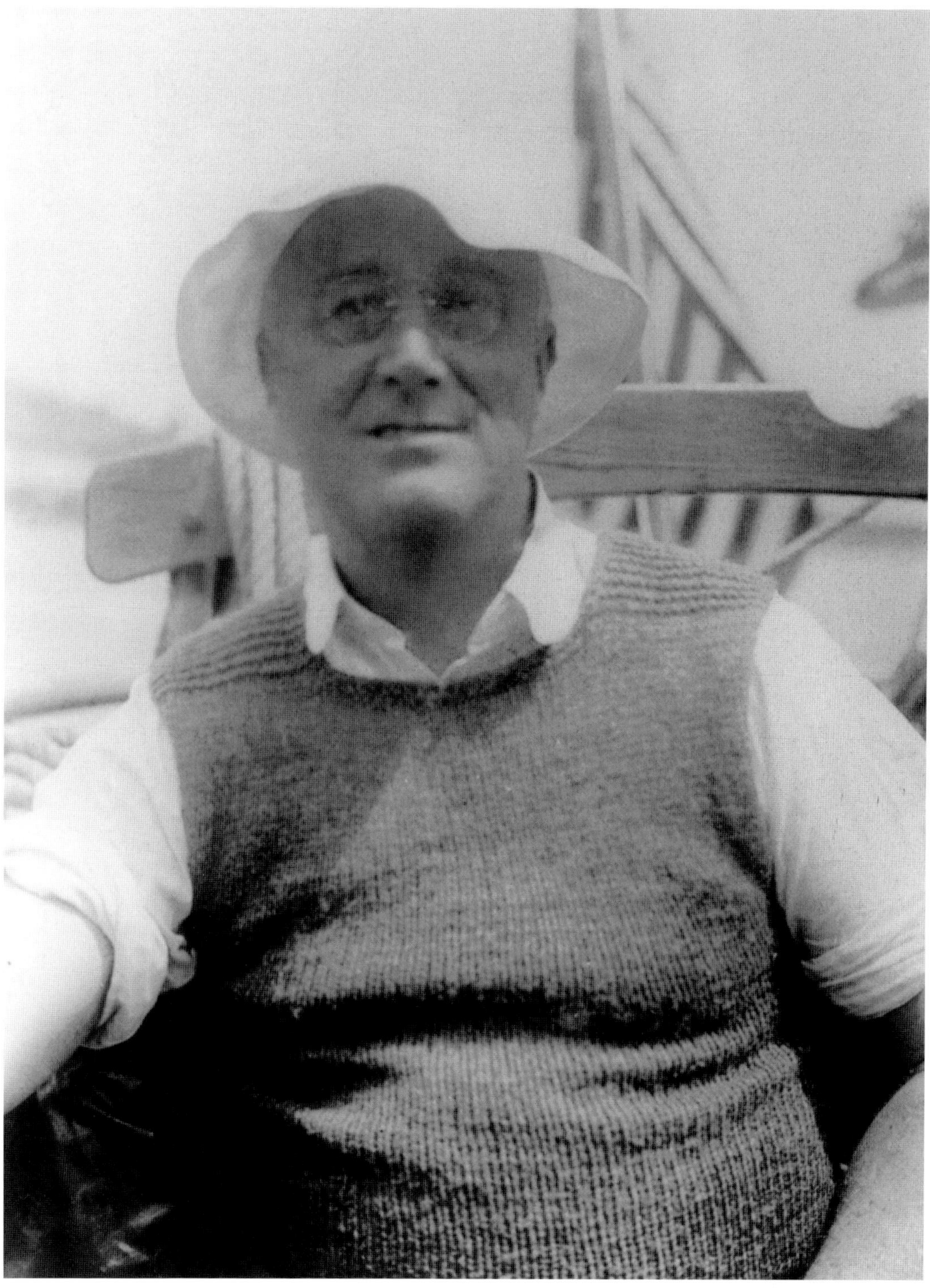

A candid portrait of FDR on vacation, sailing *Amberjack II* to Campobello. At the end of the hectic first hundred days of his administration, in June of 1933 FDR sailed the seas from Nantucket to Campobello. While vacationing, FDR kept in touch. Colonel House and Budget Director Douglas discussed pension cuts. Norman Davis stopped through on the way back from the Geneva Arms Conference. And in between business meetings, the president took time to show off the yacht to his granddaughter Sara Delano Roosevelt. (June 16, 1933)

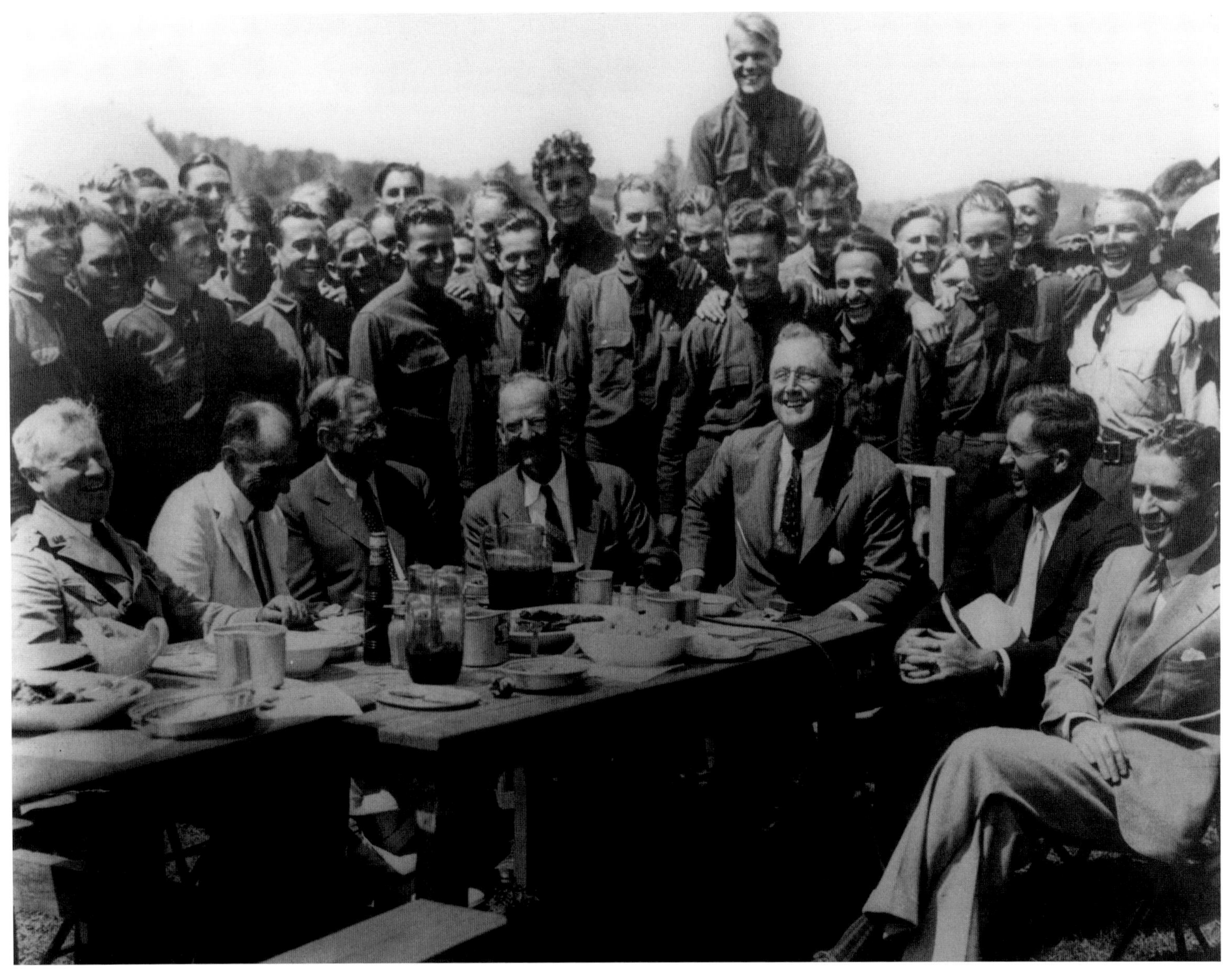

FDR amid his advisors General Paul B. Malone; Col. Louis Howe; Secretary Ickes of the Interior Department; Robert Fechner, Director of the Civilian Conservation Corps; Agriculture Secretary Henry Wallace, and Assistant Secretary of Agriculture Rexford Tugwell, in the Shenandoah Valley, Virginia, at the CCC camp, at Big Meadows, Skyland Drive. FDR remarked: "I wish I could spend a couple of months here myself. The only difference between us is that I am told you men have put on an average of twelve pounds each. I am trying to lose twelve pounds.

"It is very good to be able to visit these Virginia Civilian Conservation Corps camps. I hope that they are as inspiring all over the country as these I have seen today.

"More important, I have seen the boys themselves, and all you have to do is to look at the boys themselves to see that the camps themselves are a success." (August 12, 1933)

FDR, Eleanor Roosevelt, Sara Delano Roosevelt, and son James and his wife on the battleship USS *Indianapolis.* The *Indianapolis* acted as the platform for the president as he reviewed the Battle Fleet off New York City. FDR had an abiding interest in all things maritime; it was his uncle, President Theodore Roosevelt, who started the presidential naval review tradition in 1903. (May 31, 1934)

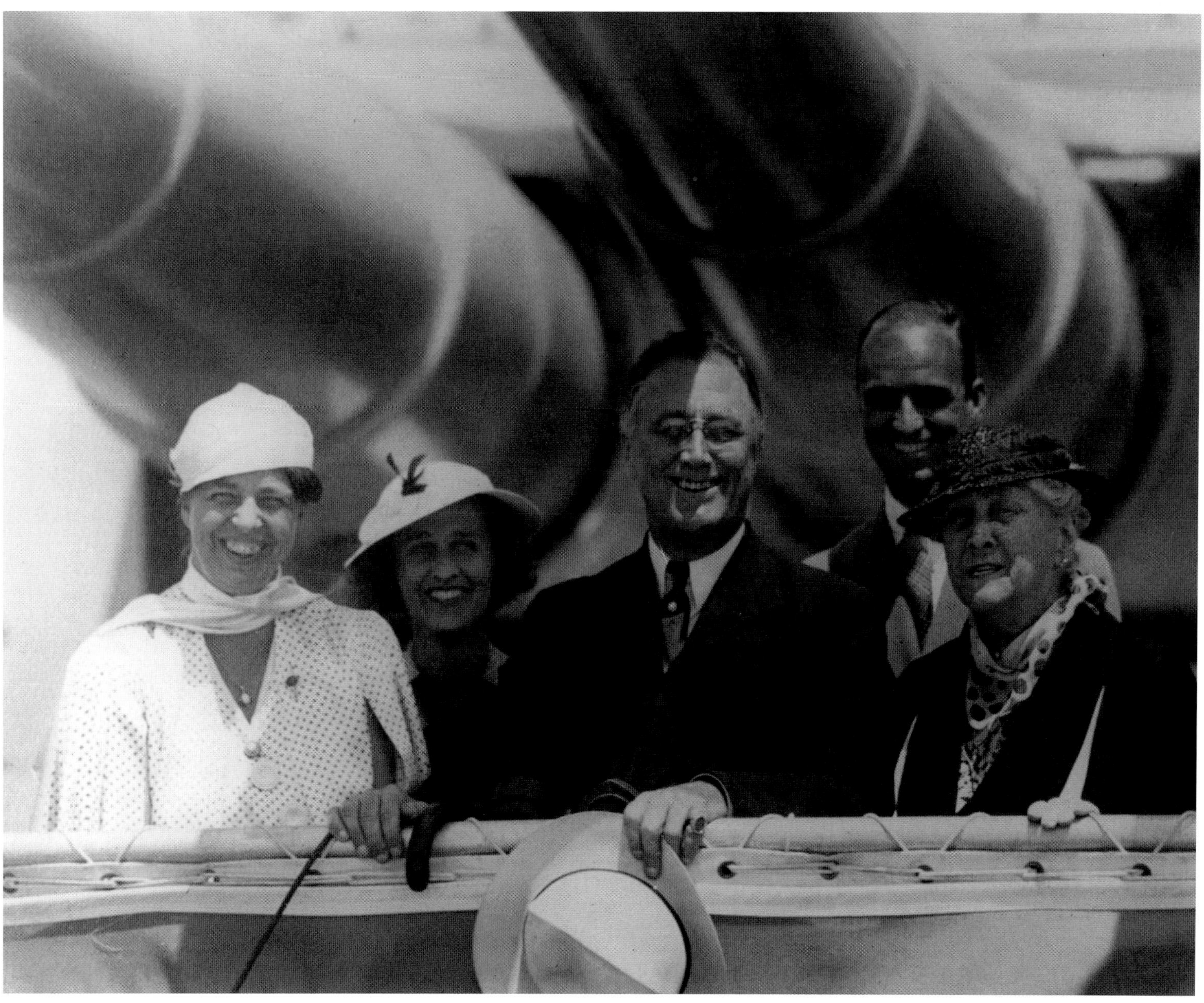

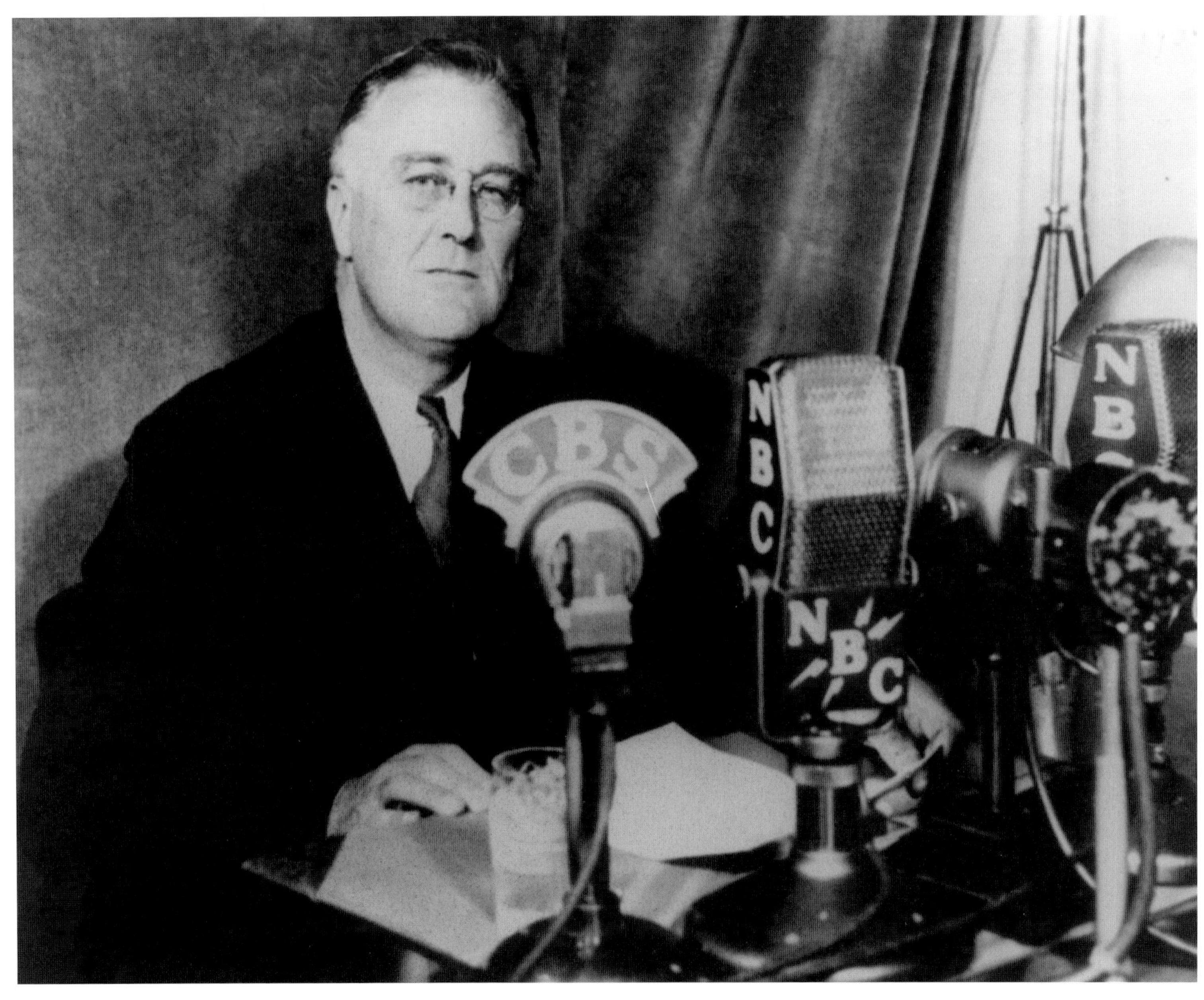

Preparing to address the nation on radio, FDR looks resolute and determined, set to convey confidence, in a fireside chat. This chat, his sixth, was entitled "On Moving Forward to Greater Freedom and Greater Security." FDR had devised this method of direct appeal to citizens as governor of New York. (September 30, 1934)

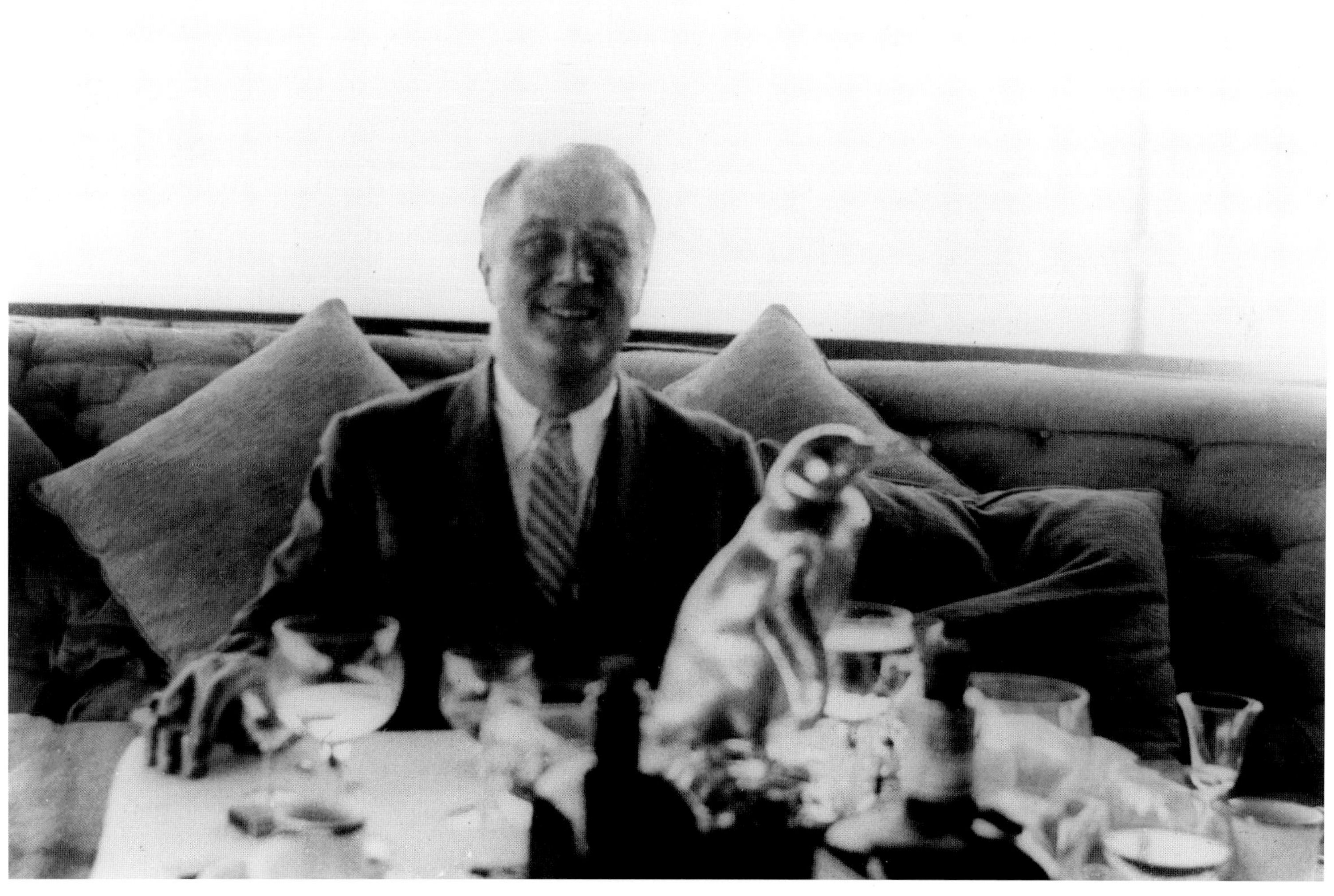

FDR on William Vincent Astor's yacht, *Nourmahal.* FDR had first visited *Nourmahal* after a failed assassination attempt in 1933 that took the life of Chicago mayor Anton Cermak. He returned yearly. "This is the only place I can get away from people, telephones and uniforms," Roosevelt wrote, yet on this trip he met the Duke and Duchess of Kent. Built by the Krup ironworks in 1928, the yacht itself was transferred to Navy then Coast Guard duty, and scrapped in 1964. Astor, a Hudson Valley neighbor, was an intimate of FDR's and also served in espionage activities. (March 27, 1935)

Eleanor and son John on horseback. Life in Hyde Park was idyllic. A cousin remarked: "We were very active, riding horses, swimming, playing games. But we, as well as my cousin John's children [who lived in Hyde Park], had to work for two to three hours a day, mowing, baling hay, splitting wood, filling fireplaces. I loved it." John, the Roosevelts' youngest child, grew up much closer to his mother than to his father. This did not prevent a break in later years when he switched his political affiliation so that he might support Eisenhower's presidential bid. (1935)

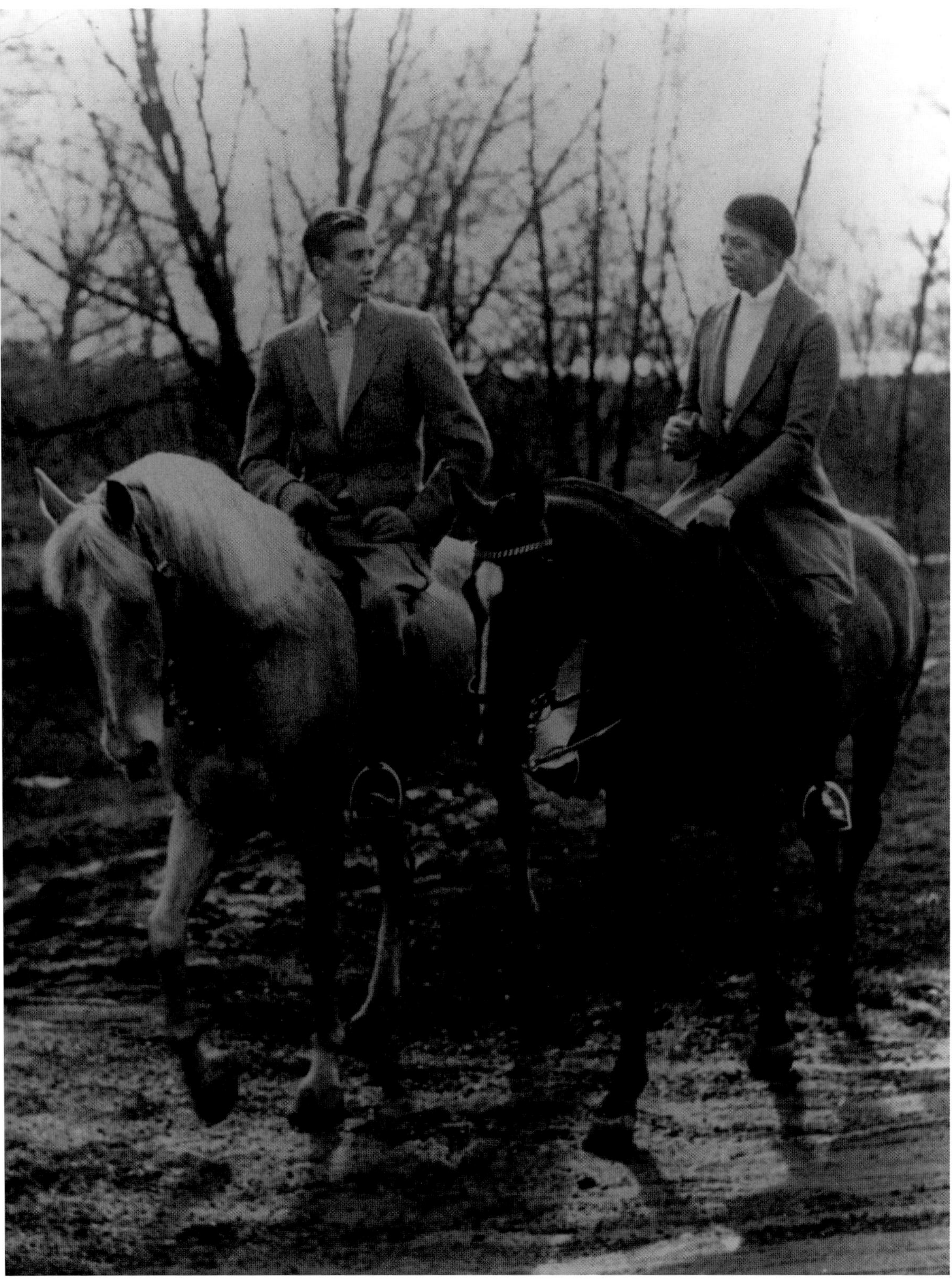

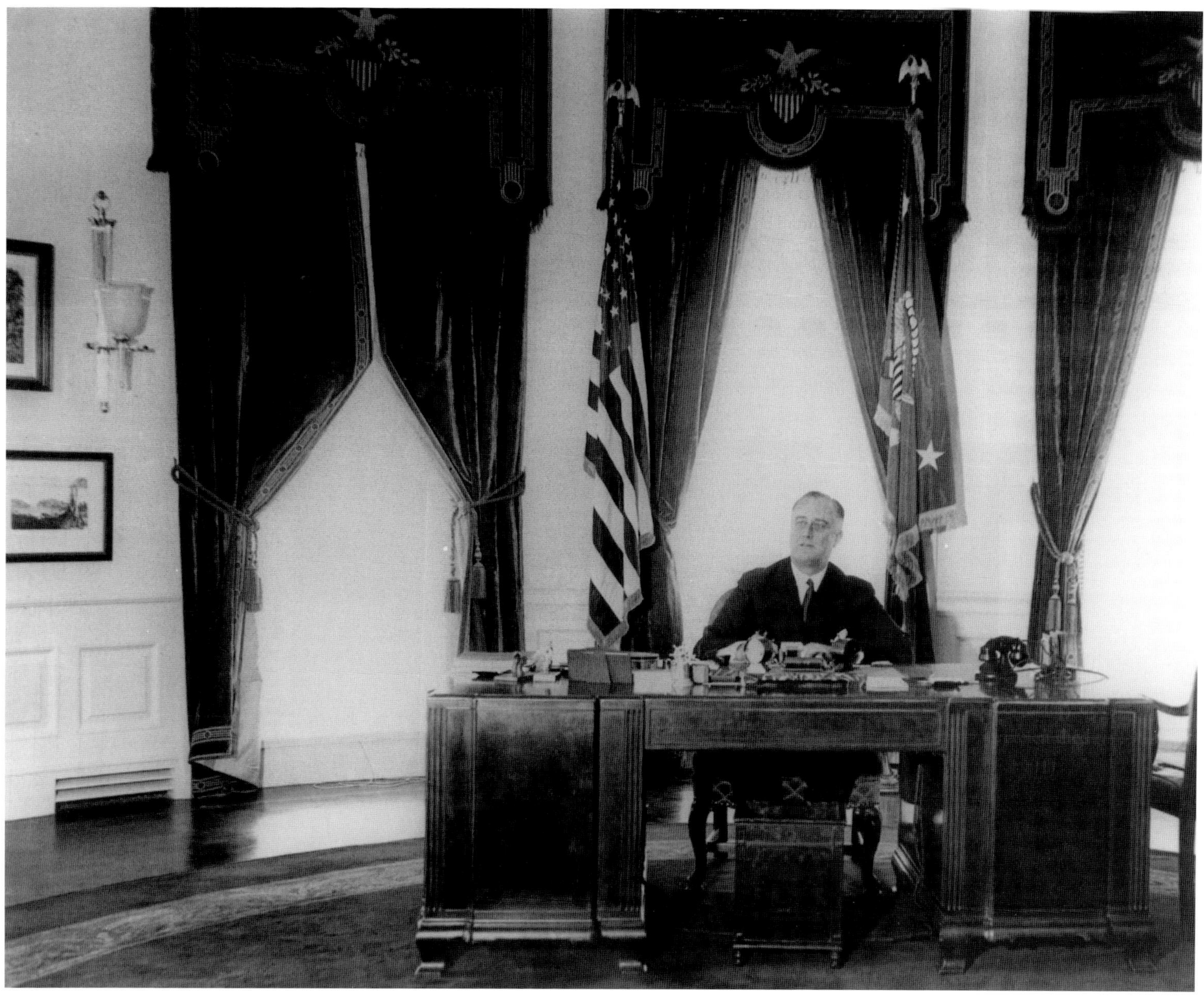

FDR in the Oval Office. His desk is not so cluttered as it had been in Albany, and his legs are carefully concealed. (1935)

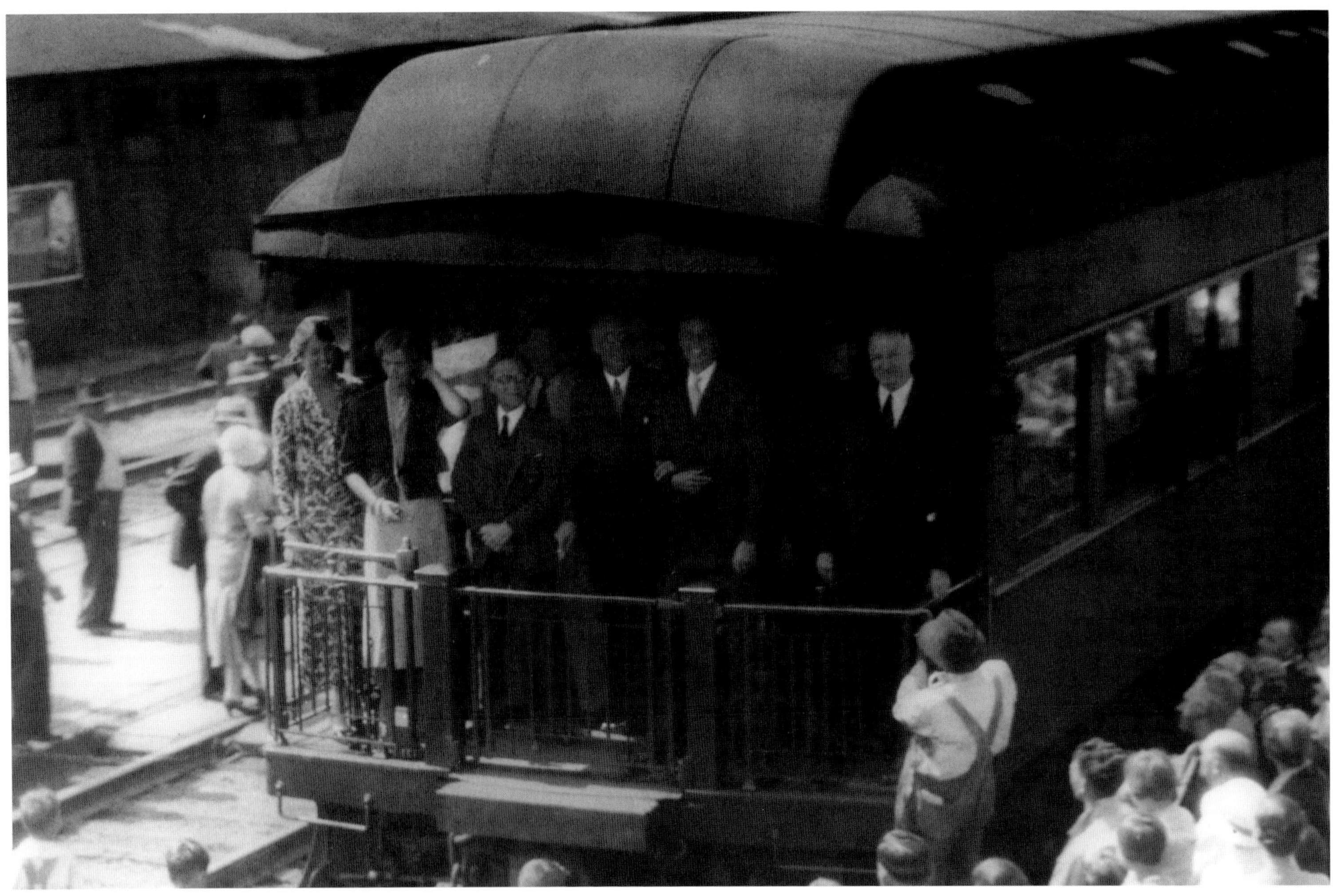

Franklin barnstorming with Eleanor, Anna, James, James Farley, and Newton D. Baker in Galion, Ohio. Farley had managed Franklin's successful campaigns for governor. Roosevelt's speech went: "My friends, I am glad to come back through Galion. I have been here many times before. I am particularly glad to see, by the expression on your faces, that you are much more cheerful than you were in 1932.

"You know, while I am theoretically a lawyer, I am also a bit of a farmer. I farm in two places, one on the Hudson River and the other down in Georgia. That is why I know something about farm prices. One reason why I think you here are more cheerful is because corn is selling at better than ten or fifteen cents a bushel and because hogs and cattle are selling at better than three or four cents a pound. . . .

"I know from personal experience that people in the cotton belt in this country cannot buy the foodstuffs produced in the North if they have to sell their cotton for four or five cents a pound. In the same way, you people cannot buy overalls made of southern cotton when you get only ten or fifteen cents a bushel for your corn.

"I have always been particularly interested in the fact that this part of Ohio has gone in for diversification in farming. The more that we can diversify our farming all through the country and not have to depend entirely on one crop, the better it will be for the Nation as a whole. In that respect, you are setting a perfectly fine example for the farmers in the State of New York and for the farmers out West and for the farmers down South.

"I am mighty glad to see you and I want to thank you on behalf of Mrs. Roosevelt for the flowers. They are perfectly beautiful, and there has not been a sunflower aboard the train yet." (October 16, 1936)

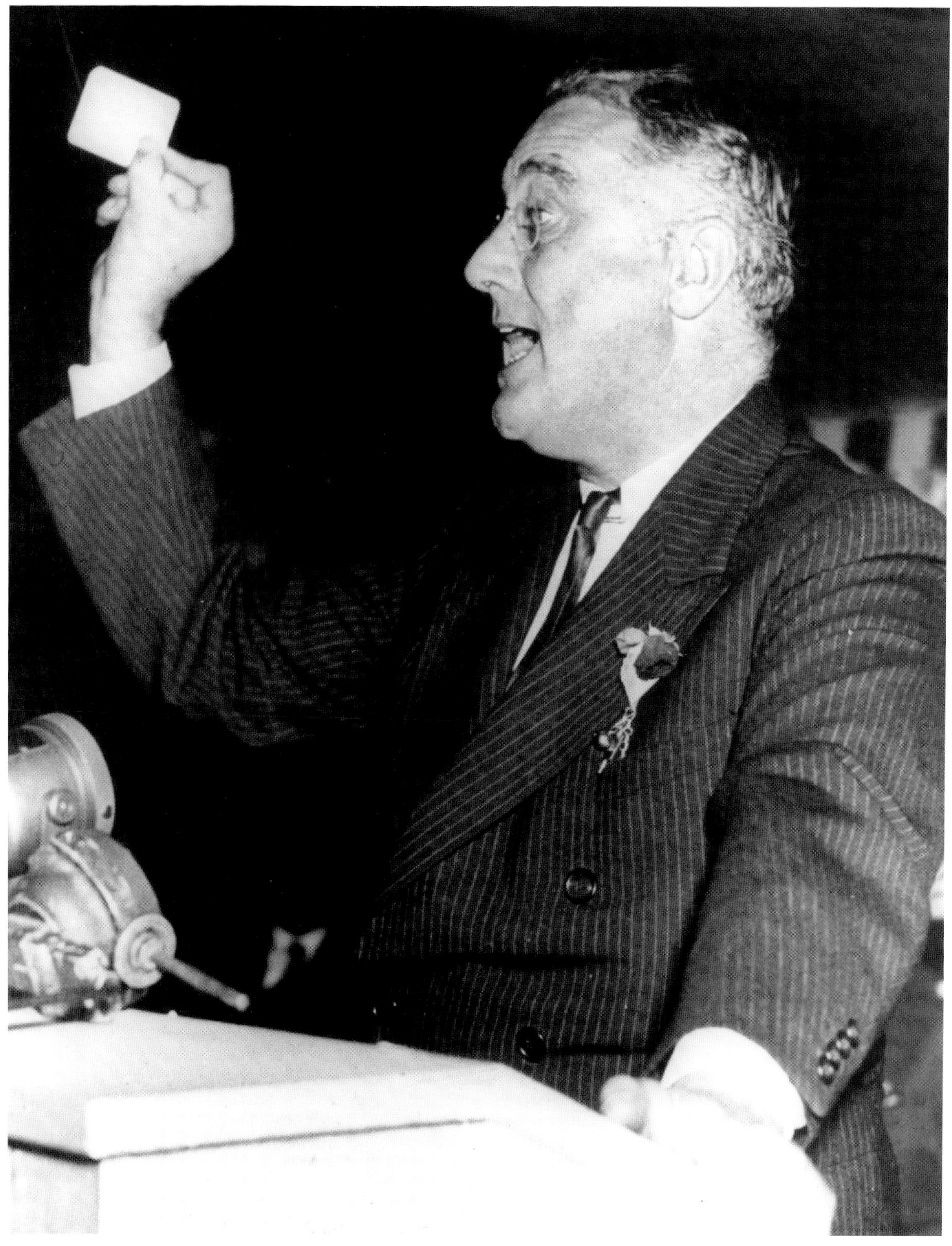

FDR at the ground-breaking ceremonies of the Queens Midtown Tunnel, New York City (38th St.), gesturing with a card. He remarked, "This card is a very essential part of this ceremony. Without it, they would not start that shovel working. . . . I am very proud of what has been done. I am proud of the privilege that we have had in Washington in helping the City of New York to start and complete a large number of very important public works, public works that will be useful, public works that are giving employment to thousands of men and women. I also want to say that these public works which have been initiated would not have been possible had it not been for an intelligent and aggressive Administration in the City of New York." (October 2, 1936)

The results of FDR's fishing exploits off Cocos Island in the Pacific. Sailing on board the USS *Houston,* during his three days at Cocos the President caught a 110-pound sailfish. Controversy followed Franklin even here—pirates had reputedly buried their treasure in the area, and Costa Rica and the British were disputing rights to recover it. (October 9, 1935)

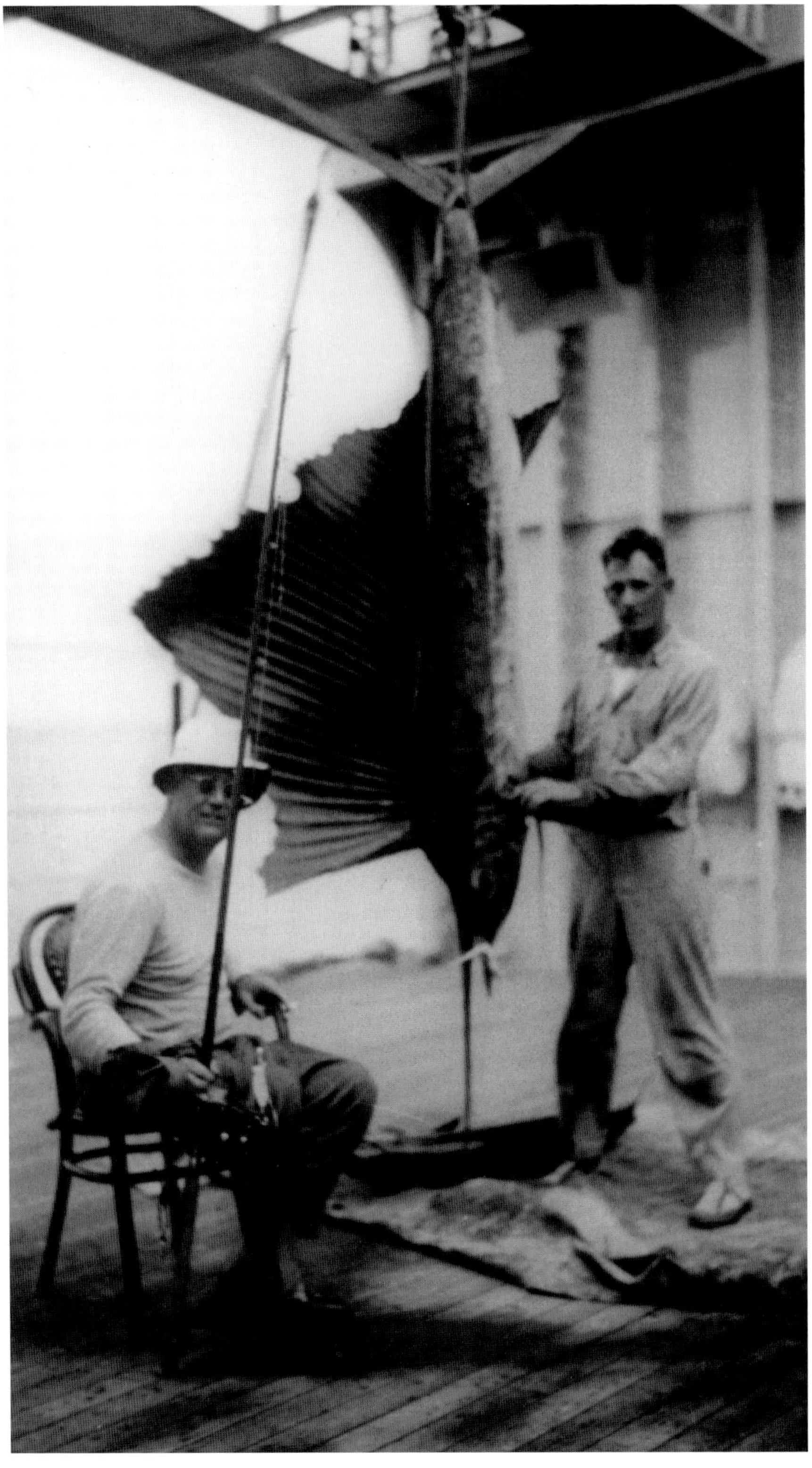

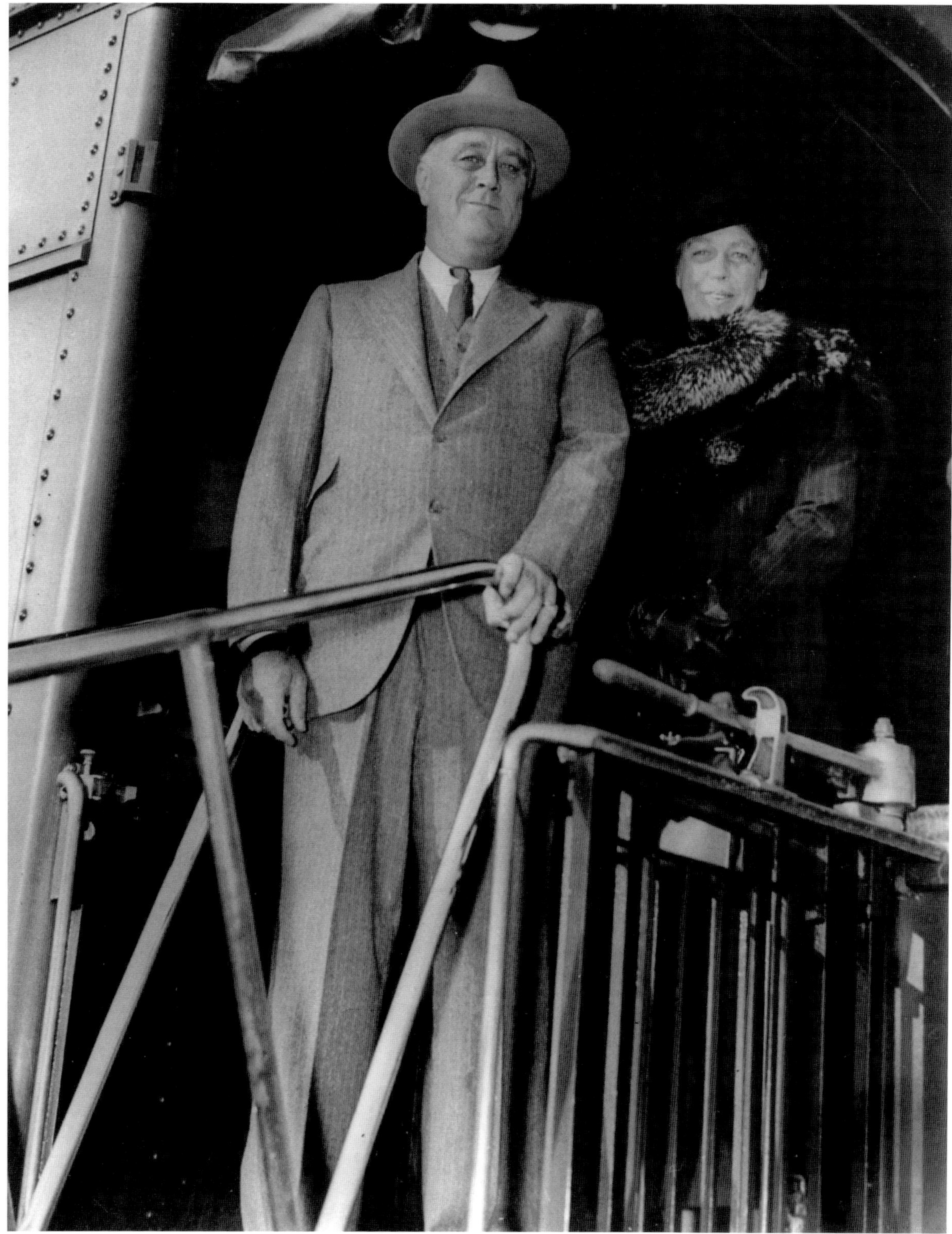

FDR and Eleanor en route to Washington. They had returned to Hyde Park to vote in the mid-term Congressional elections. Relations with Canada were being mended and a treaty would be signed in a few days ending the futile trade war then raging between the two nations. (November 8, 1935)

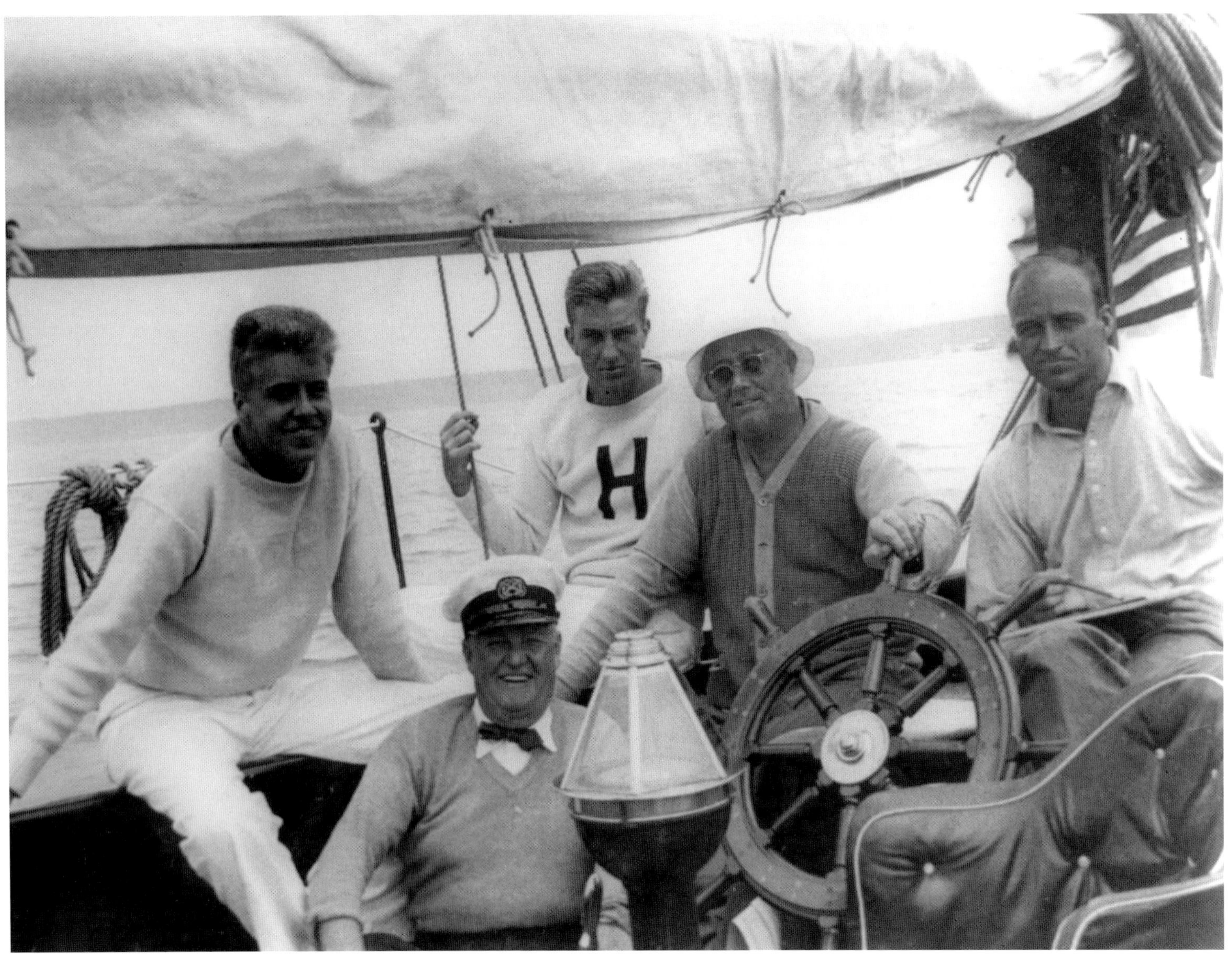

FDR and sons John, James (a Marine Lieutenant Colonel), and Franklin, Jr., on the yacht *Sewanna,* chartered from Harrison Tweed (president of the Legal Aid Society of New York) for John's use that summer. Franklin had been on vacation at his home in Hyde Park, but also delivering speeches to encourage more local interest in government: "Where communities take the greatest interest, in those places the work is most valuable, permanent and satisfactory." (July 14, 1936)

FDR at the helm of the battleship USS *Indianapolis,* on his "Good Neighbors" cruise to South America. Here standing under the eight-inch guns he receives the Argentine navy's salute. (November 29, 1936)

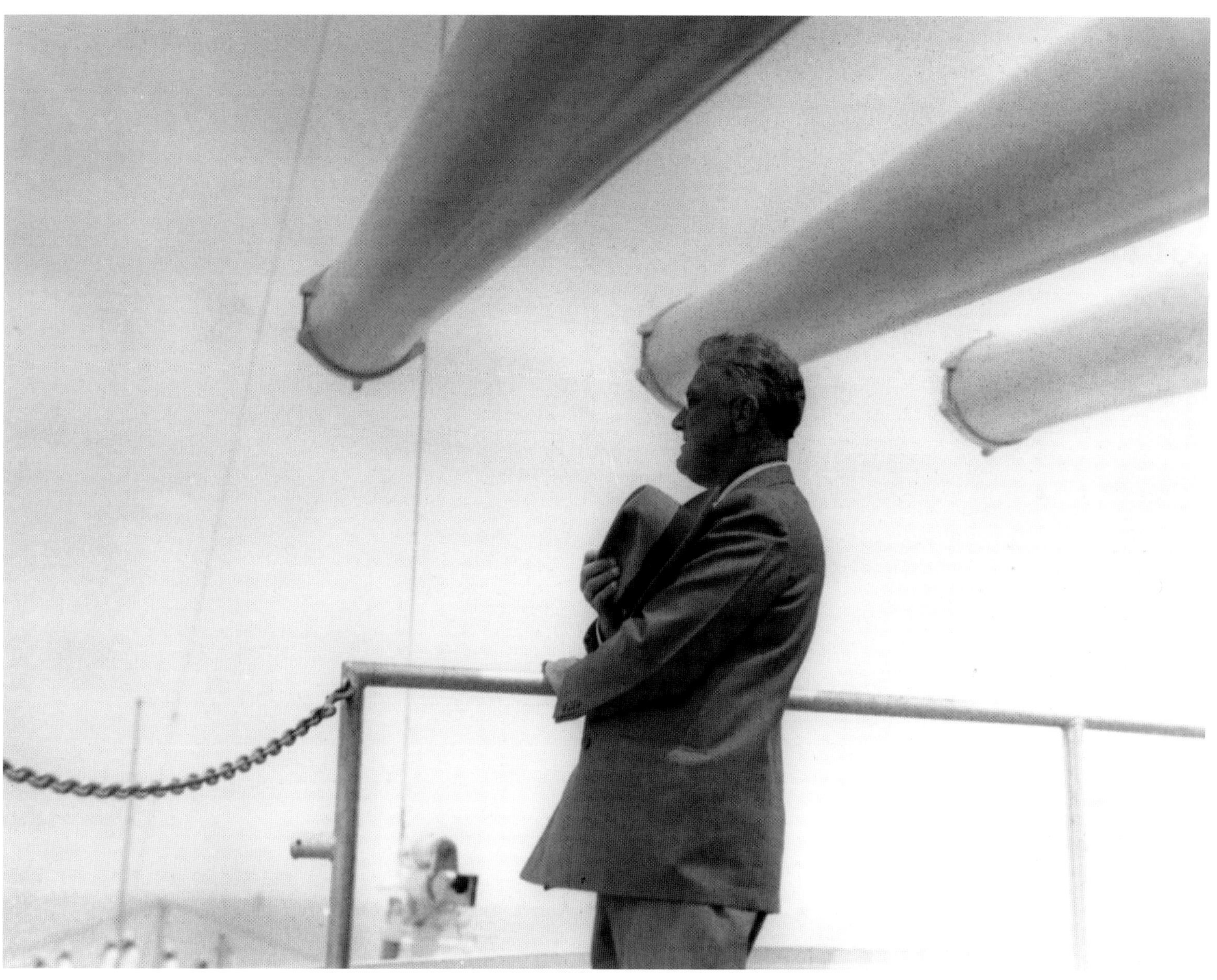

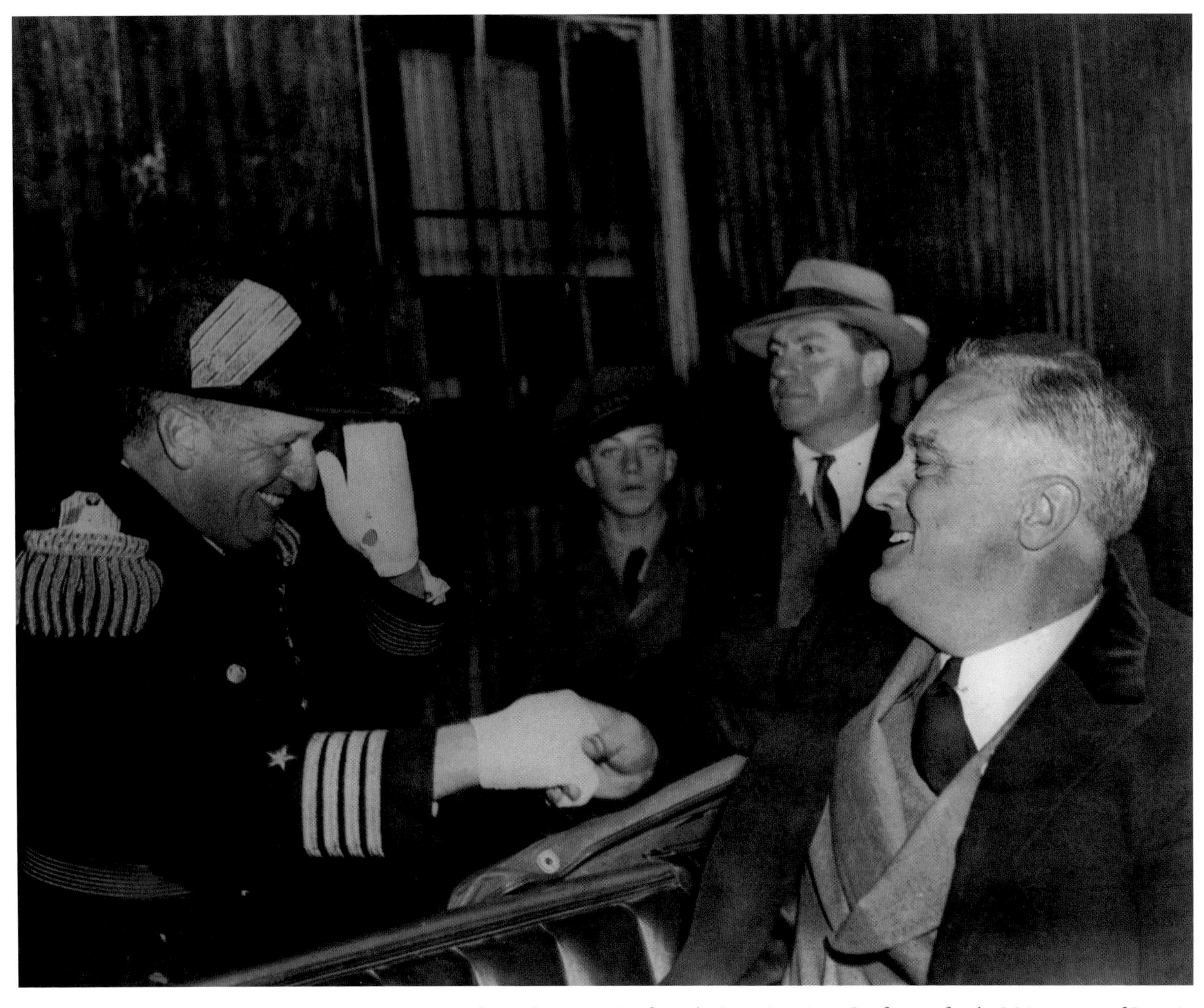

FDR in South Carolina returning from the Inter-American Conference for the Maintenance of Peace in Buenos Aires: “Good neighbors we are; good neighbors we shall remain.” It had been a triumphant year for Franklin with his re-election and a positive reception in South America. (December 15, 1936)

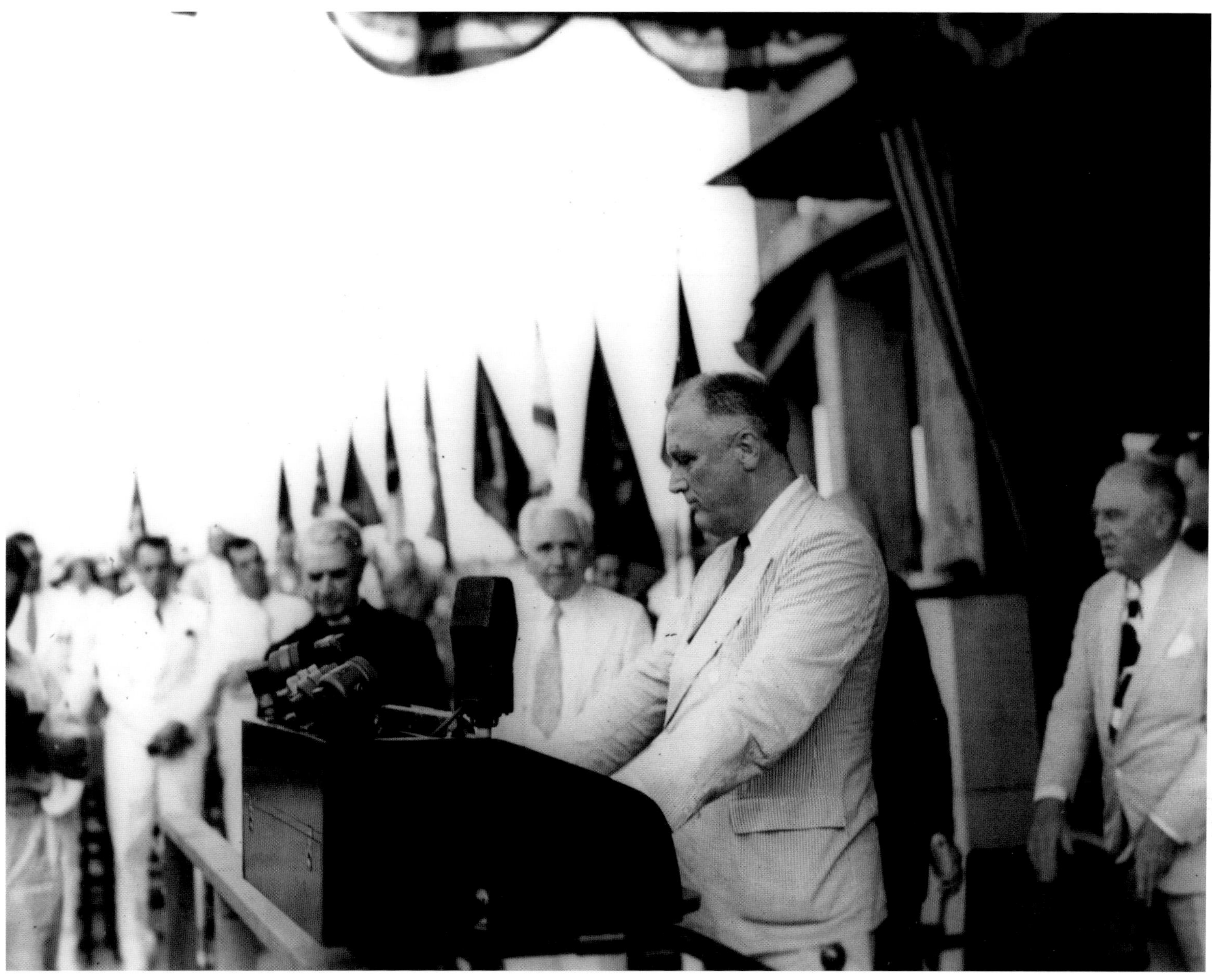

FDR laying cornerstone of the Federal Trade Commission (FTC) building, Washington, D.C. "The erection of this splendid home for the Federal Trade Commission completes the architectural unit facing on Constitution Avenue.

"Furthermore, it carries forward the plan of housing eventually in Government owned buildings all of the Departments and Agencies of the Federal Government in the District of Columbia. . . . Dictates of economy and good business sense call for a continuation of the erection of Federal buildings in order, over a comparatively short period of years, to save the taxpayers' money.

"May this permanent home of the Federal Trade Commission stand for all time as a symbol of the purpose of the Government to insist on a greater application of the Golden Rule to the conduct of corporations and business enterprises in their relationship to the body politic." (July 12, 1937)

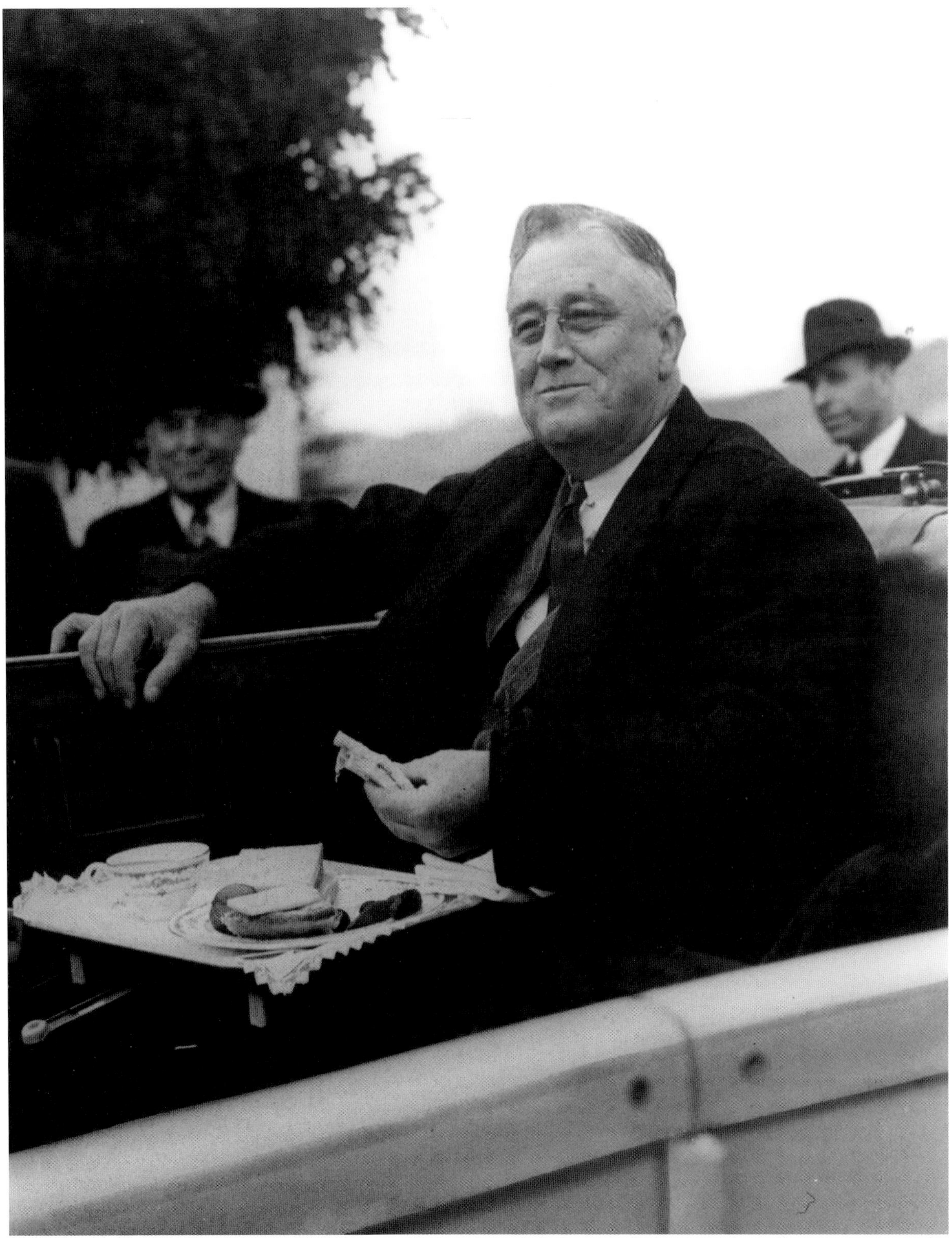

FDR at the Grand Coulee Dam in Washington. "It is a great project—something that appeals to the imagination of the whole country. There is just one other word that is worth saying from the national point of view. We think of this as something that is benefiting this part of the country primarily, giving employment to a great many people in this neighborhood. But we must also remember that one half of the total cost of this dam is paid to the factories east of the Mississippi River. In other words, it is putting to work in the steel centers and other great manufacturing centers of the east thousands of people in making the materials that go into the dam. So, in a very correct sense, it is a national undertaking and doing a national good." Franklin had also visited August 3, 1934, when construction of the dam had begun. (October 2, 1937)

FDR shares a laugh with Mayor Williams of Miami, Florida, as he prepares to go on a Caribbean fishing trip. *Time* offered some color coverage of the adventure: "After a call at the Dry Tortugas, where the President stopped to inspect the gloomy ruins of Fort Jefferson, the *Potomac* steamed slowly up the Florida Coast. Disembarking at Miami, the President was tanned and cheerful but admitted that his jaw—still so sore that Dr. McIntire thought it might be necessary to scrape the bone—had interfered with the pleasures of fishing. Prize catch of the last day—a 25-lb. barracuda—had gone to Assistant Attorney General Robert H. Jackson, who, with WPA Administrator Harry Hopkins, Secretary of the Interior Harold Ickes, and Son James Roosevelt had made up the Presidential party." (December 5, 1937)

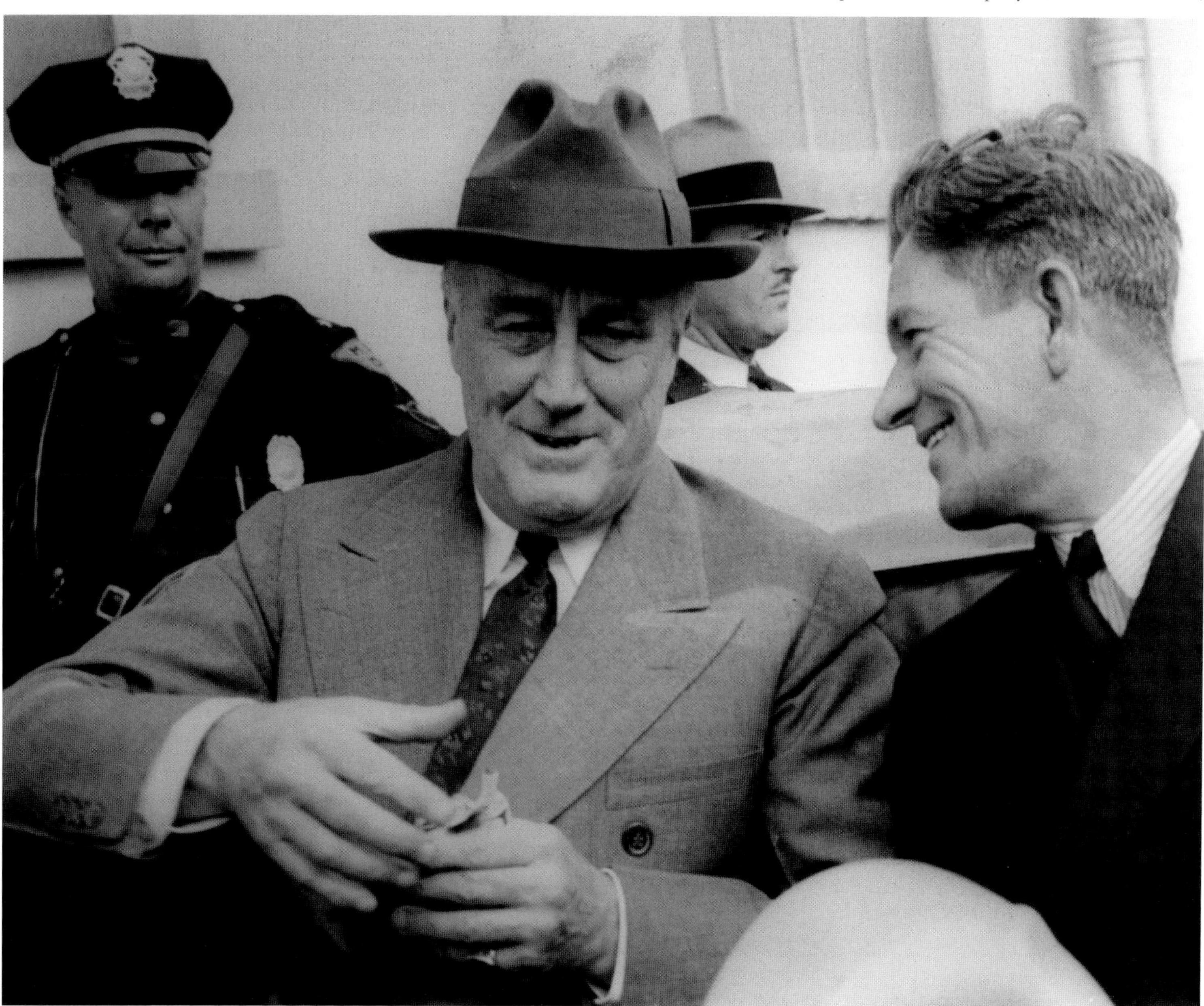

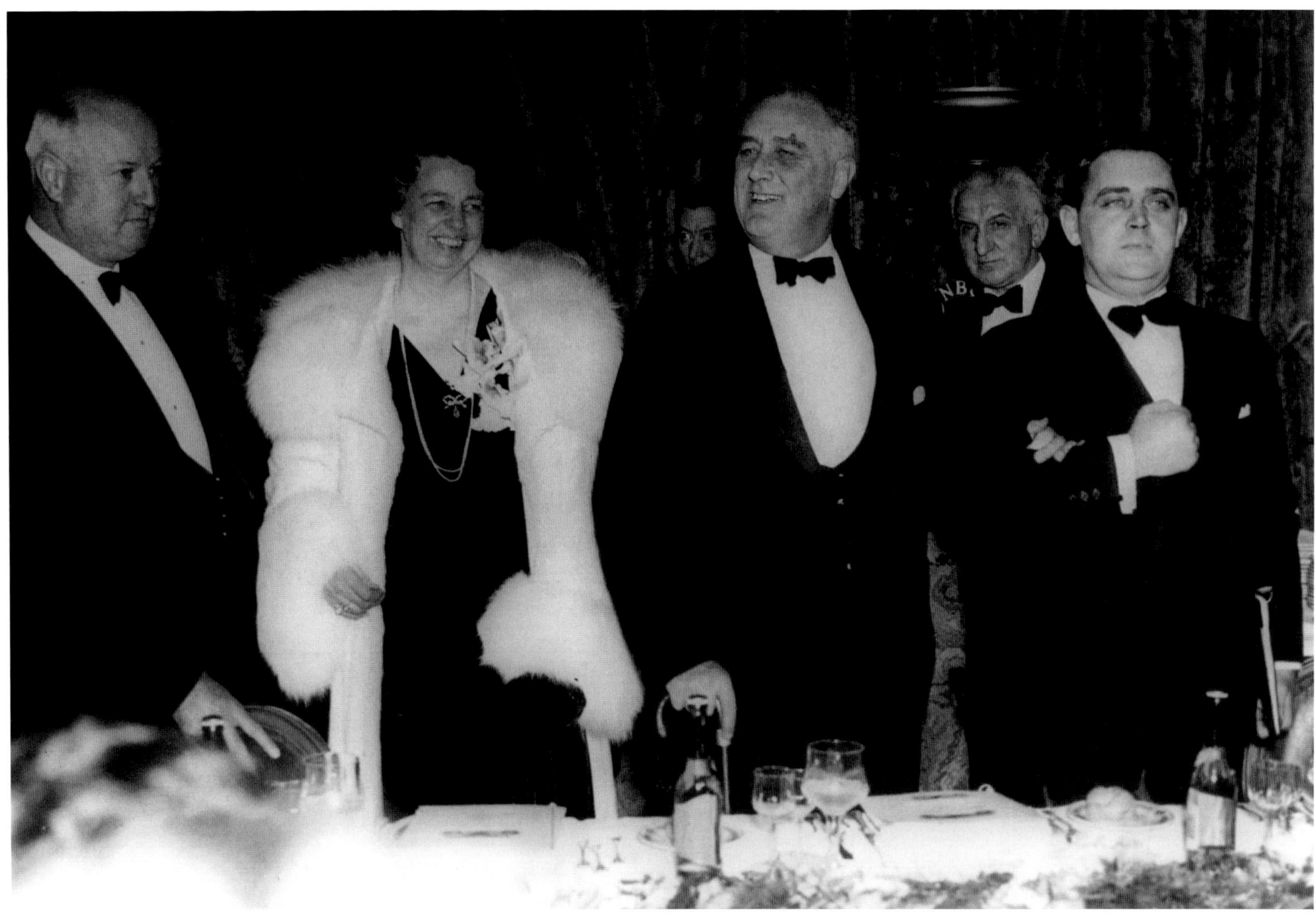

FDR and Eleanor at the Jackson banquet with James Farley and Secret Service Agent Tommy Qualters (an ex–Notre Dame football star). "When speaking before a party gathering in these modern days," said the president, "I am happy to realize that the audience is not confined to active members of my own party, and that there is less of unthinking partisanship in this country today than at any time since the Administration of George Washington.

"In the last campaign, in 1936, a very charming lady wrote me a letter. She said: 'I believe in you and in what you are trying to do for the Nation, I do wish I could vote for you—but you see my parents were Republicans and I was brought up as a Republican and so I have to vote for your opponent.'

"My reply to her ran as follows: 'My father and grandfather were Democrats and I was born and brought up as a Democrat, but in 1904, when I cast my first vote for a President, I voted for the Republican candidate, Theodore Roosevelt, because I thought he was a better Democrat than the Democratic candidate.'

"I have told that story many times, and if I had to do it over again I would not alter that vote.

"On the eighth of every January we honor Andrew Jackson for his unending contribution to the vitality of our democracy. We look back on his amazing personality, we review his battles because the struggles he went through, the enemies he encountered, the defeats he suffered and the victories he won are part and parcel of the struggles, the enmities, the defeats and the victories of those who have lived in all the generations that have followed. . . .

"Once more the head of the Nation is working with all his might and main to restore and to uphold the integrity of the morals of democracy—our heritage from the long line of national leadership from Jefferson to Wilson and preeminently from old Andrew Jackson himself." (January 8, 1938)

FDR and Eleanor at the Lincoln Memorial. He placed a four-foot wreath, one of the thirty-two wreaths at the memorial commemorating the 129th anniversary of Lincoln's birth. Captain Patrick H. Tansey placed another on behalf of the District Commissioners. Various other military organizations placed the other thirty wreaths and the GAR held services at First Congregational Church. (February 12, 1938)

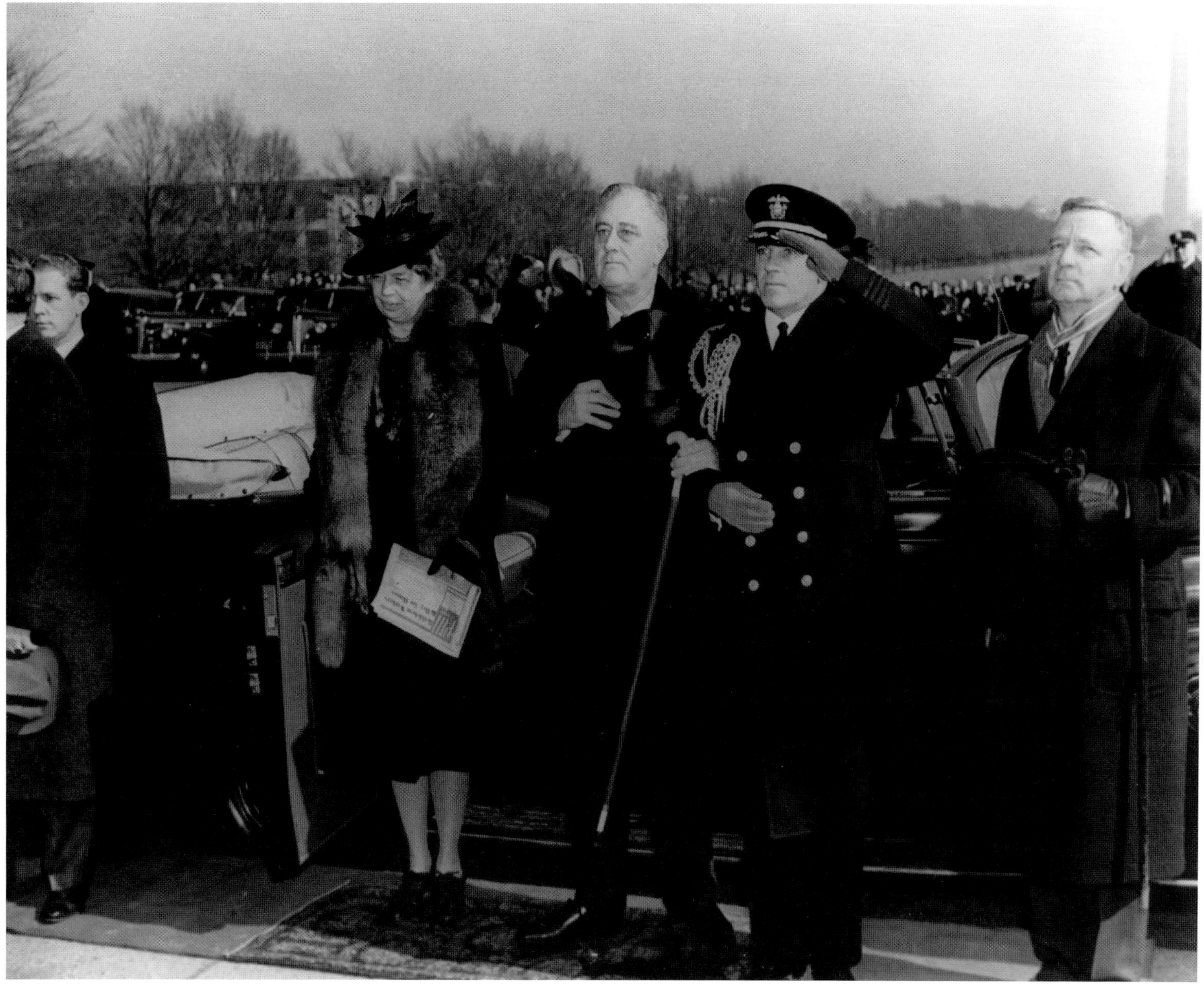

A rather jaunty-looking FDR on the USS *Houston* in Pensacola, Florida. He was in Pensacola to inspect naval aviation cadets. In July, Pensacola had seen the filming of *Wings of the Navy,* Hollywood's dramatic take on naval aviation, starring Olivia de Havilland. Earlier in the summer he had fished off the Galapagos on the *Houston,* which would become the U.S. Navy's flagship shortly after this picture was taken. The rest of its history is tragic. It was sunk by the Japanese on March 1, 1942, and the surviving sailors taken for slave labor in Southeast Asia. (August 9, 1938)

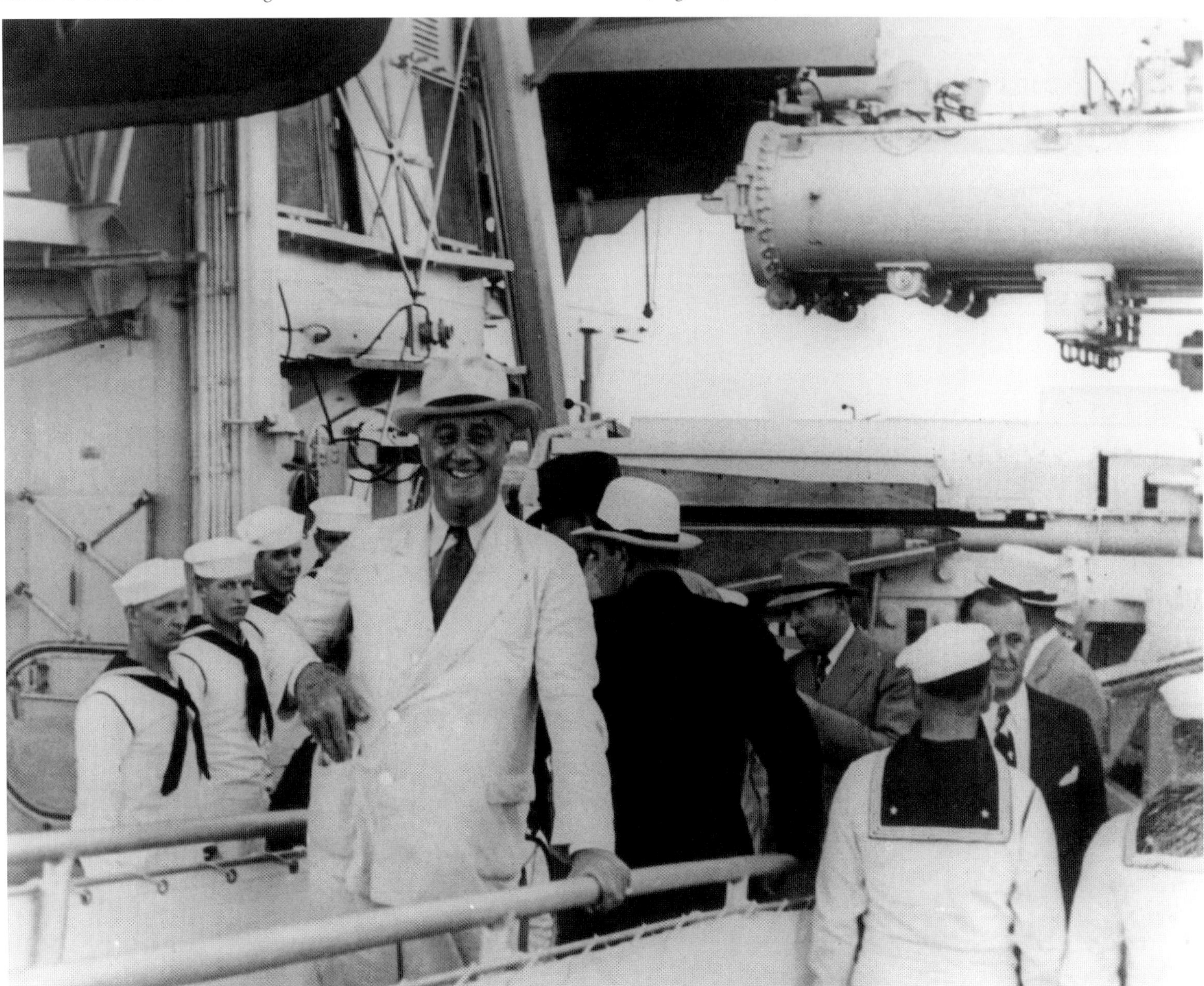

FDR speaking in Barnesville, Georgia. While there to dedicate a new Rural Electrification Administration project, which would provide dramatically cheaper electricity, he also took on Walter George, the sitting senator, urging those present to vote for his opponent. "I have no hesitation in saying that if I were able to vote in the September primaries in this State, I most assuredly should cast my ballot for Lawrence Camp." *Time* magazine reported: "When the President turned to sit down, George arose, walked over, shook F.D.R.'s hand and said: 'I want you to know that I accept the challenge.' Replied Roosevelt: 'God bless you, Walter. Let's always be friends.'" The president's unorthodox appeal did not work—the senator was handily reelected. (August 11, 1938)

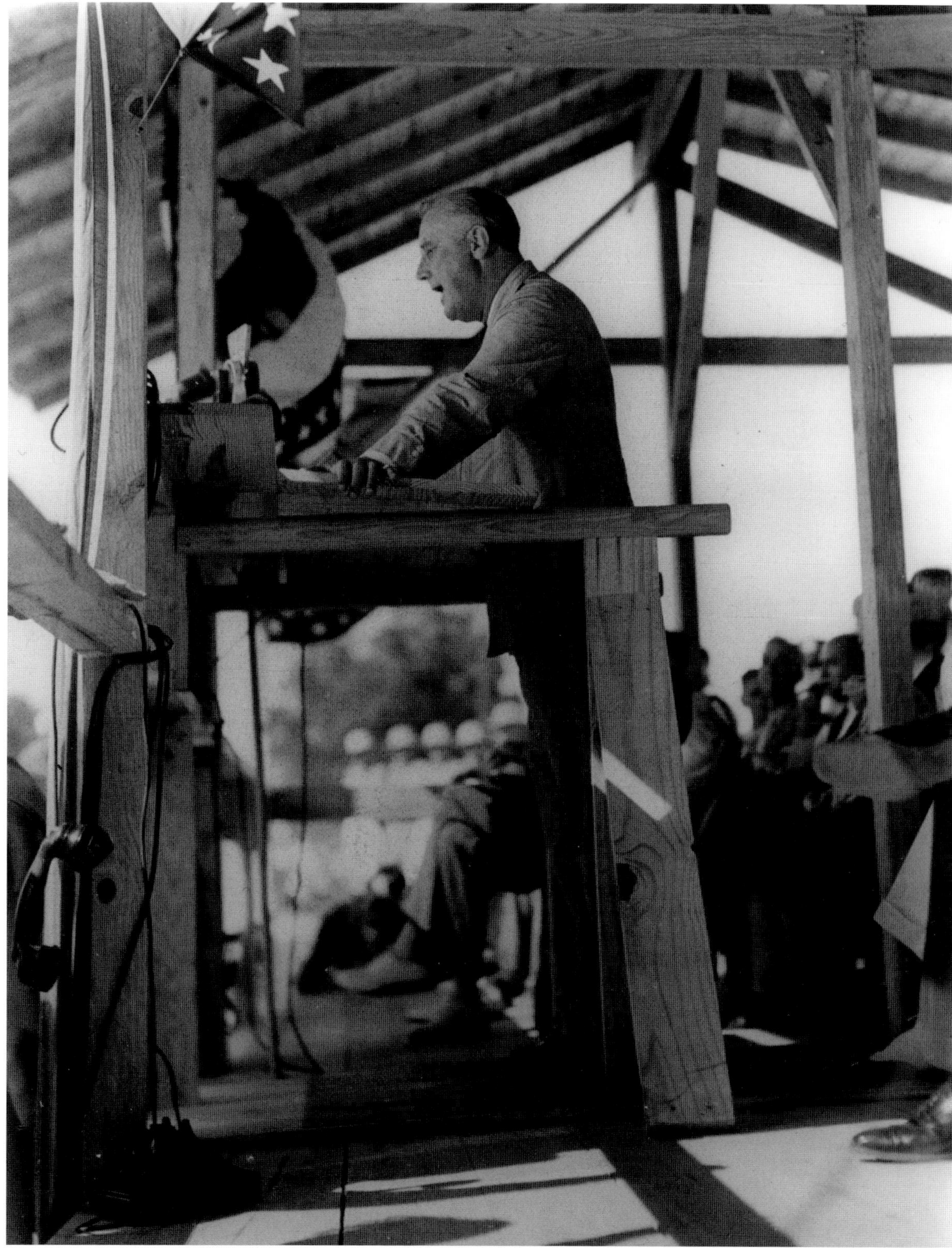

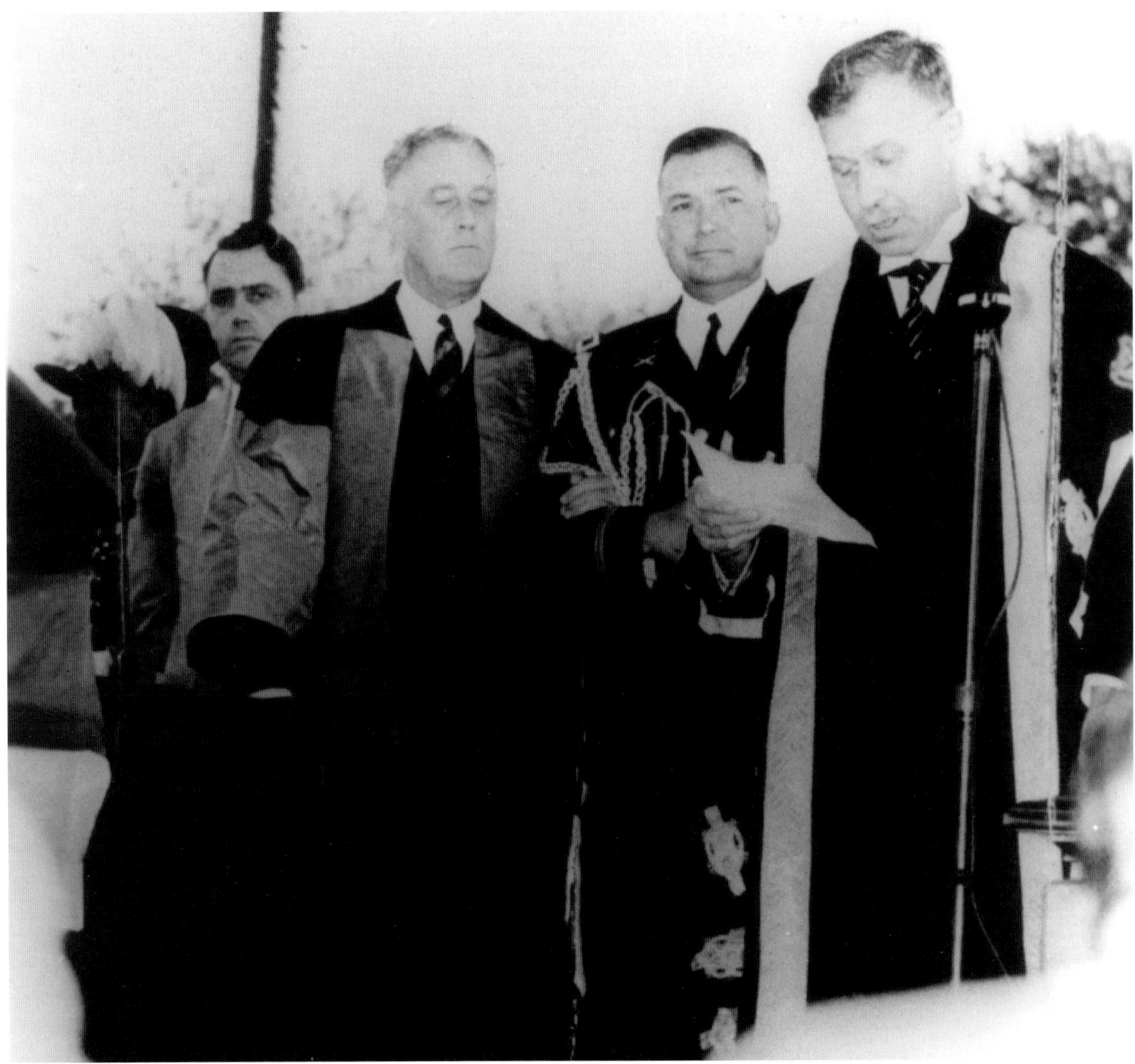

FDR at Queen's University in Kingston, Ontario, where he received an honorary degree. His address to the assembly was gracious in noting the links between the two countries. "My good friend, the Governor General of Canada, in receiving an honorary degree in June at that University at Cambridge, Massachusetts, to which Mackenzie King and I both belong, suggested that we cultivate three qualities to keep our foothold in the shifting sands of the present—humility, humanity and humor. I have been thinking in terms of a bridge which is to be dedicated this afternoon and so I could not help coming to the conclusion that all of these three qualities imbedded in education, build new spans to reestablish free intercourse throughout the world and bring forth an order in which free nations can live in peace." (August 18, 1938)

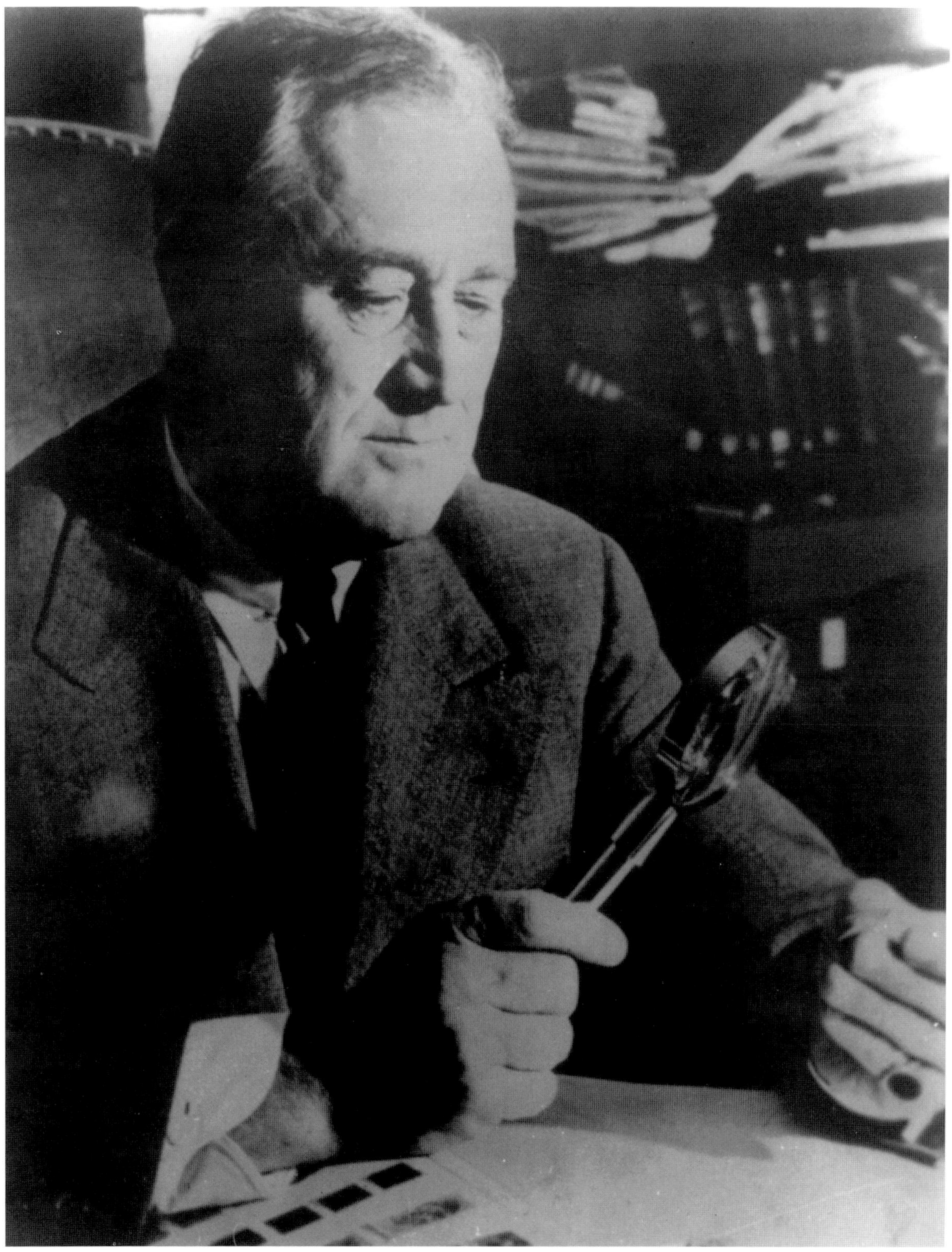

FDR examining stamps from his collection. His interest in stamps dates back to his childhood in 1891 when he was asking his aunt Dora Forbes in Macao for any exotic stamps her husband might have. He joined the American Philatelic Society when he was governor of New York. He has been dubbed the "Philatelic President" and always took a lively interest in new stamps issued by the United States, offering design suggestions and giving final approvals. Postmaster General James Farley, a longtime supporter of FDR, caused some controversy in the stamp-collecting community. He had handed out sheets of 200 stamps, unperforated, ungummed, and with his autograph to the President, cabinet members, and political friends. These sheets quickly became valuable collectors' items—worth far more than their face value—until the government reprinted the issue to quell the resulting scandal. FDR's collection was auctioned off in 1946.

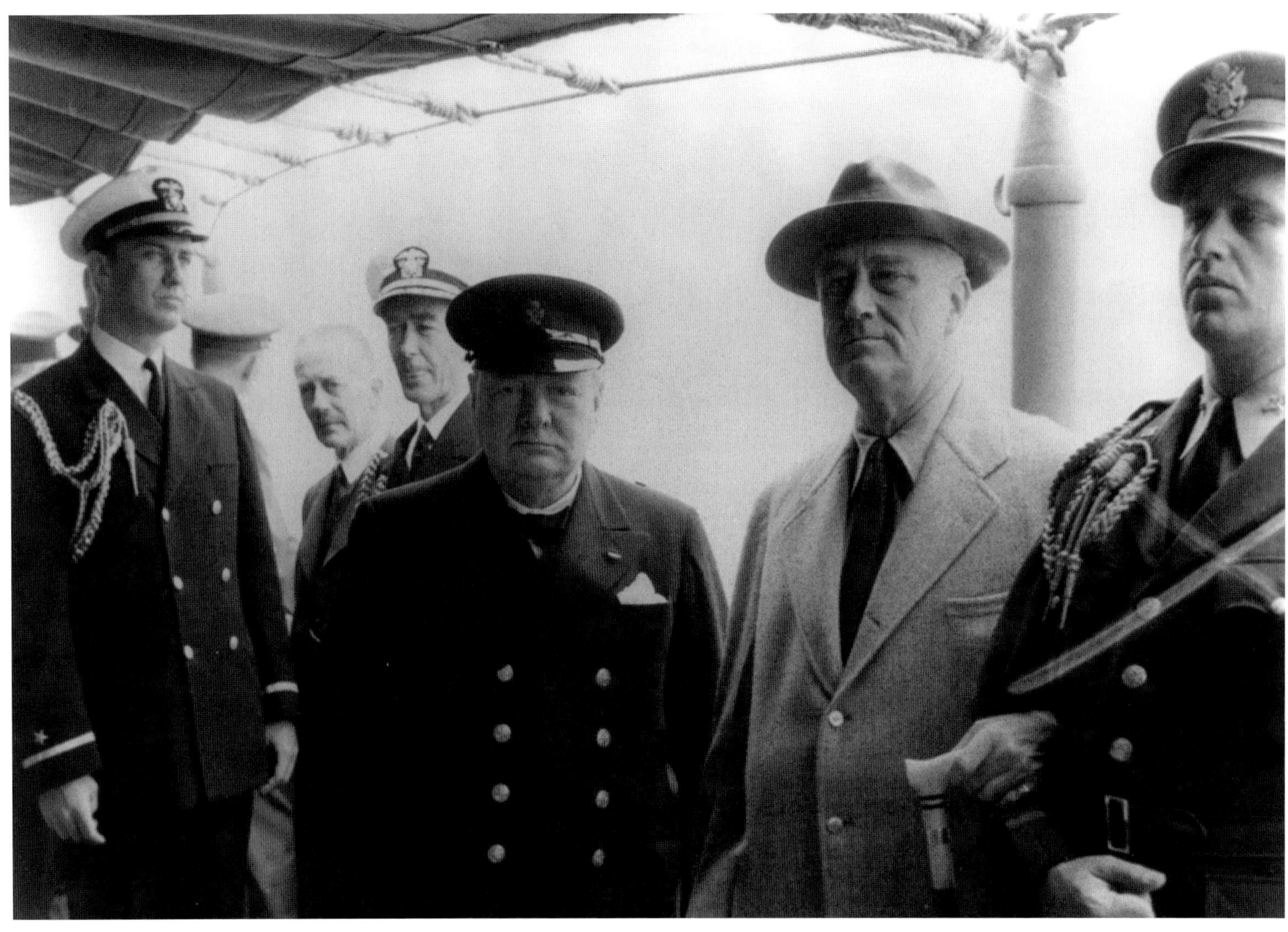

FDR greeting Winston Churchill aboard USS *Augusta* to start the Atlantic Conference, shown here with Franklin, Jr., and Elliott Roosevelt. Churchill would write back to the king: "With humble duty, I have arrived safely, and am visiting the President this morning." FDR boarded the HMS *Prince of Wales* for services, luncheon, and talks with Churchill the following day. The first meeting of FDR and Churchill in twenty-three years, and first as leaders of their countries, intricate plans had been laid to shroud this meeting in secrecy. Held in Placentia Bay, off what would soon become the American Argentia base in Newfoundland, the meeting resulted in the Atlantic Charter, a statement of principles for world order, and sparked the link between the men who would spend the next five years leading a world at war. (August 9, 1941)

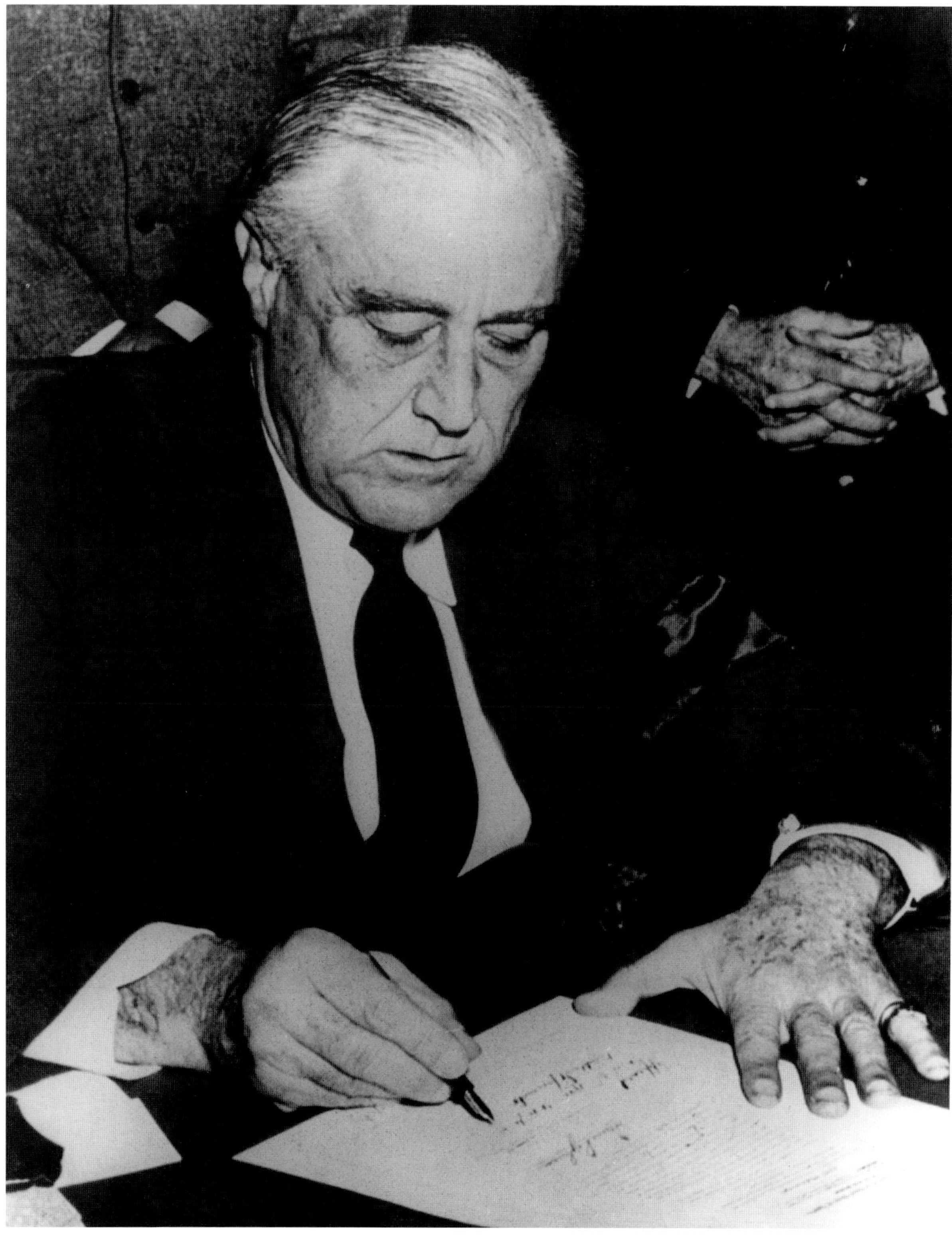

FDR signing the declaration of war against Japan. The day before, December 7, Japan had attacked the United States' naval base at Pearl Harbor. This attack drew America into war raging around the world, from the Japanese invasion of China in 1933 to Hitler's invasion of Poland in 1939. FDR's powerful rhetoric against the Japanese attack, "a date which will live in infamy," overcame criticism and the resolution passed with only a single dissenting vote. (December 8, 1941)

FDR greeting the visiting president Manuel Quezon of the Philippines, wife Dona Aurora, and son Manuel Jr., with John L. McCrea, Naval Aide to President Roosevelt. Douglas MacArthur was Quezon's military chief. It was an emotional meeting, according to the *Washington Post:* "When President Quezon saw President Roosevelt waiting for him alongside a White House automobile, his dark eyes lighted up in recognition and he almost ran to meet him. 'Mr. President—,' he cried. 'It's grand to see you,' said President Roosevelt pumping his hand." (May 13, 1942)

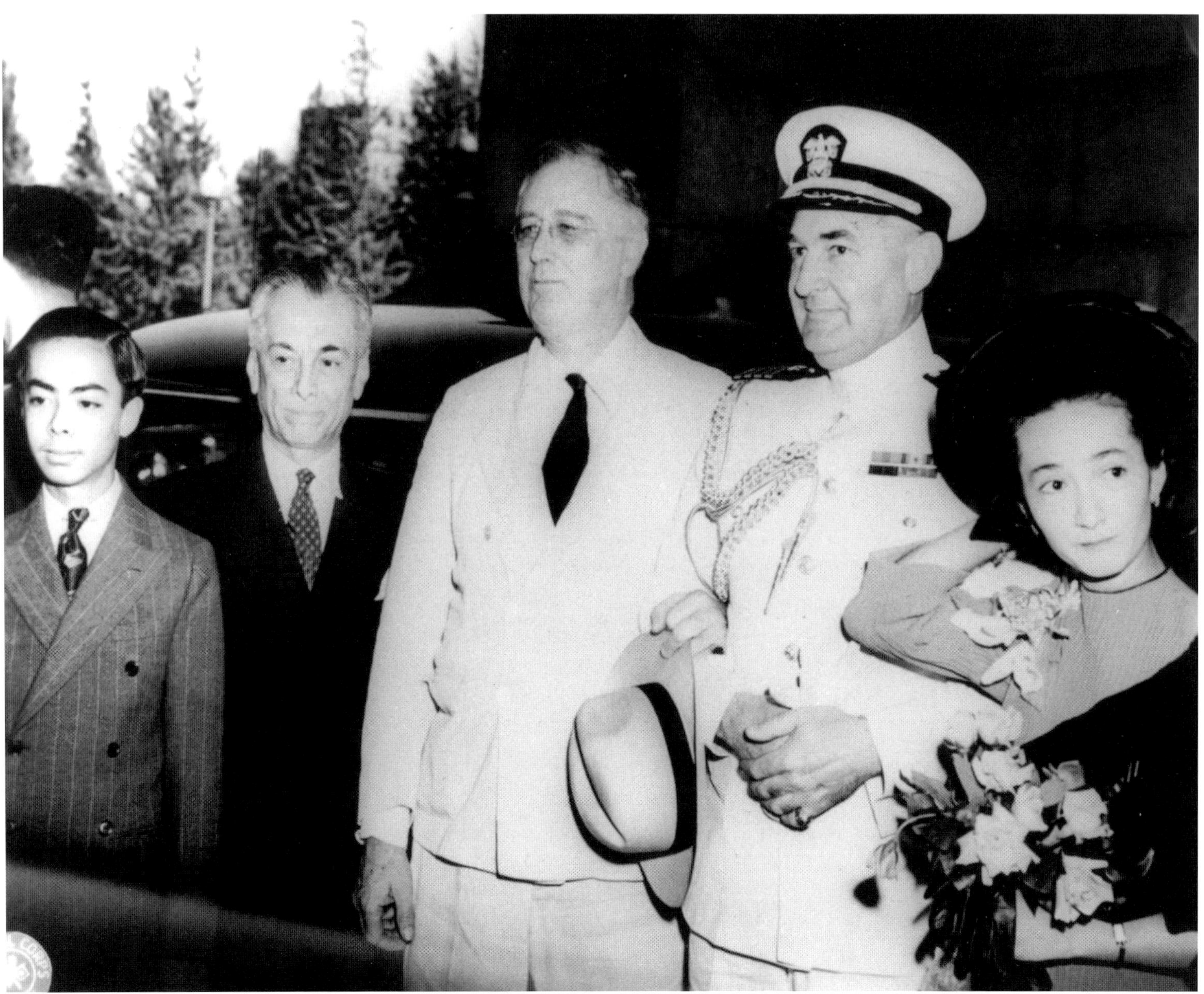

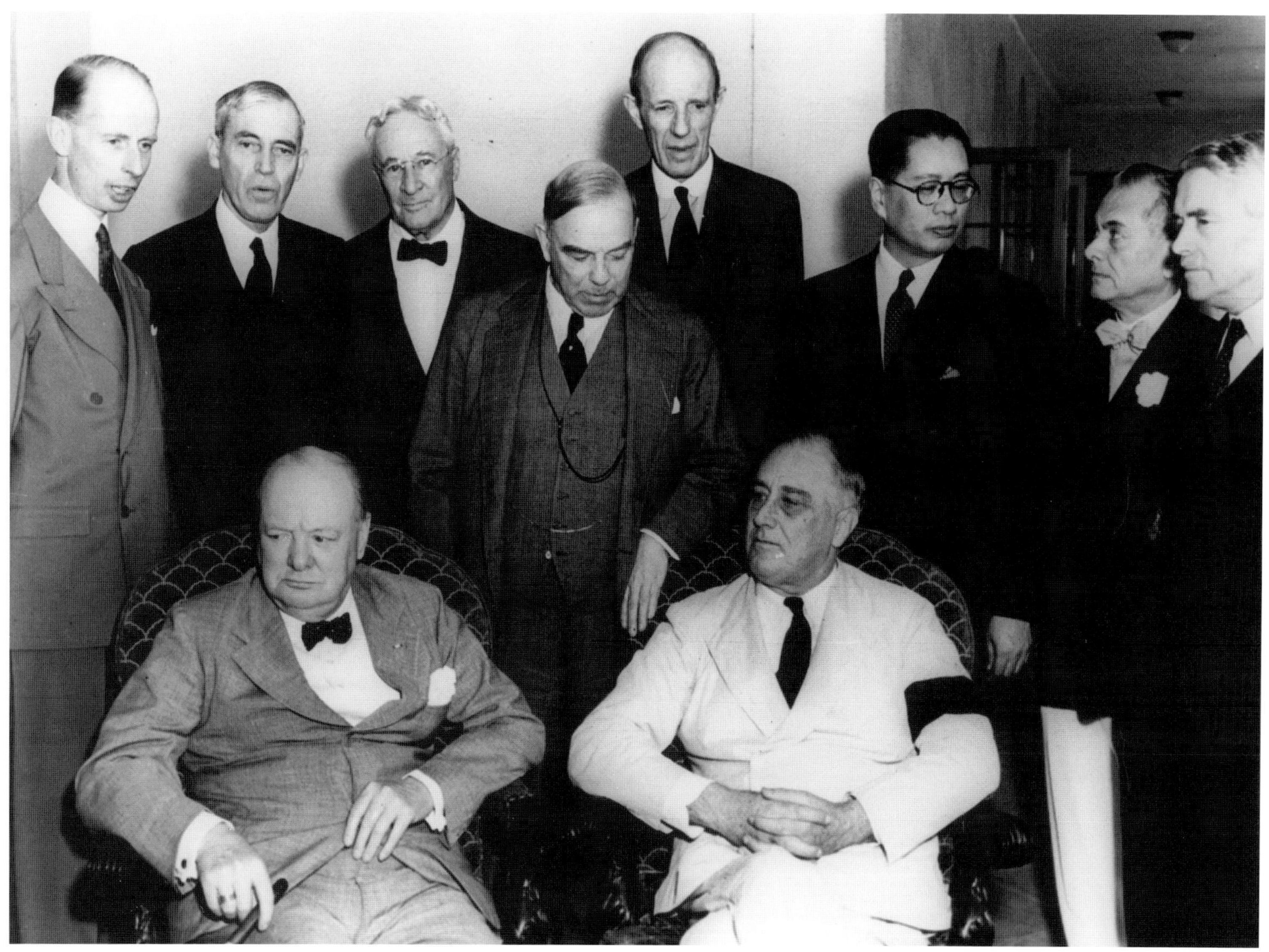

FDR and Churchill, here at the conclusion of the Second Washington war conference. Churchill flew to the United States, met with Franklin in Hyde Park, and then both returned to Washington for more meetings. The war was going badly for the Allies with the fall of Tobruk in North Africa to the Nazis. A cross-Channel invasion was made a lesser priority over attacking the periphery of Axis-controlled territory. Pictured here are Canadian ambassador Leighton McCarthy, Canadian Prime Minister Mackenzie King, Lord Halifax, British Ambassador to Washington, and Chinese envoy Dr. T. V. Soong in Washington, D.C. The statement released afterward included: "We have taken full cognizance of our disadvantages as well as our advantages. We do not underrate the task.

"We have conducted our conferences with the full knowledge of the power and resourcefulness of our enemies. . . .

"We recognize and applaud the Russian resistance to the main attack being made by Germany and we rejoice in the magnificent resistance of the Chinese Army. Detailed discussions were held with our military advisers on methods to be adopted against Japan and the relief of China.

"While exact plans, for obvious reasons, cannot be disclosed, it can be said that the coming operations which were discussed in detail at our Washington conferences, between ourselves and our respective military advisers, will divert German strength from the attack on Russia." (June 25, 1942)

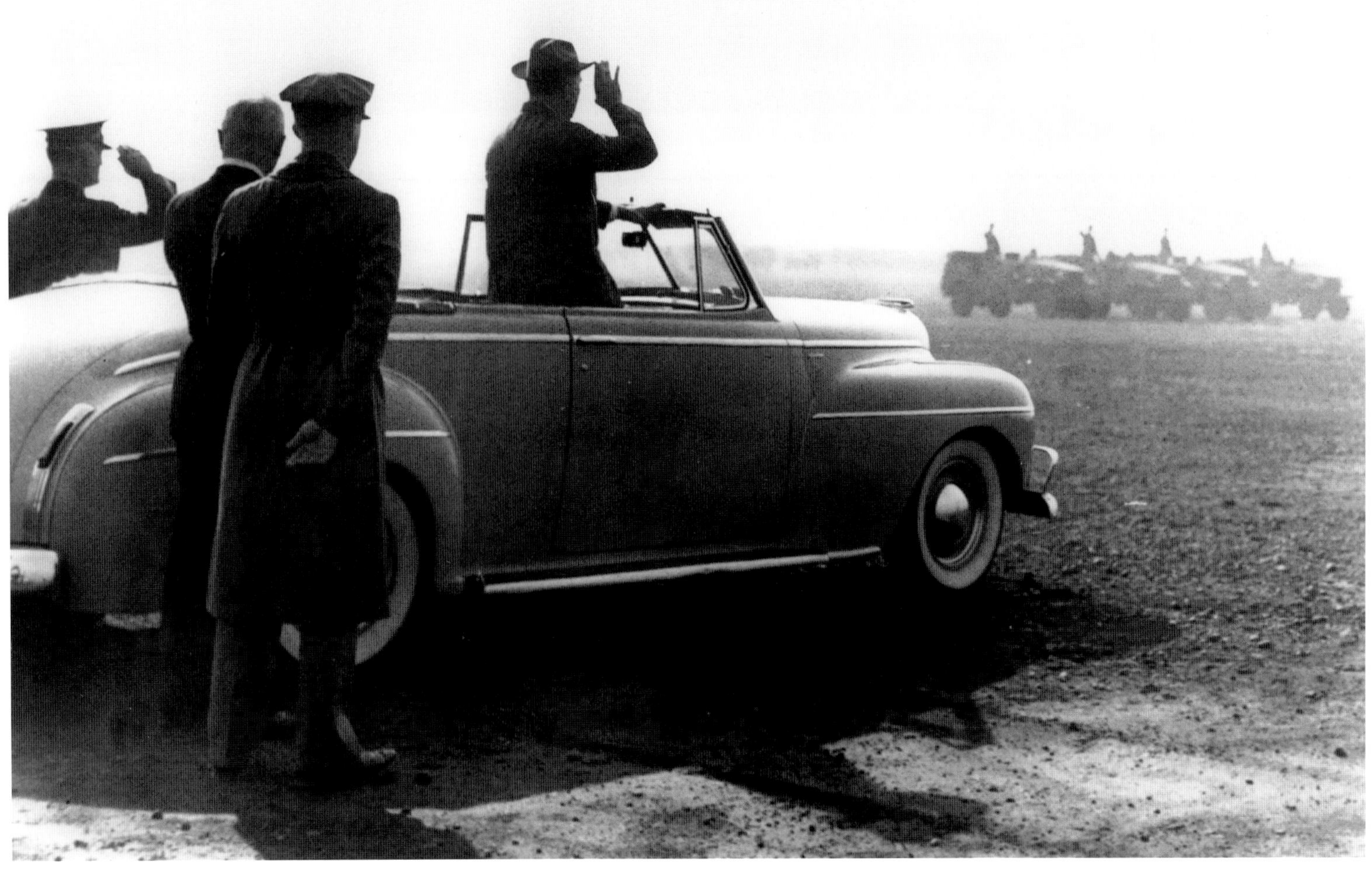

FDR at Fort Lewis, Washington, part of his two-week tour, where he visited twenty-nine war plants. The war was not going well in Europe or the Pacific, but this tour would bring attention to the strides being made in war production. In his press conference at the conclusion of the tour he noted the important contribution women were making: "Now, on impressions on the trip, I have spoken about the large number of women workers. It's an amazing thing how they are working into the production of munitions with very great success. In some of the plants we saw, these are not just stenographers in the office, these are women running machines, and inspecting parts as they come out of a machine. And some plants run 20 percent. Some of the airplane plants are running 30 percent, even—I think one of them—40 percent, and it is getting up, according to the managers and operators of these plants, so that probably within another year in very many of the plants, half of all the labor in the plants will be women." (September 22, 1942)

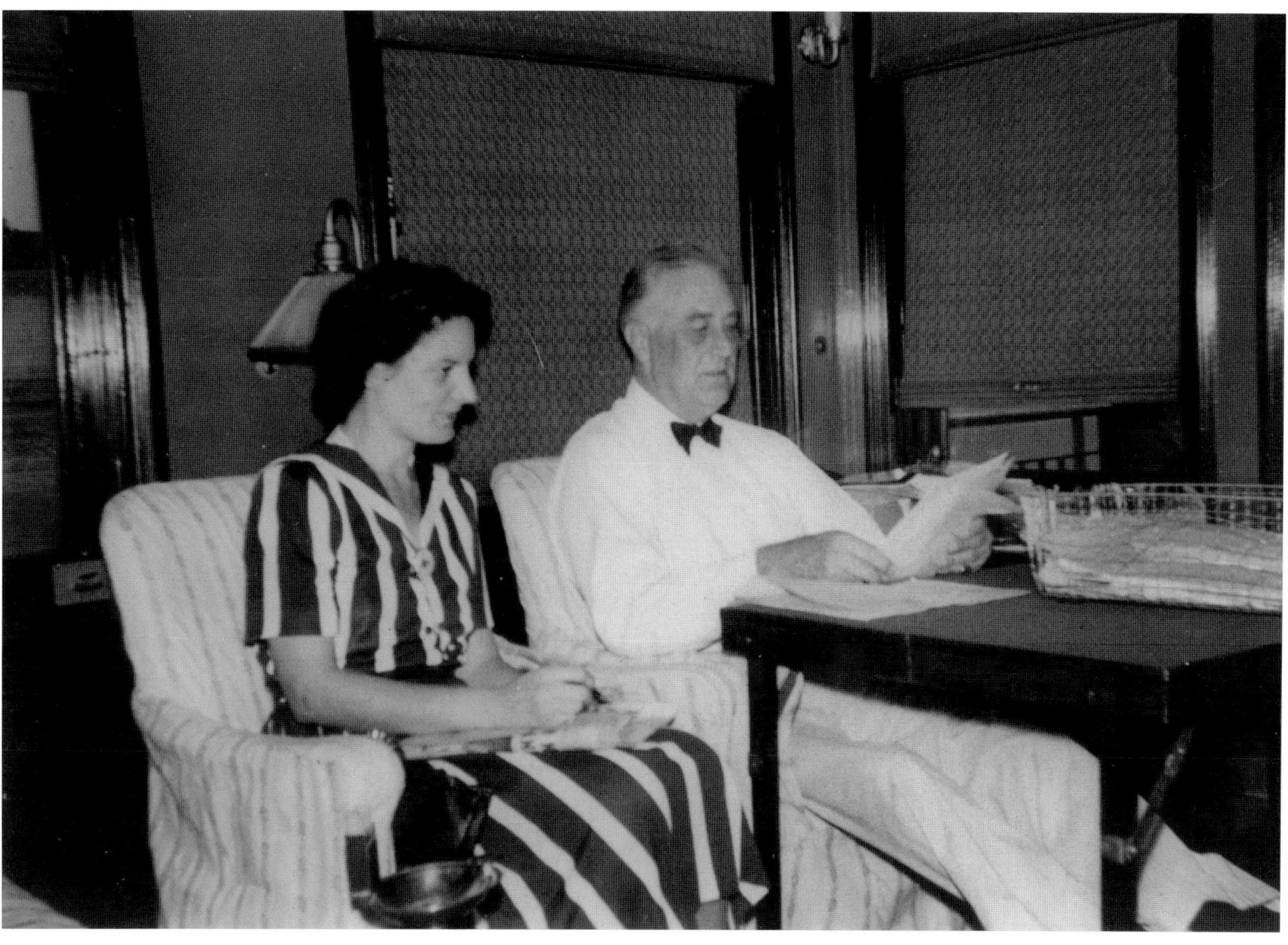

FDR and Dorothy Jones Brady, his White House secretary. Brady was Franklin's secretary from 1933 until his death in 1945. Interviewed years later, she stated, "He had a compassion that was like a magnificent obsession. Every day you were there you knew that your number one job was to help people in trouble." FDR was in the midst of a two-week inspection excursion through various defense plants and had just been to the dedication of the new Marine base, Camp Pendleton. (September 30, 1942)

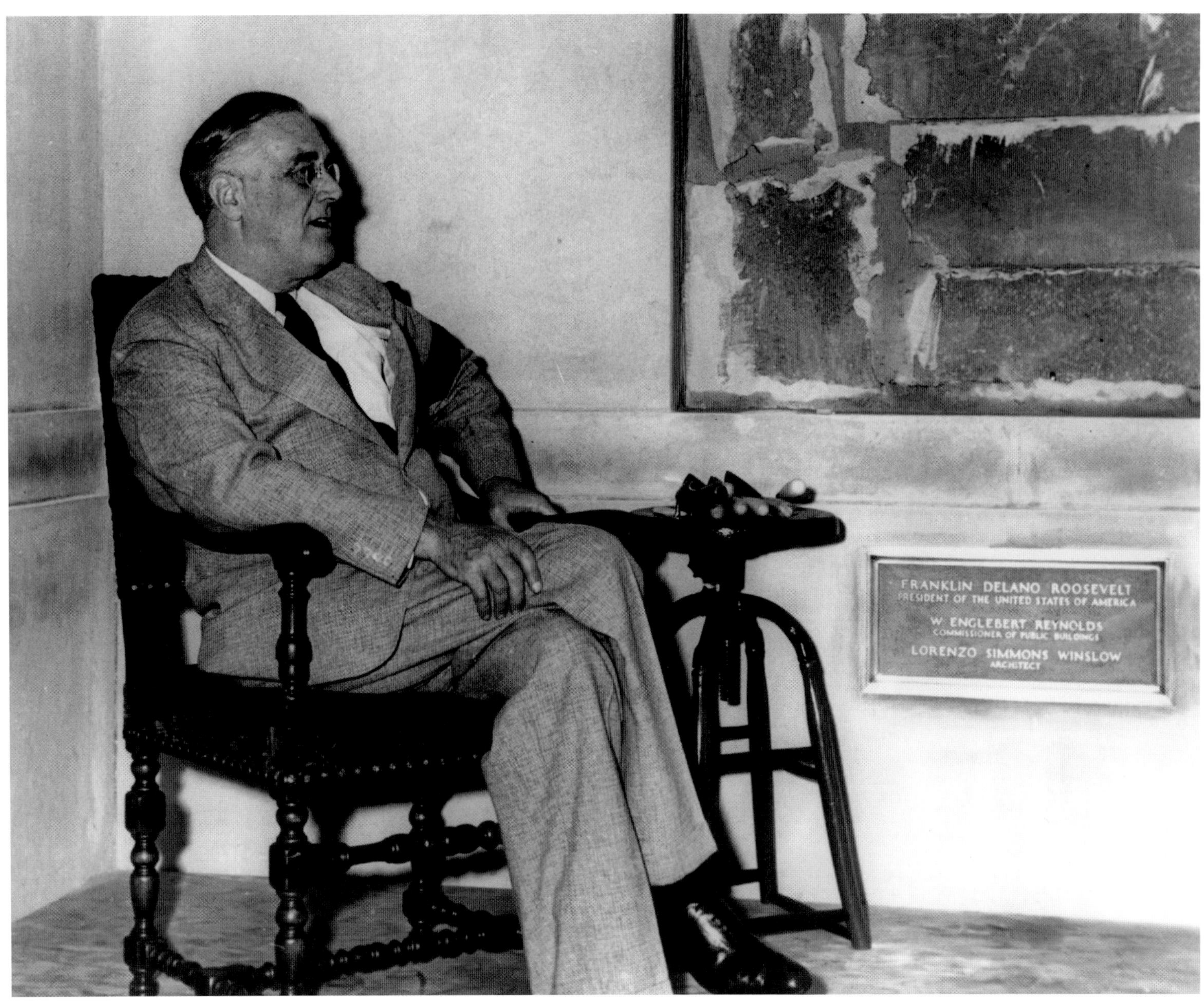

FDR unveiling White House Library renovations, done by Lorenzo Winslow. Lorenzo Simmons Winslow (1892–1976) worked as an architect in the White House for twenty years (1933-53). Projects he oversaw included the swimming pool in the West Terrace and the West Wing expansion in 1934; new roads, gates, and fences for the south grounds in 1936; and the new kitchen and pantries. He became official White House architect in 1941 and designed and oversaw the construction of the East Wing. The East Wing museum FDR planned would not materialize. (November 5, 1942)

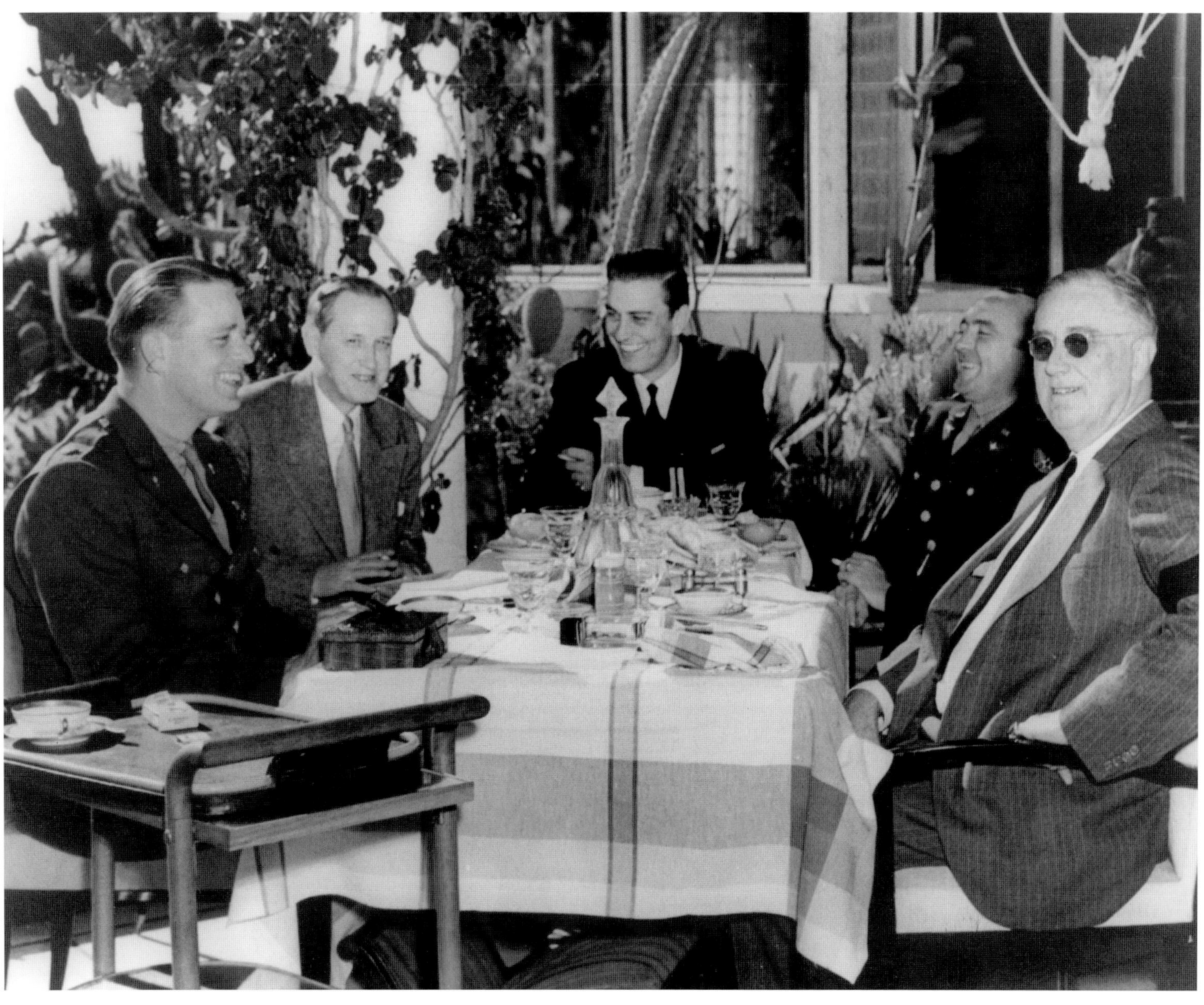

FDR at lunch with sons Elliott and Franklin, Jr., Harry Hopkins, and George Durno (of the International News Service) in Casablanca. Franklin, Jr., was serving in the Navy. It was here in Casablanca that the Allies first demanded unconditional surrender of the Axis. FDR casually espoused it and Churchill reluctantly followed suit. (January 16, 1943)

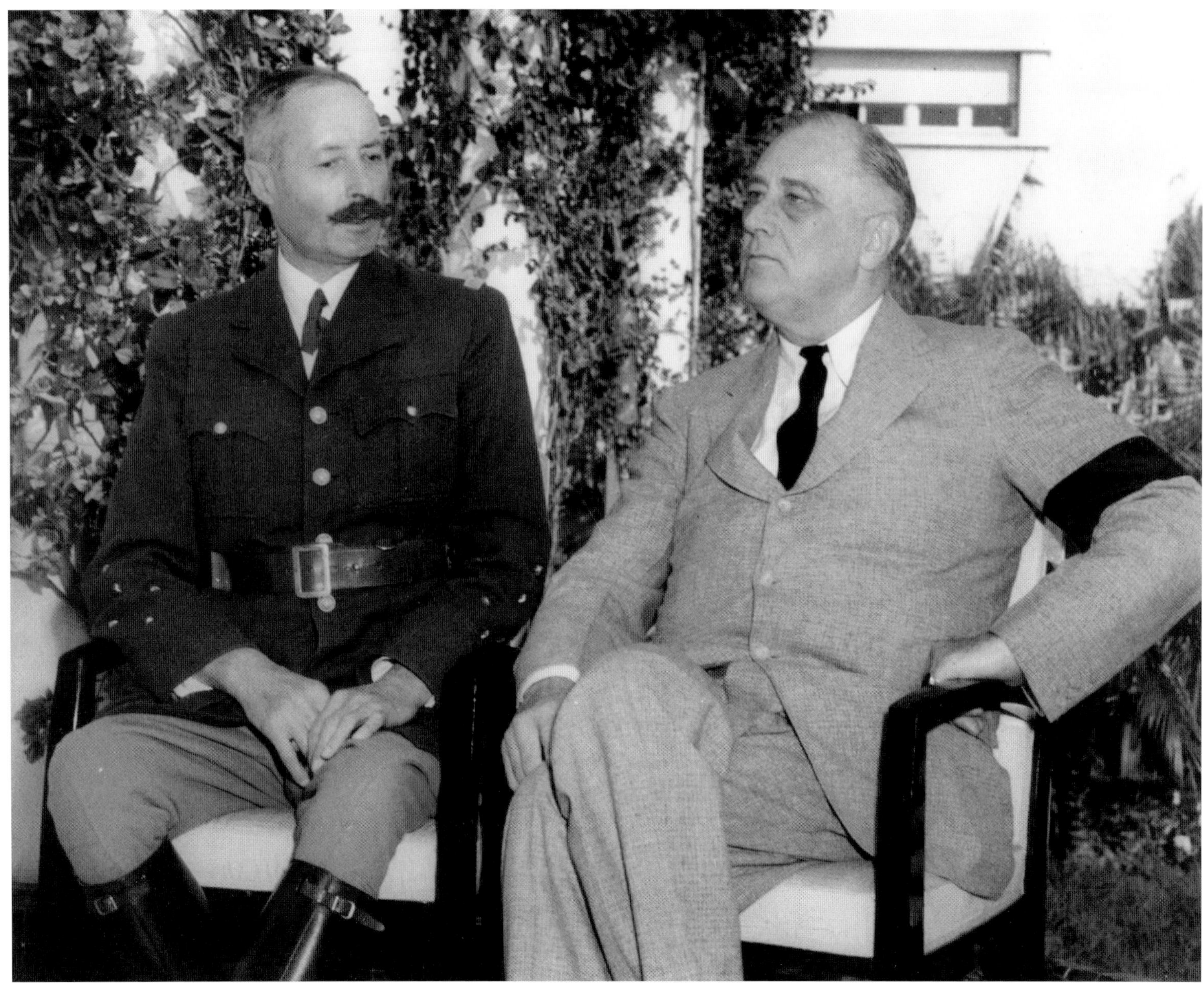

FDR and French general Henri-Honoré Giraud in Casablanca. Giraud was the military commander of the Free French forces in North Africa. He had made a spectacular escape from a German prison after two years' imprisonment. The Vichy government refused to return him to his German captors. Giraud made his way to the Allied forces in North Africa, meeting with Eisenhower in Gibraltar. He worked with Charles de Gaulle as co-president of the French Committee of National Liberation, an arrangement agreed to in June 1943 after heavy Allied pressure and six months of negotiation. But in 1944 he was ousted for maintaining his own intelligence network separate from that of the Allies. (January 19, 1943)

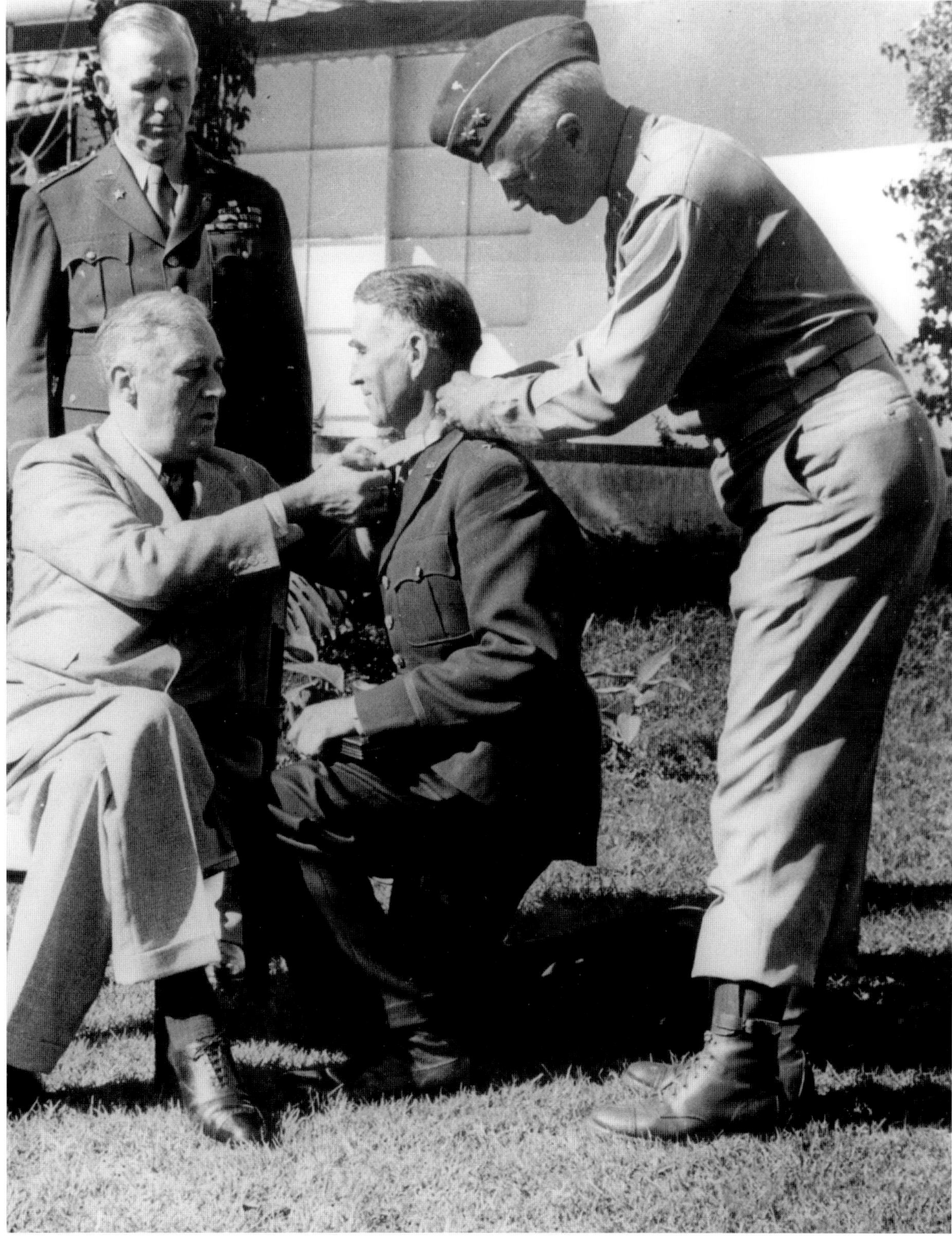

FDR decorating Colonel William Wilbur, with General Marshall and General Patton, in Casablanca. FDR awards Wilbur the Medal of Honor "for conspicuous gallantry and intrepidity in action above and beyond the call of duty." He had landed with the invading American troops, made his way through enemy lines and delivered his messages to the French in Casablanca. On his return he commandeered a tank platoon and they took out a battery harassing the invading Americans. "Col. Wilbur's conduct was voluntary and exemplary in its coolness and daring." (January 22, 1943)

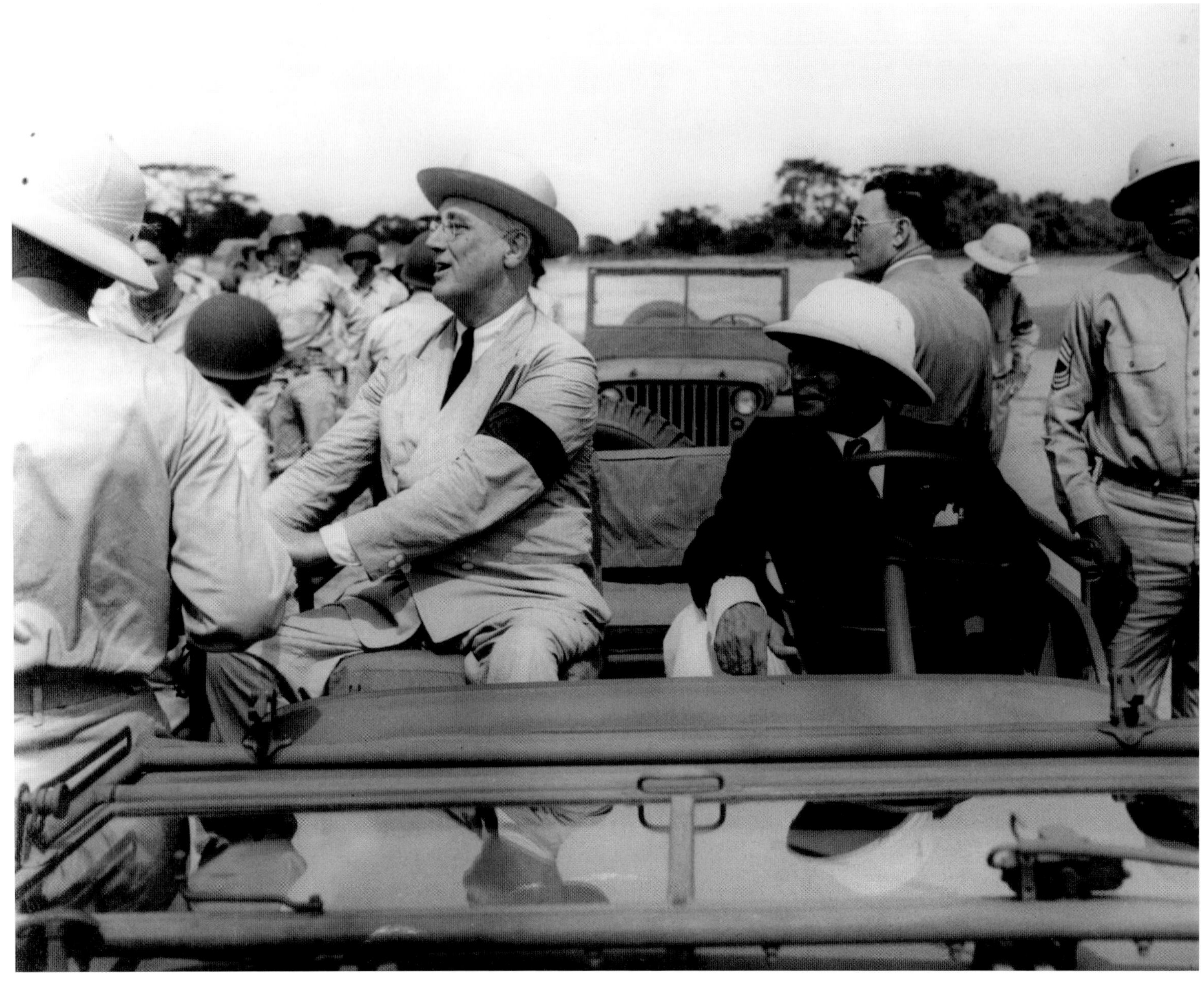

FDR in a jeep with Liberian president Edwin Barclay. In 1942, the United States established a base in Liberia. FDR visited Liberia following the Casablanca conference. Although founded by descendants of freed American slaves, Liberia had a strong German presence. The United States wooed Liberia to its side for its key supplies of natural rubber, vital to the war effort, and strategic position on the sea lanes in support of the invasion of North Africa. Barclay would repay the compliment, visiting Washington in May. (January 27, 1943)

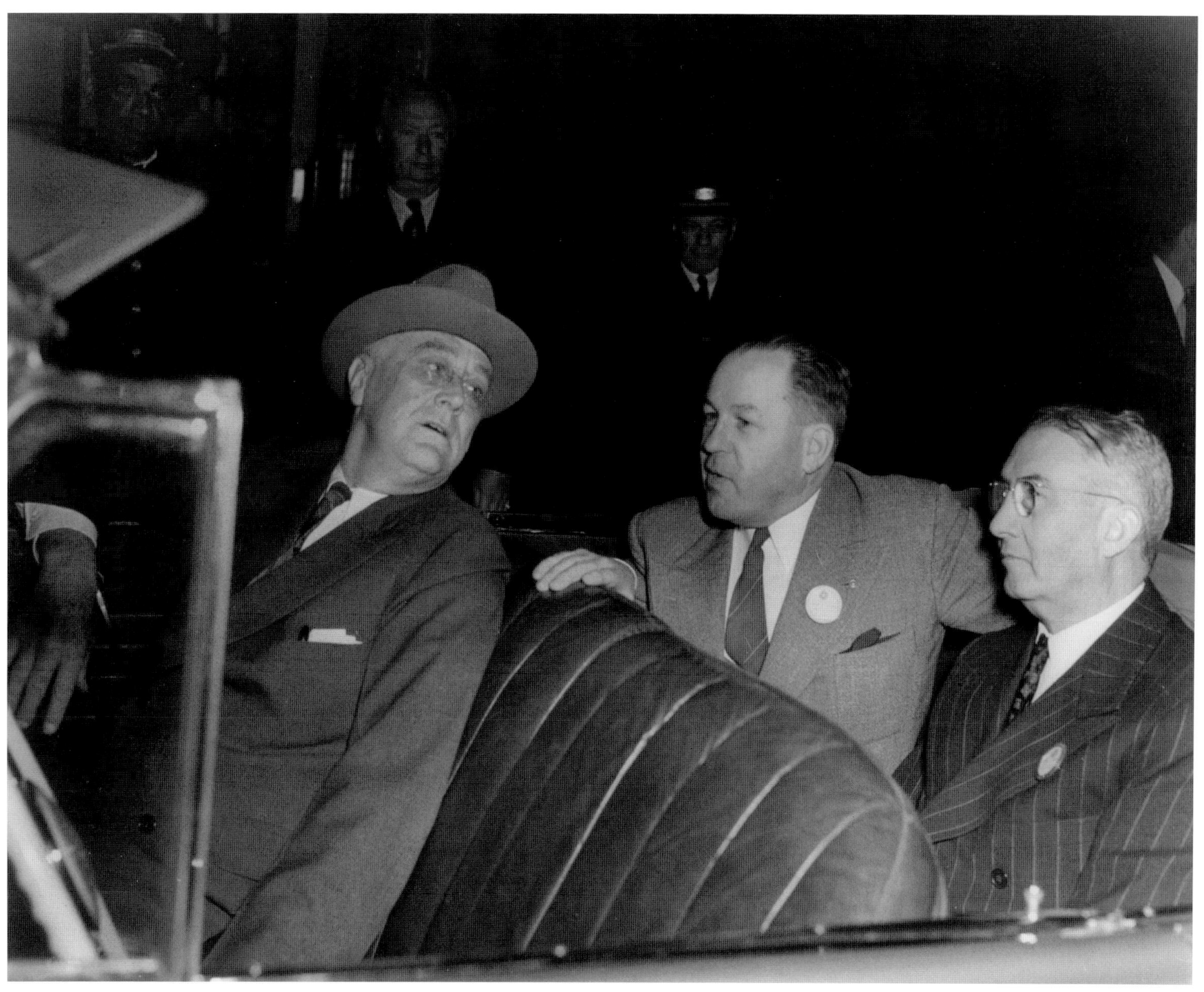

FDR consulting with Nebraska governor Dwight Griswold and Glenn L. Martin in Omaha, Nebraska. The president was visiting the Martin bomber plant, which was busy manufacturing B-26 Marauders and B-29 Superfortresses. The plant would ultimately employ more than 13,000 people (over one-third of them women). "We've taught our employees to make planes. . . . We've trained them, they have been willing to learn, and we have surrounded them with tools and procedures so that they make few mistakes. And those that do occur are caught by inspectors," said company president J. T. Hartson. It was here that the *Enola Gay* was built. (April 26, 1943)

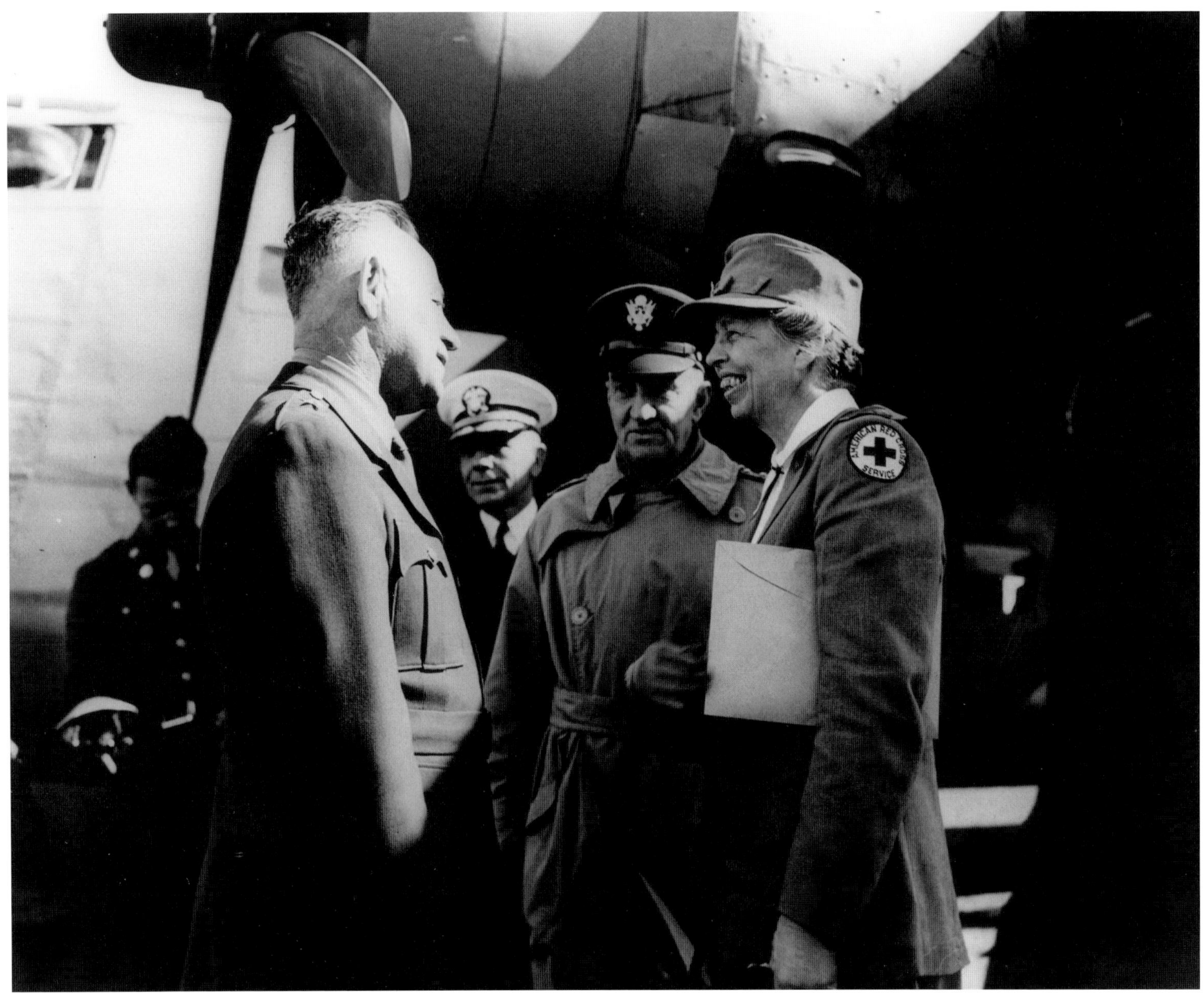

Eleanor Roosevelt greeting colleagues in Sydney, Australia. Eleanor undertook a five-week goodwill tour of the South Pacific to boost the soldiers' morale. She wears the Red Cross uniform as suggested by Norman Davis, chairman of the American Red Cross. Some in the military were not enthusiastic at the prospect of the visit, but she won them over with her energy. Admiral Halsey was impressed: "I marveled at her hardihood, both physical and mental. She saw patients who were grievously wounded. I marveled most at their expressions as she leaned over them. It was a sight I will never forget. She alone accomplished more good than any other person who passed through my area."

"The suffering of the men," she said, "left a mark from which I think I shall never be free." (August-September 1943)

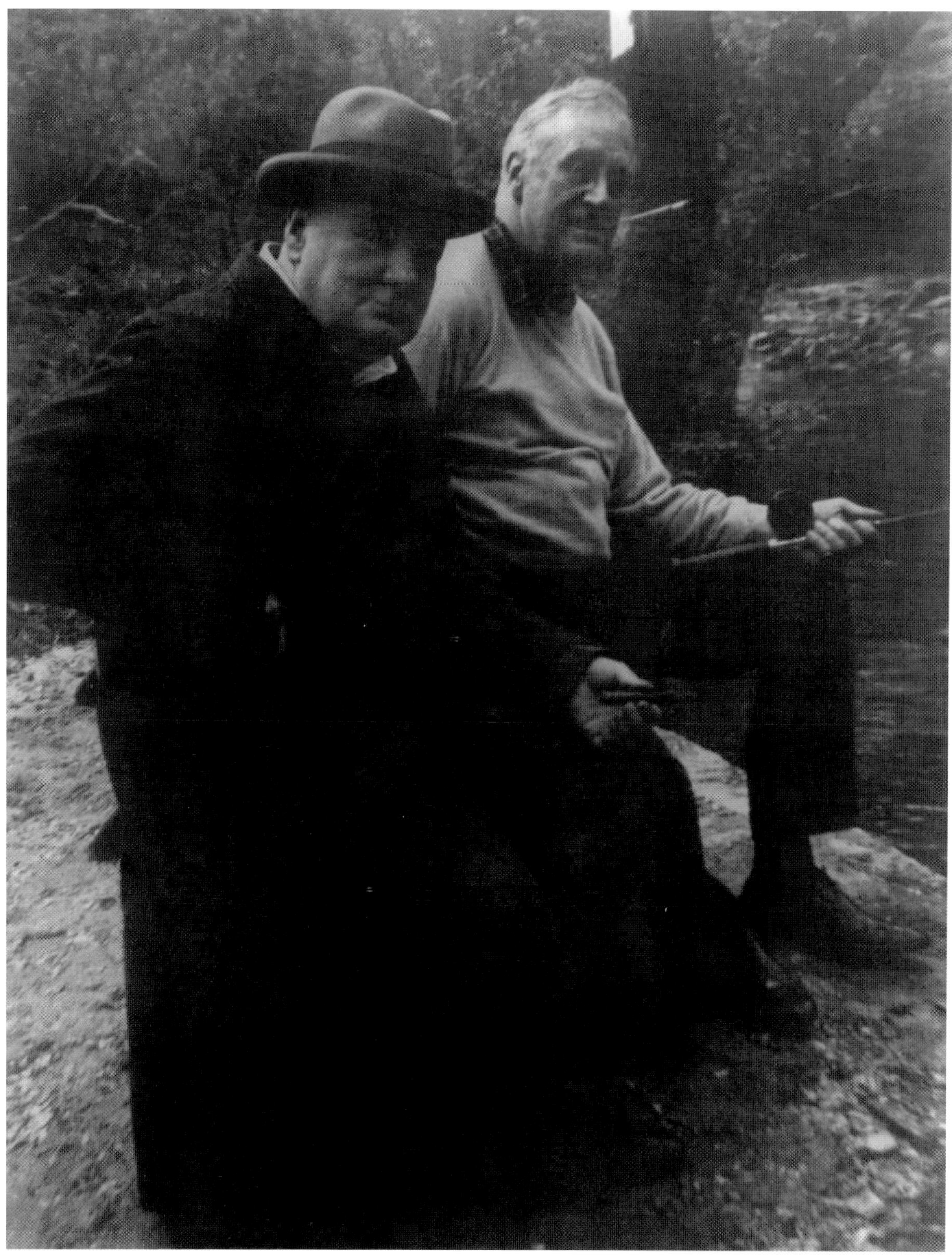

FDR (carefully posed) and Churchill fishing at Shangri La in a break during their two-week series of meetings. Churchill and Roosevelt met for the third time (a meeting code-named "Trident") here in May 1943. A whole series of decisions were reached on war in Europe and the Pacific. Roosevelt had selected this site in the Catoctin Mountains in 1942, naming his new retreat "Shangri La." Its elevation made it a full ten degrees cooler (and far less humid) than Washington. It was renamed Camp David by President Eisenhower and has served as a retreat for presidents since—a place apart from heat, humidity, and the glare of the media. (May 14, 1943)

FDR and prime minister of Canada, Mackenzie King. This, the first Quebec conference, nicknamed Quadrant, included six hundred representatives from the U.S., United Kingdom, and Canada—but no Russians. The war was distinctly turning in the Allies direction, leading to concerns about the postwar world and the role the Soviets would play. Here FDR reaffirmed his determination to share atomic secrets with the British. (August 18, 1943)

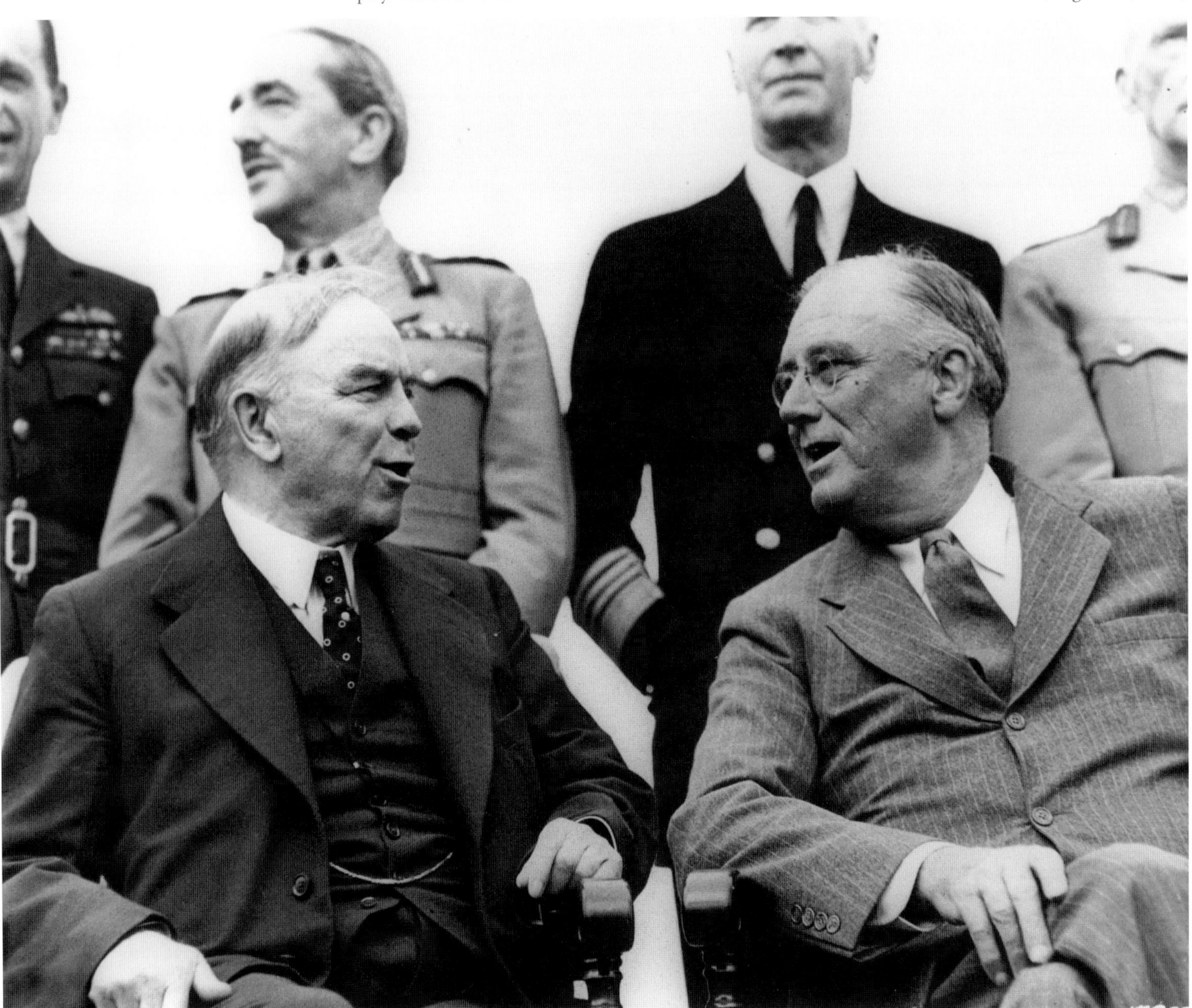

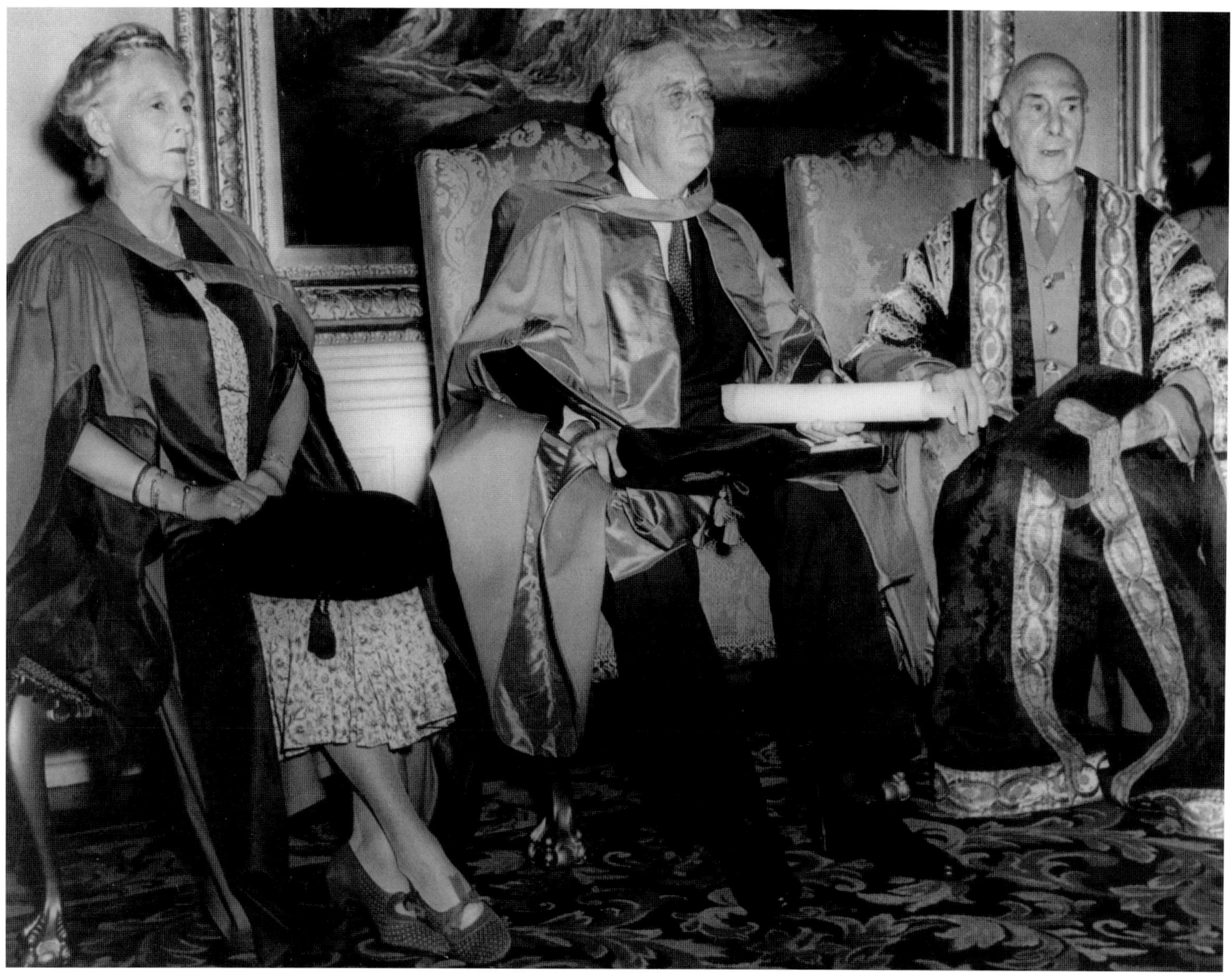

FDR in Ottawa, with the Earl of Athlone, Governor General of Canada, and his wife, Princess Alice. The Governor General and his wife played host to the attendees of the first Quebec conference. Franklin addressed the Canadian Parliament, in part: "It is no secret that at Quebec there was much talk of the postwar world. That discussion was doubtless duplicated simultaneously in dozens of nations and hundreds of cities and among millions of people.

"There is a longing in the air. It is not a longing to go back to what they call 'the good old days.' I have distinct reservations as to how good 'the good old days' were. I would rather believe that we can achieve new and better days.

"Absolute victory in this war will give greater opportunities to the world because the winning of the war in itself is proving that concerted action can accomplish things. Surely we can make strides toward a greater freedom from want than the world has yet enjoyed. Surely by unanimous action in driving out the outlaws and keeping them under heel forever we can attain a freedom from fear of violence." (August 25, 1943)

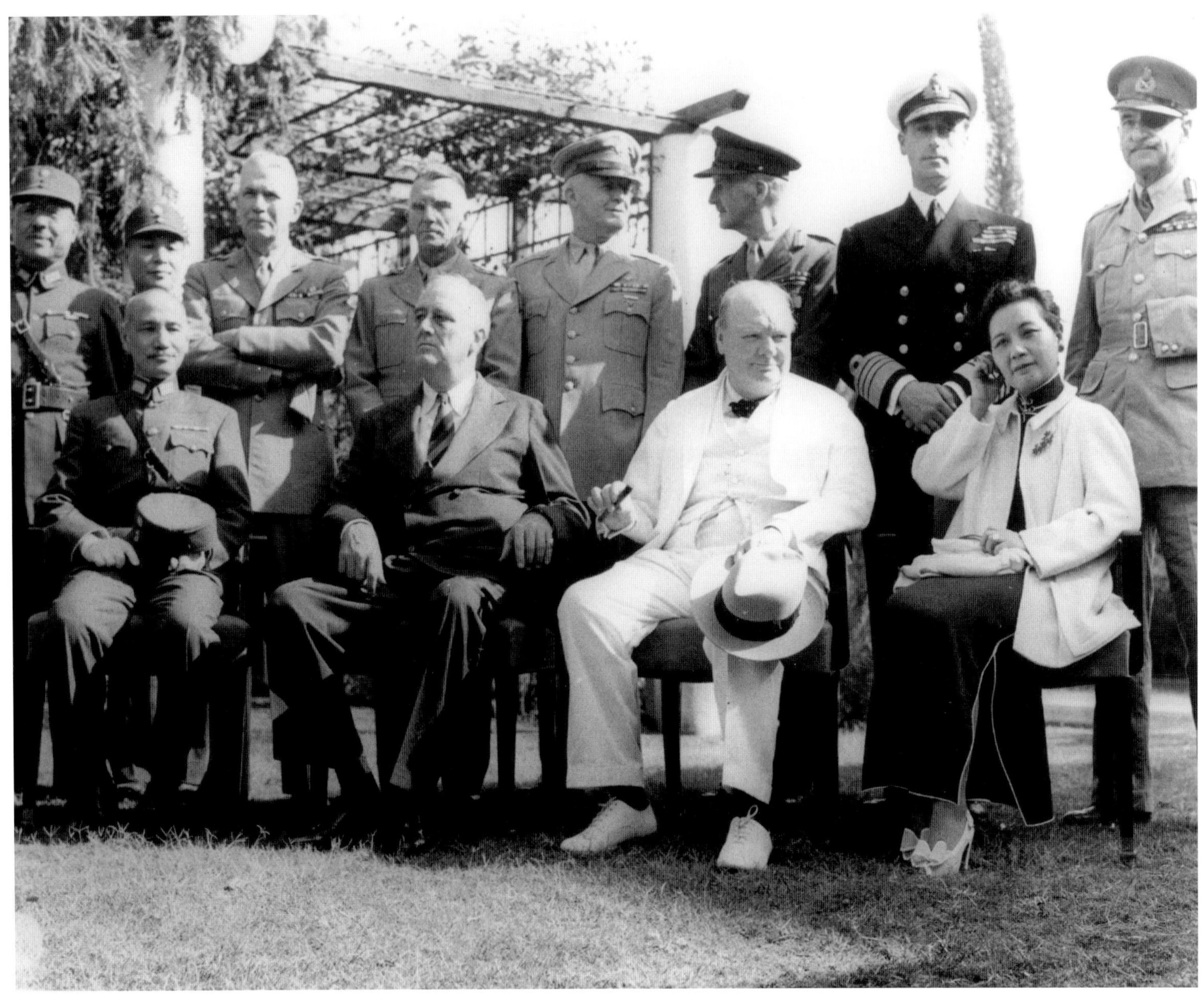

FDR, Churchill, Chiang Kai-shek, and Madame Chiang in Cairo. The meeting in Cairo was held en route to a meeting with Stalin in Teheran. This offered Chiang prestige as acknowledged postwar Chinese leader and a place at the table as a member of "the Big Four." Talks were difficult, in part because Churchill was anxious to reclaim British imperial territory from the Japanese and wanted to avoid Chinese interference. Madame Chiang Kai-shek, a formidable figure in her own right, served as her husband's English translator. The previous February she had addressed a joint session of Congress—a rare honor. She would live on until 2003. (November 25, 1943)

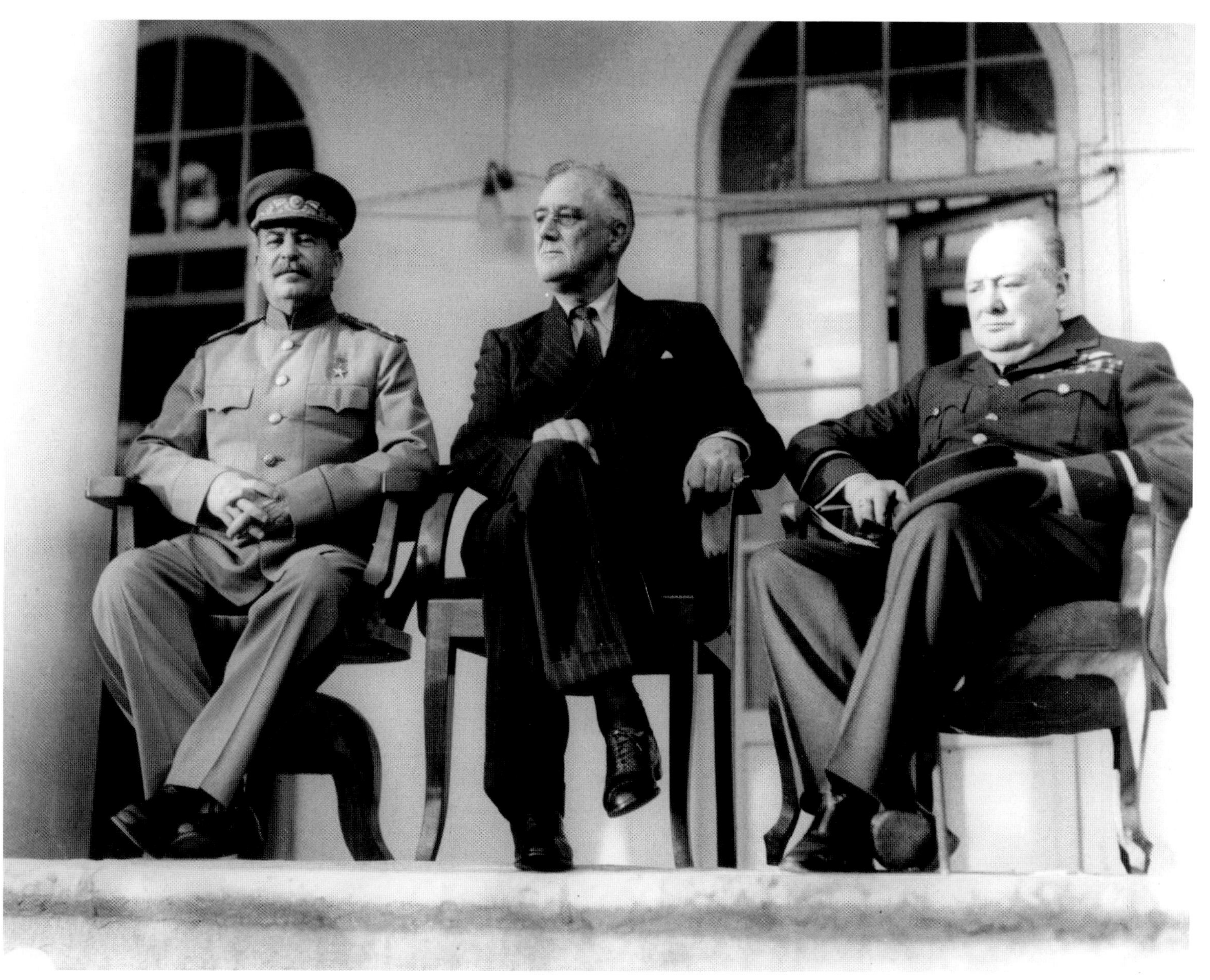

FDR, Winston Churchill, and Joseph Stalin—"the Big Three"—at the Teheran Conference "Eureka." It was the first meeting of FDR and Stalin. According to recollections by Archbishop Spellman, FDR was ready to concede much of Eastern Europe to the Soviets. The threat of assassination, as reported by Molotov, led to FDR residing in the Russian compound for the duration of the conference. To Churchill's distress, FDR discussed (perhaps naively, or perhaps ingenuously) a very wide range of issues with Stalin, including British India—with the suggestion it might be re-formed on the Soviet line. Plans for the division of influence in Eastern Europe were also discussed. (November 29, 1943)

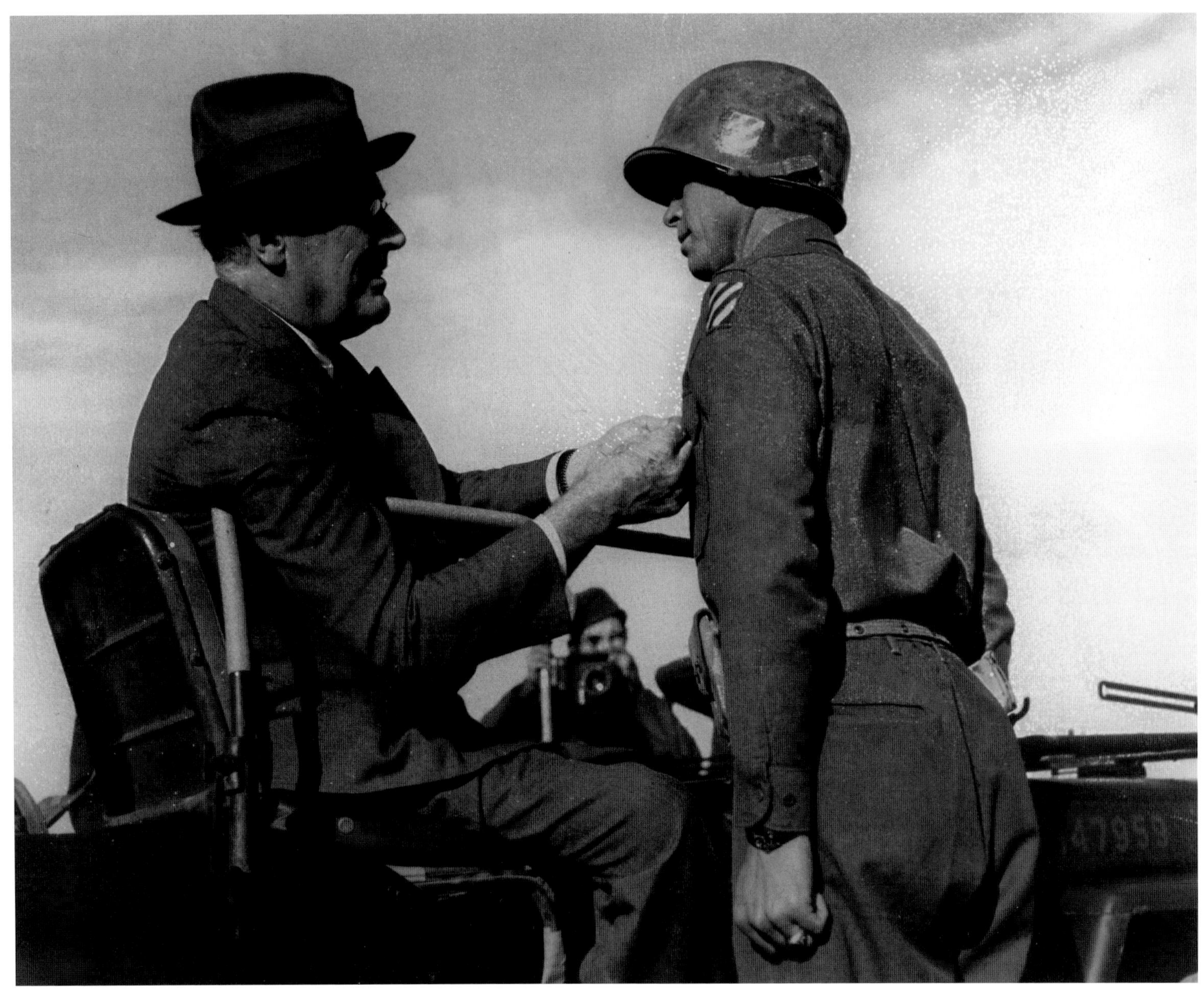

FDR decorating a soldier, Lieutenant W. W. Kellogg, at Castelvetrano, Sicily. FDR had finished a punishing sequence of meetings in Cairo (with Chiang Kai-shek and Churchill) and Teheran (with Stalin and Churchill). The president wanted to visit Naples, but his advisors considered that too close to the front line. Castelvetrano, in contrast, sits on the farthest west shore of Sicily. (December 8, 1943)

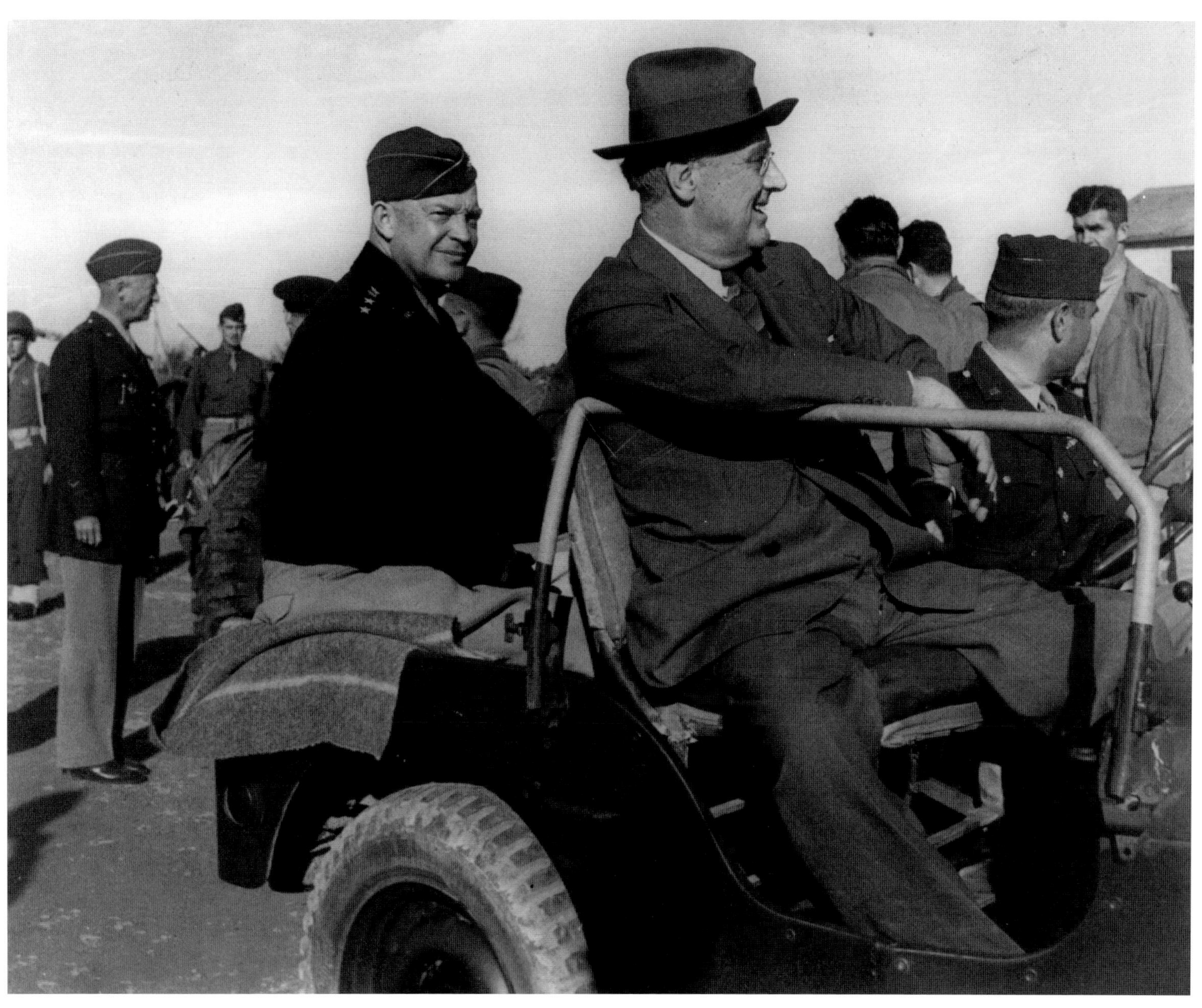

FDR with General Eisenhower and General Patton in Castelvetrano, Sicily. Following the Teheran Conference with Stalin, FDR visited troops in Sicily. At Castelvetrano airfield he met with Eisenhower and Patton. Patton had been under a cloud owing to reports of his slapping a soldier suffering battle fatigue, but FDR indicated he considered the incident closed. (December 8, 1943)

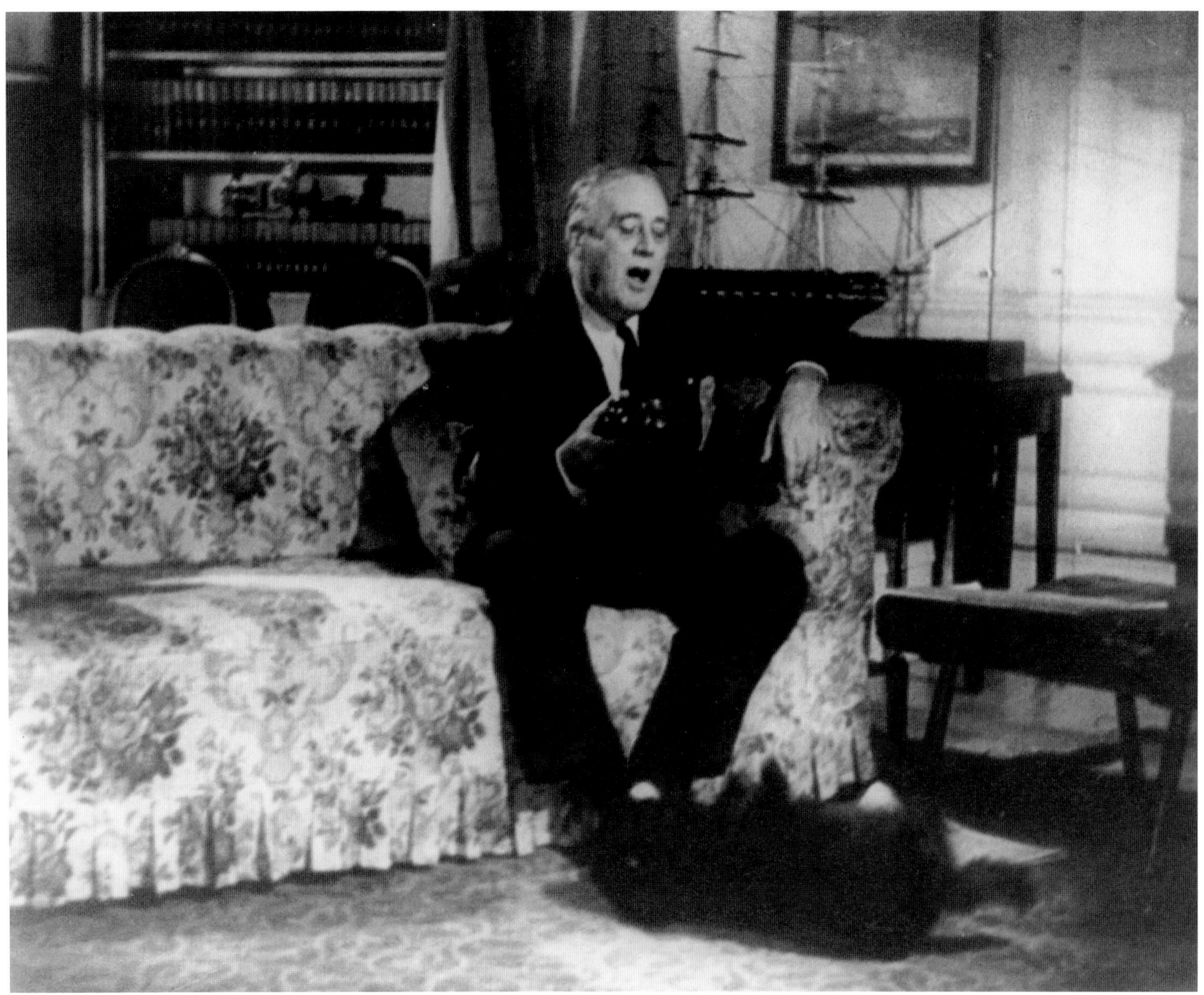

FDR with his Scottie Fala at the White House. Even Fala was not immune from political controversy: "These Republican leaders have not been content with attacks on me, or my wife, or on my sons. No, not content with that, they now include my little dog, Fala. Well, of course, I don't resent attacks, and my family doesn't resent attacks, but Fala does resent them. You know, Fala is Scotch, and being a Scottie, as soon as he learned that the Republican fiction writers in Congress and out had concocted a story that I had left him behind on the Aleutian Islands and had sent a destroyer back to find him—at a cost to the taxpayers of two or three, or eight or twenty million dollars—his Scotch soul was furious. He has not been the same dog since. I am accustomed to hearing malicious falsehoods about myself—such as that old, worm-eaten chestnut that I have represented myself as indispensable. But I think I have a right to resent, to object to libelous statements about my dog." (September 23, 1944)

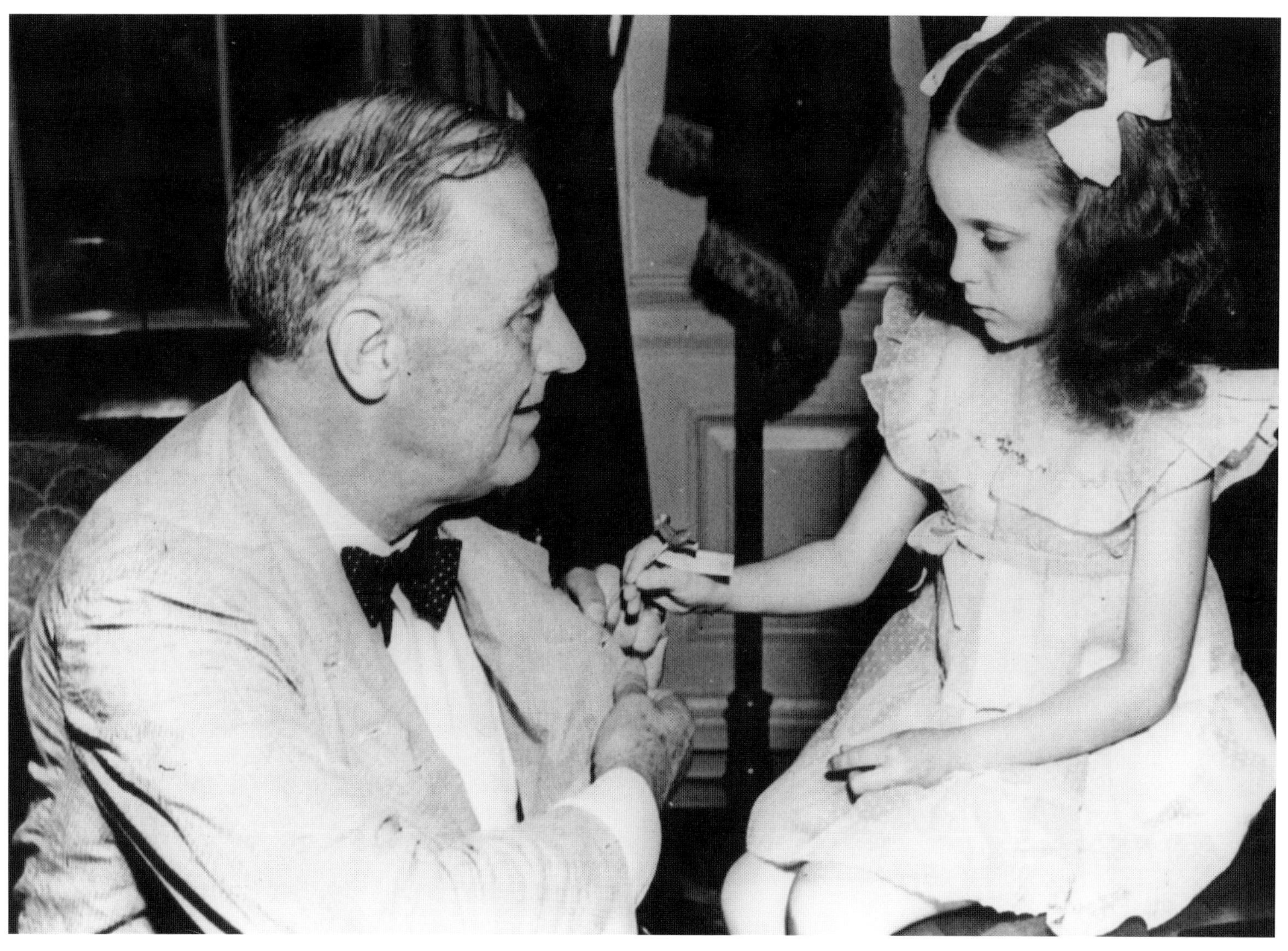

FDR buys a poppy from six-year-old Phyllis Fay Firebaugh, Memorial Day, 1944. Inspired by the poem which made famous the poppies that bloom in the World War I Flanders battlefields, the "Buddy Poppy" was first distributed in 1922, to raise funds to support disabled veterans. (May 27, 1944)

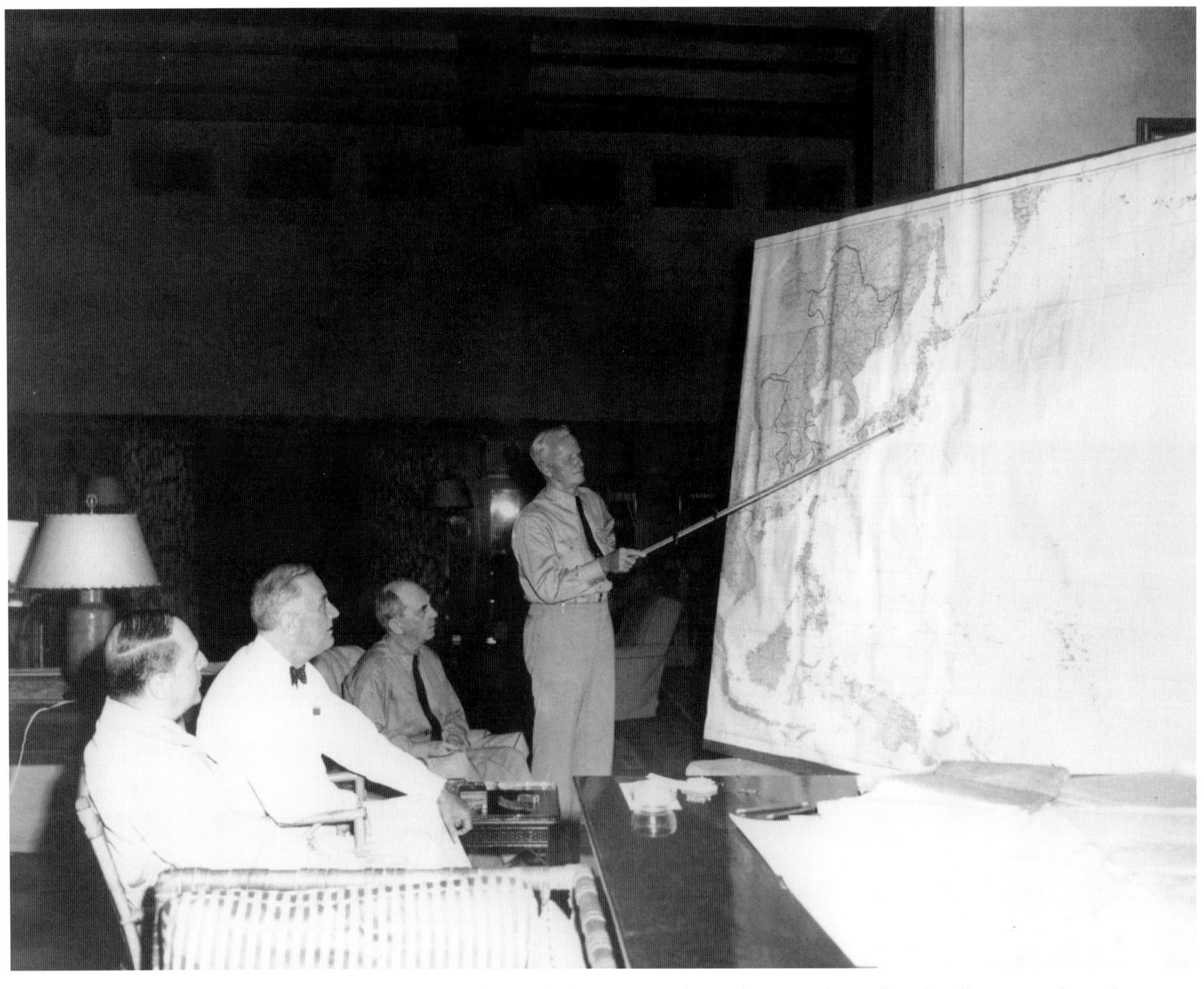

The Waikiki conference, with FDR receiving a briefing on the Pacific theater, General Douglas MacArthur, Admiral William D. Leahy, and Admiral Chester W. Nimitz. Admiral Nimitz is at the map, pointing out potential landing sites on the Japanese mainland. (July 28, 1944)

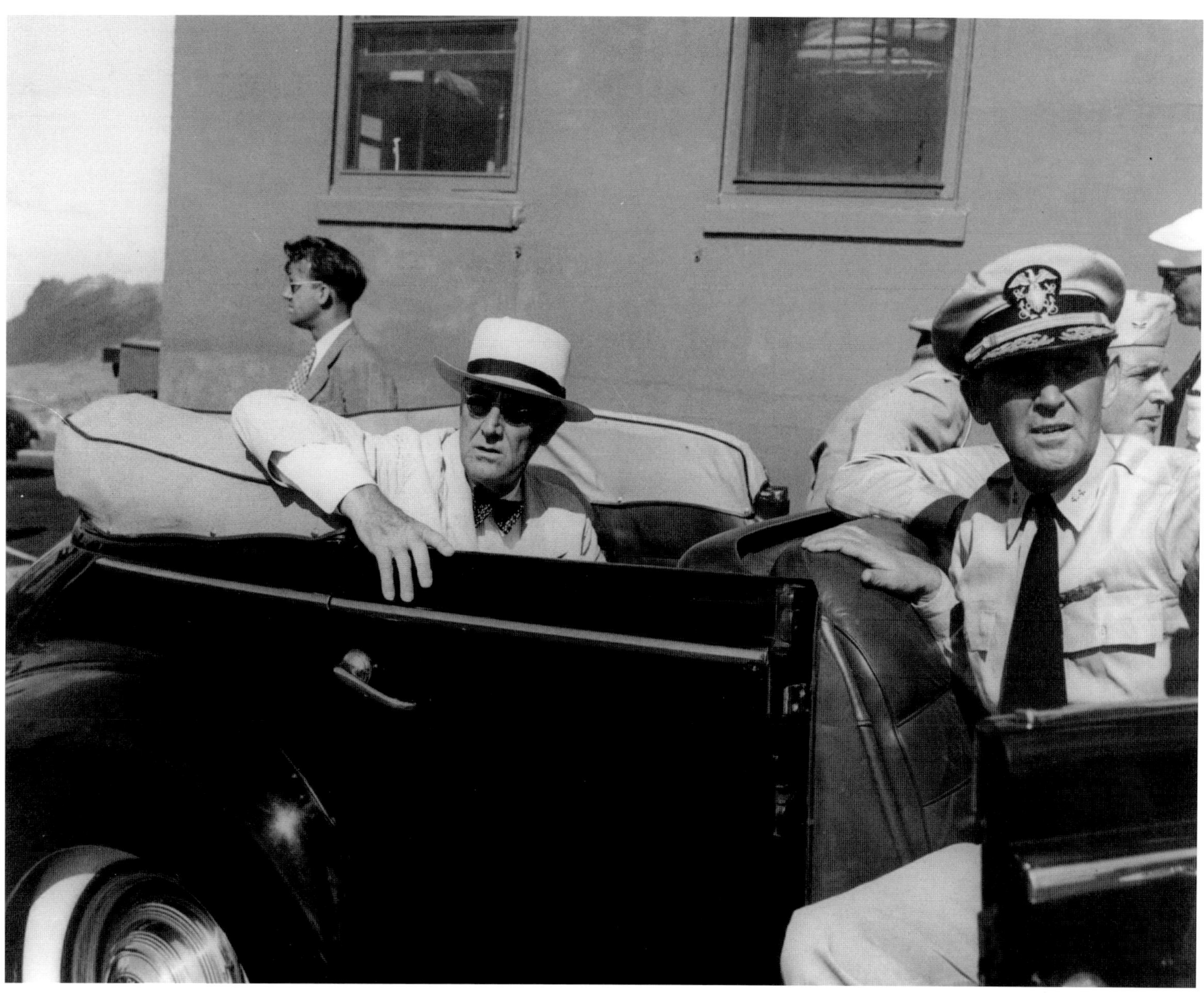

FDR with Admiral John D. Price in Kaneohe Bay, Hawaii. FDR was touring Hawaiian military installations, sailing on the *Baltimore.* The United States had made strides in throwing back the Japanese, and continued to do so. This trip was a means of publicizing that fact, since the war in Europe was dominating the news coverage. FDR met with his naval commanders to discuss conduct and strategy in the Pacific theater, debating the order of liberation of the Philippines and Formosa. Here he also managed to form a more cordial relationship with General MacArthur. (July 29, 1944)

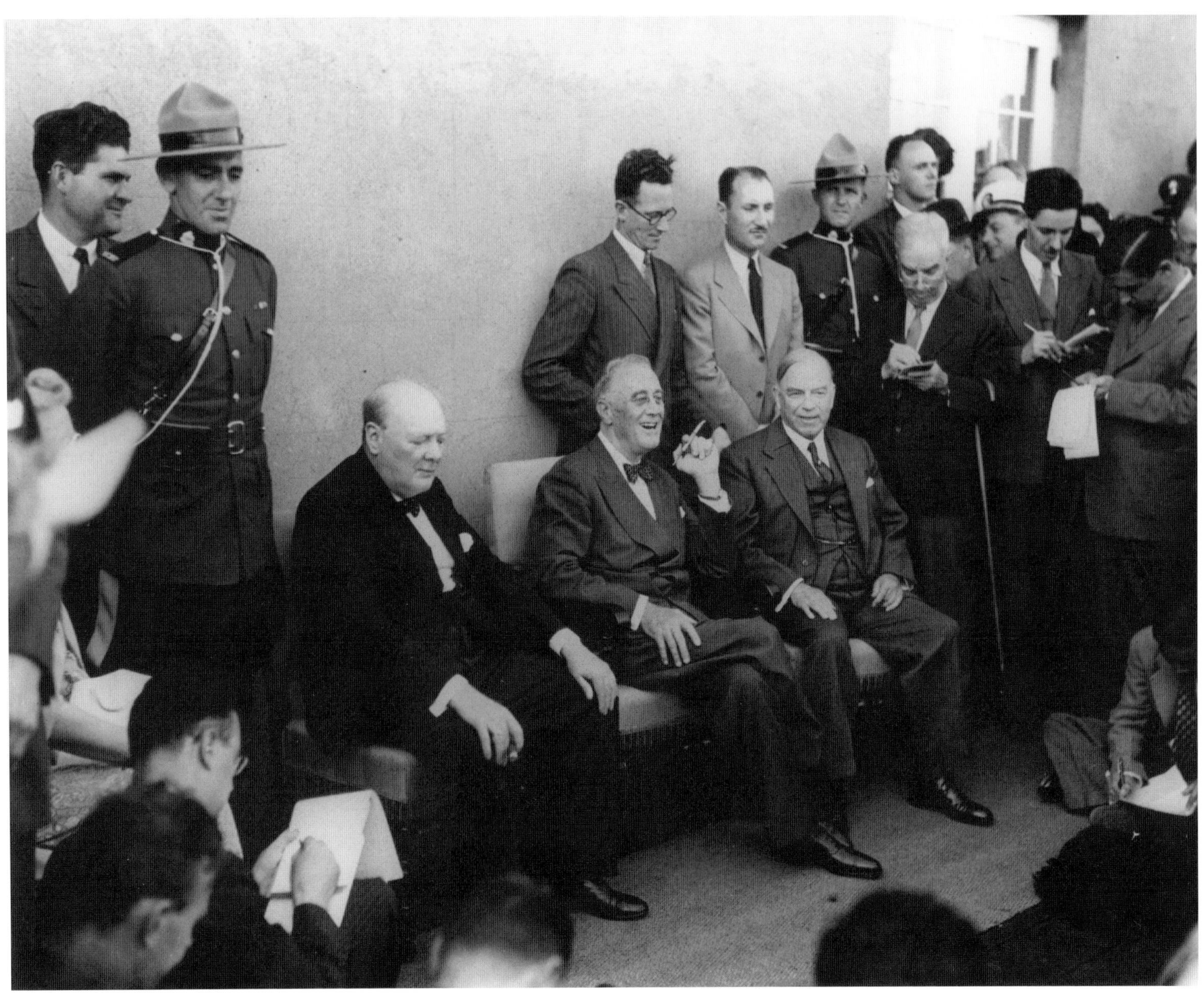

FDR, Churchill, and Canadian prime minister Mackenzie King briefing the press. Roosevelt seems to dominate the scene, Churchill looking a bit ill-at-ease. This was the second Quebec conference, nicknamed "Octagon." Churchill sought additional Lend-Lease aid from the United States, and in turn gave naval support to the American fleet in the Pacific. Here the partition of postwar Germany was promoted, by Henry Morganthau. King, the host, Canada's longest-serving Prime Minister, recorded in his diary that "it was rather amusing to see nations competing for a chance to get at the enemy." (September 16, 1944)

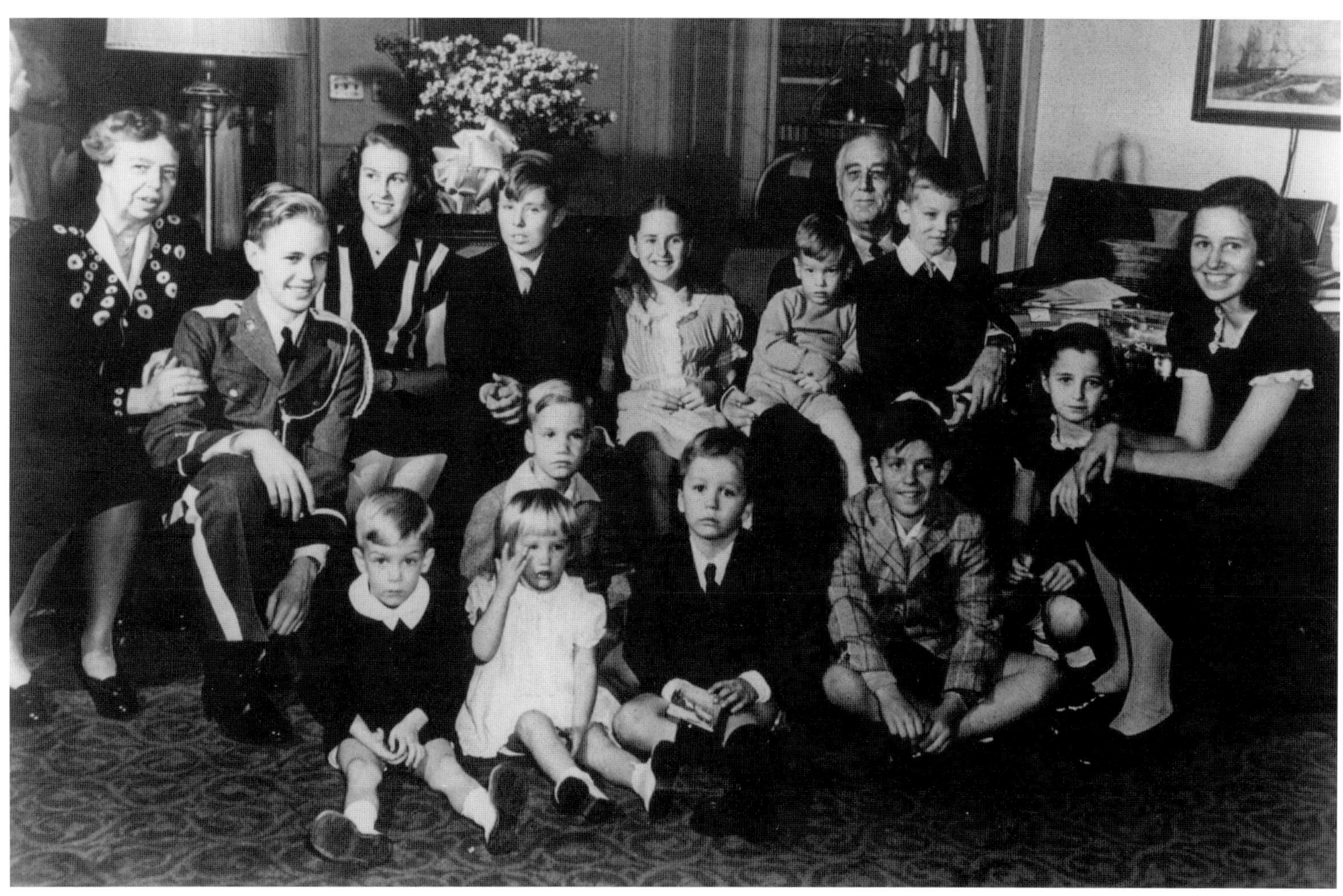

Eleanor, FDR, and their thirteen grandchildren visiting at the White House. With FDR ill and in declining health, this would be the last gathering of grandparents and grandchildren. He made sure they were all present to witness and celebrate the inauguration. Roosevelt died just four months after this family photograph was made, taken in celebration of his unprecedented fourth inauguration. (January 20, 1945)

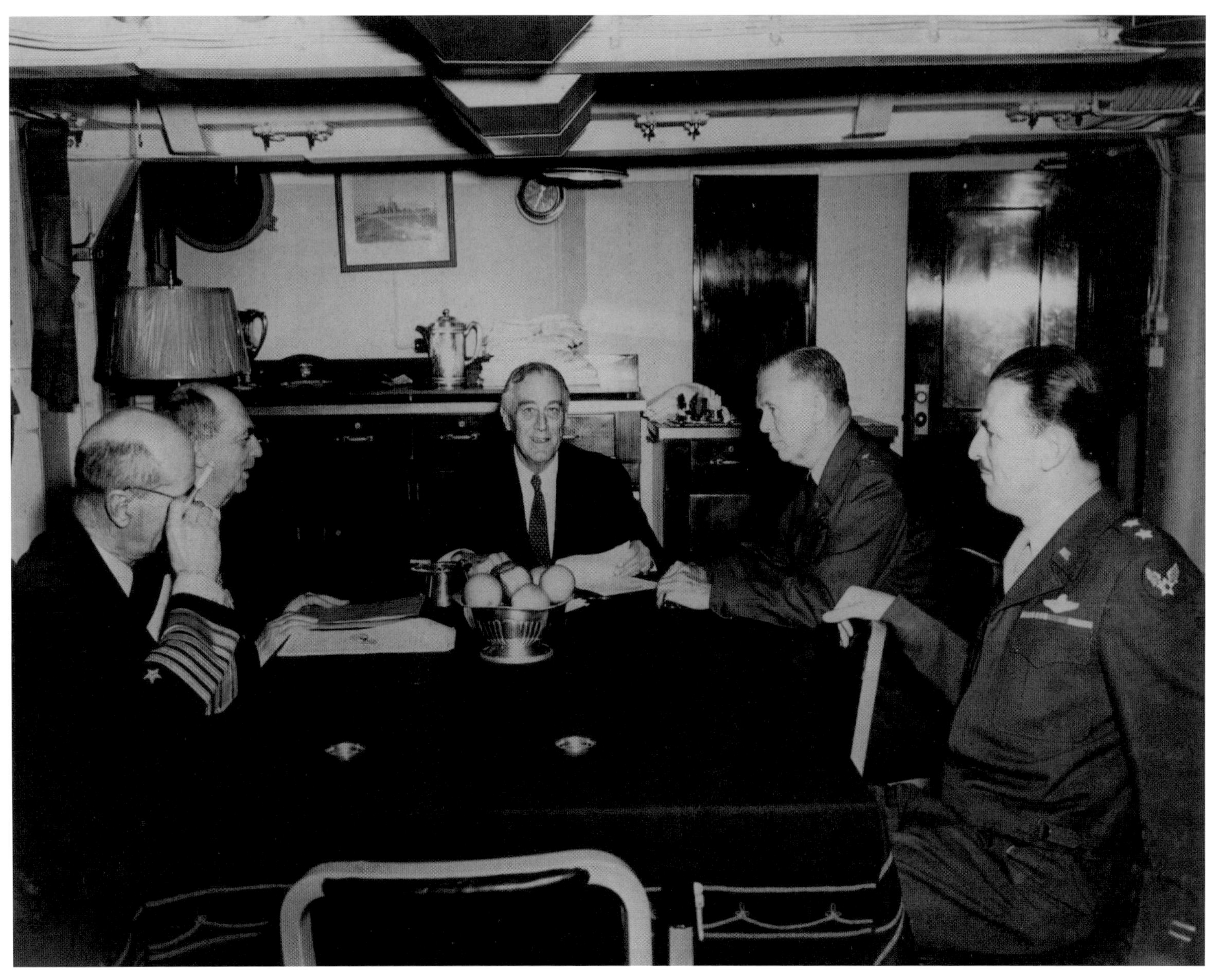

FDR consulting with William D. Leahy, Admiral Ernest J. King, General George C. Marshall, and Air Force General Laurence S. Kuter in Malta preparing for the Yalta talks with Joseph Stalin. The British were alarmed at FDR's declining health. Franklin suffered in particular from sinusitis, giving him a deceptively vacuous look. (February 2, 1945)

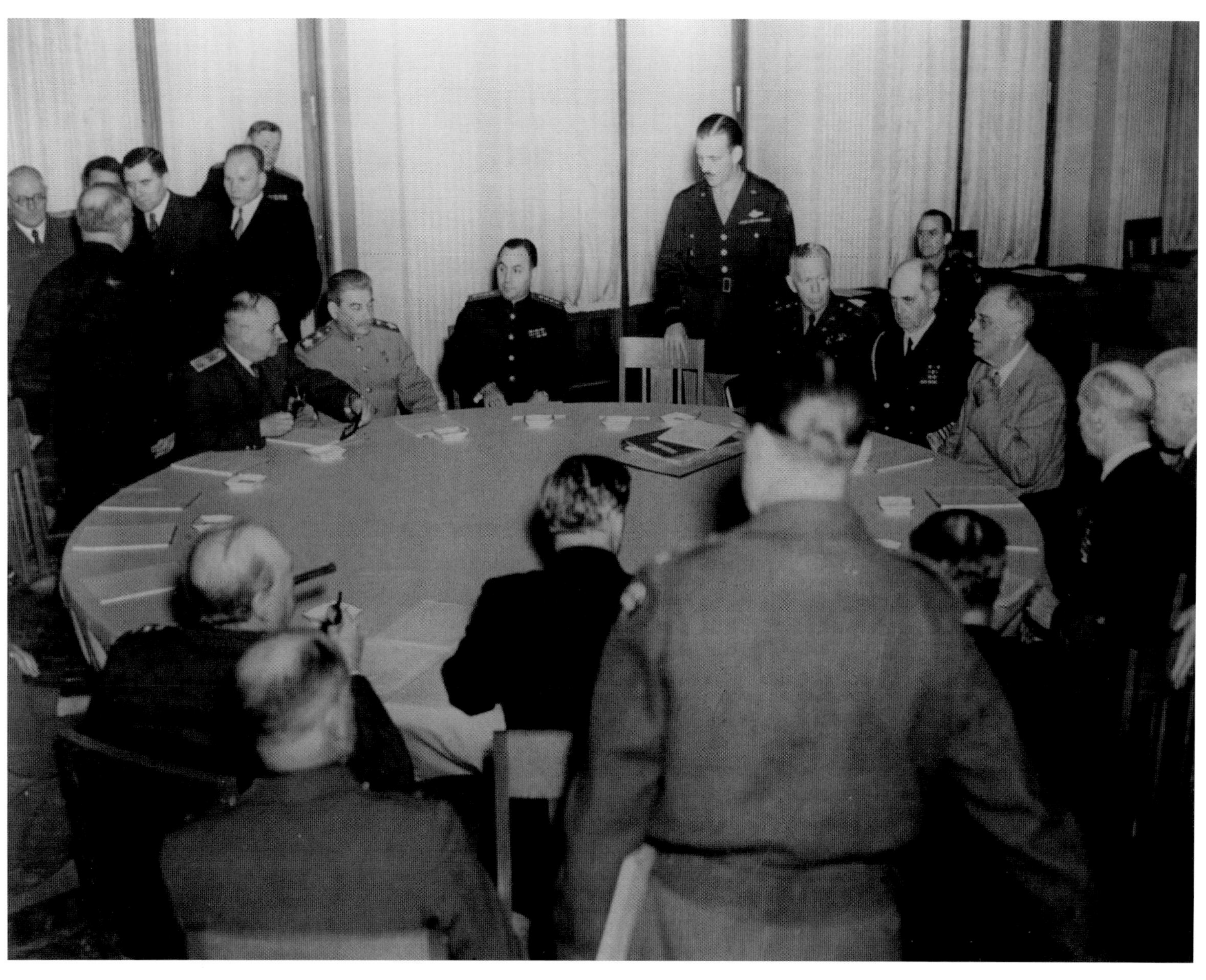

The big round table at Yalta with FDR, Stalin, and Churchill. Despite health concerns, FDR revived, perhaps braced by the ocean voyage, to gracefully preside over the Yalta talks. (February 4, 1945)

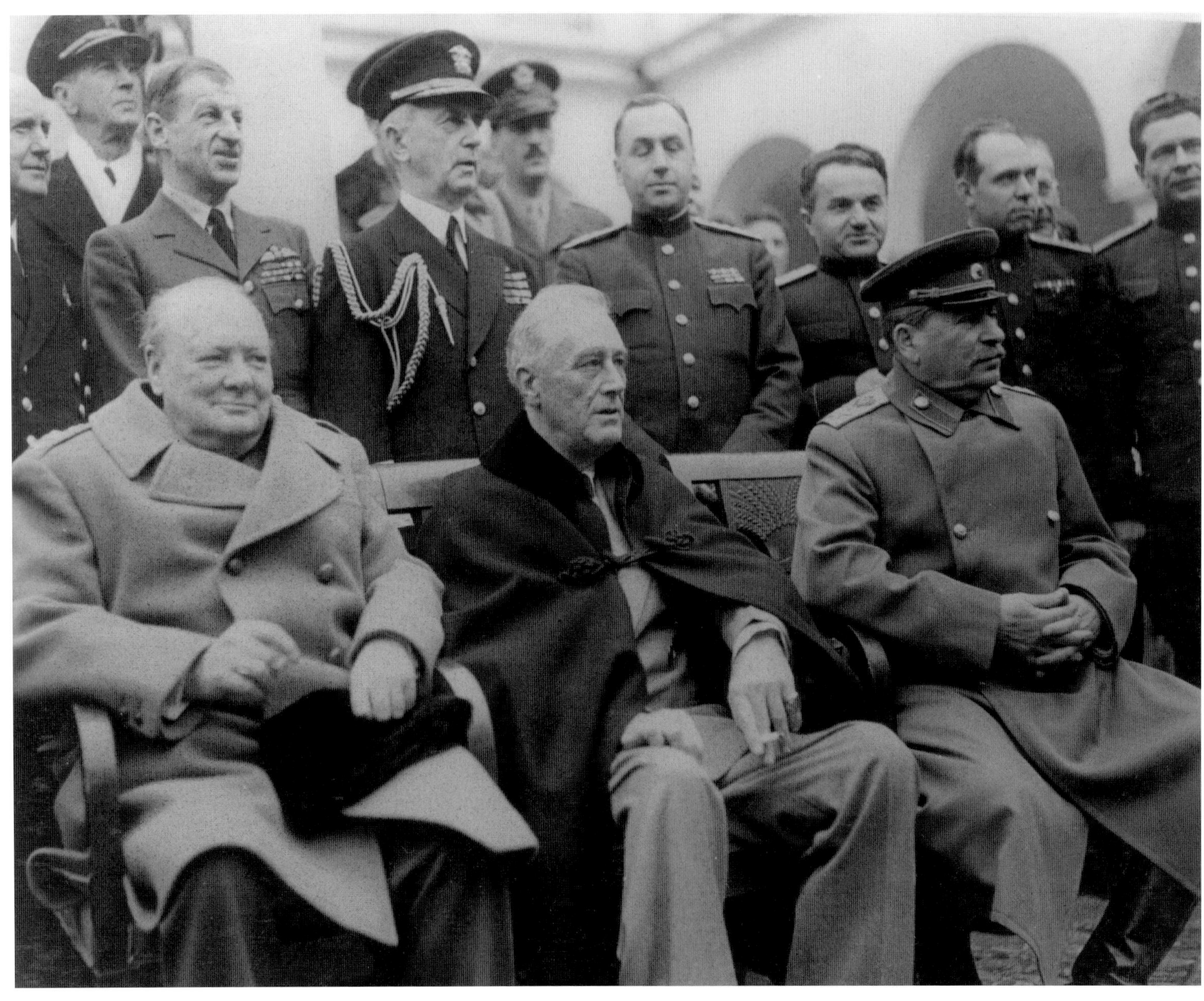

FDR, Churchill, and Stalin at Yalta. (February 9, 1945)

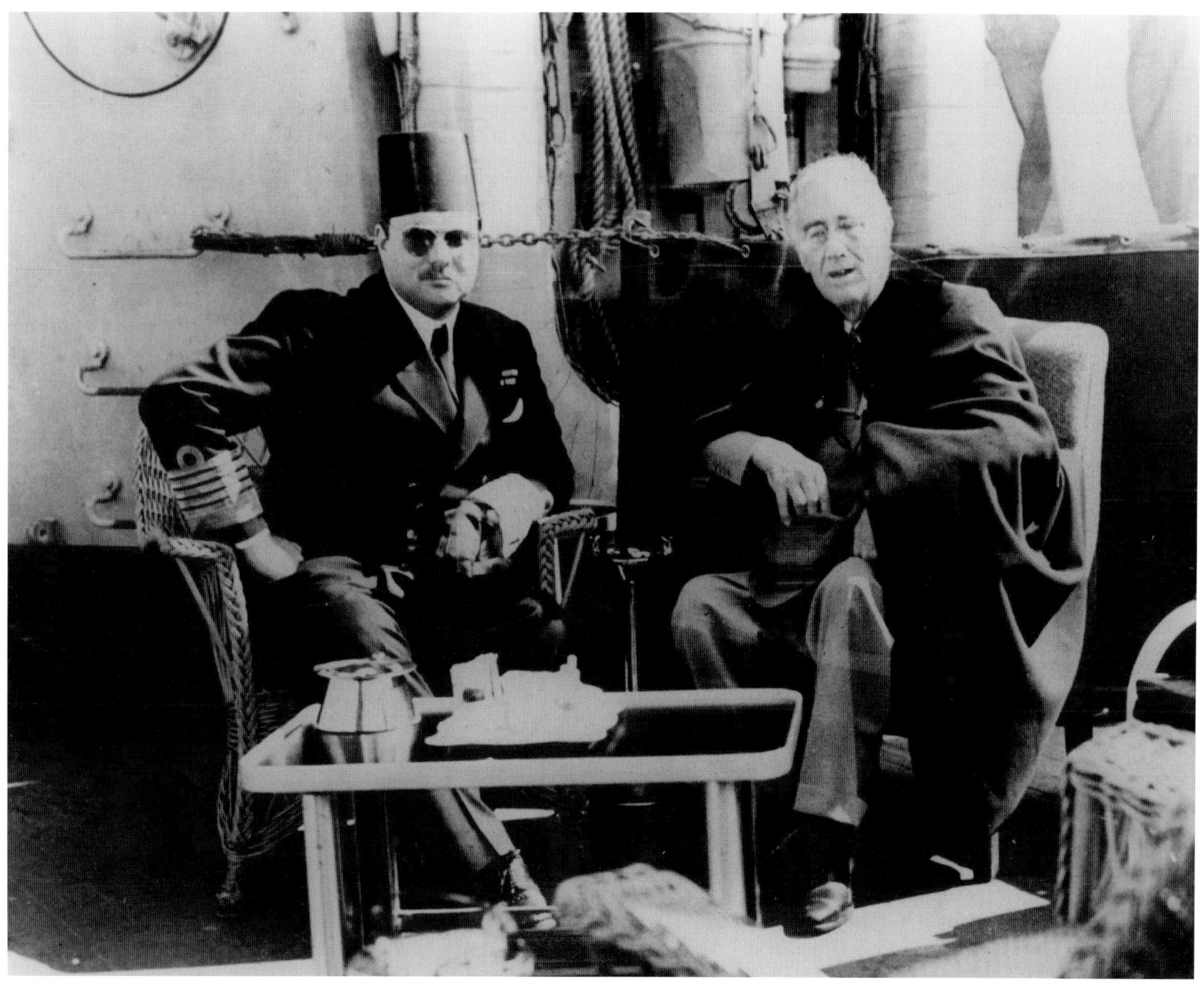

FDR with King Farouk. Farouk, even more than Ibn Saud, was the embodiment of exotic Orientalism to the visiting Americans. FDR was anchored in the Suez Canal following the Yalta conference. The Middle East, long the province of the European powers, would be nearing a crossroads. It seemed likely that the British mandate would expire in Palestine after the war. The potential for conflict made it of concern to America. (February 13, 1945)

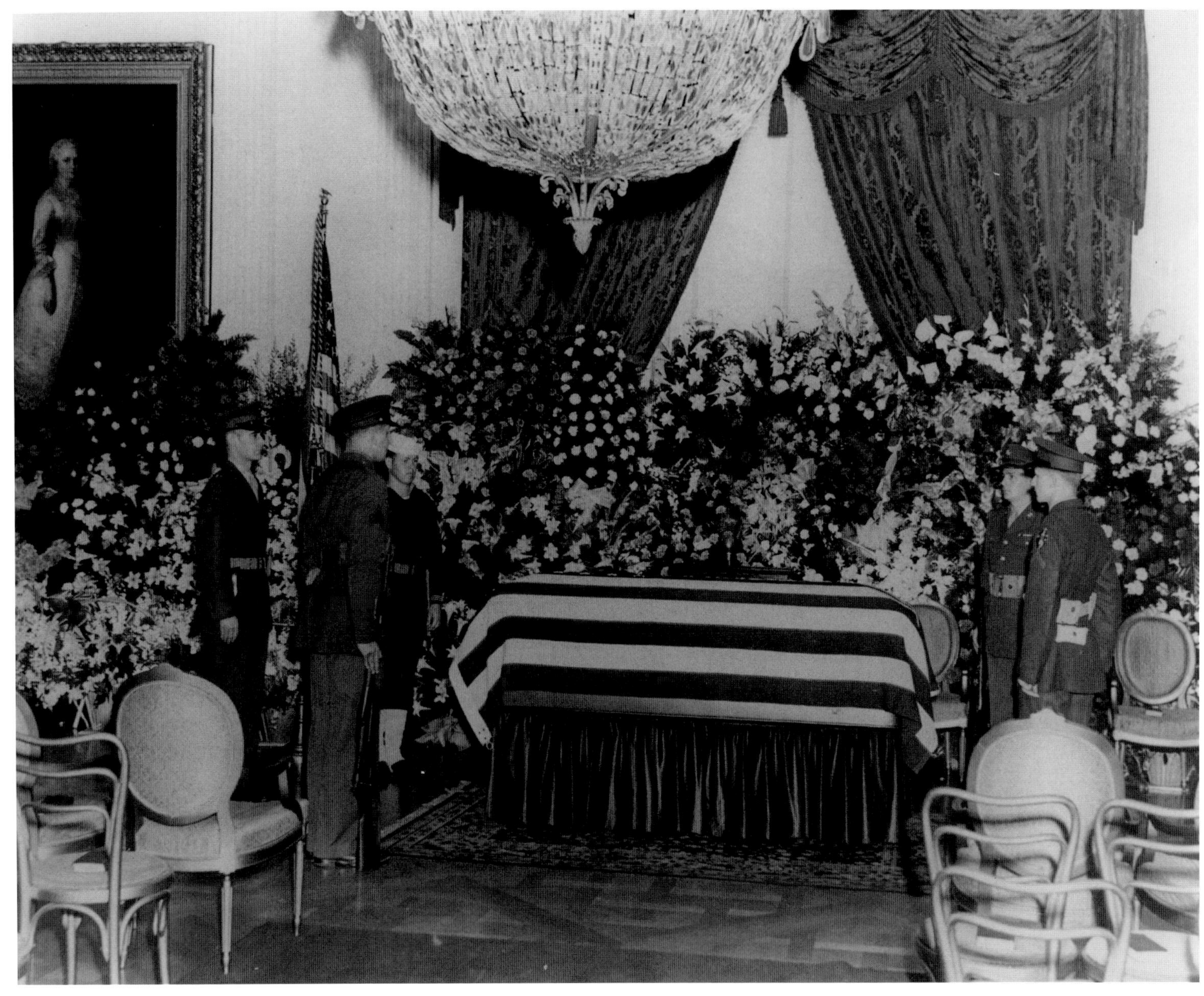

FDR's flag-draped coffin at the White House following its long train journey from Warm Springs. The funeral was held in the East Room of the Executive Mansion with Angus Dun, Episcopal Bishop of Washington, Howard S. Wilkinson of St. Thomas's Episcopal Church, and John G. McGee of St. John's presiding. St. Thomas Episcopal was where FDR worshiped when in Washington and where he had been a vestryman. The body was then transported to Hyde Park for burial. (1945)

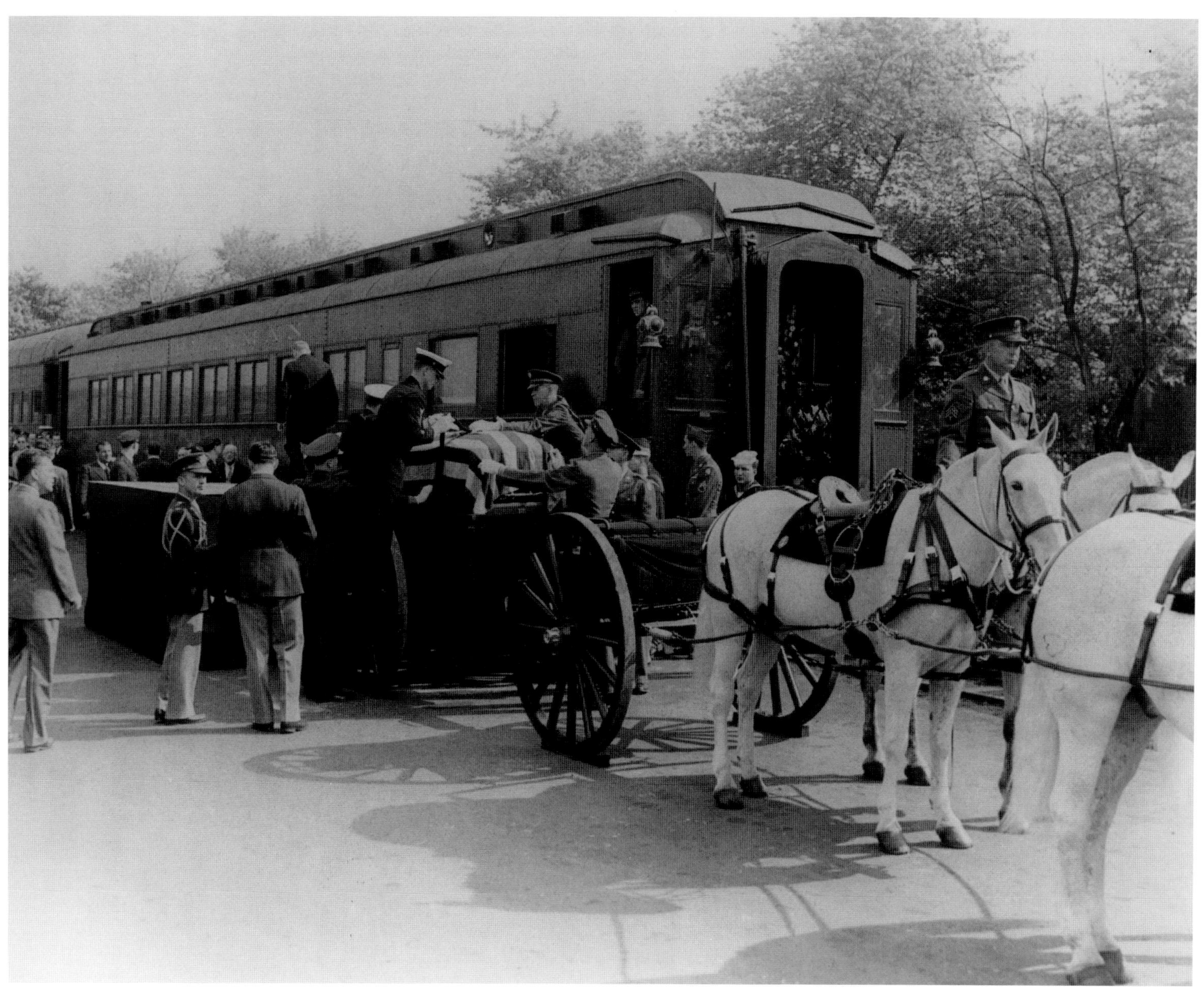

FDR's coffin is loaded onto the train in Washington, D.C., for the return to his family home. (April 1945)

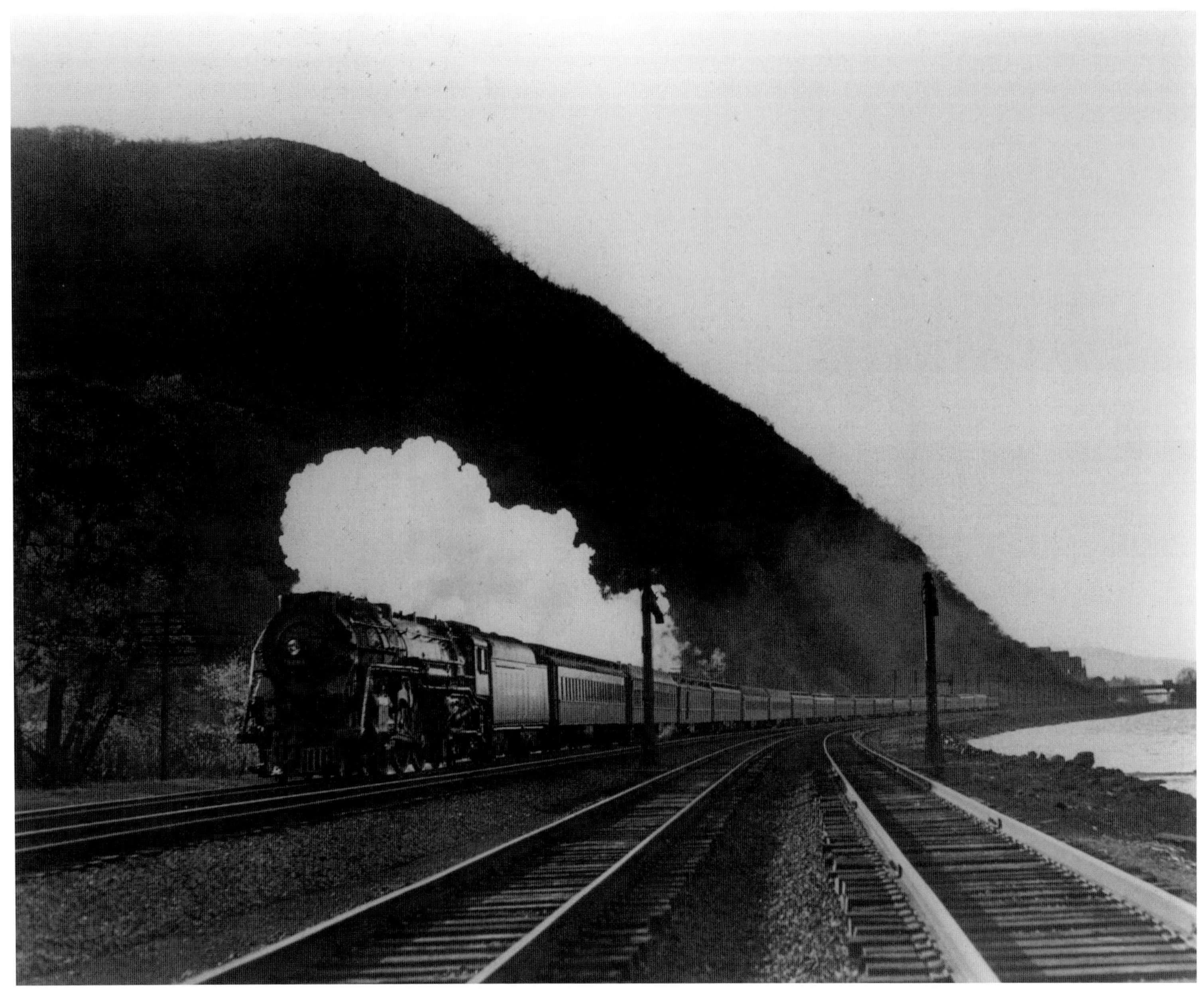

Train taking FDR for burial at home in Hyde Park. Eleanor accompanied the body on the train. Franklin would be laid to rest in the rose garden at the family home, Springwood. (April 15, 1945)

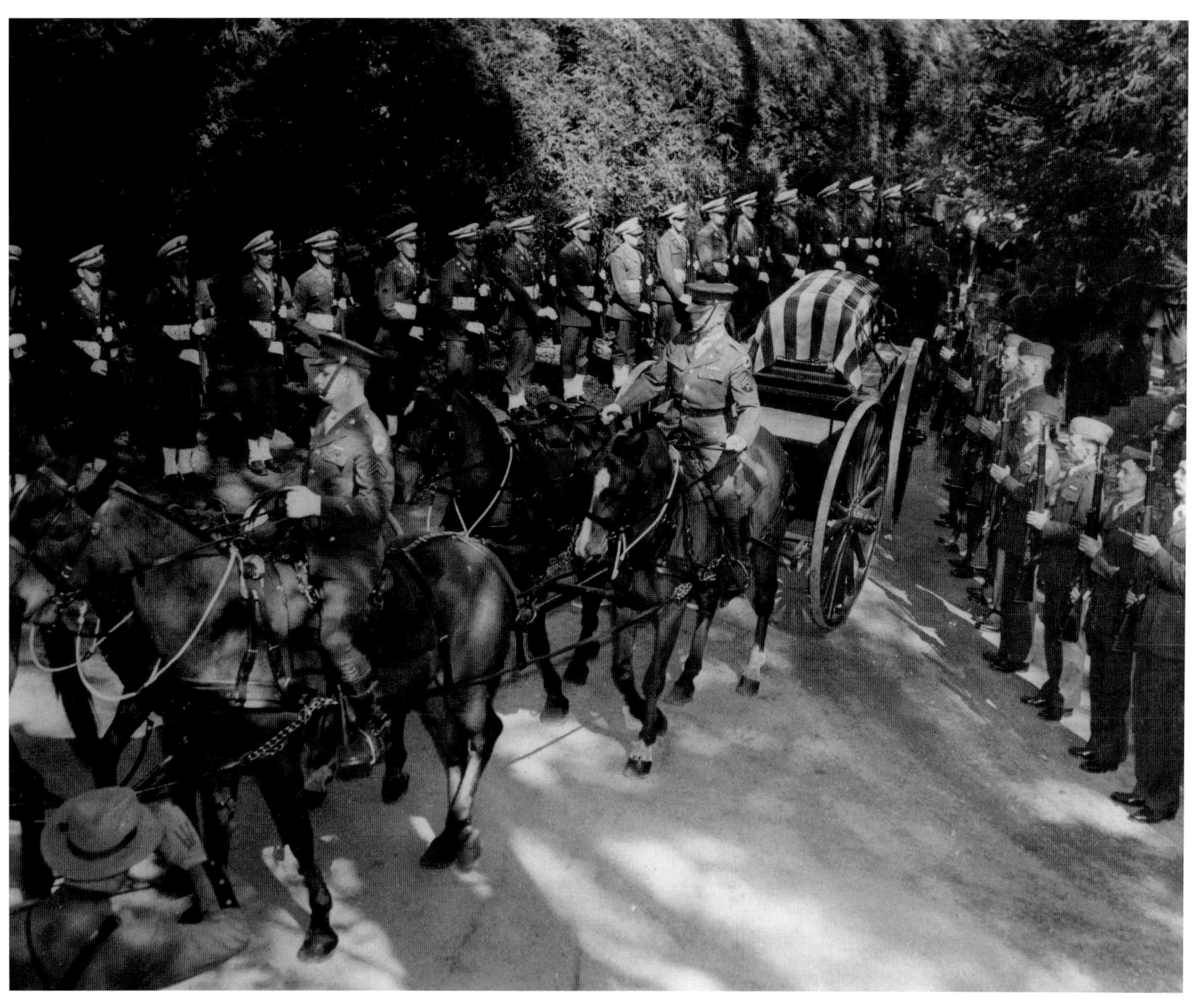

FDR's coffin on the caisson, on the way to Springwood for burial. (April 15, 1945)

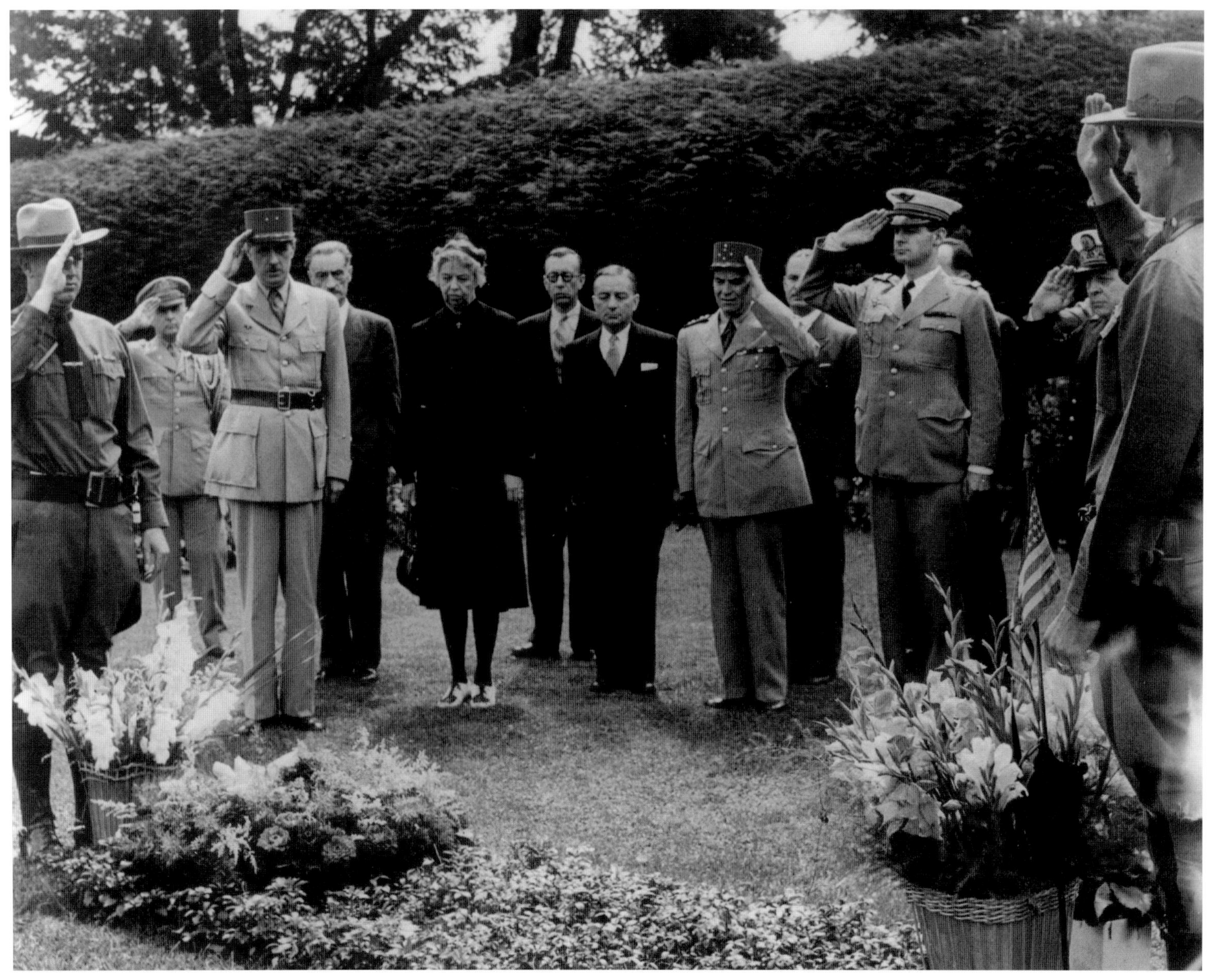

Mourners paying their respects. Eleanor would thank them in her column: "And now I want to say one personal word of gratitude to the many people who have sent messages of affection and condolence during these last days. My children and I are deeply grateful. I want to say too that the people who waited in the stations and along the railroad to pay their last respects have my deep appreciation.

"And now there abideth these three—faith, hope, charity, but the greatest of these is charity." (1945)

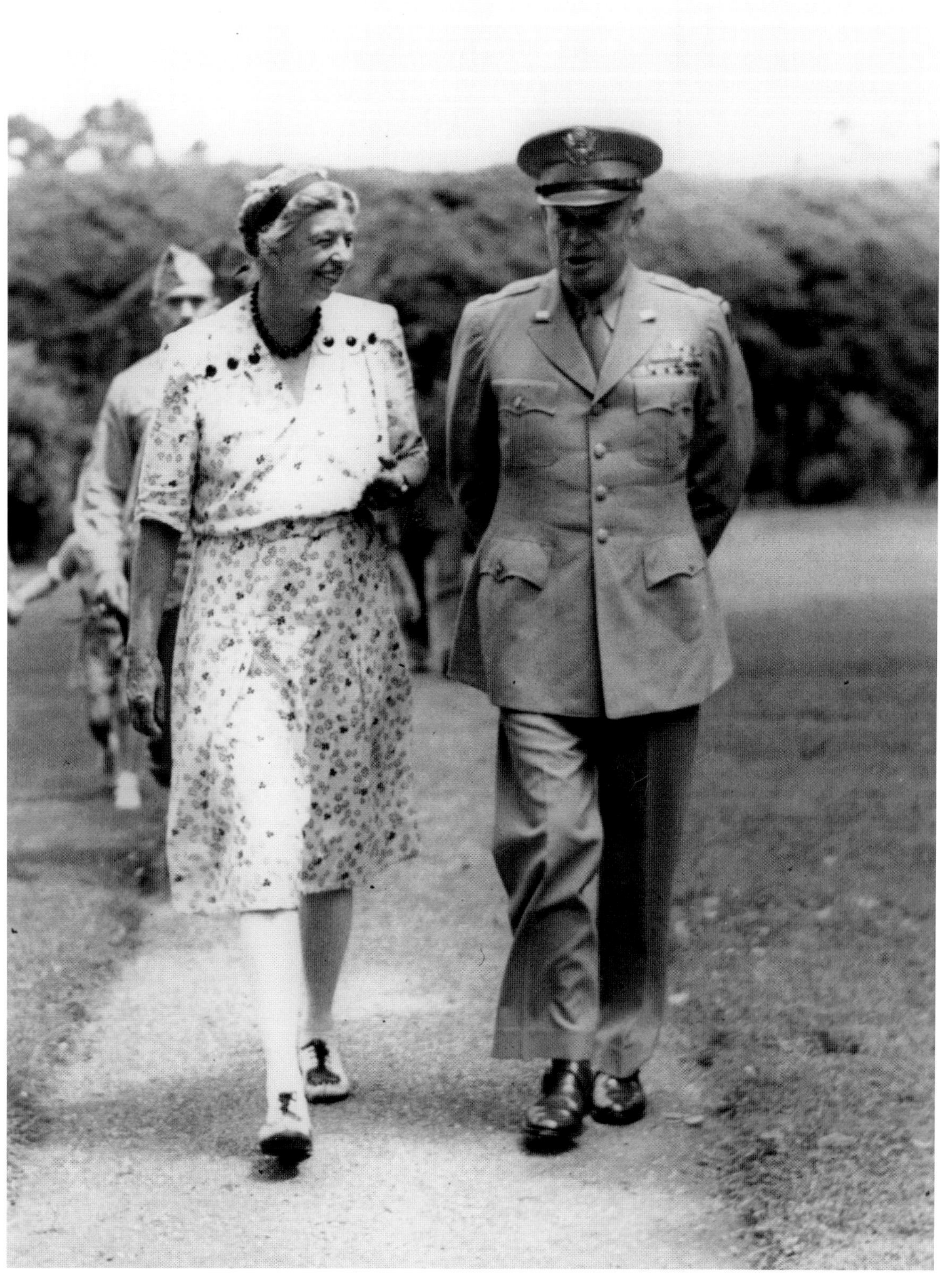

Eleanor and Eisenhower chatting in Hyde Park, some months following FDR's death. Eleanor recounts the meeting in her column "My Day": "Yesterday morning, with my grandchildren and Miss Thompson, I went over to the big house to meet General Eisenhower. He had sent us word that he was flying up from Washington to lay a wreath on my husband's grave, but the weather was stormy last night and for a time we wondered whether he would really get here. He arrived just before noon, however, with Mrs. Eisenhower and their son, Lieutenant Eisenhower, who recently graduated from West Point. It was Mrs. Eisenhower's first flight and I thought her very courageous, since I have often found the flying weather bad between here and Washington." (July 10, 1945)

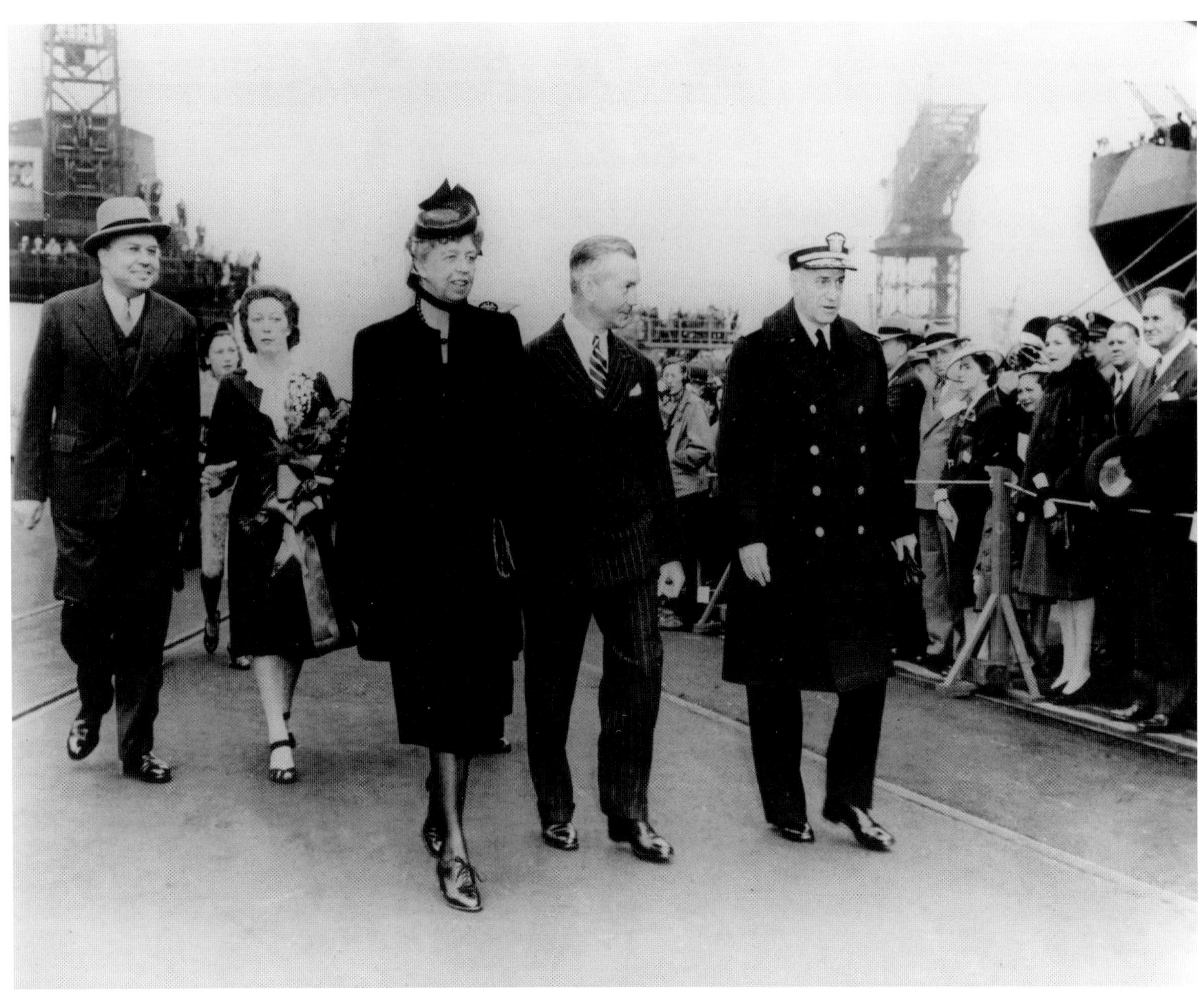

Mourning advisors and confidants launch the USS *Franklin D. Roosevelt,* a 45,000-ton Midway class large aircraft carrier, in New York City, just two weeks after the President's funeral. Originally called the *Coral Sea,* the *Franklin D. Roosevelt* would serve as an expression of American military power for the next thirty years, until its decommissioning in 1977. (1945)

Notes on the Photographs

These notes, listed by page number, attempt to include all aspects known of the photographs. Each of the photographs is identified by the page number, photograph's title or description, photographer and collection, archive, and call or box number when applicable. Although every attempt was made to collect all available data, in some cases complete data was unavailable due to the age and condition of some of the photographs and records.

II **FDR Speaking**
Franklin D. Roosevelt Library
47961005

VI **Formal Portrait**
Franklin D. Roosevelt Library
4794620

X **On the Amberjack II**
Franklin D. Roosevelt Library
47961812

2 **Five-year-old FDR**
Franklin D. Roosevelt Library
621

3 **Franklin with Sara Delano Roosevelt**
Franklin D. Roosevelt Library
47962103

4 **FDR and Playfellows**
Franklin D. Roosevelt Library
5962

5 **Piloting at Campobello**
Franklin D. Roosevelt Library
48224182

6 **Papa's 80th Birthday**
Franklin D. Roosevelt Library
479615

7 **Pet Goat**
Franklin D. Roosevelt Library
48224137

8 **FDR and Friends in Campobello**
Franklin D. Roosevelt Library
4822386419

9 **FDR on Welsh Pony**
Franklin D. Roosevelt Library
43183141

10 **Formal Portrait of FDR**
Franklin D. Roosevelt Library
4796152

11 **Formal Portrait of FDR and Sara**
Franklin D. Roosevelt Library
47963858

12 **FDR with Father**
Franklin D. Roosevelt Library
4796170

13 **Loon Lake, N.Y.**
Franklin D. Roosevelt Library
47963825

14 **Self**
Franklin D. Roosevelt Library
4822398254

15 **Group School Portrait**
Franklin D. Roosevelt Library
425612

16 **Other Side of the Camera**
Franklin D. Roosevelt Library
482242401

17 **Candid Portrait**
Franklin D. Roosevelt Library
47484

18 **FDR, Father, Niece, Friend**
Franklin D. Roosevelt Library
4822361811

19 **FDR, Frances Pell, and Helen Roosevelt**
Franklin D. Roosevelt Library
4822361819

20 **FDR and Family**
Franklin D. Roosevelt Library
4822361830

21 **Groton Baseball Team**
Franklin D. Roosevelt Library
6628

22 **Groton Football Team**
Franklin D. Roosevelt Library
479655

23 **Bopaddy in School Play**
Franklin D. Roosevelt Library
48224260

24 **Performance**
Franklin D. Roosevelt Library
479657

25 **In Campobello**
Franklin D. Roosevelt Library
4822361870

26 **FDR, Father, and Family Dog**
Franklin D. Roosevelt Library
4822361880

27 **FDR and Helen Roosevelt**
Franklin D. Roosevelt Library
48224157

28 **Birthday Party, New London, Conn.**
Franklin D. Roosevelt Library
4822361944

29 **FDR, Mother, and Young Lady**
Franklin D. Roosevelt Library
4822361935

30 **FDR and Camera**
Franklin D. Roosevelt Library
4822361934

31 **Collegiate**
Franklin D. Roosevelt Library
4796187

32 **Harvard Crimson**
Franklin D. Roosevelt Library
4792124646

33 **Yachting**
Franklin D. Roosevelt Library
4796112

34 **Class Day Officers**
Franklin D. Roosevelt Library
4796200

35 **FDR and Aunt and Uncle**
Franklin D. Roosevelt Library
4822361990

36 **Hyde Park on the Hudson**
Franklin D. Roosevelt Library
4796244

37 **FDR and Eleanor**
Franklin D. Roosevelt Library
635336

38 **Delano Family Gathering**
Franklin D. Roosevelt Library
48223619126

39 **Driving Cart**
Franklin D. Roosevelt Library
479653

40 **Saint Moritz, Switzerland**
Franklin D. Roosevelt Library
47964927

41 **Wedding of Frances Pell to Sir Martin Archer-Shee**
Franklin D. Roosevelt Library
4822362695

42 **Picnic**
Franklin D. Roosevelt Library
5953

43 **Newlyweds**
Franklin D. Roosevelt Library
48224140

44 **FDR with Friends**
Franklin D. Roosevelt Library
7420202923

45 **Family Outing**
Franklin D. Roosevelt Library
744131

46 **Happy Couple with Baby**
Franklin D. Roosevelt Library
4796480428

47 **Canoeing at Campobello**
Franklin D. Roosevelt Library
744149

48 **Camping**
Franklin D. Roosevelt Library
744148

49 **FDR Shouldering New Daughter**
Franklin D. Roosevelt Library
4796480433

50 **Piloting Yacht**
Franklin D. Roosevelt Library
4797252

51 **FDR and Mother on Yacht**
Franklin D. Roosevelt Library
4796118

52 **FDR on Horseback**
Franklin D. Roosevelt Library
4796480458

53 **Harvard Class of 1904**
Franklin D. Roosevelt Library
4822L386875A

54 **Waiting in Eastport**
Franklin D. Roosevelt Library
7420469

55 **Piloting Yacht**
Franklin D. Roosevelt Library
48223619212

56 **Group Portrait**
Franklin D. Roosevelt Library
4796113

57 **Teasing Jean Delano**
Franklin D. Roosevelt Library
4796108

58 **FDR and Baby Elliott**
Franklin D. Roosevelt Library
47978

60 **FDR Electioneering**
Franklin D. Roosevelt Library
4822401422

61 **Flag Day**
Franklin D. Roosevelt Library
48223868708

62 **Brooklyn Naval Yard**
Franklin D. Roosevelt Library
4822368836

63 **Assistant Secretary of the Navy**
Franklin D. Roosevelt Library
4822368867

64 **Shooting in Winthrop, Maryland**
Franklin D. Roosevelt Library
4822368874

65 **Visiting London**
Franklin D. Roosevelt Library
4822401412

66 **USS Texas**
Franklin D. Roosevelt Library
4796543

67 **Philadelphia Navy Yard**
Franklin D. Roosevelt Library
482236676

68 **Perfect Family**
Franklin D. Roosevelt Library
47962024

69 **Campaigning in Dayton, Ohio**
Franklin D. Roosevelt Library
48224196

70 **FDR and Eleanor in Campobello**
Franklin D. Roosevelt Library
47964863196

71 **Campaigning in Hyde Park**
Franklin D. Roosevelt Library
4822362655

72 **Whistle-Stop Campaigning**
Franklin D. Roosevelt Library
49833

73 **Family**
Franklin D. Roosevelt Library
47962210

74 **Intimate Portrait**
Franklin D. Roosevelt Library
4796767

75 **Formal Portrait 1924**
Franklin D. Roosevelt Library
47961044

76 **Ship Models**
Franklin D. Roosevelt Library
47961475

77 **Politicians**
Franklin D. Roosevelt Library
482240142

78 **FDR on Crutches**
Franklin D. Roosevelt Library
4849323

79 **Houseboat Larooco**
Franklin D. Roosevelt Library
482239837

80 **Fish**
Franklin D. Roosevelt Library
5931

81 **Driving**
Franklin D. Roosevelt Library
7711121

82 **Addressing Crowd**
Franklin D. Roosevelt Library
4822362652

83 **Olean Speech**
Franklin D. Roosevelt Library
47961000

84 **Democratic Party Workers**
Franklin D. Roosevelt Library
4822370410

85 **Induction into Scottish Rite Freemasonry**
Franklin D. Roosevelt Library
482237019

86 **Posed at Car in Warm Springs**
Franklin D. Roosevelt Library
47961015

87 **FDR, Missy and Eleanor**
Franklin D. Roosevelt Library
48223868674

88 **Celebrating in Peekskill**
Franklin D. Roosevelt Library
60286

89 **Advisors and Consultants**
Franklin D. Roosevelt Library
922

90 **Jaunty FDR**
Franklin D. Roosevelt Library
47961467

91 **Golf at Warm Springs**
Franklin D. Roosevelt Library
827129

92 **Albany**
Franklin D. Roosevelt Library
482237024

93 **Gubernatorial Inauguration**
Franklin D. Roosevelt Library
4822418558

94 **Final Touches**
Franklin D. Roosevelt Library
4822418571

95 **FDR and Five Colleagues**
Franklin D. Roosevelt Library
482240165

96 **Business in Warm Springs**
Franklin D. Roosevelt Library
482240151

97 **Seven Democratic Party Colleagues**
Franklin D. Roosevelt Library
48223868593

98 **FDR with Eleanor and John**
Franklin D. Roosevelt Library
47962004

99 **Addressing New York State Assembly**
Franklin D. Roosevelt Library
4796971

100 **FDR Celebrating**
Franklin D. Roosevelt Library
47961047

103 **Honoring Admiral Byrd**
Franklin D. Roosevelt Library
47961023

104 **FDR and Admiral Byrd**
Franklin D. Roosevelt Library
47961021

105 **Friends and Colleagues in Albany**
Franklin D. Roosevelt Library
47961844

106 **Laying Cornerstone in Hudson**
Franklin D. Roosevelt Library
47961456

107 **Albany Inauguration Portrait**
Franklin D. Roosevelt Library
4796904

108 **Warm Springs, Georgia**
Franklin D. Roosevelt Library
4796964

109 **Shipboard**
Franklin D. Roosevelt Library
4796958

110 **Port Authority of New York Groundbreaking**
Franklin D. Roosevelt Library
482237037

111 Trademark Grin
Franklin D. Roosevelt Library
482237035

112 FDR with Harriet Golden
Franklin D. Roosevelt Library
4822370332

113 Greeting Crowds in Ithaca
Franklin D. Roosevelt Library
4822370330

114 Signing
Franklin D. Roosevelt Library
4796986

115 FDR with Military Aides
Franklin D. Roosevelt Library
47961453

116 In New York City
Franklin D. Roosevelt Library
4796984

117 New Cottage Retreat in Warm Springs
Franklin D. Roosevelt Library
4822372427

118 Listening to His Nomination
Franklin D. Roosevelt Library
48223868589

119 Congratulatory Telegram
Franklin D. Roosevelt Library
4822370413

120 At Albany
Franklin D. Roosevelt Library
48224264

121 FDR in Peekskill
Franklin D. Roosevelt Library
482240133

122 FDR in Hampton Beach
Franklin D. Roosevelt Library
47961291

123 FDR with John Nance Garner
Franklin D. Roosevelt Library
482240136

124 Handshake
Franklin D. Roosevelt Library
48224468

125 FDR in Seattle
Franklin D. Roosevelt Library
47961477

126 FDR, Judge, and Daughter
Franklin D. Roosevelt Library
464411

127 FDR and Warm Springs Institute for Rehabilitation
Franklin D. Roosevelt Library
482237041

128 New Albany, Indiana
Franklin D. Roosevelt Library
47961471

129 FDR at Greenway Ranch, Arizona
Franklin D. Roosevelt Library
48223704277

130 Grinning
Franklin D. Roosevelt Library
48223704422

131 FDR Greeting Youth
Franklin D. Roosevelt Library
48223704429B

132 Photograph of FDR and George Cardinal Mundelein Archbishop of Chicago
Franklin D. Roosevelt Library
48221888

133 Speaking on Campaign Trail
Franklin D. Roosevelt Library
57636

134 At Work
Franklin D. Roosevelt Library
7755101

135 Official Portrait of the New President
Franklin D. Roosevelt Library
4796915

136 Inauguration Day
Franklin D. Roosevelt Library
4849330

137 Back from the Capitol
Franklin D. Roosevelt Library
65501

138 First Ball at the Washington Nationals
Franklin D. Roosevelt Library
47961745

139 President and First Lady
Franklin D. Roosevelt Library
57680

140 FDR and Mother
Franklin D. Roosevelt Library
47962006

141 Candid
Franklin D. Roosevelt Library
47961538

142 FDR amid Advisors
Franklin D. Roosevelt Library
54499

143 On the Battleship USS Indianapolis
Franklin D. Roosevelt Library
4822370653

144 National Radio Address
Franklin D. Roosevelt Library
47961783

145 Nourmahal
Franklin D. Roosevelt Library
47961598

146 Eleanor and John
Franklin D. Roosevelt Library
47962487

147 FDR in Oval Office
Franklin D. Roosevelt Library
57648

148 Galion, Ohio
Franklin D. Roosevelt Library
4822370498A

149 Ground-Breaking Ceremonies of the Queens Midtown Tunnel
Franklin D. Roosevelt Library
47961858

150 **Fishing Exploits, off Cocos Island**
Franklin D. Roosevelt Library
482242224

151 **En Route to Washington**
Franklin D. Roosevelt Library
56131742

152 **On the Yacht Sewanna**
Franklin D. Roosevelt Library
47961792

153 **FDR at the Helm**
Franklin D. Roosevelt Library
48223868230

154 **FDR in South Carolina**
Franklin D. Roosevelt Library
48223868334

155 **Laying Cornerstone of the Federal Trade Commission**
Franklin D. Roosevelt Library
48223709100

156 **On the Grand Coulee Dam**
Franklin D. Roosevelt Library
5322743

157 **FDR and Mayor Williams**
Franklin D. Roosevelt Library
48223868201

158 **Banquet**
Franklin D. Roosevelt Library
4822362624

159 **Lincoln Memorial**
Franklin D. Roosevelt Library
781832

160 **FDR on the USS Houston**
Franklin D. Roosevelt Library
48223710237

161 **Speaking in Barnesville, Georgia**
Franklin D. Roosevelt Library
5322756

162 **FDR at Queen's University in Kingston, Ontario**
Franklin D. Roosevelt Library
48223710258

163 **Stamps**
Franklin D. Roosevelt Library
49659

164 **FDR Greets Winston Churchill**
Franklin D. Roosevelt Library
48223616

165 **Signing Declaration of War**
Franklin D. Roosevelt Library
48224041

166 **Greetings**
Franklin D. Roosevelt Library
4315112

167 **FDR and Churchill**
Franklin D. Roosevelt Library
48223868736

168 **FDR at Fort Lewis**
Franklin D. Roosevelt Library
4313049

169 **FDR and Dorothy Jones Brady**
Franklin D. Roosevelt Library
482239789

170 **White House Library Renovations**
Franklin D. Roosevelt Library
431641

171 **FDR with Sons**
Franklin D. Roosevelt Library
59122

172 **FDR and French General**
Franklin D. Roosevelt Library
482289

173 **FDR Decorating General William Wilbur, General Marshall**
Franklin D. Roosevelt Library
4822218

174 **FDR in Jeep**
Franklin D. Roosevelt Library
4822100

175 **Consulting**
Franklin D. Roosevelt Library
4822656

176 **Eleanor Greeting Colleagues in Sydney**
Franklin D. Roosevelt Library
47893

177 **FDR and Churchill Fishing**
Franklin D. Roosevelt Library
47961535

178 **FDR and Prime Minister Mackenzie King of Canada**
Franklin D. Roosevelt Library
4822362210

179 **In Ottawa**
Franklin D. Roosevelt Library
482242573

180 **In Cairo**
Franklin D. Roosevelt Library
48223715100

181 **The Big Three**
Franklin D. Roosevelt Library
48223715107

182 **Decorating a Soldier**
Franklin D. Roosevelt Library
482282

183 **FDR and General Eisenhower**
Franklin D. Roosevelt Library
482279

184 **FDR with Scottie, Fala**
Franklin D. Roosevelt Library
48224265

185 **Buddy Poppy**
Franklin D. Roosevelt Library
61253

186 **The Waikiki Conference**
Franklin D. Roosevelt Library
48223868478

187 **FDR with Admiral John D. Price**
Franklin D. Roosevelt Library
4822714

188 Quebec Conference
Franklin D. Roosevelt Library
4822365439

189 Thirteen Grandchildren
Franklin D. Roosevelt Library
47962062

190 Preparation for Talks
Franklin D. Roosevelt Library
4822365910

191 Round Table
Franklin D. Roosevelt Library
4822365955

192 In Yalta
Franklin D. Roosevelt Library
4822365969

193 FDR and King Farouk
Franklin D. Roosevelt Library
6116811

194 Funeral
Franklin D. Roosevelt Library
7218423

195 Return Trip
Franklin D. Roosevelt Library
7218411

196 Funeral Train
Franklin D. Roosevelt Library
4691

197 Coffin on Caisson
Franklin D. Roosevelt Library
4822371952

198 Mourners
Franklin D. Roosevelt Library
48223724290

199 Eleanor and Eisenhower
Franklin D. Roosevelt Library
46813

200 Launching of USS Franklin D. Roosevelt
Franklin D. Roosevelt Library
48223821347